Beginning Oracle Database 11*g* Administration

From Novice to Professional

Iggy Fernandez

Beginning Oracle Database 11g Administration: From Novice to Professional

Copyright © 2009 by Iggy Fernandez

ISBN-10 (pbk): 1-59059-968-3

ISBN-13 (pbk): 978-1-59059-968-6

ISBN-13 (electronic): 978-1-4302-0628-6

Printed and bound in the United States of America 9 8 7 6 5 4 3 2 1

Trademarked names may appear in this book. Rather than use a trademark symbol with every occurrence of a trademarked name, we use the names only in an editorial fashion and to the benefit of the trademark owner, with no intention of infringement of the trademark.

Lead Editor: Jonathan Gennick
Development Editor: Douglas Pundick
Technical Reviewer: Bob Bryla
Editorial Board: Clay Andres, Steve Anglin, Mark Beckner, Ewan Buckingham, Tony Campbell, Gary Cornell, Jonathan Gennick, Michelle Lowman, Matthew Moodie, Jeffrey Pepper, Frank Pohlmann, Ben Renow-Clarke, Dominic Shakeshaft, Matt Wade, Tom Welsh
Project Manager: Richard Dal Porto
Copy Editors: Jim Compton, Sharon Wilkey
Associate Production Director: Kari Brooks-Copony
Production Editor: Kelly Gunther
Compositor and Artist: Kinetic Publishing Services, LLC
Proofreader: Nancy Sixsmith
Indexer: Broccoli Information Management
Cover Designer: Kurt Krames
Manufacturing Director: Tom Debolski

Distributed to the book trade worldwide by Springer-Verlag New York, Inc., 233 Spring Street, 6th Floor, New York, NY 10013. Phone 1-800-SPRINGER, fax 201-348-4505, e-mail orders-ny@springer-sbm.com, or visit http://www.springeronline.com.

For information on translations, please contact Apress directly at 2855 Telegraph Avenue, Suite 600, Berkeley, CA 94705. Phone 510-549-5930, fax 510-549-5939, e-mail info@apress.com, or visit http://www.apress.com.

Apress and friends of ED books may be purchased in bulk for academic, corporate, or promotional use. eBook versions and licenses are also available for most titles. For more information, reference our Special Bulk Sales–eBook Licensing web page at http://www.apress.com/info/bulksales.

The information in this book is distributed on an "as is" basis, without warranty. Although every precaution has been taken in the preparation of this work, neither the author(s) nor Apress shall have any liability to any person or entity with respect to any loss or damage caused or alleged to be caused directly or indirectly by the information contained in this work.

The source code for this book is available to readers at http://www.apress.com.

For Michelle.

"Oh Fame!—if I e'er took delight in thy praises,
'Twas less for the sake of thy high-sounding phrases,
Than to see the bright eyes of the dear one discover
She thought that I was not unworthy to love her."
          —*Lord Byron*

And for all the IT colleagues and friends who, over the years,
have asked me to teach them the basics of Oracle Database.

Contents at a Glance

PART I ■ ■ ■ Database Concepts

PART II ■ ■ ■ Database Implementation

PART III ■ ■ ■ Database Support

PART IV ■ ■ ■ Database Tuning

Contents

PART I ■■■ Database Concepts

PART II ■ ■ ■ Database Implementation

PART III ■ ■ ■ Database Support

PART IV ■ ■ ■ Database Tuning

Foreword

There are so many computer books in the world. A few of them are lousy, most of them are pretty good, and several are excellent.

Fortunately for the Gross National Products of nations, we all buy many of these books.

Unfortunately, most of these books are never read, just skipped through and left to gather dust on the shelves with all the other good books (and course materials) that we never revisited.

So many wise words, wise thoughts, funny and instructive stories, and so many years of experience collected in these books. And so many people willing to commit (!) the same mistakes over and over again because they never read the books, but instead perform the famous skip/skim procedure.

Many authors ask for the skip/skim treatment of their books because, unlike Iggy, they either quote extensively from manuals or try to advise the reader about the chapters he or she can skip or skim.

The few people who actually read a handful of good Oracle database books from cover to cover, including trying out stuff on their test system as they read—they will have a much easier and more entertaining work life with Oracle's database.

Iggy is a workhorse. He wrote this book while holding down a day job at Database Specialists, editing the journal of the Northern California Oracle Users Group (NoCOUG), and making presentations at the RMOUG, IOUG, and Hotsos conferences. He's also a thinking man, who decided (I think) to write the book he wished he'd had when he started with databases.

So when I looked through the sections and chapters (all of them very useful, by the way), I saw a pattern:

Section I contains information you can easily find in manuals on http://tahiti.oracle.com or a good textbook on database theory. The information in Section II could also be extracted from the manuals if you knew what you were looking for in the first place—and had the many hours required at your disposal.

Sections III and IV, however, could only be written by someone who has acquired experience, has made mistakes (and learned from them), and has thought about his job and his role in the database world—and discussed it with others.

This is a very good book, Iggy. I want a signed copy of it.

Mogens Nørgaard
CEO of Miracle A/S and cofounder
of the OakTable Network

About the Author

IGGY FERNANDEZ has been working in the IT industry for more than 20 years. He has more than 10 years of experience as an Oracle Database administrator supporting databases big and small, for companies big and small, including a stint as the manager of the Oracle Database administration team of a large application services provider (ASP). His favorite part of Oracle Database administration is performance tuning because it can often be a puzzle that requires a creative solution.

In his spare time, he edits the *NoCOUG Journal*—the quarterly journal of the Northern California Oracle Users Group—for which he also writes a column called "SQL Corner." He is also a frequent speaker at Oracle User Group conferences.

About the Technical Reviewer

BOB BRYLA is an Oracle 9*i*, 10*g*, and 11*g* Certified Professional with more than 20 years of experience in database design, database application development, training, and Oracle database administration. He is the primary Internet database designer and an Oracle DBA at Lands' End in Dodgeville, Wisconsin.

In his spare time, he is a technical editor for a number of Oracle Press and Apress books, in addition to authoring several certification study guides for Oracle Database 10*g* and 11*g*. He has also been known to watch science fiction movies and dabble in videography in his spare time.

Acknowledgments

I would like to thank to Bill Schwimmer, my manager at MCI Systemhouse, for giving me the chance to become an Oracle Database administrator many years ago; Jonathan Gennick at Apress for offering me the opportunity to write this book; technical reviewer Bob Bryla for his thorough and insightful reviews; my old friends Ravi Kulkarni and Sumit Sengupta for constant encouragement and patient listening; Ian Jones at Database Specialists for providing feedback on so many chapters; and the entire production team at Apress—especially project manager Richard Dal Porto, copy editors Jim Compton and Sharon Wilkey, and production editor Kelly Gunther—who turned my unpolished scribblings into a finished product.

I would also like to thank all the colleagues and friends who helped me with this project, including Allen Tran, David Wolff, Gary Sadler, Malathy Thiruloganathan, Manoj Joshi, Raghav Vinjamuri, Rajesh Talreja, Rich Headrick, Scott Alexander, and Terry Sutton.

Introduction

In the ancient Chinese classic text *Tao Te Ching*, Lao Tzu ("Old Master") says, *"The tree which fills the arms grew from the tiniest sprout; the tower of nine stories rose from a (small) heap of earth; the journey of a thousand [miles] commenced with a single step."* I wrote *Beginning Oracle Database 11g Administration* to help you take the first steps of your Oracle Database journey. It's the book I wish I'd had when I first started using Oracle Database so many years ago. It's the book that I would have liked to have given to the many IT colleagues and friends who, over the years, have asked me to teach them the basics of Oracle Database.

I started my own journey more than 10 years ago when my manager at the time, Bill Schwimmer, gave me the chance to become an Oracle Database administrator back in the days of Oracle 7. Books on Oracle Database were fewer then, and I relied on printed copies of the manuals, which I had to share with the rest of the team; this was in the days before Google, when Netscape Navigator had just appeared on the scene.

Today the Oracle Database manuals can be downloaded for free from the Oracle website. But their size has grown tremendously over the years. The Oracle Database 7.3 SQL reference manual had about 750 pages; the 11g version is twice that size. You definitely don't want to be carrying a printed copy of that in your backpack!

The book that you have in your hands is not an exhaustive reference manual by any stretch of the term; it is a more manageable introduction to key Oracle Database administration topics, including planning, installation, monitoring, troubleshooting, maintenance, backups, and performance tuning—to name just a few. You'll be getting the benefit of my experience not just the party line found in the manuals. For example, for reasons explained inside, I emphasize the Statspack tool instead of Automatic Workload Repository (AWR).

In this book, you'll find information that you won't find in other books on Oracle Database. Here you'll find not just technical information but guidance on the work practices that are as vital to your success as technical skills. The most important chapter in the book is "The Big Picture and the Ten Deliverables." If you take the lessons in that chapter to heart, you can quickly become a much better Oracle database administrator than you ever thought possible.

Who This Book Is For

I was a C programmer before I became a database administrator. For lack of a text like this, it took me quite a while to adjust to my new role. If you are an IT professional who has been thrust into an Oracle Database administration role without the benefit of formal training, or just want to understand how Oracle Database works, then I wrote this book for you.

How This Book Is Structured

The chapters of this book are logically organized into four parts that closely track the way your database administration career will naturally evolve. Part I is a necessary back-grounder in relational database theory and Oracle Database concepts, Part II will teach you how to implement an Oracle Database correctly, Part III will expose you to the daily routine of a database administrator, and Part IV will introduce you to the fine art of performance tuning. Each chapter has a section of exercises that are designed to help you apply the lessons of the chapter. Each chapter also includes a list of reference works that contain more information on the topic of the chapter.

Part I: Database Concepts

You may be in a hurry to learn how to create a database but I hope you will take the time to first understand the underlying theory. You won't regret it.

Chapter 1: Relational Database Management Systems

Leonardo da Vinci said, *"Those who are in love with practice without knowledge are like the sailor who gets into a ship without rudder or compass and who never can be certain [where] he is going. Practice must always be founded on sound theory."* How can you competently administer a relational database management system like Oracle if you don't really know what makes a "relational" database relational or what a database management system manages for you? This chapter will help you find your bearings and prepare you for what is to come in the rest of the book.

Chapter 2: SQL and PL/SQL

All database user activity is conducted in Structured Query Language (SQL), and therefore database administrators need to be intimately familiar with it. The greatest potential for performance improvement usually lies within the software application, not within the database where the application stores its data or within the physical infrastructure where the database is housed. An equally important reason why database administrators need to be intimately familiar with SQL is that all database administration activities such as database maintenance and user management are also conducted in SQL. A third reason is that SQL has deficiencies that must be guarded against. These deficiencies include redundancy, problems introduced by nullable data items, and the absence of prohibitions on duplicate data records.

Chapter 3: Oracle Architecture

Just as an automobile engine has a lot of interconnected parts that must all work well together, and just as an automobile mechanic must understand the individual parts and how they relate to the whole, the Oracle database engine has a lot of interconnected parts, and the database administrator must understand the individual parts and how they relate to the whole. This chapter provides a short overview of the Oracle engine.

Part II: Database Implementation

After spending some time on database theory, you'll be eager to create your first database. I hope that you take the opportunity to install Oracle on your own XP or Vista laptop—the best way to learn is by doing.

Chapter 4: Planning

Your goal as Oracle administrator is not simply to create a database but to be on time, on budget, and to meet the availability and performance targets of the business. As with any goal, careful planning is the key to success. You have little control over a number of factors that affect the success of your database; for example, application design and testing. This chapter discusses three important issues that are definitely within your circle of influence and that you cannot afford to ignore: licensing, architecture, and sizing.

Chapter 5: Software Installation

In this chapter, I'll go over a few prerequisites such as obtaining the software, installation guides, and reference manuals. I'll also discuss the installation of software that precedes the creation of a database. I'll show you how I installed the Oracle software on my laptop running Windows XP Professional.

Chapter 6: Database Creation

Database creation is easier that you would think; it's the tasks that come before and after that take a lot of time. In this chapter, I'll first discuss the "Next-Next-Next; click Finish" method of creating a database. I'll then briefly discuss some tasks that you should consider performing after you create a database; specifically, installing the RDA and Statspack tools and disabling database features that have not been licensed. Finally, I'll introduce the manual method of database creation and some basic administrative tasks.

Chapter 7: Physical Database Design

Performance considerations can come to the forefront at any time during the life of the database; new queries can be introduced at any time. Database administrators must therefore understand the mechanisms that can be used to improve performance, and this chapter discusses three broad categories. *Indexes* can be used to quickly find the data. *Partitions* and *clusters* can be used to organize the data. Finally, *materialized views* and *denormalized tables* can be used to perform expensive operations like Joins ahead of time.

Chapter 8: User Management and Data Loading

Your job does not end when you create a database; you still have to get the data into it and ensure that those who have a need to use it can do so. This chapter discusses how to control users and how to get large amounts of data in and out of databases. User management and data loading are two common chores performed by database administrators.

Part III: Database Support

The easy part is over. You have created a database and loaded it with data. Now you have to turn your attention to the care and feeding of it.

Chapter 9: Taking Control

If you are going to be responsible for a database, you need to know what it contains and how it is being used. Which are the biggest tables? How are the data files, control files, and log files laid out? How many people have database accounts? How many people use the database at a time? Your first action when you acquire responsibility for a database should be to thoroughly explore it.

In this chapter, you'll learn about form-based tools such as Enterprise Manager, SQL Developer, and Remote Diagnostic Agent which make it easy to explore the database and simplify the task of database administration.

Chapter 10: Monitoring

When I was growing up, I was sometimes wakened at night by the sound of a walking stick tapping on the ground—it was the night watchman patrolling the neighborhood. He would have had a better chance of surprising any burglars if he'd crept up on them quietly, but I never questioned why he advertised his presence so loudly. Armed only with a walking stick, he would have to rely on strong lungs to wake up the neighborhood if he saw any burglars, so perhaps it was best to advertise his presence and hope that burglars would flee when they heard him coming. Nevertheless, the sound of his stick was comforting—it was good to know that someone trustworthy was watching the neighborhood while we slept.

The database administrator is responsible for watching the database. If something goes wrong with the database that could have been prevented, there is nobody else to blame. As you'll learn in this chapter, database availability, changes, security, growth, backups, workload, performance, and capacity are some of the areas that should be monitored.

Chapter 11: Fixing Problems

In this chapter, you will watch a real-life problem as it progresses from detection to resolution. You will learn a five-step systematic approach to problem-fixing and the difference between *incident management* and *problem management*. I will cover the variety of Internet resources that are available to you, introduce an Oracle knowledge base called MetaLink, and explain how to get technical support from Oracle Corporation. Finally, I will discuss some common database problems.

Chapter 12: Backups

American national hero Benjamin Franklin often wrote anonymous letters to the *Pennsylvania Gazette,* a prominent newspaper that he himself owned and edited. In one such letter he coined the famous phrase *"an ounce of prevention is worth a pound of cure"* and, in addition to making several suggestions for the prevention of fires, he suggested that Philadelphia imitate his native Boston in establishing fire stations and employing firefighters; not only should all efforts be made to prevent fires but the city should be adequately prepared to handle the next inevitable fire.

Backups are to a database what fire stations and fire fighters are to a city; we may protect the database against damage the best we can, but we must be prepared if the database ever gets damaged, through user or operator error or hardware failure, and needs to be repaired. In this chapter you'll learn about the different kinds of backups and the tools used to create them.

Chapter 13: Recovery

In the previous chapter, you learned how to make backup copies of the database; you will now turn your attention to repairing the database if it gets damaged.

Chapter 14: Database Maintenance

In *The Little Prince* by Antoine de Saint-Exupéry, the protagonist meets a little prince whose home was on an asteroid. In one of their discussions, the little prince talked about the importance of proper maintenance, saying *"Sometimes, there is no harm in putting off a piece of work until another day. But when it is a matter of baobabs, that always means a catastrophe. I knew a planet that was inhabited by a lazy man. He neglected three little bushes …"* You can quite imagine what might happen to an asteroid if three little bushes are allowed to grow into immense baobab trees.

In this chapter, we go over the maintenance that is needed to keep your database in peak operating condition.

Chapter 15: The Big Picture and the Ten Deliverables

This is the most important chapter in this book—I discuss the big IT picture and offer very specific guidance in the form of the database administration role's ten deliverables. Few, if any, other books address this topic. If you take the lessons in this one chapter to heart, you can quickly become a better Oracle Database administrator than you thought possible.

Competency in Oracle technology is only half of the challenge of being a database administrator. If you had very little knowledge of Oracle technology but knew exactly *what* needed to be done, you could always find out *how* to do it—there is Google and there are online manuals a-plenty. Too many Oracle database administrators don't know *what* to do and what they have when they are through is "just a mess without a clue."

Part IV: Database Tuning

There's no such thing as a completely self-tuning car and there's no such thing as a completely self-tuning database. Performance tuning can often be a puzzle that requires a creative solution.

Chapter 16: Instance Tuning

Database tuning can be a complex exercise but it can be facilitated by a systematic approach. This chapter describes a systematic five-step approach to performance tuning. It also presents the most important tools provided by Oracle to help with performance tuning; Statspack is emphasized because newer tools such as AWR and ADDM require costly licenses and are not available at most sites. In particular, you will learn a powerful method of mining the Statspack repository for data on performance trends. A highlight of this chapter is the very detailed performance tuning exercise at the end; it will reinforce the lessons of the chapter.

Chapter 17: SQL Tuning

Perhaps the most complex problem in database administration is SQL tuning, and it is not a coincidence that I left it for the very end. The paucity of books devoted to SQL tuning is evidence of the difficulty of the topic. The only ways to interact with Oracle, to retrieve data, to change data, to administer the database, are via SQL. Oracle itself uses SQL to perform all the work that it does behind the scenes. SQL performance is therefore the key to database performance; all database performance problems are really SQL performance problems even if they express themselves as contention for resources.

In this chapter, I will present some of the causes of inefficient SQL and some of the common techniques of making SQL more efficient. Most of the time will be spent working through a case study; I will show you a fairly typical SQL statement and improve it in stages until it hits the theoretical maximum level of performance that is possible to achieve.

Source Code and Updates

As you work through the examples in this book, you may decide that you prefer to type in all the code by hand. Many readers choose to do this because it is a good way to get familiar with the coding techniques that are being used.

Whether you want to type the code in or not, all the source code for this book is available in the Source Code section of the Apress web site (http://www.apress.com). If you like to type in the code, you can use the source code files to check the results you should be getting—they should be your first stop if you think you might have typed in an error. If you don't like typing, then downloading the source code from the Apress web site is a must! Either way, the code files will help you with updates and debugging.

Errata

Apress makes every effort to make sure that there are no errors in the text or the code. However, to err is human, and as such we recognize the need to keep you informed of any mistakes as they're discovered and corrected. Errata sheets are available for all our books at http://www.apress.com. If you find an error that hasn't already been reported, please let us know.

The Apress web site acts as a focus for other information and support, including the code from all Apress books, sample chapters, previews of forthcoming titles, and articles on related topics.

Contacting the Author

Please send any comments and suggestions to BeginningOracle11gDBA@yahoo.com.

PART I

Database Concepts

CHAPTER 1

∎∎∎

Relational Database Management Systems

Those who are in love with practice without knowledge are like the sailor who gets into a ship without rudder or compass and who never can be certain [where] he is going. Practice must always be founded on sound theory.

—The Discourse on Painting by Leonardo da Vinci

When I was a junior programmer, quite early in my career, my friends and I were assigned to work on a big software development project for which we would have to use unfamiliar technologies, though we were promised that training would be provided before the project started. All we knew in advance was that the operating system was something called VAX/VMS; we did not know which programming language or database would be used. The very first thing the instructor said was (paraphrasing) "First you have to insert your definitions into the CDD," and he walked to the chalkboard and wrote the commands that we needed for the purpose. Needless to say, we were quite flustered because we had no idea what those "definitions" might be or what a "CDD" was and how it fit into the big picture.

I've been told that the first thing I should tell you is how to create an Oracle 11*g* database. Well, if you really must know, the necessary command is `CREATE DATABASE` followed by your choice of name for the database—anybody can type that command and create an Oracle 11*g* database. But the mere knowledge of a few Oracle commands (or even a lot of Oracle commands) will not make anyone an Oracle database administrator. What Leonardo said is so important that I'll quote it again: "*Those who are in love with practice without knowledge are like the sailor who gets into a ship without rudder or compass and who never can be certain [where] he is going. Practice must always be founded on sound theory.*" How can you competently administer a relational database management system like Oracle if you don't really know what makes a "relational" database relational or what a database management system manages for you?

What Is a Database?

Chris Date was the keynote speaker at one of the educational conferences organized by the Northern California Oracle Users Group (NoCOUG), of whose journal I am the editor. The local television news station sent out a crew to cover the event because Chris Date is a well-known database theoretician and one of the associates of Dr. Edgar Codd, the inventor of relational database theory. The news reporter cornered me and asked me if I was willing to answer a few questions for the camera. I was quite flattered but when the reporter pointed the camera at me and asked "Why are databases important to society?" all I could think of to say was (paraphrasing) "Well, they're important because they're, like, *really* important, you know." Ten years of database administration under my belt and I still flunked the final exam!

I'd therefore like us to spend just a few minutes at the outset considering what the word *database* signifies. An understanding of the implications of the word and the responsibilities that go along with them will serve you well as a good database administrator.

We might begin by saying that databases can contain data that is confidential and must be protected from prying eyes. Only authorized users should be able to access the data, their privileges must be suitably restricted, and their actions must be logged. Even if the data in the databases is for public consumption, we might still need to restrict who can update the data, who can delete from it, and who can add to it. Competent *security management* is therefore part of your job.

We might also say that databases can be critical to the ability of the organization to function properly. Organizations such as banks and e-commerce web sites require their databases to be available around the clock. Competent *availability management* is therefore an important part of your job. In the event of a disaster such as flood or fire, the databases may have to be relocated to an alternative location using backups. Competent *continuity management* is therefore another important part of your job. We also need competent *change management* to protect the database from unauthorized or badly tested changes, *incident management* to detect problems and restore service quickly, *problem management* to provide permanent fixes for known issues, *configuration management* to document infrastructure components and their dependencies, and *release management* to bring discipline to the never-ending task of applying patches and upgrades to software and hardware.

We might also observe that databases can be very big. The first database I worked with, for the semiconductor manufacturing giant Intel, was less than 100 megabytes in size and only had a few dozen data tables. Today, databases used by enterprise application suites like Peoplesoft, Siebel, and Oracle Applications are tens or hundreds of gigabytes in size and might have ten thousand tables or more. One reason databases are now so large is that advancements in magnetic disk storage technology have made it feasible to efficiently store and retrieve large quantities of nontextual data such as pictures and sound.

We might also note that databases can grow rapidly and that we need to plan for growth. We might also see that database applications might consume huge amounts of computing resources. *Capacity management* is therefore another important part of your job, and you need a capacity plan that accommodates both continuous data growth and increasing needs for computing resources.

When we stop thinking in terms of Oracle commands such as CREATE DATABASE *and start thinking in terms such as security management, availability management, continuity management, change management, incident management, problem management, configuration management, release management, and capacity management, the business of database administration begins to make coherent sense and we become more effective database administrators. These terms are the part of the standard jargon of the IT Infrastructure Library (ITIL), a suite of best practices used by IT organizations throughout the world.*

Now would you like to take a stab at answering the question that floored me in the television interview: *Why are databases important to society?*

What Is a *Relational* Database?

Relational database theory was invented by Dr. Edgar Codd in 1970 in a paper titled "A Relational Model for Data for Large Shared Data Banks."[1] He based his theory on rigorous mathematical principles and used the correct mathematical term relation to describe what we loosely refer to as a *table*. The word *table* is not a mathematical term, but *relation* is a precisely defined mathematical term, and a lot of good mathematics can be built around its definition.

Definition of the Term *Relation*

In simple terms, a relation is an association of the members of two or more sets. Here is the precise definition found in Dr. Codd's paper:

> *Given sets S1, S2,..., Sn (not necessarily distinct), R is a relation on these n sets if it is a set of n-tuples each of which has its first element from S1, its second element from S2, and so on.*

---

1. Codd, Edgar. "A Relational Model for Data for Large Shared Data Banks," *Communications of the ACM*, Volume 13, Issue 6 (June 1970).

Well, this just seems to be a boring mathematical way of complicating a simple concept like a table and does not explain why the relational approach swept aside all that came before it. To understand why the relational approach was revolutionary, we have first to understand the technologies that came before it and how they were deficient. We must then study the "relational operators" that produce new relations from old.

Network Databases

An example of a pre-relational database technology was the "network database" technology, one of the best examples of which was DEC/DBMS, created by Digital Equipment Corporation for the VAX/VMS and OpenVMS platforms—it still survives today as Oracle/DBMS. Yes, it's strange but it's true—Oracle Corporation, the maker of the world's dominant relational database technology, also sells a prerelational database technology. According to Oracle Corporation, Oracle/DBMS is a very powerful, reliable and sophisticated database technology that has continued relevance and that Oracle is committed to supporting. Here are some quotes from Oracle Corporation's web site.

> CODASYL DBMS is a multiuser, CODASYL-compliant database management system for OpenVMS operating systems. CODASYL DBMS is designed for databases of all levels of complexity, ranging from simple hierarchies to sophisticated networks with multilevel relationships. CODASYL DBMS provides a reliable operating platform for application environments where stability, high availability, and throughput are essential. ... Oracle's strategy for CODASYL DBMS beyond Release 7 is continued emphasis on availability, VLDB capabilities, and performance. ... Our overall objective is that of continuous support and enhancement to ensure DBMS keeps its reputation for stability and quality.[2]

In a network database, data records are linked together in chains. Consider an example involving three record types: SUPPLIER, PART, and QUOTE; each SUPPLIER record stores information about a supplier, each PART record stores information about a part, and each QUOTE record stores the price quoted by a supplier for a part. Figure 1-1 shows how records might be linked together. We see that hammers are supplied by three different suppliers and that New Yankee Workshop, Inc. has quoted the lowest price.

---

2. CODASYL is the Conference on Data Systems Languages, an industry consortium that wrote the specifications for the COBOL programming language.

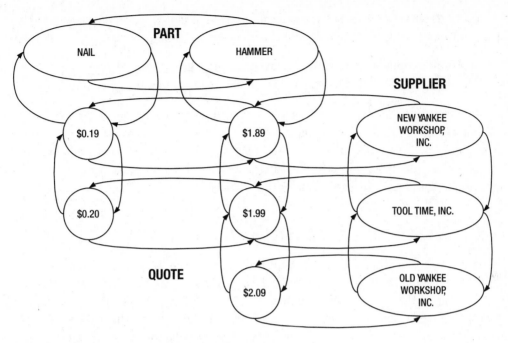

Figure 1-1. *Relationship between suppliers and parts*

Assuming that the chains of quotes are sorted in ascending order and that individual PART records and SUPPLIER records can be quickly located using the *hash* technique,[3] the database organization shown in Figure 1-1 allows us to accomplish the following tasks.

1. List all the information available for a specified part—the hash indexing method allows us to retrieve the required PART record quickly.

2. List all the information available for a specified supplier—the hash indexing method also allows us to retrieve the required SUPPLIER record quickly.

3. List all parts—this can be answered by traversing the chain of PART records from the beginning to the end.

4. List all suppliers—this can be answered by traversing the chain of SUPPLIER records from the beginning to the end.

5. List all suppliers of a specified part—this can be answered by traversing the chain of QUOTE records linked to the specific PART record.

---

3. *Hash* techniques are used to compute a numeric value from a nonnumeric value such as a part code. A data record can then be stored at the address corresponding to this numeric value and can be found at this address at a future time. Hash techniques thus serve the same purpose as an index.

6. List all parts supplied by a specified supplier—this can be answered by traversing the chain of QUOTE records linked to the specific SUPPLIER record.

7. List the supplier who has quoted the lowest price for a specified part—this can be answered by finding the first QUOTE record linked to the specific PART record.

But other tasks such as "list the suppliers who supply all parts," "list the parts that are supplied by all suppliers," and "list the suppliers who supply all the parts supplied by a specified supplier at cheaper prices" cannot be easily accomplished using the network database structure diagrammed in Figure 1-1. But they are easily accomplished with a relational database, as we shall soon see.

Definition of a *Relational* Database

Relational database technology swept aside the older technologies precisely because it proved flexible enough to answer all kinds of questions; not just a small set of questions. This is because relational databases come with *relational operators* that produce new relations from old. Here, then, is a "rough and ready" definition (slightly paraphrased) of a relational database from C.J. Date's *An Introduction to Database Systems, Eighth Edition* (Addison-Wesley, 2003):

> *A relational database is a database in which: The data is perceived by the user as tables (and nothing but tables)[4] and the operators available to the user for (for example) retrieval are operators that derive "new" tables from "old" ones.*

Relational Operators

Let's examine some relational operators and use them to answer the question: *Which suppliers supply all parts?* But first, we need to organize our data into tables. Tables 1-1 through 1-3 list the contents of a sample database that we'll use to explore the workings of relational operators.

Table 1-1. *The Part Table*

PartName
HAMMER
NAIL

---

4. Having explained the origin of the word *relation*, we can start using the more common term *table* wherever we are referring to a relation.

Table 1-2. *The Supplier Table*

SupplierName
NEW YANKEE WORKSHOP, INC.
OLD YANKEE WORKSHOP, INC.
TOOL TIME, INC.

Table 1-3. *The Quote Table*

SuppplierName	PartName	Quote
NEW YANKEE WORKSHOP, INC.	HAMMER	$1.89
NEW YANKEE WORKSHOP, INC.	NAIL	$0.19
OLD YANKEE WORKSHOP, INC.	HAMMER	$2.09
TOOL TIME, INC.	HAMMER	$1.99
TOOL TIME, INC.	NAIL	$0.20

Table 1-4 lists the definitions of five relational operators, four of which we will need to answer the question: *Which suppliers supply all parts?*

Table 1-4. *Five Relational Operators*[5]

Operator	Definition
Selection	Form another table by extracting a subset of the rows of a table of interest using some criteria.
Projection	Form another table by extracting a subset of the columns of a table of interest. Any duplicate rows that are formed as a result of the projection operation are eliminated.
Union	Form another table by selecting all rows from two tables of interest. If the first table has 10 rows and the second table has 20 rows, then the resulting table will have at most 30 rows, because duplicates will eliminated from the result.
Difference	Form another table by extracting only those rows from one table of interest that do not occur in a second table.
Join	Form another table by concatenating records from two tables of interest. For example, if the first table has 10 rows and the second table has 20 rows, then the resulting table will have 200 rows—and if the first table has 10 columns and the second table has 20 columns, then the resulting table will have 30 columns.

We can compute the answer to the question *"Which suppliers supply all parts?"* in a sequence of five steps. At each step, we use one of the relational operators just listed and create an intermediate result table.

---

5. It is possible to create new operations by combining the listed operations. For example, "Natural Join" is the result produced by a Join operation on two tables followed by a Selection operation on the resulting intermediate table.

1. In the first step, we use the Join operation and form an intermediate result table by concatenating records from the Suppliers table and the Parts table. All combinations of SupplierName and PartName occur in this table. Table 1-5 shows the result.

Table 1-5. *All SupplierName and PartName Combinations*

SupplierName	PartName
NEW YANKEE WORKSHOP, INC.	HAMMER
NEW YANKEE WORKSHOP, INC.	NAIL
OLD YANKEE WORKSHOP, INC.	HAMMER
OLD YANKEE WORKSHOP, INC.	NAIL
TOOL TIME, INC.	HAMMER
TOOL TIME, INC.	NAIL

2. In the second step, we use the Projection operation and form another intermediate result table by extracting the SupplierName and PartName columns from the Quotes table. The result in Table 1-6 is the list of valid SupplierName and PartName combinations.

Table 1-6. *Valid SupplierName and PartName Combinations*

SupplierName	PartName
NEW YANKEE WORKSHOP, INC.	HAMMER
NEW YANKEE WORKSHOP, INC.	NAIL
OLD YANKEE WORKSHOP, INC.	HAMMER
TOOL TIME, INC.	HAMMER
TOOL TIME, INC.	NAIL

3. In the third step, we use the Difference operation and form a third intermediate result table, shown in Table 1-7, by extracting only those rows from the intermediate result table created in the first step that are not to be found in the intermediate result table created in the second step. The occurrence of a certain combination of SupplierName and PartName in this new intermediate table indicates that the supplier in question does not supply the indicated part.

Table 1-7. *Invalid SupplierName and PartName Combinations*

SupplierName	PartName
OLD YANKEE WORKSHOP, INC.	NAIL

4. In the fourth step, we use the Projection operation and form yet another intermediate result table by extracting only the first column from the intermediate result
table created in the third step. The result, shown in Table 1-8, is the list of suppliers who do not supply at least one part.

Table 1-8. *Suppliers Who Do Not Supply All Parts*

SupplierName
OLD YANKEE WORKSHOP, INC.

5. In the fifth and final step, we use the Difference operation once again and obtain
the final result we were seeking by extracting only those rows from the Suppliers
table that do not occur in the intermediate result table of the fourth step. Table 1-9
shows the final result, which is the required list of suppliers who do supply all parts!

Table 1-9. *Suppliers Who Supply All Parts*

SupplierName
NEW YANKEE WORKSHOP, INC.
TOOL TIME, INC.

RELATIONAL ALGEBRA EXPRESSIONS

Just as numbers and arithmetical symbols such as addition and multiplication can be combined into an
arithmetical expression, so also can tables and table operators be combined into a relational algebra
expression. We can specify the previous sequence of steps in a single expression as shown here.

```
Supplier MINUS PROJECTION((Part JOIN Supplier) MINUS PROJECTION(Quote))
```

Structured Query Language

The specification of relational algebra expressions is facilitated by an English-like language
called Structured Query Language or SQL. As an example, let's look at the SQL formulation of
the query *Which suppliers supply all parts?* Multiple formulations are possible, and the one
shown in Listing 1-1 uses a technique called *subquery factoring* to produce the intended
result using the same series of short steps that was used in the previous section.

Listing 1-1. *Suppliers Who Supply All Parts*

```
WITH

-- Step 1: Join operation
    supplierpart AS
    (SELECT suppliername, partname
        FROM supplier, part),

-- Step 2: Projection operation
    validsupplierpart AS
    (SELECT suppliername, partname
        FROM quote),

-- Step 3: Difference operation
    invalidsupplierpart AS
    (SELECT suppliername, partname
        FROM supplierpart
     MINUS
     SELECT suppliername, partname
        FROM validsupplierpart),

-- Step 4: Projection operation
    unwantedsupplier AS
    (SELECT suppliername
        FROM invalidsupplierpart),

-- Step 5: Difference operation
    wantedsupplier AS
    (SELECT suppliername
        FROM supplier
     MINUS
     SELECT suppliername
        FROM unwantedsupplier)

SELECT suppliername
  FROM wantedsupplier;
```

The SQL statement shown in Listing 1-1 is fairly English-like and self-explanatory, and we will resume the discussion of SQL in the next chapter. For now, note how the formatting improves readability—the elegantly formatted version with vertical "rivers" and capitalized "reserved words"[6] shown in Listing 1-1 was produced using a tool called Toad and is completely equivalent to the unreadable version shown in Listing 1-2.

Listing 1-2. *Unreadable SQL Query*

```
with supplierpart as (select suppliername, partname from supplier, part),
validsupplierpart as (select suppliername, partname from quote),
invalidsupplierpart as (select suppliername, partname from supplierpart minus
select suppliername, partname from validsupplierpart), unwantedsupplier as (select
suppliername from invalidsupplierpart), wantedsupplier as (select suppliername from
supplier minus select suppliername from unwantedsupplier) select suppliername from
wantedsupplier;
```

Efficiency of Relational Operators

You may have noticed that the discussion in the previous section made no mention of efficiency. The definitions of the table operations do not explain how the results can be efficiently obtained. This is, in fact, intentional and is one of the greatest strengths of relational database technology—*it is left to the database management system to provide efficient implementations of the table operations*. In particular, the selection operation depends heavily on indexing schemes and Oracle Database provides a host of such schemes, including B-tree indexes, index-organized tables, partitioned tables, partitioned indexes, function indexes, reverse-key indexes, bitmap indexes, table clusters, and hash clusters. We'll discuss indexing possibilities as part of physical database design in Chapter 7.

Query Optimization

Perhaps the most important aspect of relational algebra expressions is that, except in very simple cases, they can be rearranged in different ways to gain a performance advantage without changing their meaning or causing the results to change. The following two expressions are equivalent, except perhaps in the order in which data columns occur in the result—a minor presentation detail, not one that changes the meaning of the result.

Listing 1-3. *Joining Two Tables*

```
Table_1 JOIN Table_2
Table_2 JOIN Table_1
```

---

6. Words that have special meaning in SQL.

The number of ways in which a relational algebra expression can be rearranged increases dramatically as the expressions grow longer. Even the relatively simple expression (Table_1 JOIN Table_2) JOIN Table_3 can be arranged in the following 12 equivalent ways that produce results differing only in the order in which columns are presented—a cosmetic detail that can be easily remedied before the results are shown to the user.

Listing 1-4. *Joining Three Tables*

```
(Table_1 JOIN Table_2) JOIN Table_3
(Table_1 JOIN Table_3) JOIN Table_2
(Table_2 JOIN Table_1) JOIN Table_3
(Table_2 JOIN Table_3) JOIN Table_1
(Table_3 JOIN Table_1) JOIN Table_2
(Table_3 JOIN Table_2) JOIN Table_1


Table_1 JOIN (Table_2 JOIN Table_3)
Table_1 JOIN (Table_3 JOIN Table_2)
Table_2 JOIN (Table_1 JOIN Table_3)
Table_2 JOIN (Table_3 JOIN Table_1)
Table_3 JOIN (Table_1 JOIN Table_2)
Table_3 JOIN (Table_2 JOIN Table_1)
```

It is not obvious at this stage what performance advantage, if any, is gained by rearranging relational algebra expressions. Nor is it obvious what criteria should be used while rearranging expressions. Suffice it to say that a relational algebra expression is intended to be a *nonprocedural* specification of an intended result and the *query optimizer* may take any actions intended to improve the efficiency of query processing as long as the result is not changed. Relational query optimization is the subject of much theoretical research, and the Oracle query optimizer continues to be improved in every release of Oracle Database. We shall return to the subject of SQL query tuning in Chapter 17.

What Is a Database Management System?

Database management systems such as Oracle are the interface between users and databases. Database management systems differ in the range of features they provide, but all of them offer certain core features such as *transaction management*, *data integrity*, and *security*. And, of course, they offer the ability to create databases and to define their structure, as well as to store, retrieve, update, and delete the data in the database.

Transaction Management

A *transaction* is a unit of work that may involve several small steps, all of which are necessary in order not to compromise the integrity of the database. For example, a *logical* operation such as inserting a row into a table may involve several *physical* operations such as index updates, *trigger* operations,[7] and *recursive* operations.[8] A transaction may also involve multiple logical operations. For, example transferring money from one bank account to another may require that two separate rows be updated. A DBMS needs to ensure that transactions are *atomic, consistent, isolated*, and *durable.*

The Atomicity Property of Transactions

It is always possible for a transaction to fail at any intermediate step. For example, the user may lose his or her connection to the database or the database may run out of space and may not be able to accommodate new data that the user is trying to store. If a failure occurs, the database management system performs automatic *rollback* of the work that has been performed so far. Transactions are therefore *atomic* or indivisible from a logical perspective. The end of a transaction is indicated by an explicit instruction such as COMMIT.

The Consistency Property of Transactions

Transactions also have the *consistency* property. That is, they do not compromise the integrity of the database. However, it is easy to see that the database may be *temporarily* inconsistent during the operation of the transaction. In the previous example, the database is in an inconsistent state when money has been subtracted from the balance in the first account but has not yet been added to the balance in the second account.

The Isolation Property of Transactions

Transactions also have the *isolation* property; that is, concurrently occurring transactions must not interact in ways that produce incorrect results. A database management system must be capable of ensuring that the results produced by concurrently executing transactions are *serializable;* that is, the outcome must be the same as if the transactions were executed in serial fashion instead of concurrently.

    For example, suppose that one transaction is withdrawing money from a bank customer's checking account, and another transaction is simultaneously withdrawing money from

---

7. Trigger operations are operations that are automatically performed when the triggering event occurs. For example, an attempt to update data in one table may cause a *log record* to be written to another table.

8. Recursive operations are *management operations* that are performed by the database in order to support user operations. For example, an attempt to insert new data into a table might necessitate that additional space be allocated to accommodate the new data.

the same customer's savings account. Let's assume that negative balances are permitted as long as the *sum* of the balances in the two accounts is not negative. Suppose that the operation of the two transactions proceeds in such a way that each transaction determines the balances in both accounts before either of them has had an opportunity to update either balance. Unless the database management system does something to prevent it, this can potentially result in a negative sum. This kind of problem is called *write skew*.

A detailed discussion of isolation and serializability properly belongs in an advanced course on application development, not in a beginner text on database administration. The interested reader will find more information online, in the *Oracle 11g Advanced Application Developer's Guide,* available at `http://www.oracle.com/technology/documentation/index.html`.

The Durability Property of Transactions

Transactions also have the *durability* property. This means that once all the steps in a transaction have been successfully completed and the user notified, the results must be considered permanent even if there is a subsequent computer failure, such as a damaged disk. We will return to this topic in the chapters on database backups and recovery; for now, we note that the end of a transaction is indicated by an explicit command such as `COMMIT`.

Data Integrity

Data loses its value if it cannot be trusted to be correct. A database management system provides the ability to define and enforce *integrity constraints*. The database management system will reject any attempt to violate the integrity constraints when inserting, updating, or deleting data records and will typically display an appropriate error code and message. In fact, the very first Oracle error code, "ORA-00001," relates to attempts to violate an integrity constraint. It is possible to enforce arbitrary constraints using trigger operations; these can include checks that are as complex as necessary, but the more common types of constraints are *check constraints*, *uniqueness constraints*, and *referential constraints*.

Check Constraints

Check constraints are usually simple checks on the values of a data item. For example, a price quote must not be less than $0.00.

Uniqueness Constraints

A uniqueness constraint requires that some part of a record be unique. For example, two employees may not have the same employee number. A unique part of a record is called a *candidate key,* and one of the candidate keys is designated as the *primary key*. Intuitively, we expect every record to have at least one candidate key; otherwise, we would have no way of specifying which records we needed. Note that the candidate key can consist of a single item from the data record, a combination of items, or even all the items.

Referential Constraints

Consider the example of an employee database in which all payments to employees are recorded in a table called Salary. The employee number in a salary record must obviously correspond to the employee number in some employee record; this is an example of a *referential constraint*.[9]

Data Security

A database management system gives the owners of the data a lot of control over their data—they can delegate limited rights to others if they choose to. It also gives the database administrator the ability to restrict and monitor the actions of users. For example, the database administrator can disable the password of an employee who leaves the company, to prevent him or her from gaining access to the database. Relational database management systems use techniques such as *views* (virtual tables defined in terms of other tables) and *query modification* to give individual users access to just those portions of data they are authorized to use.

Oracle offers extensive query modification capabilities under the name of Virtual Private Database (VPD), but here is a simple example of the technique from a database management system called Ingres. A manager named Solomon Grundy is being given permission to retrieve and update the name, age, and salary of just those employees that he manages. When he tries to retrieve records from the employee data table, the following additional clauses are silently appended to his query:

```
employee.departmentnumber = department.departmentnumber
and department.managername = "Solomon Grundy"
```

---

9. Database management systems are a perpetual work in progress and each new version offers new features. Strange as it may sound, the Oracle database management system did not enforce "referential integrity" constraints until Version 7 was released in the 1990s (by which time it was already the world's largest database company). It would not, for example, prevent a salary from being inadvertently paid to a non-existent employee. The following quote from an article published in *Software* magazine in 1989 alludes to a time when network database management systems outclassed relational database management systems in areas such as data integrity:

> "About six or seven years ago when I worked for a vendor that made a [network] DBMS called Seed, I spoke at a conference. Also speaking was Larry Rowe, one of the founders of Relational Technology, Inc. and one of the developers of the relational DBMS Ingres. We were about to be clobbered by these new relational systems. He suggested to me that the best way to compete against the relational systems was to point out that they did not support referential integrity."

This filters out rows of data that Solomon Grundy is not allowed to see by joining each employee record with the corresponding department record and checking that the manager of the department is none other than Solomon Grundy. Furthermore, as shown in Listing 1-5, Solomon Grundy can only get access to the data from terminal "tta2" and only from 8 a.m. to 5 p.m. on weekdays.

Listing 1-5. *Query Modification*

```
define permit retrieve, replace of employee (employeename, age, salary)
to sgrundy at "tta2" from 8:00 to 17:00 on mon to fri
where employee.departmentnumber = department.departmentnumber
and department.managername = "Solomon Grundy"
```

We shall return to the subject of data security in a future chapter.

What Makes a Relational Database Management System Relational?

Having already discussed the meaning of both *relational database* and *database management system*, it might appear that the subject is settled. But the natural implications of the relational model are so numerous and profound that critics contend that, even today, a "truly relational" database management system does not exist. For example, Dr. Edgar Codd, the inventor of relational database theory, wanted the database management system to treat "views" in the same manner as "base tables" whenever possible but the problem of view updateability is unsolved to the present day. Dr. Codd listed more than 300 separate requirements that a database management system must meet in order to fulfill his vision properly, and we have time for just one of them—*physical data independence*. Here is the relevant quote from Dr. Codd's book (*The Relational Model for Database Management: Version 2*. Addison Wesley, 1990):

> *RP-1 Physical Data Independence: The DBMS permits a suitably authorized user to make changes in storage representation, in access method, or in both—for example, for performance reasons. Application programs and terminal activities remain logically unimpaired whenever any such changes are made.*

Summary

I hope that you now have an appreciation for the theoretical foundations of Oracle 11g. More information on the subjects we touched upon can be found in the books mentioned in the bibliography at the end of the chapter. Here is a short summary of the concepts we discussed in this chapter.

- A database is an information repository that must be competently administered using the principles laid out in the IT Infrastructure Library (ITIL) including *security management, availability management, continuity management, change management, incident management, problem management, configuration management, release management,* and *capacity management.*

- A *relation* is a precise mathematical term for what we loosely call a data table. Relational database technology swept aside earlier technologies because of the power and expressiveness of *relational algebra* and because it made performance the responsibility of the database management system instead of the application developer.

- A database management system provides efficient algorithms for the processing of table operations as well as indexing schemes for data storage. The *query optimizer* rearranges relational algebra expressions in the interests of efficiency but without changing the meaning or the results that are produced.

- A *database management system* is defined as a software layer that provides services such as *transaction management, data security,* and *data integrity.*

- A *transaction* is a logical unit of work characterized by *atomicity, consistency, isolation,* and *durability.*

- Relational database theory has many consequences including that of *logical data independence,* which implies that changes to the way in which data is stored or indexed should not affect the logical behavior of application programs.

Exercises

The following exercises, based on this chapter's supplier-part example, will help you appreciate the expressive power of relational algebra; in each case, you will need only the table operators that are described in this chapter.

- List the parts that are supplied by all suppliers.

- List the parts that are supplied by OLD YANKEE WORKSHOP, INC. as well as by TOOL TIME, INC.

- List the suppliers who supply at least one part that is not supplied by a specified supplier.

- List the suppliers who do not supply at least one part that is supplied by a specified supplier.

- List the suppliers who supply all the parts supplied by a specified supplier but no others.

- List the suppliers who supply all the parts supplied by a specified supplier at cheaper prices.

- List the parts that are only supplied by a specified supplier.

These exercises are a good preparation for the discussion of Structured Query Language in the next chapter.

Further Reading

Silberschatz, Abraham; Korth, Henry; Sudarshan S. *Database Systems Concepts, Fifth Edition.* McGraw-Hill, 2005. If you had to buy just one book on database theory, this is the one that I would recommend. This standard college textbook, now in its fifth edition, offers not only a fair amount of theory but also coverage of three of the leading commercial relational database management systems: Oracle, IBM DB2 Universal Database, and Microsoft SQL Server. It also covers the leading open-source relational database management system, PostgreSQL.

Date, C. J. *An Introduction to Database Systems, Eighth Edition.* Addison Wesley, 2003. This well-known work, now in its eighth edition, whose author is one of the world's foremost database theoreticians and an associate of Dr. Edgar Codd, takes an extremely rigorous and theoretical approach, which makes the book suitable only for the most dedicated students of relational database technology.

Codd, E. F. *The Relational Model for Database Management: Version 2.* Addison Wesley, 1990. This famous book, now out of print, by the inventor of relational database technology lists more than 300 requirements that a relational database management system must meet in order to fulfill his vision. It makes fascinating reading but, like Date's book, is suitable only for the most dedicated students of relational database technology.

CHAPTER 2

SQL and PL/SQL

A number of our established "powerful" programming language features, even beloved ones, could very well turn out to belong rather to "the problem set" than to "the solution set."

—Dutch computer scientist Edsger Dijkstra, advocate of structured programming and winner of the 1972 Turing Award, in "Correctness Concerns and, Among Other Things, Why They Are Resented"

All database activity is conducted in SQL, and therefore database administrators need to be intimately familiar with it. Figure 2-1 illustrates that the greatest potential for performance improvement usually lies within the software application, not within the database where the application stores its data or within the physical infrastructure where the database is housed.[1]

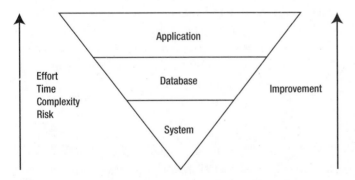

Figure 2-1. *The performance improvement pyramid*

---

1. Based on a discussion in *Oracle Rdb Guide to Database Performance and Tuning*. Rdb is another relational database management system sold by Oracle—Oracle acquired it from Digital Equipment Corporation together with DEC/DBMS, a network database management system.

As an example, consider the following queries in Listing 2-1, both of which retrieve the names of parts supplied by TOOL TIME, INC. The first query does not allow Oracle to use an index of the values of suppliername (if one exists) because it uses the UPPER function to transform the supplier name. If Oracle cannot use an index, it has to retrieve and examine every single record in the data table in question, an expensive proposition. Such transformations should be performed within the application program, before the query is submitted for processing.[2]

Listing 2-1. *Inefficient and Efficient SQL Queries*

```
SELECT partname
  FROM quote
 WHERE suppliername = UPPER('Tool Time, Inc.');

SELECT partname
  FROM quote
 WHERE suppliername = 'TOOL TIME, INC.';
```

An equally important reason why database administrators need to be intimately familiar with SQL is that all database administration activities such as database maintenance and user management are also conducted in SQL. It should come as no surprise, therefore, that the *Oracle Database 11*g *SQL Language Reference* has almost 1,500 pages— compare this with the fewer than 50 pages in this chapter. Fortunately, you can go online and search the SQL manual or download the electronic version free of charge.[3] You can purchase a printed copy if you like having a mountain of paper on your desk.

A third reason why database administrators need to be intimately familiar with SQL is that it has deficiencies that must be guarded against. These deficiencies include redundancy, problems introduced by nullable data items, and the absence of prohibitions on duplicate data records. We will return to this subject later in this chapter.

TRUE STORY

One day an irate software developer submitted a high-priority request that my colleagues and I find out why Oracle was not responding to "simple queries." We found that that he had submitted a query that indiscriminately joined seven tables, that is, a query of the form SELECT ... FROM Table#1, Table#2, Table#3, Table#4, Table#5, Table#6, Table#7.[4] The number of rows produced by

---

2. It is possible to create a *function-based index* of the values of the expression UPPER(suppliername).

3. The URL is http://www.oracle.com/technology/documentation.

4. Such a query is called a *cartesian product*.

such a query equals the product of the number of rows in each table; if each specified table contained 1,000 rows, the query would produce 100 trillion rows.

When we asked the software developer why he had not specified any joining criteria, he said that he first wanted to determine whether Oracle could handle a "simple" query before submitting a "complex" query!

It happened to me—it could happen to you!

Railroad Diagrams

SQL statements have a dizzying array of optional clauses, and Oracle reference works use *railroad diagrams* as a visual aid. Figure 2-2 is an example of a railroad diagram for a hypothetical ROW command.

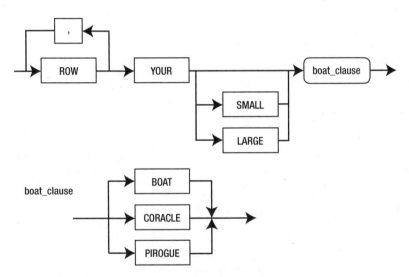

Figure 2-2. *A railroad diagram for a hypothetical* ROW *command*

Travel the railroad track from left to right, unless there is an explicit arrow pointing from right to left. Along the way you will encounter mandatory words and clauses as well as optional words and clauses and subdiagrams.

The preceding diagrams indicate that the ROW command can take the forms indicated in Listing 2-2.

Listing 2-2. *Examples of* ROW *Commands*

```
ROW YOUR BOAT
ROW, ROW YOUR BOAT
ROW, ROW, ROW YOUR CORACLE
ROW, ROW, ROW, ROW YOUR PIROGUE
ROW, ROW, ROW, ROW, ROW YOUR LARGE CORACLE
```

Figure 2-3 is a greatly simplified version of the railroad diagram for the SELECT statement. It is obvious, even from this simplified version, that SELECT statements can range from the very simple to the staggeringly complex.

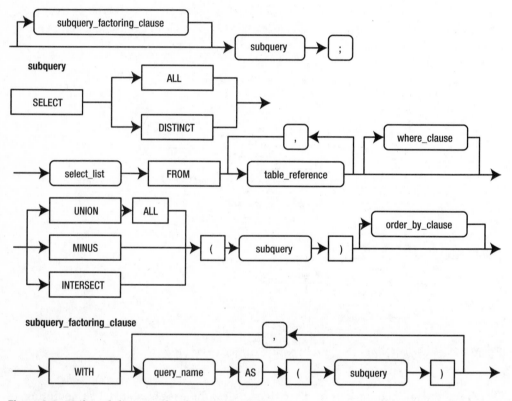

Figure 2-3. *Railroad diagram for the* SELECT *statement*

The diagram starts out with an optional *subquery factoring clause* of the kind you encountered in the first chapter. Mandatory clauses include a SELECT list and a list of tables to be joined. A SELECT list is some combination of data items from the data records that are joined together. Optional clauses include a WHERE clause and an ORDER BY clause; the WHERE clause specifies criteria satisfied by the data items in the records that are joined together, and the ORDER BY clause sorts the results of the query.

Assuming that supplier records include a data item called supplierstatus, the SQL statement conforms to the diagrams in Figure 2-3 and lists the status of suppliers who supply at least one part, as shown in Listing 2-3. If a supplier does not supply any parts, the Join operation will fail and the supplier will not be listed.

Listing 2-3. *Suppliers Who Supply at Least One Part*

```
SELECT DISTINCT supplier.suppliername,
                supplier.supplierstatus
          FROM supplier,
               quote
         WHERE quote.suppliername = supplier.suppliername
      ORDER BY suppliername;
```

The FROM clause specifies that records from which the Supplier and Quote tables are to be joined together for investigation. The WHERE clause specifies that only those records that have matching values of the suppliername data item are to be retained. The SELECT list specifies that the only data items that are really of interest are those in the supplier record itself. The ORDER BY clause specifies how the results should be sorted. The DISTINCT qualifier is required because SQL does not automatically eliminate duplicates (unlike relational algebra).

The most interesting thing about the subquery diagram is that it references *itself*:

- Just before the ORDER BY clause, you can optionally specify a UNION, INTERSECT, or MINUS clause followed by another subquery.

- If you check the Table Reference subdiagram, you will see that a table reference can itself be a subquery. This kind of subquery is called an inline view.

- Subqueries that produce a single value can be used in any place where a single value is indicated. This kind of subquery is called a scalar subquery. In particular, scalar subqueries can be used in a SELECT list and in a WHERE clause.

Types of SQL

Only a small fraction of the SQL reference manual is devoted to the sort of SQL statements that you have encountered so far. SQL statements are commonly classified into Database Manipulation Language (DML) statements to modify data, and Database Definition Language (DDL) statements to create and modify the different types of objects that compose an Oracle database. The SQL reference manual also describes commands that can be used to create and modify databases and to perform database administration activities such as stopping and starting databases.

Data Definition Language

A large portion of the Oracle 11*g* SQL reference manual is devoted to DDL: commands that are used to create, alter, and drop different types of database objects such as tables and indexes.

Listing 2-4 shows the DDL commands that can be used to create the Supplier, Part, and Quote tables used in the first chapter. These commands specify a data type such as *variable character* (VARCHAR) or numeric for each data item, the length of each data item, and, in the case of numeric data items, the precision. VARCHAR(32) indicates no more than 32 data characters, and NUMBER(8, 2) indicates a decimal number with no more than eight digits, two of which are to the right of the decimal point. Each of the three tables has a *primary key*, and the Quote table is linked to the other two tables by *foreign keys*. All data items in this example are specified to be NOT NULL, which simply means that their values cannot be left unspecified. Finally, note that each SQL statement is followed by a terminating semicolon.

Listing 2-4. *DDL Commands to Create the Supplier, Part, and Quote Tables*

```
CREATE TABLE supplier (
  suppliername VARCHAR(32) NOT NULL,
  PRIMARY KEY (suppliername)
);

CREATE TABLE part (
  partname VARCHAR(32) NOT NULL,
  PRIMARY KEY (partname)
);

CREATE TABLE quote (
  suppliername VARCHAR(32) NOT NULL,
  partname VARCHAR(32) NOT NULL,
  quote NUMBER(8,2) NOT NULL,
  PRIMARY KEY (suppliername, partname),
  FOREIGN KEY (suppliername) REFERENCES supplier,
  FOREIGN KEY (partname) REFERENCES part
);
```

Database Manipulation Language

You have already seen several examples of the SELECT statement. Next, let's consider the INSERT, UPDATE, DELETE, and MERGE statements.

The INSERT Statement

Listing 2-5 shows the INSERT statements that can be used to create the data required for the examples in the first chapter. Note that character strings, such as the supplier names and part names used in the example, are enclosed with single quote marks.

Listing 2-5. *DML Commands to Populate the Supplier, Part, and Quote Tables*

```
INSERT INTO part
     VALUES ('HAMMER');
INSERT INTO part
     VALUES ('NAIL');

INSERT INTO supplier
     VALUES ('NEW YANKEE WORKSHOP, INC.');
INSERT INTO supplier
     VALUES ('OLD YANKEE WORKSHOP, INC.');
INSERT INTO supplier
     VALUES ('TOOL TIME, INC.');

INSERT INTO quote
     VALUES ('NEW YANKEE WORKSHOP, INC.', 'HAMMER', '1.89');
INSERT INTO quote
     VALUES ('NEW YANKEE WORKSHOP, INC.', 'NAIL', '0.19');
INSERT INTO quote
     VALUES ('OLD YANKEE WORKSHOP, INC.', 'HAMMER', '2.09');
INSERT INTO quote
     VALUES ('TOOL TIME, INC.', 'HAMMER', '1.99');
INSERT INTO quote
     VALUES ('TOOL TIME, INC.', 'NAIL', '0.20');
```

The UPDATE Statement

The UPDATE statement enables us to specify a subset of data rows and instructions for modifying them. In Listing 2-6—an example of how arithmetic can be used in SQL statements—all price quotes from TOOL TIME, INC. are being increased by 10 percent.

Listing 2-6. *DML Command to Modify the Values of Data Items*

```
UPDATE quote
   SET quote = 1.1 * quote
 WHERE suppliername = 'TOOL TIME, INC.';
```

The DELETE Statement

The DELETE statement enables us to specify a subset of data rows to delete. The statement shown in Listing 2-7 removes the entry for TOOL TIME, INC.

Listing 2-7. *DML Command to Delete a Data Record from the Supplier Table*

```
DELETE FROM supplier
 WHERE suppliername = 'TOOL TIME, INC.';
```

Note that the preceding DELETE statement will fail because of the presence of child records in the Quote table. Presumably, the intention is to also remove these records, in which case you need to delete them first by using a similar command.

The MERGE Statement

MERGE is a powerful statement that combines the capabilities of the INSERT statement, the UPDATE statement, and the DELETE statement. Consider the following example. Suppose you have new quotes in a table called Newquote. If a revised quote has been provided for a part that was previously supplied by a supplier, the corresponding record in the Quote table has to be updated. If a quote has been provided for a part that was not previously supplied by a supplier, a new record has to be inserted into the Quote table. Finally, a quote of 0 indicates that the supplier no longer supplies the part. You can merge the contents of the Newquote table into the Quote table by using the MERGE statement—inserting, updating, or deleting records as necessary—as shown in Listing 2-8.

Listing 2-8. *DML Command to Merge the Contents of One Table into Another Table*

```
MERGE INTO quote q
   USING newquote n
   ON (    q.suppliername = n.suppliername
      AND q.partname = n.partname)
   WHEN MATCHED THEN
      UPDATE
         SET quote = n.quote
      DELETE
         WHERE q.quote = 0
   WHEN NOT MATCHED THEN
      INSERT
      VALUES (n.suppliername, n.partname, n.quote);
```

Embedded SQL

Application programs written by application software developers can communicate with an Oracle database only by using SQL. These application programs must therefore be linked with Oracle-supplied routines that give them the capability to communicate with an Oracle database.

Listing 2-9 shows an example of SQL statements embedded in a Java program. Each embedded SQL statement is prefixed with the phrase #sql. The program lists the names of all parts supplied by a specified supplier and the price quote in each case; the account name and password required to connect to the database have to be provided to the program at runtime.

Listing 2-9. *SQL Commands Embedded in a Java Program*

```
import sqlj.runtime.*;
import sqlj.runtime.ref.*;
import java.sql.*;

public class PrintQuote
{
  public static void main(String[] args)
  {
    Connection connection = null;

    #sql iterator quote_iterator (
      String partname,
      double quote);

    quote_iterator quote = null;

    try
    {

      // Connect to the database
      // The account name and password are provided to the program by the user

      DriverManager.registerDriver(
        new oracle.jdbc.driver.OracleDriver());
      connection = DriverManager.getConnection(
        "jdbc:oracle:thin:@localhost:1521:ORCL",
        args[0],
        args[1]);
```

```
DefaultContext.setDefaultContext(
  new DefaultContext(connection));

// Retrieve the data for one supplier
// The supplier's name is provided to the program by the user

String suppliername = args[2];

#sql quote = {
   SELECT partname,
          quote
     FROM quote
    WHERE suppliername = :suppliername
   ORDER BY partname};

// Print one row of data on each line

while (quote.next()) {
  System.out.printf(
    "%-40s%10.2f\n",
    quote.partname(),
    quote.quote());
}

connection.close();

}
catch (SQLException exception) {
  exception.printStackTrace();
}
}
}
```

SQL*Plus and SQL Developer

Oracle provides a command-line tool called *SQL*Plus* that enables you to interact with the database without having to embed SQL in an application program; this is the tool that database administrators most frequently use in their work. An easy-to-use GUI tool called *SQL Developer* was introduced in Oracle Database 9*i*, but the advantage of a command-line tool such as SQL*Plus is that it can be used to automate tasks—that is, a series of SQL statements can be placed in a file and automatically executed at prescribed times.

The SQL*Plus utility can also be used as a simple report-writing tool to produce neatly formatted reports. The commands in Listing 2-10 cause the entire Quote table to be listed—notice the use of the ORDER BY clause to sort the data records retrieved by the SQL query. Listing 2-11 shows the output produced by the commands in Listing 2-10.

Figure 2-4 shows the SQL Developer tool, which I will have more to say about in Chapter 9.

Listing 2-10. *An SQL*Plus Program to Produce a Neatly Formatted Report*

```
-- Specify the dimensions of the printed page
SET linesize 78
SET pagesize 60

-- Print page titles and a closing line
TTITLE center "QUOTE LISTING" right "Page:" sql.pno skip 1
REPFOOTER skip 1 center "END OF REPORT"

-- Print suitable titles for each column of information
COLUMN suppliername format a32 heading "Supplier Name"
COLUMN partname format a32 heading "Part Name"
COLUMN quote format 99999990.00 heading "Quote"

-- Print the supplier name only once and skip a line when the supplier name changes
BREAK on suppliername skip 1

-- Print the number of parts supplied by each supplier
COMPUTE count of partname on suppliername

-- Print all information in the quote table
  SELECT suppliername, partname, quote
    FROM quote
ORDER BY suppliername, partname;
```

Listing 2-11. *A Neatly Formatted Report with Page Headings, Column Headings, and Summary Lines*

```
                              QUOTE LISTING                Page:        1

Supplier Name                 Part Name                              Quote
-------------------------     -----------------------------    ------------
NEW YANKEE WORKSHOP, INC.     HAMMER                                  1.89
                              NAIL                                    0.19
*****************************  ---------------------------------
count                                                       2


OLD YANKEE WORKSHOP, INC.     HAMMER                                  2.09
*****************************  ---------------------------------
count                                                       1


TOOL TIME, INC.               HAMMER                                  1.99
                              NAIL                                    0.20
*****************************  ---------------------------------
count                                                       2



                              END OF REPORT
```

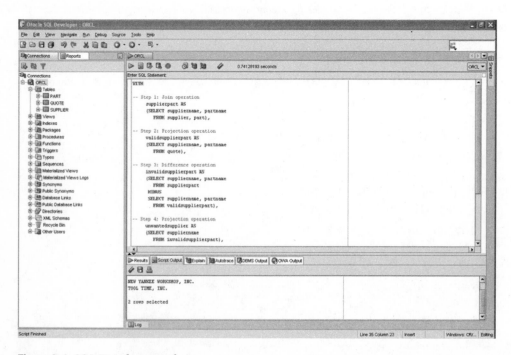

Figure 2-4. *SQL Developer tool*

Criticisms of SQL

The IBM team that developed SQL made certain decisions that violated relational principles—chief among them that duplicate rows were allowed. The inventor of relational database technology, Dr. Ted Codd, was not part of IBM's development team and, despite his urging, these deficiencies were not corrected in subsequent revisions of the language. In the opinion of some commentators, the gap then continued to widen. Nevertheless, no one has been successful in providing an alternative to SQL, and we must learn to live with its deficiencies. Chris Date makes the point very forcefully in *An Introduction to Database Systems*:

> SQL is now so far from being a true embodiment of relational principles—it suffers from so many sins of both omission and commission—that I would frankly prefer not to discuss it at all! However, SQL is obviously important from a commercial point of view; thus, every database professional needs to have some familiarity with it . . .

Duplicates

The SQL standard allows tables to contain duplicate data records and does not require that duplicates be eliminated from the results of a Projection or Union operation, thus violating the principles laid down by Codd. Chris Date has published an example in which 12 formulations of a certain SQL query returned 9 different results because duplicate data rows existed in the tables in question. Not only does this become a programming nightmare, but Date points out that this is one of the reasons why the query optimizer cannot always rewrite queries into alternative forms that are more efficient—the optimizer cannot be sure that the result will be unaffected by the rewrite.

Redundancy

Redundancy is not a violation of relational principles but creates a serious performance problem that database administrators must understand. There are usually many ways to rephrase the same SQL query. For various reasons (such as the one described in the previous section), the query optimizer might not find the optimal query execution plan in all cases even though all of the plans retrieve the same data and, therefore, the query plan that is optimal in one case is equally optimal in all other cases. Assuming that supplier records include a data item called Supplierstatus, the following listings show ten ways to express the query *List the status of all suppliers who supply hammers.*[5]

---

5. The ideas for this section are taken from a 1988 paper titled "SQL Redundancy and DBMS Performance" by well-known relational theorist Fabian Pascal.

The version in Listing 2-12 is the only one that conforms to the simplified railroad diagram in Figure 2-3 and is obviously an abbreviated way of specifying the application of three separate relational algebra operators: Join, Restriction, and Projection. Please refer to *Oracle Database 11g SQL Language Reference* for the complete diagram.

Listing 2-12. *Status of All Suppliers Who Supply Hammers—Traditional Formulation*

```
SELECT supplier.suppliername, supplier.supplierstatus
  FROM supplier, quote
 WHERE supplier.suppliername = quote.suppliername
   AND quote.partname = 'HAMMER';
```

The versions in Listing 2-13 are modern variants of Listing 2-12. They do not conform to the simplified railroad diagram in Figure 2-3—you will have to refer to *Oracle Database 11g SQL Language Reference* for the complete diagram.

Listing 2-13. *Status of All Suppliers Who Supply Hammers—Modern Formulations*

```
SELECT suppliername, supplier.supplierstatus
  FROM supplier NATURAL JOIN quote
 WHERE quote.partname = 'HAMMER';

SELECT suppliername, supplier.supplierstatus
  FROM supplier JOIN quote USING (suppliername)
 WHERE quote.partname = 'HAMMER';

SELECT supplier.suppliername, supplier.supplierstatus
  FROM supplier JOIN quote ON (supplier.suppliername = quote.suppliername)
 WHERE quote.partname = 'HAMMER';
```

The next two solutions in Listing 2-14 are not based on relational algebra at all and use a *subquery*.

Listing 2-14. *Status of All Suppliers Who Supply Hammers—Examples of Subqueries*

```
SELECT suppliername, supplierstatus
  FROM supplier
 WHERE suppliername IN (SELECT suppliername
                          FROM quote
                         WHERE partname = 'HAMMER');

SELECT suppliername, supplierstatus
  FROM supplier
```

```
WHERE suppliername = ANY (SELECT suppliername
                            FROM quote
                           WHERE partname = 'HAMMER');
```

The next three solutions, shown in Listing 2-15, use a mechanism called the *correlated subquery* to produce the same results as the previous solutions; correlated subqueries cannot be processed independently of the main query.

Listing 2-15. *Status of All Suppliers Who Supply Hammers—Examples of Correlated Subqueries*

```
SELECT suppliername, supplierstatus
  FROM supplier
 WHERE 'HAMMER' IN (SELECT partname
                      FROM quote
                     WHERE suppliername = supplier.suppliername);


SELECT suppliername, supplierstatus
  FROM supplier
 WHERE 'HAMMER' = ANY (SELECT partname
                         FROM quote
                        WHERE suppliername = supplier.suppliername);


SELECT suppliername, supplierstatus
  FROM supplier
 WHERE EXISTS (SELECT suppliername
                 FROM quote
                WHERE suppliername = supplier.suppliername
                  AND partname = 'HAMMER');
```

Listing 2-16 uses a correlated subquery in conjunction with an *aggregate function* to count quote records and determine whether the supplier under consideration supplies hammers.

Listing 2-16. *Status of All Suppliers Who Supply Hammers: An Example of Aggregation*

```
SELECT suppliername, supplierstatus
  FROM supplier
 WHERE (SELECT COUNT (suppliername)
          FROM quote
         WHERE suppliername = supplier.suppliername
           AND partname = 'HAMMER') > 0;
```

In Chapter 1, you saw the SQL answer to the problem *List the suppliers who supply all parts*. Listing 2-17 shows three alternative formulations—the first formulation uses correlated subqueries, while the next two formulations use aggregate functions.

Listing 2-17. *Alternative Solutions to the Problem: List the Suppliers Who Supply All Parts*

```
SELECT suppliername
  FROM supplier
 WHERE NOT EXISTS (
          SELECT partname
            FROM part
           WHERE NOT EXISTS (
                   SELECT *
                     FROM quote
                    WHERE suppliername = supplier.suppliername
                      AND partname = part.partname));


SELECT suppliername
  FROM supplier
 WHERE (SELECT COUNT (*)
          FROM quote
         WHERE suppliername = supplier.suppliername) = (SELECT COUNT (*)
                                                          FROM part);


SELECT    suppliername
    FROM quote
GROUP BY suppliername
  HAVING COUNT (*) = (SELECT COUNT (*)
                        FROM part);
```

Nullable Data Items

Sometimes the value of a data item is not known. If we permit a record to be stored even if the values of some data items are not known, those data items are said to be *nullable*. Missing information leads to "fuzzy" logic in which there is a third alternative—unknown—to truth and falsehood of a statement such as STATUS='A'. Nullable data items are commonly used by database designers, but three-valued logic is not intuitive. I will illustrate this with an example.

Suppose the Supplierstatus data item in supplier records is nullable and suppose we do not know the status of TOOL TIME, INC. Also suppose that the only valid values of the Supplierstatus item are A and B, and that this is enforced by Oracle by a *check constraint*, as shown in Listing 2-18.

Listing 2-18. *A Check Constraint*

```
ALTER TABLE supplier
ADD supplierstatus VARCHAR(4)
CHECK (supplierstatus = 'A' OR supplierstatus = 'B');

UPDATE supplier
   SET supplierstatus = 'A'
 WHERE suppliername != 'TOOL TIME, INC.';
```

In the preceding scenario, how many records are retrieved by the SQL query in Listing 2-19?

Listing 2-19. *An SQL Query with Counterintuitive Results*

```
SELECT suppliername
  FROM supplier
 WHERE supplierstatus = 'A' OR supplierstatus = 'B';
```

Intuitively, we expect to retrieve all rows in the table, because the only valid values of Supplierstatus are A and B and because that rule is enforced by a check constraint. However, Oracle will nevertheless retrieve only *two* rows. This is not a sensible result.

Counterintuitively, the queries in Listing 2-20 also retrieve only two data records.

Listing 2-20. *Two More Examples of SQL Queries with Counterintuitive Results*

```
SELECT suppliername
  FROM supplier
 WHERE supplierstatus = supplierstatus;

SELECT suppliername
  FROM supplier
 WHERE supplierstatus = 'A' OR supplierstatus != 'A';
```

The reasoning offered for these counterintuitive results is that the status of TOOL TIME, INC. is unknown and, therefore, the answer to every question involving the status of TOOL TIME, INC. is also unknown. To retrieve the third record, you need to add the clause OR supplierstatus IS NULL to the preceding SQL queries; you can find more information on the problems created by nullable data items in any good book on SQL.

Introduction to PL/SQL

Oracle gives us the ability to store programs in the database—and these programs are often written by using a proprietary Oracle language called *Procedural Language/SQL*, or *PL/SQL*. PL/SQL offers the entire suite of structured programming mechanisms such as condition checking, loops, and subroutines. Of course, just like programs written in other languages, PL/SQL programs communicate with Oracle by using SQL.

Here is an example of a PL/SQL program to delete a supplier record and any associated quote records—first a flow chart in Figure 2-5, and then the actual program itself in Listing 2-21.[6]

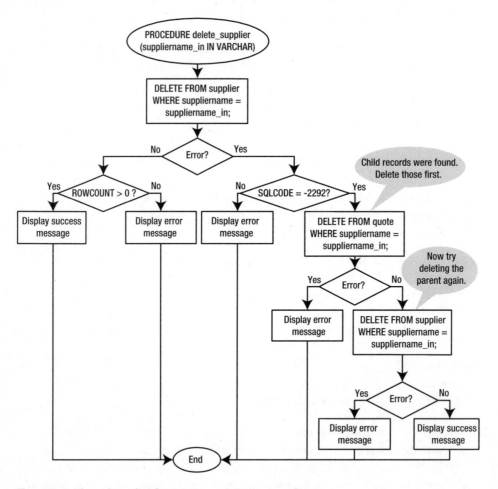

Figure 2-5. *Flow chart for the* delete_supplier *procedure*

---

6. If the Supplier and Quote tables are related by referential constraints and the ON DELETE CASCADE option is included in the definition of the Quote table, Oracle will automatically delete a Quote record when the corresponding Supplier record is deleted. For the purposes of this example, we assume that this option has not been used.

Listing 2-21. *PL/SQL Program to Delete a Supplier Record and All Associated Quote Records*

```
PROCEDURE delete_supplier (suppliername_in IN VARCHAR)
IS
BEGIN
   DELETE FROM supplier
         WHERE suppliername = suppliername_in;

   IF SQL%ROWCOUNT > 0
   THEN
      DBMS_OUTPUT.put_line ('Supplier deleted: ' || suppliername_in);
   ELSE
      DBMS_OUTPUT.put_line ('Supplier does not exist: ' || suppliername_in);
   END IF;
EXCEPTION
   WHEN OTHERS
   THEN
      /* Child records were found. Delete those first. */
      IF SQLCODE = -2292
      THEN
         BEGIN
            DELETE FROM quote
                  WHERE suppliername = suppliername_in;

            /*Now try deleting the parent again. */
            BEGIN
               DELETE FROM supplier
                     WHERE suppliername = suppliername_in;

               DBMS_OUTPUT.put_line ('Supplier deleted: ' || suppliername_in);
            EXCEPTION
               WHEN OTHERS
               THEN
                  DBMS_OUTPUT.put_line ('Error deleting supplier; ' || SQLERRM);
            END;
         EXCEPTION
            WHEN OTHERS
            THEN
               DBMS_OUTPUT.put_line ('Error deleting supplier; ' || SQLERRM);
         END;
      ELSE
         DBMS_OUTPUT.put_line ('Error deleting supplier; ' || SQLERRM);
      END IF;
END;
```

Storing programs in the database has many advantages. Special PL/SQL programs called *triggers* can be executed whenever a user performs a specified action. This gives us the ability to enforce business rules, control access to data, and keep records of who accessed the data and how it changed. Storing sequences of commands in the database greatly reduces the amount of communication between client and server and thus improves efficiency. Also, PL/SQL functions can be utilized in SQL statements; this increases the power and flexibility of SQL.

Much Ado About Suppliers

This section provides SQL solutions for the queries listed in the "Exercises" section of Chapter 1. Other solutions exist; remember that most SQL statements can be written in various ways. In this chapter's "Exercises" section, you will be asked to rewrite these statements without using query factoring and without using the MINUS operator.

Parts That Are Supplied by All Suppliers

The answer to this problem looks similar to the answer to the problem *List the suppliers who supply all parts*. All we have to do is to interchange the roles of suppliers and parts, as shown in Listing 2-22.

Listing 2-22. *Parts That Are Supplied by All Suppliers*

```
WITH

-- Step 1: Join operation
    supplierpart AS
    (SELECT suppliername,
            partname
      FROM supplier,
           part),

-- Step 2: Projection operation
    validsupplierpart AS
    (SELECT suppliername,
            partname
      FROM quote),
```

```
-- Step 3: Difference operation
    invalidsupplierpart AS
    (SELECT suppliername,
            partname
      FROM supplierpart
    MINUS
     SELECT suppliername,
            partname
      FROM validsupplierpart),

-- Step 4: Projection operation
    unwantedpart AS
    (SELECT partname
      FROM invalidsupplierpart),

-- Step 5: Difference operation
    wantedpart AS
    (SELECT partname
      FROM part
    MINUS
     SELECT partname
      FROM unwantedpart)

SELECT  partname
  FROM wantedpart;
```

Parts Supplied by OLD YANKEE WORKSHOP, INC. as Well as by TOOL TIME, INC.

The answer to this problem is similar to the answer to the previous problem. Instead of the entire Part table, we have to consider only two parts, as shown in Listing 2-23.

Listing 2-23. *Parts Supplied by OLD YANKEE WORKSHOP as Well as by TOOL TIME, INC.*

```
WITH

-- Step 1: Join operation
    supplierpart AS
    (SELECT suppliername,
            partname
```

```
          FROM (SELECT 'OLD YANKEE WORKSHOP, INC.' AS suppliername
                  FROM DUAL
                UNION
                SELECT 'TOOL TIME, INC.' AS suppliername
                  FROM DUAL),
             part),

-- Step 2: Projection operation
     validsupplierpart AS
     (SELECT suppliername,
             partname
       FROM quote),

-- Step 3: Difference operation
     invalidsupplierpart AS
     (SELECT suppliername,
             partname
       FROM supplierpart
      MINUS
      SELECT suppliername,
             partname
       FROM validsupplierpart),

-- Step 4: Projection operation
     unwantedpart AS
     (SELECT partname
        FROM invalidsupplierpart),

-- Step 5: Difference operation
     wantedpart AS
     (SELECT partname
        FROM part
       MINUS
       SELECT partname
         FROM unwantedpart)

SELECT partname
  FROM wantedpart;
```

Suppliers Who Supply at Least One Part That Is Not Supplied by a Specified Supplier

Notice the inline view that occurs in Listing 2-24. Also notice the use of the keyword DIS-TINCT—it is required because SQL does not automatically eliminate duplicates. The & in &suppliername indicate that suppliername is a variable element. Oracle will request a value for suppliername when you execute this statement.

Listing 2-24. *Suppliers Who Supply at Least One Part That Is Not Supplied by a Specified Supplier*

```
WITH temp AS
    (SELECT suppliername,
            partname
      FROM supplier,
            (SELECT partname
              FROM quote
             WHERE suppliername = '&suppliername'))

SELECT DISTINCT suppliername
          FROM (SELECT suppliername,
                       partname
                  FROM quote
                MINUS
                SELECT suppliername,
                       partname
                  FROM temp);
```

Suppliers Who Do Not Supply at Least One Part That Is Supplied by a Specified Supplier

The answer to this problem is similar to the answer to the previous problem. All that changes is the order in which one table is subtracted from the other, as shown in Listing 2-25. Notice that we have to once again use the DISTINCT keyword to eliminate duplicates.

Listing 2-25. *Suppliers Who Do Not Supply at Least One Part That Is Supplied by a Specified Supplier*

```
WITH temp AS
    (SELECT suppliername,
            partname
```

```
            FROM supplier,
                 (SELECT partname
                    FROM quote
                   WHERE suppliername = '&suppliername'))

SELECT DISTINCT suppliername
        FROM (SELECT suppliername,
                     partname
                FROM temp
              MINUS
              SELECT  suppliername,
                      partname
                FROM quote);
```

Suppliers Who Supply All the Parts Supplied by a Specified Supplier but No Other Parts

The answer to this problem draws on the answers provided in Listings 2-24 and 2-25. We discard any supplier who supplies at least one part that is not supplied by the specified supplier, as shown in Listing 2-26. We also discard any supplier who does not supply at least one part that is supplied by the specified supplier.

Listing 2-26. *Suppliers Who Supply All the Parts Supplied by a Specified Supplier but No Other Parts*

```
WITH temp AS
     (SELECT suppliername,
             partname
        FROM supplier,
             (SELECT partname
                FROM quote
               WHERE suppliername = '&suppliername'))

SELECT suppliername
  FROM supplier
 WHERE NOT (suppliername = '&suppliername')
MINUS
SELECT suppliername
  FROM (SELECT suppliername,
               partname
          FROM quote
        MINUS
```

```
        SELECT suppliername,
               partname
          FROM temp)
MINUS
SELECT suppliername
  FROM (SELECT suppliername,
               partname
          FROM temp
        MINUS
        SELECT  suppliername,
               partname
          FROM quote);
```

Suppliers Who Supply All the Parts Supplied by a Specified Supplier at Cheaper Prices

The answer to this problem is interesting because the Quote table has to be joined to itself. We use aliases—q1 and q2—for the two copies in order to differentiate them, as shown in Listing 2-27.

Listing 2-27. *Suppliers Who Supply All the Parts Supplied by a Specified Supplier at Cheaper Prices*

```
WITH temp AS
     (SELECT suppliername,
             partname
        FROM supplier,
             (SELECT partname
                FROM quote
               WHERE suppliername = '&suppliername'))

SELECT suppliername
  FROM supplier
 WHERE NOT (suppliername = '&suppliername')
MINUS
SELECT suppliername
  FROM (SELECT suppliername,
               partname
          FROM temp
        MINUS
```

```
        SELECT suppliername,
               partname
          FROM quote)
MINUS
SELECT q2.suppliername
  FROM quote q1,
       quote q2
 WHERE q1.suppliername = '&suppliername'
   AND q2.suppliername != '&suppliername'
   AND q2.partname = q1.partname
   AND q2.quote >= q1.quote;
```

Parts That Are Supplied by Only a Specified Supplier

The answer to this problem is far less complex than the answers to the previous problems. Two tables are subtracted from each other, and each table is produced by using simple Selection and Projection operations, as shown in Listing 2-28.

Listing 2-28. *Parts That Are Supplied by Only a Specified Supplier*

```
SELECT partname
  FROM quote
 WHERE suppliername = '&suppliername'
MINUS
SELECT partname
  FROM quote
 WHERE suppliername != '&suppliername';
```

Summary

The database administrator needs to understand SQL in all its forms. Many Oracle experts have devoted their entire careers to the study of SQL, and I have hardly been able to scratch the surface in this chapter. I highly recommend the books listed at the end of this chapter and, of course, the official Oracle reference works can always be downloaded from the Oracle web site. Here is a short summary of the concepts discussed in this chapter:

- All database activity, including database administration activities, are transacted in SQL.

- Oracle reference works use railroad diagrams to teach the SQL language. Railroad diagrams can include subdiagrams and can even refer to themselves in recursive fashion. For instance, a table reference can be an entire subquery—this kind of subquery is called an *inline view*. The SELECT list can include *scalar subquery expressions*—subqueries that return exactly one data item from exactly one data row.

- SQL is divided into Data Manipulation Language (DML) and Data Definition Language (DDL). DML includes the SELECT, INSERT, UPDATE, MERGE, and DELETE statements. DDL includes the CREATE, ALTER, and DROP statements for the different classes of objects in an Oracle database. The SQL reference manual also describes commands that can be used to perform database administration activities such as stopping and starting databases.

- SQL needs to be embedded into software application programs so they can communicate with the database.

- SQL has been criticized because it does not prohibit duplicates; the absence of a prohibition against duplicates causes queries that are seemingly equivalent to produce differing results and inhibits the query optimization process.

- The use of nullable data items can lead to results that contradict common sense.

- SQL queries can usually be formulated in several different ways. The Oracle optimizer may not always choose the same query execution plan in all cases, even though the query plan that is most efficient in one case is obviously the most efficient for all other cases.

- Programs written in PL/SQL can be stored in an Oracle database. The use of these programs has many advantages, including efficiency, control, and flexibility. PL/SQL offers a full complement of structured programming mechanisms such as condition checking, loops, and subroutines.

Exercises

- Review the subquery factoring example in the first chapter and satisfy yourself that it conforms to the diagram in Figure 2-3. Answer the following questions:

    - How many subqueries have been used? (Ten)

    - How many subqueries have been explicitly named? (Five)

    - How many SELECT lists have been used? (Eight)

    - Which parts of the statement don't conform to the railroad diagram? (The interspersed comments)

- Download *Oracle Database 11g SQL Language Reference* from http://www.oracle.com/technology/documentation. Review the railroad diagram for the SELECT statement and all the subdiagrams.

- Try to rewrite the SQL statements in Listings 2-22 through 2-28 by using the NOT EXISTS clause instead of the MINUS operator and without using subquery factoring. Ask a database administrator in your organization for help testing these statements against a real database by using SQL*Plus or SQL Developer. Note that SQL*Plus does not automatically handle blank lines—you have to use the SET sqlblanklines on command to tell it to do so.

Further Reading

Oracle Corporation. *Oracle 11g PL/SQL User's Guide and Reference*. Oracle Corporation, 2007. Searchable or downloadable free of charge at http://www.oracle.com/technology/documentation/index.html.

Oracle Corporation. *Oracle Database 11g Application Developer's Guide—Fundamentals*. Oracle Corporation, 2007. This book is required reading for everybody who wants to create software application programs that interact with an Oracle database. It is searchable or downloadable free of charge at http://www.oracle.com/technology/documentation.

Oracle Corporation. *Oracle Database 11g SQL Language Reference*. Oracle Corporation, 2007. An exhaustive reference to every aspect of SQL—it has nearly 2,000 pages. Searchable or downloadable free of charge at http://www.oracle.com/technology/documentation.

Oracle Corporation. *Oracle Database 11g SQL*Plus User's Guide and Reference.* Oracle
　　Corporation, 2007. Searchable or downloadable free of charge at http://www.oracle.
　　com/technology/documentation.

De Haan, Lex. *Mastering Oracle SQL and SQL*Plus.* Apress, 2004. Written by a well-known
　　Oracle expert and teacher, this book may be more understandable than the official
　　Oracle reference work.

Gennick, Jonathan. *Oracle SQL*Plus: The Definitive Guide.* O'Reilly, 2004. Oracle refer-
　　ence works are very good at documenting every detail of a product but not as good at
　　describing how to use the product to maximum advantage. This book will help you
　　do that.

Feuerstein, Steven. *Oracle PL/SQL for DBAs.* O'Reilly, 2005. DBAs often find a need for
　　a PL/SQL procedure, and this book, written especially for DBAs, is a good introduc-
　　tory text. Methods of improving performance of PL/SQL code are given prominence.

Feuerstein, Steven. *Oracle PL/SQL Developer's Workbook.* O'Reilly, 2000. For the dedi-
　　cated student.

Feuerstein, Steven. *Oracle PL/SQL Language Pocket Reference, 4th Edition.* O'Reilly, 2007.
　　For when you want to quickly refresh your memory.

Feuerstein, Steven. *Oracle PL/SQL Programming, 4th Edition.* O'Reilly, 2005. Steven Feuer-
　　stein has devoted his life to the study of PL/SQL, and well-thumbed copies of his
　　books can be seen on the desk of every PL/SQL program developer.

Feuerstein, Steven. *PL/SQL Best Practices, 2nd Edition.* O'Reilly, 2007. The title says it all,
　　and the author needs no introduction.

CHAPTER 3

■■■

Oracle Architecture

Try to imagine, how Confucius, Buddha, Jesus, Mohammed or Homer would have reacted when they had been offered a [computer].

—Edsger Dijkstra, advocate of structured programming and winner of the 1972 Turing Award, in "Correctness Concerns and, Among Other Things, Why They Are Resented"

Just as an automobile engine has a lot of interconnected parts that must all work well together, and just as an automobile mechanic must understand the individual parts and how they relate to the whole, the Oracle database engine has a lot of interconnected parts, and the database administrator must understand the individual parts and how they relate to the whole. This chapter provides a short overview of the Oracle engine. Of course, it is impossible to document the workings of a complex piece of machinery in a short chapter—for a full treatment, you will have to refer to *Oracle Database 11*g *Concepts* which, like all the reference manuals, is searchable and downloadable for free at the Oracle web site.

As an introduction, Figure 3-1 shows an interesting diagram of the inner workings of the Oracle database engine. This diagram was produced by a software tool called Spotlight from Quest Software. The name of the database—Training—is seen in the upper-right corner of the diagram. The arrows show the flow of information between database components.

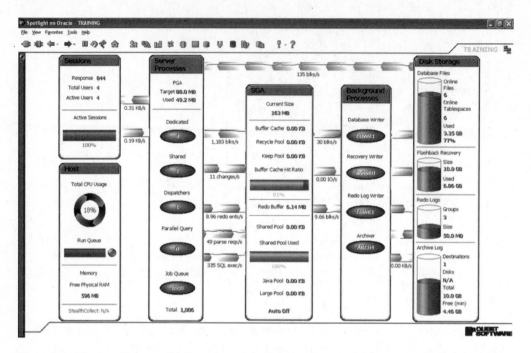

Figure 3-1. *The Spotlight tool's diagrammatic representation of the Oracle engine*

- The *Sessions* panel represents the users who are using the database.

- The *Host* panel represents the host computer of the database.

- The *Server Processes* panel represents the computer processes on the host computer that are performing all the work requested by the users.

- The *SGA* panel represents an area of computer memory that is used as a work area by the database. *SGA* stands for *System Global Area*.

- The *Background Processes* panel represents a core set of computer processes that are independent of the user sessions and perform specialized tasks such as storing information about transactions in the redo log files.

- The *Disk Storage* panel represents the files in which the data is stored and supporting files such as redo log files and archived redo log files.

The other terms used in the diagram are explained in the following sections.

Database vs. Instance

In Oracle terminology, the word *database* is used to collectively indicate the data files and supporting files on the storage disks attached to the host computer, and the word *instance* is used to describe the various computer processes resident in computer memory and memory areas shared by these processes. This is in contrast to database architectures such as Microsoft SQL Server and IBM DB2, for which the word *instance* indicates a collection of databases that share common memory resources—that is, the relationship between instances and databases is *one-to-many*. The relationship between Oracle instances and databases, on the other hand, is either *one-to-one* (one instance per database) or *many-to-one* (multiple instances per database). The many-to-one configuration is called Real Application Clusters (RAC)—the database lives on shared disks, and instances on multiple computers attach to the database.

In Figure 3-1, the database is represented by the panel on the far right labeled Disk Storage. The three blocks in the middle—labeled Server Processes, SGA, and Background Processes—represent the instance.

Database

The most concrete aspect of a database is the files on the storage disks connected to the database host. In this section, I briefly discuss each category of file. Placement, sizing, and other configuration details are discussed in Chapters 5 and 6.

Software

The location of the database software is called the *Oracle home* and is usually stored in the environment variable ORACLE_HOME. There are two species of database software: server software and client software. *Server software* is necessary to create and manage the database and is required only on the database host. *Client software* is necessary to utilize the database and is required on every user's computer—the most common example is the SQL*Plus command-line tool.

Configuration Files

The most important database configuration file is the one containing the settings used during database startup. It comes in two versions: a text version called a *pfile* and a binary version called an *spfile*. You will see an example in Chapter 6. The pfile and spfile specify such details as the amount of computer memory that Oracle may use during operation. The pfile is traditionally referred to as the init.ora file.

Another important configuration file is the listener.ora file. It controls the operation of the *listener*—an important process that comes into play when users start a database session. You will see an example of this in Chapter 6 as well. The tnsnames.ora file contains location information for databases. You will see an example later in this chapter.

Data Files

The biggest component of the database is usually the files where data is stored. You could create a database with just one data file if you wanted to prove a point, but most databases have dozens of data files.

Data files are logically grouped into *tablespaces* and are usually given descriptive names such as DATA, INDEX, UNDO, and TEMP that indicate their intended purpose. You should use a tablespace only for the purpose indicated by its name—for example, the SYSTEM tablespace is intended to store only the *data dictionary* (tables containing information about the rest of the database). Except for the SYSTEM and SYSAUX tablespaces, which are always created and whose names are mandated by Oracle, the number and names of the other tablespaces are left to you.

Each Oracle table and index is assigned to a single tablespace, and their growth is therefore limited by the availability of space in that assigned tablespace. They share the space with all the other tables or indexes also assigned to the tablespace. Data files can grow automatically as required but, for reasons associated with manageability, it is recommended that you limit how big they can grow. You can also choose to create large data files of fixed size and you can create additional data files at any time during the life of the database.

The names chosen for data files typically include the name of the tablespace and an extension of dbf or ora (for example, SYSTEM01.dbf might be the name given to the first data file in the SYSTEM tablespace), but this is only a convention, not a requirement, and you are free to invent your own convention or not to have one at all.

The space within data files is organized into *data blocks* (sometimes called *pages*) of equal size; 2, 4, 8, 16, 32, or 64 kilobytes (KB). 8KB is a commonly used block size. Each block contains data from just one table. The size of data records should be taken into consideration when deciding what size block to use. Oracle allows data records to span data blocks, but it is more efficient to retrieve one data block instead of multiple blocks from different locations on the storage disks. All the data files in one tablespace use blocks of the same size, and the block size should be a factor in the decision to assign a table or index to a particular tablespace. When a table needs more space, it grabs a contiguous range of data blocks called an *extent*; it is conventional to use uniformly sized extents for all tables in the same tablespace.

Temporary Files

Each Oracle server process uses a private work area called a Program Global Area in computer memory to hold intermediate results, for example, data that needs to be sorted. The temporary files are used for intermediate storage when sufficient memory is unavailable.

Redo Log Files

Redo log files help Oracle ensure that the effects of a user's transaction are durable even if there is a computer failure. Before any data in the data files is changed, the *log writer* (LGWR) process stores a copy of the old data (undo information) and the new data (redo information) in the redo log file. In the event of a computer failure, the redo log files enable Oracle to undo the effects of incomplete transactions (uncommitted transactions) and verify the changes of completed transactions (committed transactions).

The sizes of the redo log files are decided by the database administrator. It is conventional but not required for all redo log files to be of the same size. An Oracle database needs at least two redo log files. Oracle uses the redo log files in round-robin fashion; when one redo log file is completely filled, Oracle begins filling the next one, and so on.

Because the redo log files defend the database against computer failure, they must be well protected. It is typical to mirror each redo log file; a mirrored set of redo log files is referred to as a *redo log group*. It is also typical to put each member of a redo file group on a different storage disk. All the members of a redo file group have the same size; the log writer process stores the same information in all members of a redo file group. Oracle can therefore continue to operate as long as at least one member of each redo file group is undamaged.

Archived Redo Log Files

When a redo file fills up, an Oracle component called the *archiver* makes one or more copies of it in locations specified by the database administrator. Multiple copies improve the chances that at least one will survive if the storage disks are damaged.

These copies make it possible to reconstruct data files if they are ever damaged. If a data file is damaged, the database administrator can first restore the most recent backup copy of the data file, and the information contained in the archived redo files can be systematically processed to reproduce the effects of all the transactions that modified the data file since the backup copy was created.

Control File

Oracle uses the *control file* while starting the database. This file contains information about the rest of the database, such as the names and locations of the data files. It also contains information—such as the names and locations of the archived redo log files—needed for recovery of damaged data files. It is continuously updated during the operation of the database.

Because of the criticality of the control file, it is conventional to have multiple copies, that is, mirrors. Oracle keeps all copies in perfect synchronization.

Event Logs

Oracle records important events in various log files. Events such as startup and shutdown, important Data Definition Language (DDL) operations such as ALTER TABLESPACE ADD DATAFILE, and space shortages are some of the events that are recorded in the *alert log*. A record is written to the *listener log* every time a user establishes a connection to the database. A detailed *trace file* is produced every time certain severe errors occur; examples include the ORA-600 error, which usually indicates that an Oracle bug has been encountered. You will see examples of event logs in Chapters 10 and 11.

Database Backups

Storage disks can fail at any time, and it is important to protect the database by creating backup copies of the data files. If enough disk space is unavailable, backup copies of the data files can be stored on magnetic tapes. If enough disk space is available, backup copies can be stored on the disks, though they should not be stored on the disks where data files are stored. The location of the backup copies is traditionally referred to as the *flashback recovery area*. The backups stored on disk are usually copied to tapes for added safety.

We will return to the topic of database backups in Chapters 12 and 13.

Instance

The Oracle instance is the engine that processes requests for data from the database—it is composed of foreground processes, background processes, and a large shared memory area called the System Global Area (SGA).

System Global Area

The *System Global Area* (SGA) is typically a very large memory area shared by all Oracle processes. It is divided into distinct areas such as the buffer cache, the shared pool, and the log buffer, whose sizes are specified in the database configuration file (pfile or spfile). The various Oracle processes coordinate their access to these areas by using an inter-process communication (IPC) mechanisms called *latches*.

Buffer Cache

Typically, the *buffer cache* is the largest portion of the SGA. For reasons of efficiency, copies of data blocks (block buffers) are cached in computer memory whenever possible. Whenever a foreground process needs a data block, it first checks the buffer cache, hoping to find the block there. If a block is not found in the cache, query processing has to be delayed until the foreground process retrieves the block from the storage disks.

When the buffer cache fills up, the least-recently-used blocks are removed to make space for new requests. Various strategies can be attempted to improve the efficiency of the cache. A special *keep pool* can be created within the buffer cache to store data blocks from frequently used data tables, for example, lookup tables. A *recycle pool* can be created to store blocks that are rarely reused. Other techniques include partitioning and clusters—more information is provided in Chapter 7.

Shared Pool

The *shared pool* is another large component of the SGA and has many uses. The best-known use is caching *query execution plans* for potential reuse by the user who first submitted the query or by any another user who submits the identical query—this is done in an area called the *shared SQL area*. Another well-known use is caching of information from the data dictionary—this is done in an area within the shared pool called the *dictionary cache*.

Log Buffer

The *log buffer* is a queue of undo entries and redo entries. The *log writer* wakes up periodically and copies any accumulated undo and redo entries to the redo log file. Typically, the size of this area is only a few megabytes.

Foreground Processes

A dedicated *foreground process* is typically started whenever a user connects to the database—it performs all the work requested by the user. An alternative model called *multithreaded server* (MTS), in which all user connections are serviced by a small set of dispatchers and shared servers, is also available but is not very suitable for general-purpose use and is not widely used.

The foreground process performs activities such as checking whether the user has permission to access the data, generating a query execution plan for the SQL query submitted by the user, and retrieving data blocks into the buffer cache and modifying them. Before changing the contents of block buffers, it gains exclusive control to them by using a latch (as noted earlier, this is an inter-process communication, or IPC, mechanism). Before modifying a data block, the foreground process first makes a copy of the block in an undo segment in the undo tablespace; it also creates the undo and redo entries that the log writer will store in the redo log files.

A dedicated foreground process is terminated when the corresponding database session is terminated.

Background Processes

Unlike dedicated foreground processes, *background processes* live from database startup until database shutdown. The following are some of the better-known categories of background processes:

- The *database writer (DBWR)* process is responsible for transferring all modified data blocks in the data caches to the data files. Multiple database writer processes can be created if necessary to share the load.

- The *log writer (LGWR)* process is responsible for transferring all undo and redo entries in the log buffer to the redo log files.

- The *archiver (ARCH)* process is responsible for making copies of the redo log files when they fill up. These archived redo log files will be required if a data file is damaged and needs repair. Multiple archiver processes can be created if necessary to share the load.

- When a data block in the data cache is modified, the change blocks are not immediately transferred to the data files. In the interest of efficiency, it is better to copy changes in batches—this is the function of the database writer processes. However, at frequent intervals, the contents of the data caches are synchronized with the data files. Any modified data blocks remaining in memory are flushed to disk, and the file headers are updated with a special indicator called the *system change number (SCN)*. This activity is called a *checkpoint*, and the task of coordinating this activity is performed by a dedicated process called the *checkpoint process (CKPT)*.

- The *process monitor (PMON)* watches the progress of database connections. If a connection terminates abnormally, the process monitor initiates the necessary rollback activity on behalf of any transaction that was in progress at the time.

- The *system monitor (SMON)* is responsible for any cleanup activities necessary if the database is restarted after an abnormal shutdown resulting from system failure. It uses the contents of the redo logs to perform the necessary cleanup activity. It also performs certain space management activities during normal database operation.

Life Cycle of a Database Session

Now let's consider the life cycle of a database session, from initiation to termination. For simplicity, I am restricting the example to a traditional client-server connection[1] and assume the use of dedicated servers instead of shared servers. Here are the phases that each database session goes through:

1. The program residing on the user's computer tries to connect to a database. One of the methods it can use to determine the location of the database is to refer to the tnsnames.ora file in the ORACLE_HOME/network/admin directory on the user's computer. There, it finds the name of the database host computer and the number of the network port where connections are being accepted. Here is an example of an entry in the tnsnames.ora file; it refers to a database called ORCL on a host called IGGY:

```
ORCL =
  (DESCRIPTION =
    (ADDRESS = (PROTOCOL = TCP)(HOST = IGGY)(PORT = 1521))
    (CONNECT_DATA =
      (SERVER = DEDICATED)
      (SERVICE_NAME = ORCL)
    )
  )
```

2. The user's program sends a message to the port number specified in the tnsnames.ora file. The Oracle listener process receives the message and creates a dedicated server process to process the user's requests.

3. The user's program then provides the user's credentials (name and password) to the dedicated server process. The dedicated server checks the data dictionary and verifies that the user's credentials are valid and that the user has permission to access the database.

---

1. A form of connection used in modern e-commerce applications is the three-tier connection: the user interacts with an application server, which acts as an intermediary between the user and the database server.

4. The user's program sends an SQL statement to the dedicated server for processing.

5. The dedicated server prepares the SQL statement for execution. First it verifies that the SQL statement is syntactically correct. Then it verifies that the tables mentioned in the SQL statement actually exist and that the user has permission to access those tables. Then it creates a query execution plan for the SQL statement. The query execution plan is saved in the plan cache in the shared SQL area so that it can be reused later by the same user or another user.

6. The dedicated server checks whether the required blocks of data are in the buffer cache. If the needed blocks are not in the buffer cache, the dedicated server retrieves them from the data files.

7. If the SQL statement does not involve any modifications to the data, the required data rows are transmitted to the user. If the SQL statement involves modification to the data, the dedicated server first copies the relevant blocks of data to a rollback segment. It also creates undo and redo entries in the log buffer. The log writer wakes up periodically and copies any accumulated undo and redo entries to the redo log files.

8. If the SQL statement involved modification to the data, the user's program sends a COMMIT command to the dedicated server process. The dedicated server process puts the COMMIT instruction in the log buffer and waits for confirmation from the log writer that it has recorded the COMMIT instruction in the redo log files—this guarantees the *durability* of the modifications.

9. The database writer wakes up periodically and copies any modified data blocks that it finds in the data cache to the data files. The checkpoint process wakes up periodically and initiates a systematic synchronization procedure on all data files that includes updating the system change number in the heading of each data file.

10. If the undo and redo entries fill up the current redo log file, the log writer closes the file and opens the next one. The archiver subsequently makes a copy of the closed file in case a data file ever gets damaged and needs to be repaired.

11. The user's program disconnects from the database. This terminates the dedicated server process.

Summary

The information in this chapter is a summary of the contents of *Oracle 11g Concepts*. Here is a short summary of the concepts we touched on:

- In Oracle terminology, the word *database* is used to collectively indicate the data files and supporting files on the storage disks attached to the host computer. The word *instance* is used to indicate the various computer processes resident in computer memory and memory areas shared by these processes.

- Unlike in Microsoft SQL Server or IBM DB2, the relationship between Oracle instances and databases is either one-to-one (one instance per database) or many-to-one (multiple instances per database).

- The location of the database software is called the Oracle home and is usually stored in the environment variable ORACLE_HOME.

- Well-known configuration files include init.ora, listener.ora, and tnsnames.ora.

- Data files are logically grouped into tablespaces. Each Oracle table or index is assigned to one tablespace and shares the space with the other tables assigned to the same tablespace. Data files can grow automatically if the database administrator wishes. The space within data files is organized into equally sized blocks; all data files belonging to a tablespace use the same block size. When a data table needs more space, it grabs a contiguous range of data blocks called an extent; it is conventional to use the same extent size for all tables in a tablespace.

- Temporary files are used if a large work area does not fit in available computer memory.

- Redo log files are used to store the undo and redo entries needed to guarantee atomicity and durability of a transaction. Redo logs are of fixed size and are mirrored for safety. Oracle fills the redo logs in round-robin fashion. The redo logs should be archived when they fill up—this makes it possible to repair data files if they get damaged.

- The control file is used by Oracle while starting the database; it contains the names and locations of the data files, among other things.

- Oracle records important events and errors in the alert log. A detailed trace file is created when a severe error occurs.

- The System Global Area (SGA) is composed of the buffer cache, the shared pool, and the log buffer. The best-known use of the shared pool is to cache query execution plans. It is also used to store information from the data dictionary.

- A dedicated server is started whenever a user connects to the database; it is terminated when the user disconnects from the database. In the multithreaded server (MTS) mode of operation, all user connections are serviced by a small number of dispatchers and shared servers.

- Background processes are not tied to user connections and live from database startup until database shutdown. The best-known background processes are the database writer (DBWR), the log writer (LGWR), the archiver (ARCH), the checkpoint process (CKPT), the process monitor (PMON), and the system monitor (SMON).

Exercises

- Download *Oracle Database 11g SQL Language Reference* from `http://www.oracle.com/technology/documentation/index.html` and find out how to augment the table creation commands listed in Chapter 2 with tablespace assignment instructions and extent sizing instructions.

- Ask a database administrator in your company for a listing of the database configuration files discussed in this chapter. Search the Oracle documentation at `http://www.oracle.com/technology/documentation/index.html` for an explanation of their contents.

- Search Figure 3-1 for any terms that have not been explained in this chapter. Search the Oracle documentation at `http://www.oracle.com/technology/documentation/index.html` for the definitions. A good place to start is *Oracle Database 11g Master Glossary*.

Further Reading

Oracle Corporation. *Oracle Database 11g Concepts.* Oracle Corporation, 2007. Required reading for Oracle database administrators. Searchable or downloadable free of charge at `http://tahiti.oracle.com` or `http://www.oracle.com/technology/documentation/index.html`. Printed copies can also be purchased from Oracle's online store.

Alapati, Sam. *Expert Oracle Database 11g Administration.* Apress, 2008. A useful reference for the intermediate to experienced database administrator.

PART II

Database Implementation

CHAPTER 4

■ ■ ■

Planning

2. Start with the end in mind.

—*The Seven Habits of Highly Effective People* by Stephen Covey

Your goal as Oracle administrator is not simply to create a database but to be on time, on budget, and to meet the availability and performance targets of the business. As with any goal, careful planning is the key to success. You have little control over a number of factors that affect the success of your database; for example, application design and testing. This chapter discusses three important issues that are definitely within your circle of influence and that you cannot afford to ignore: licensing, architecture, and sizing.

Licensing

Oracle provides a choice of licenses, ranging from free licenses to licenses for basic functionality or more advanced functionality, and a long range of individually priced extra-cost options. Furthermore, Oracle software does not require licensing keys to unlock it; anyone may freely download software from the Oracle web site and begin using it. This is an unusual practice that separates Oracle from other software vendors and has probably contributed to Oracle's success in the marketplace. It is, therefore, very easy to make the mistake of using software for which one does not have the required licenses. Oracle software is not cheap, so to avoid nasty surprises, make sure the licensing question is answered as early in the software development project as possible.

Practical Example

Suppose we are considering using a high-end configuration of four Sun SPARC Enterprise T5220 servers—each with four 1.2GHz UltraSPARC T2 4-Core CPUs—for an e-commerce web site. For extra horsepower and reliability, the production database will be handled by two servers clustered together using Oracle Real Application Clusters (RAC) technology. For protection against catastrophes such as fire or flood, the third server will be located in a separate data center and will handle a *standby* database, which is kept synchronized with the production database using Oracle's Data Guard technology; the standby database can also be used for reporting purposes and backups if the Active Data Guard option is purchased. The fourth server is needed to house multiple development and testing databases.

Table 4-1 shows the license and support fees I calculated using the pricing document on the Oracle web site when I wrote this chapter; the prices are subject to change, so you should always download the latest version of the pricing document. I've included typical options that you might consider licensing, such as *table partitioning*—a performance and management feature that we will discuss in Chapter 7—and new features of Oracle Database 11*g* such as Active Data Guard and Total Recall. I've also included some extra-cost database administration tools such as Diagnostics Pack and Tuning Pack. I had to multiply the number of CPU cores by a factor of 0.75 to compute the number of *equivalent CPUs* that must be licensed. More information on the treatment of multicore CPUs can be found in the pricing document listed at the end of this chapter; AMD and Intel CPUs are treated differently than Sun CPUs.

Table 4-1. *Oracle Licensing Cost for a High-End Configuration*

Description	License Cost per Single-Core CPU	Number of Licensed Servers	Number of Licensed CPUs	Number of Cores	Number of Equivalent CPUs	Cost
Enterprise Edition	$47,500	4	16	64	48	$2,280,000
Real Application Clusters	$23,000	2	8	32	24	$552,000
Partitioning Option	$11,500	4	16	64	48	$552,000
Active Data Guard	$5,800	3	12	48	36	$208,800
Total Recall	$5,800	3	12	48	36	$208,800
Diagnostics Pack	$3,500	3	12	48	36	$126,000
Tuning Pack	$3,500	3	12	48	36	$126,000
Configuration Management Pack	$3,500	4	16	64	48	$168,000
Provisioning Pack	$3,500	4	16	64	48	$168,000
Total Purchase Price						**$4,389,600**
Annual Support Fees						**$965,712**

The total cost of Oracle licenses for the configuration that I chose is $4,389,600, and the annual support fee is $965,712. The high cost of licenses and support may cause you to select a different hardware configuration or to license fewer software options that you would prefer. Table 4-2 shows the prices I calculated for a low-end configuration consisting of four Dell PowerEdge 2900 III servers, each with two 2.5GHz Intel Xeon E5420 4-core CPUs.

Table 4-2. *Oracle Licensing Cost for a Low-End Configuration*

Description	License Cost per CPU	Number of Licensed Servers	Number of Licensed CPUs	Cost
Standard Edition (SE)	$17,500	4	8	$140,000
Real Application Clusters	Included with SE[1]			
Partitioning Option	Unavailable with SE			
Active Data Guard	Unavailable with SE			
Total Recall	Unavailable with SE			
Diagnostics Pack	Unavailable with SE			
Tuning Pack	Unavailable with SE			
Configuration Management Pack	Unavailable with SE			
Provisioning Pack	Unavailable with SE			
Total Purchase Price				**$140,000**
Annual Support Fees				**$30,800**

Even though a significant discount will probably be forthcoming for large purchases, the cost of Oracle Database can exceed that of some other widely used commercial technologies such as Microsoft SQL Server. Oracle Database technology is arguably superior to the alternatives, but prudence requires a cost-benefit analysis. Free alternatives to commercial technologies are *open source* technologies like MySQL and PostgreSQL, which don't require license payments but may not have all the features of the commercial technologies. However, licensing costs, support fees, and feature sets are not the only considerations when making technology choices; development costs, personnel costs, hardware compatibility, and performance benchmarks are some of the other considerations.

---

1. Real Application Clusters is included with Standard Edition if there are no more than four CPUs in the cluster.

Free to Download, Free to Learn, Unlimited Evaluation

You can freely download Oracle database software from the Oracle web site and use it for self-education, evaluate its suitability for a project, or develop a prototype of an application. The following language is found at `http://www.oracle.com/technology/software/index.html`:

> *"All software downloads are free, and each comes with a Development License that allows you to use full versions of the products at no charge while developing and prototyping your applications (or for strictly self-educational purposes)."*[2]

No license keys are required to unlock Oracle database software, there is no limit to the length of the evaluation period, there are no restrictions on the use of the product, and you don't need to provide information about yourself or your company if you don't want to do so. Oracle does not appear to be worried about the potential for illegal use of its software and stands alone in the software industry in allowing its product to be downloaded and used in this way; some of its commercial success can undoubtedly be traced to its liberal download and usage policies.

Database Editions

Just as Microsoft does with Windows Vista, Oracle packages its software into different versions. Those who need only basic database functionality can buy a less expensive edition than a large international corporation that needs the high-end features. Here are some of the editions that you can choose from:

Oracle Express Edition: Provides a significant subset of Oracle Database functionality—comparable to that of *Standard Edition,* described next—as a free starter edition. There are significant restrictions on its use—for example, the database size is restricted to four gigabytes—but Express Edition can be used without charge even in commercial settings—for example, a starter database bundled with a software product—and formal classroom settings. A significant attraction is its ease of deployment; it is provided as a *self-extracting executable* for Windows or an *RPM package* for Linux.

Standard Edition: Includes a significant subset of Oracle Database functionality. There are no restrictions on the size of the database, but there is a restriction on the size of the server; Standard Edition can only be installed on servers with a maximum capacity of four CPUs. It is not suitable for the largest databases, because performance and

---

2. Please review the precise terms of the development license at `http://www.oracle.com/technology/software/popup-license/standard-license.html`.

management options such as Partitioning are not included; they can only be licensed along with Enterprise Edition, described next. *Management packs* such as Configuration Management and Change Management are also not available with Standard Edition. However, in an effort to promote the use of Real Application Clusters (RAC) technology (a high-availability feature), Oracle permits its use with Standard Edition if there are no more than four CPUs in the cluster.

Enterprise Edition: Includes performance and management features required by the largest and most demanding databases, such as parallel query, query results caching, parallel backup and recovery, and so on. Enterprise Edition costs much more than Standard Edition: $47,500 per single-core CPU, at time of writing. However, there are a number of features that are not included even with Enterprise Edition and cost even more, the most significant being RAC and partitioning (a management and performance feature needed when dealing with the largest data tables). Other important features that also require additional license fees are the management packs, such as Configuration Management Pack, Change Management Pack, Provisioning Pack (for release management), Diagnostic Pack, and Tuning Pack.

Oracle licenses can be purchased on the Web at `http://store.oracle.com`. However, it is conventional to contact an Oracle sales representative so that discounts can be negotiated on large purchases. If your organization already uses Oracle, you will already have an assigned sales representative. If your organization is using Oracle for the first time, you can get in touch with a sales representative by calling the toll-free number listed on the Oracle web site.

■**Note** Further licensing topics this book must omit for lack of space include the *named user* metric, Personal Edition, Standard Edition One, and *term licenses*. I also do not have space to list the features that are bundled in the various editions and the restrictions on each edition. The documents containing all this information are listed at the end of this chapter.

As already indicated, Oracle software can be freely downloaded from the Oracle web site. *Media packs* (CD sets) can also be ordered from the online store for a nominal price. Reference manuals can also be downloaded in PDF format from the Oracle web site and there is no charge, whether or not you buy licenses for Oracle software. Of particular interest to you at this stage are the installation guides for various operating system platforms. Printed copies of the reference manuals can be purchased if really necessary, but they are quite expensive.

Architectural Choices

Oracle provides a variety of architectural choices to suit every need. The choice of architecture is determined by factors such as performance, availability, and scalability. For example, if you require very high availability, you could consider Oracle's Data Guard architecture. If you need to start small and scale to very high volumes, you could consider Oracle's Real Application Clusters (RAC) architecture. The following sections explore the most common architectural choices for Oracle databases.

Dedicated Server

This is the simplest Oracle configuration as well as the most common. It requires that each connection to the database be handled by a dedicated Oracle process; if 100 users were connected to the database, then 100 Oracle processes would be required to handle them.

You will use dedicated server architecture when creating a database on your laptop in Chapter 6.

Shared Server

The Dedicated Server architecture does not work well for large numbers of connections because the Oracle Database processes contend for the limited amount of RAM. Large numbers of database connections are typically observed in Online Transaction Processing (OLTP) situations, but most of the connections are typically idle most of the time.

For example, suppose that all the employees of a company use the same computer program on their individual workstations to do their daily work. They remain connected to the database throughout the day but each of them usually makes a very reasonable number of requests for information during the course of the day. The total time required to process each user's requests is usually a very small fraction of the time the user is connected.

In such a situation, shared Oracle Database processes can be used to conserve RAM. The program running on the user's workstation communicates with an Oracle Database *dispatcher* process instead of a dedicated Oracle Database process. The dispatcher process places the request on a *request queue*. Any available shared process handles the request and places the results on a *response queue*. The dispatcher then communicates the results to the user. Any information that has to be preserved until the next request—that is, any *state information*—is preserved in the SGA.

Connection Pooling

An even more efficient use of resources can be achieved when the application is *stateless*. This is typically the case with e-commerce applications. As an example, consider a web store such as Amazon.com. The user browses the selections in the web store and adds items to a shopping cart. Each addition to the shopping cart is an autonomous task that results in a modification to the database. When the user has finished browsing and has committed to a purchase, he or she specifies shipping and payment details. This could happen hours or days after the user first began browsing. This mode of operation is said to be *stateless* in the sense that any information generated by the autonomous tasks (that is, information describing the current state of the operation) is not preserved in RAM for use by successor tasks—the information is saved in the form of a *cookie* on the user's computer or in the database itself.

Connection pooling can be used if the application is stateless in the sense just described. Prior to Oracle Database 11g, connection pooling could only be implemented in the *application tier*; that is, a modestly sized set of shared application processes handled all the requests. Each of these application servers maintained a persistent connection to the database. During periods of heavy activity, there might not be enough application processes to handle all the work, and delays might occur in handling requests.

Modern e-commerce applications need to be able to handle thousands of concurrent requests. The database can quickly become a bottleneck if every request requires that information be read from the database or that the database be modified. Various strategies can be used to prevent the database from becoming a bottleneck. After all, the database is limited by the number of CPUs and other factors and can only handle a relatively modest number of requests at a time. For example, information that does not change frequently such as product specifications and pictures can be cached in the application tier.

A typical application tier consists of a pool of application servers called a *server farm*. Each server in the server farm may have hundreds of application processes, each of which needs to connect to the database. However, if each application process is handled by a dedicated Oracle Database process, the number of Oracle Database processes can become unmanageable. Oracle Database 11g provides a feature called Database Resident Connection Pooling (DRCP) to improve scalability in such situations.

With DRCP, the processes in the application tier communicate not with dedicated Oracle Database processes but with a *connection broker*. The connection broker hands off each request to any available Oracle Database process in a *connection pool*. When the application process completes its task, it releases the Oracle Database process back to the connection pool. This mode of operation is made possible because the tasks are stateless in the sense described earlier.

Real Application Clusters

A computer can efficiently handle only a certain number of requests at a time; this number is greatly dependent on the number of CPUs and the amount of RAM. As the number of requests increases beyond a certain threshold, processes begin competing for scarce resources and all of them suffer. The easiest solution is to increase the number of CPUs and the amount of RAM, but large and powerful computers are also very expensive.

Real Application Clusters is a technology that combines the resources of more than one computer. Two or more Oracle Database instances share access to the same set of disks and coordinate with each other over a fast network. Additional instances can be added to the cluster as the workload increases. This allows us to start with cheap commodity hardware and "scale out" as the workload increases instead of "scaling up" to a more powerful (and more expensive) computer.

RAC also has implications for database availability. For example, any single instance can be shut down for hardware maintenance or OS patching without affecting the availability of the database. In some cases, it is even possible to apply Oracle patches in *rolling upgrade* fashion.

Standby Database

A *standby database* can improve application availability. In this scenario, redo information from the main database is shipped and applied to another database, called the standby. In the event of a primary database outage, applications can use the standby database. Applications can also be switched to the standby database when hardware maintenance or operating system maintenance needs to be performed on the primary database; *even the outages associated with Oracle patch sets and upgrades can be avoided*. Note that the maintenance of the standby database can be automated and simplified using an Oracle product called Data Guard, which is part of Enterprise Edition.

To save money, it is typical for the standby database to have fewer hardware resources (CPU and memory) than the primary database; it is also typical to use a non-RAC standby database for an RAC primary database. Another interesting option is to use an *active-active* configuration of two or more computers. A typical active-active configuration has two databases, each on a separate server; the standby database of the first database is placed on the second server and the standby database of the second database is placed on the first server. Each server thus hosts a primary database as well as a standby database. If one server suffers an outage, the standby database on the other node can be activated; this is a very cost-effective way of using hardware resources.

Maximum Available Architecture (MAA)

Maximum Available Architecture (MAA) can be used when both availability and performance are important and budgets are generous. The typical standby configuration uses fewer hardware resources for the standby database since the probability of a switchover is low; that is, there will be some amount of degradation in performance if the applications are pointed to the standby database. The MAA configuration combines RAC technology with standby technology and uses identically configured primary and secondary sites; in other words. The primary and standby databases both have the same number of RAC nodes.

MAA can be extended to the application tier too; the details are in the white paper listed at the end of this essay. Of course, identically configured primary and secondary sites (both database and application tiers) can be extremely expensive.

Sizing

The hardware resources your database needs depend on a number of factors such as the characteristics of the application (for example, OLTP vs. OLAP), the expected amount of activity, and the performance targets (such as the response time of business-critical transactions). However, it is rare to get good information on the expected amount of activity; ask how many simultaneously active sessions can be expected on average and you might get a blank stare in return. Even if you have good information, sizing can still be tricky. Here are some strategies that you can use:

- Ask vendors for help. Both hardware and software vendors have a great deal of experience in hardware sizing.

- Use the results obtained from volume testing during the development phase.

- Use information about similar systems in the enterprise; for example, an enterprise may own several brands, each of which has a similar e-commerce database.

- Early in the exercise, set the expectation that the hardware sizing is only a "best guess" and additional hardware might have to be procured once the initial results are in.

- Be very generous in your estimates, if you are not on a tight budget. You could also use this strategy if the application is critical to the enterprise; in such cases it is preferable to be oversized than undersized.

- Ensure that there is room for expandability; for example, ensure that the system can accommodate more CPUs and memory if the estimates are found to be inadequate.

A very good discussion of sizing issues is *Sizing Oracle on Microsoft Windows and Dell PowerEdge Servers* by Larry Pedigo (Dell, 2004). The discussion is based on Dell and Windows but is certainly applicable to other environments. Here are some of the considerations you should keep in mind when sizing your system.

Disk Sizing

It is easy to underestimate the amount of space you need for the database. Another common mistake is not to leave sufficient room for growth. The following sections describe the different types of files that you have to worry about in forecasting disk space needs for a database.

Data Files

Data files store your tables and indexes, and therefore you need to have some idea of how much data will be stored in tables in the foreseeable future. To estimate the amount of space required for a table, you have to estimate the average size of each row of data and the number of rows in the table. A reasonable thumb rule is to allow as much room for indexes as you allow for tables. There is a fair amount of "overhead space" and "white space" in tables and indexes and it would not be unreasonable to estimate that only 50% of the allocated space is usable. To summarize: estimate the amount of space required for tables, then double the number to allow for indexes, then double the number again to allow for overhead space and white space.

You also need to allow room for the SYSTEM and SYSAUX tablespaces used by Oracle. Oracle uses the SYSTEM tablespace to store the data dictionary and the SYSAUX tablespace for other kinds of management information; for example, Active Workload Repository (AWR).

If you do not have a license for AWR, you will probably use Statspack to collect performance data. In this case, you should reserve a sufficient amount of space for Statspack data. Statspack data is purged after 14 days by default, but you should consider storing as much data as you possibly can.

You must also allow a sufficient amount undo and temporary space. *Undo* refers to a copy of a data block that is made before the block is changed; it is used to restore the block in case the transaction does not commit its work. Temporary space is used for sorting operations during SQL queries.

Don't forget to leave a margin of error, especially if your estimates are not very reliable.

Control Files and Online Redo Logs

The space required for control files and online redo log files is usually modest; two gigabytes should suffice for most databases. In a highly demanding OLTP environment, you should pay careful attention to the placement of these files since they can quickly become a performance bottleneck.

Archived Redo Logs

Redo logs contain the information necessary to redo the database; they contain a record of all changes to the database. When redo logs fill up, they have to be copied to the archive destination before they can be reused. The amount of space required for the storage of archived redo logs depends on the amount of activity in the database; it also depends on retention preferences. An amount of space equal to the size of the database would not be unreasonable for a busy OLTP database.

Backups and Exports

Allocating an area twice the size of the database for backups would not be an unreasonable thing to do, unless you plan to put backups directly onto tape.

Software Executables and Related Files

Some space must be allocated for the Oracle software and for various categories of error logs such as the *alert log, listener log,* and *trace files*. Four gigabytes of space is a reasonable rule of thumb for most databases.

Other Disk Considerations

There's more to worry about when it comes to files than just the amount of space they will take. Usable space, file placement, and disk speed are some of the issues to consider.

Usable space

When specifying the amount of space required for the data, be clear that you are talking about usable space. For data protection, most disks utilize some form of RAID (Redundant Array of Inexpensive Disks) layout which reduces the amount of usable space. RAID 10 (mirroring plus striping) reduce the amount of usable space by 50%. RAID 5 has the most usable space but reduces write performance; the details are outside the scope of this book. RAID 10 is the best choice for databases.

File Placement

Some attention must be paid to the placement of different categories of files; for example, data files should not be placed on the same file system where software, archived redo log files, or backups are stored. *Optimal Flexible Architecture* (OFA) is a set of recommendations provided by Oracle for the placement of different categories of files. OFA is automatically used by Database Configuration Assistant (DBCA) when creating databases.

Disk Speed

Pay attention to your disk ratings because disk I/O can be a big performance bottleneck. If it takes 10 milliseconds to retrieve one data block (typically 8 KB in size), then an SQL query may not be able to read more than 100 data rows per second, because the required rows will more likely than not be spread out over as many data blocks.

Memory Sizing

Memory sizing is heavily dependent on the characteristics of your application. The amount of space you need in order to meet performance targets is very difficult to estimate unless you have good information, such as the results of volume testing. The cost of memory is a consideration, but memory becomes cheaper every year and it is no longer unusual to find databases using many gigabytes of memory. Here are the main considerations when planning memory requirements:

Buffer Cache: You need to allow enough space for Oracle to cache data blocks in memory because disk I/O can slow down your application tremendously. Note that you must a use a 64-bit operating system and the 64-bit version of Oracle in order to create very large buffer caches because the 32-bit versions cannot handle large amounts of memory.

Shared Pool: The shared pool contains the *library cache* and the *dictionary cache*. Query execution plans are stored in the library cache, and information about database objects is stored in the dictionary cache. It is rare to find a database that needs more than 1 GB of memory for the shared pool.

Stack Space: You need to provide stack space for each Oracle connection. A commonly used rule of thumb is 512 KB for each connection, for example, 50 MB for 100 connections.

CPU Sizing

The number of CPUs you need depends not only on the speed of the CPUs—the faster the CPUs, the fewer you need—but also on the application load. A good rule of thumb is as many CPUs as the average number of simultaneously active sessions during the critical period of the day; the database for a big e-commerce application may require 16 CPUs to meet performance targets.

Note that if you use more than four CPUs, you will need to purchase Oracle Enterprise Edition, which is far costlier than Oracle Standard Edition.

Network Sizing

Finally, you must give some consideration to network requirements. A database that services hundreds of connections might require multiple network cards in order to meet performance targets. Fast connections are required to the *storage area network* (SAN) and between the nodes in an RAC cluster.

■**Tip** A large number of approved hardware and software configurations are listed at `http://www.oracle.com/technology/tech/linux/validated-configurations/index.html`. Each listed configuration has been tested and approved by Oracle and includes storage, network, and operating system details. You can safely use any one of these configurations as a starting point to design a system that meets your requirements.

Summary

Here is a short summary of the concepts touched upon in this chapter.

- Oracle offers a variety of licensing options. *Standard Edition* is attractively priced but can only be used on servers with a maximum capacity of four CPUs. *Enterprise Edition* is expensive but offers high-end features such as parallelism and SQL results caching. Certain other features that are only available with Enterprise Edition require additional fees; the list includes features such as partitioning, management packs such as Diagnostics Pack and Tuning Pack, and new features introduced in Oracle Database 11g such as *Active Standby* and *Total Recall*.

- Oracle software can be used free of charge for prototyping and self-education. Oracle documentation is freely downloadable and searchable at `http://tahiti.oracle.com`.

- The *dedicated server* configuration is the most common configuration; each user session is handled by a dedicated process.

- The *shared server* configuration conserves resources; a small set of shared processes and *dispatchers* handles all sessions.

- *Connection pooling* can be used in the application tier or in the database tier if the application is *stateless*; for example, an Internet-based application. Oracle Database 11g offers *database resident connection pooling* to supplement connection pooling in the application tier.

- Real Application Clusters (RAC) involve multiple Oracle instances connecting to the same database. This allows us to use cheap "commodity hardware" and "scale out" as the workload increases instead of "scaling up" to a more powerful (and more expensive) computer. RAC databases can improve application availability; for example, hardware maintenance can be performed on one node of the RAC database without affecting the availability of the application.

- A *standby database* can improve application availability. In this scenario, redo information from the main database is shipped and applied to another database.

- *Maximum Available Architecture* (MAA) requires identically configured primary and standby sites; for example, if the primary database uses RAC, then the standby database also uses RAC. The redundancy is extended to the application tier. MAA maximizes availability but can be very expensive.

- Sizing is a difficult task involving a lot of best guesses. Strategies to use include: asking vendors for help, using results obtained from volume testing, studying similar systems in the enterprise, set expectations correctly, estimating generously, oversizing when possible, and ensuring that there is room for expansion.

- Disk sizing must take the following categories of files into account: data files, control files, online redo logs, archived redo logs, backups, exports, software, error logs, and trace files. The use of RAID layouts is standard practice but reduces the amount of usable space. Raid 10 is the best choice for databases. Certain categories of files must be separated from each other.

- The main categories of memory usage to consider are the buffer cache, the shared pool, and stack space for user sessions.

- Oracle provides a large number of pretested hardware and software configurations, which you can use as a starting point for designing a system that meets your requirements.

Exercises

- Audit an Oracle installation in your enterprise. Use Database Configuration Assistant (DBCA) to determine what software products have been installed. Determine whether the installation is properly licensed. Also determine whether it is over-licensed; for example, if it has a license for Enterprise Edition but no features of Enterprise Edition are being used.

- Create an Oracle Technology Network (OTN) account for yourself and download the Oracle Database 11*g* software for Windows.

- Download the Oracle Database 11*g* documentation from `http://tahiti.oracle.com`. Review the licensing manual.

- Study the various architectures described in this chapter and determine which one facilitates business continuity (a.k.a. disaster recovery).

- Study an Oracle installation in your enterprise and attempt to determine if it has sufficient capacity (CPU, memory, and disk) for the near to medium term. Also attempt to determine if it is oversized for current and future requirements.

Further Reading

Oracle Corporation. *Oracle 9i Maximum Availability Architecture*. Oracle Corporation, 2004. Discusses how to use Real Application Clusters and Data Guard for maximum performance and availability. Written for Oracle Database 9*i*, it is also applicable to Oracle Database 10*g* and Oracle Database 11*g*. Available at `http://www.oracle.com/technology/deploy/availability/pdf/MAA_WP.pdf`. Numerous other materials on MAA are available at `http://www.oracle.com/technology/deploy/availability/htdocs/maa.htm`.

Oracle Corporation. *Oracle Database 11*g *Licensing*. Oracle Corporation, 2007. Describes the various bundles, extra-cost options, and licensing restrictions. Searchable or downloadable free of charge at `http://tahiti.oracle.com` or `http://www.oracle.com/technology/documentation/index.html`. Printed copies can be purchased from Oracle's online store.

Oracle Corporation. *Oracle Technology Global Price List*. Oracle Corporation, 2008. Lists the prices of the various bundles and the extra cost options; it is updated whenever prices change. Available at `http://www.oracle.com/corporate/pricing/technology-price-list.pdf`.

Oracle Corporation. *Software Investment Guide*. Oracle Corporation, 2008. Provides a management overview of licensing options. Available at `http://www.oracle.com/corporate/pricing/sig.html`.

Pedigo, Larry. *Sizing Oracle on Microsoft Windows and Dell PowerEdge Servers*. Dell, 2004. A Windows-centric and Dell-centric discussion of sizing issues but the discussion is applicable to other environments. Available at `http://www.dell.com/downloads/global/solutions/Oracle%20on%20Windows%20Sizing.pdf`.

CHAPTER 5

■ ■ ■

Software Installation

The third little pig met a man with a load of bricks, and said, "Please, man, give me those bricks to build a house with;" so the man gave him the bricks, and he built his house with them. So the wolf came, as he did to the other little pigs, and said,—
"Little pig, little pig, let me come in."
"No, no, by the hair of my chiny chin chin."
"Then I'll huff, and I'll puff, and I'll blow your house in."
Well, he huffed, and he puffed, and he huffed, and he puffed, and he puffed, and he huffed; but he could not *get the house down.*

> —*The Nursery Rhymes of England, Fifth Edition*, by James Orchard Halliwell (Frederick Warne and Co., 1886)

We're almost ready to create a database. Chapter 4 covered the planning process. In this chapter, I'll go over a few prerequisites such as obtaining the software, installation guides, and reference manuals. I'll also discuss the installation of software that precedes the creation of a database. I'll show you how I installed the Oracle software on my laptop running Windows XP Professional. I hope that you take the opportunity to install Oracle on your own XP or Vista laptop—the best way to learn is by doing.

You'll go through the process of creating your first database in Chapter 6.

Oracle Technology Network

One of the reasons that Oracle dominates the database market is that it makes its software and its software manuals available for download without any artificial restrictions such as license keys and limited trials. Oracle's motto is *free to download, free to learn, unlimited evaluation.* All one needs is an Oracle Technology Network (OTN) account, available free of charge.

In addition to software and software manuals, OTN offers forums, articles, sample code, and tutorials. Go to `http://www.oracle.com/technology/index.html` and create an account for yourself; there's no reason not to do so.

The Forgotten Manuals

Beginning with Oracle Database 8, Oracle discontinued the practice of providing free printed copies of reference manuals to customers who purchased database licenses. In the early days of the Internet, when broadband access was not common, Oracle put the manuals on a CD. Today, broadband access is the rule, and you can search and read the manuals online; they are available in both HTML and PDF format. For convenience, you can also download selected manuals—or the entire set of manuals—to your laptop computer for offline reading. You can purchase printed copies of the manuals at `http://store.oracle.com`, but be warned that they are immense. *Oracle Database 11g SQL Language Reference* alone is almost 1,500 pages, twice the size of the Oracle Database 7 version.

The manuals for Oracle Database 11g are available at `http://www.oracle.com/technology/documentation/index.html`; the manuals for older database versions are also available, all the way back to Oracle Database 7.[1] For this chapter, you need the installation guides for your operating system—separate guides are available for client installations and server installations.

▪Note A short version of the guide, labeled a *Quick Installation Guide*, is also available in each case; it covers the most common scenarios. The quick installation guide for Windows is only 14 pages long.

Prerequisites and Preinstallation Requirements

You will need to pay attention to the sections of the installation guides that discuss prerequisites and preinstallation requirements. If you have chosen a complex architecture such as Real Application Clusters (RAC), these prerequisites will themselves be fairly complex; they are outside the scope of this introductory work.

In a Unix or Linux environment, you will need to install and run Oracle using a dedicated account. In a Windows environment, you can use any account belonging to the Administrators group. In Unix and Linux environments, you will have to solve the problems of mounting the product disks and enabling an X Windows environment for the

---

1.   You can also find manuals for other Oracle offerings including Application Server, BEA, E-Business Suite, PeopleSoft, JD Edwards, Retek, and database technologies such as Times Ten, Berkeley DB, Oracle Rdb, and CODASYL DBMS.

use of Oracle Universal Installer (OUI); you will also need to use the "root" account to perform a few tasks such as modifying the kernel settings. And of course, a common prerequisite for all operating systems is adequate space for database files, archived redo logs, and backups.

Client Installations

A *client installation* refers to the software that needs to be installed on every machine from which a connection to the database is initiated. This could be a user's laptop or an application server. In this section, I'll show you two types of client installations—Instant Client and SQL Developer—and demonstrate how to install them on a Windows server.

Instant Client

Prior to Oracle 10*g*, a typical client installation was a bloated collection of software including dozens of features—such as the Oracle XML Development Kit—which are rarely needed. Installation was a time-consuming process that required the use of OUI.

Beginning with Oracle Database 10*g*, Oracle provides the most essential software in a bundle called an *instant client*. OUI is not needed for installation; you can simply copy a few files to a directory of choice. The entire process takes only a few minutes:

1. Use your OTN account to download the necessary zipped files from Oracle Technology Network. Several choices are offered. The most common choices are Basic and SQL*Plus. The *Basic* package contains the dynamic link libraries required by Oracle applications, and *SQL*Plus* is the traditional command-line tool favored by database administrators.

2. Unzip the files and copy the contents to a directory of choice, as shown in Listing 5-1. The highlighted entries are the ones from the SQL*Plus package.

Listing 5-1. *Contents of the Instant Client Software Directory*

```
C:\Documents and Settings\anyuser>dir "C:\Program Files\instantclient_11_1"
 Volume in drive C has no label.
 Volume Serial Number is 904B-26D5

 Directory of C:\Program Files\instantclient_11_1

11/09/2008  11:29 AM    <DIR>          .
11/09/2008  11:29 AM    <DIR>          ..
10/03/2007  06:48 PM            13,824 adrci.exe
10/03/2007  06:48 PM             3,363 adrci.sym
```

```
10/03/2007  06:49 PM                    315 BASIC_README
10/03/2007  06:48 PM                 29,696 genezi.exe
10/03/2007  06:48 PM                 13,027 genezi.sym
01/13/2006  12:36 AM                    342 glogin.sql
05/17/2005  12:48 PM              1,060,864 mfc71.dll
05/09/2005  05:29 AM                348,160 msvcr71.dll
10/03/2007  06:38 PM                516,096 oci.dll
10/03/2007  06:38 PM                246,731 oci.sym
09/10/2007  12:57 PM                 77,824 ocijdbc11.dll
09/10/2007  12:57 PM                 13,143 ocijdbc11.sym
10/03/2007  04:03 PM                 18,944 ociw32.dll
10/03/2007  04:03 PM                  4,516 ociw32.sym
07/25/2007  10:47 AM              1,879,924 ojdbc5.jar
07/25/2007  10:48 AM              1,977,444 ojdbc6.jar
10/03/2007  05:04 AM              1,388,544 orannzsbb11.dll
10/03/2007  05:04 AM                295,819 orannzsbb11.sym
10/03/2007  06:33 PM                868,352 oraocci11.dll
10/03/2007  06:49 PM                258,636 oraocci11.sym
10/03/2007  06:43 PM            109,096,960 oraociei11.dll
10/03/2007  06:43 PM              2,860,504 oraociei11.sym
09/06/2007  09:55 AM              1,699,840 Orasqlplusic11.dll
09/06/2007  09:55 AM                757,760 sqlplus.exe
10/03/2007  06:50 PM                 30,135 sqlplus.sym
10/03/2007  06:50 PM                    319 SQLPLUS_README
11/08/2008  09:33 PM                    174 tnsnames.ora
11/09/2008  11:28 AM    <DIR>             vc71
11/09/2008  11:28 AM    <DIR>             vc8
              27 File(s)    123,461,256 bytes
               4 Dir(s)  48,632,463,360 bytes free
```

3. Next, use any text editor to create a file called tnsnames.ora containing an entry that describes an existing database. The sample file shown in Listing 5-2 describes a database called ORCL on a host called IGGY; the Oracle listener is listening on port 1521.

Listing 5-2. *A Sample* tnsnames.ora *File*

```
C:\Documents and Settings\anyuser>type "C:\Program Files\instantclient_11_1\➥
tnsnames.ora"
ORCL =
  (DESCRIPTION =
    (ADDRESS = (PROTOCOL = TCP)(HOST = IGGY)(PORT = 1521))
    (CONNECT_DATA =
```

```
      (SERVER = DEDICATED)
      (SERVICE_NAME = ORCL)
  )
 )
```

4. Finally, add the location of the client software to the PATH variable and define a variable called TNS_ADMIN to tell Oracle where you have placed the tnsnames.ora file—typically in the same location as the Instant Client software. You'll then be ready to connect to the desired database, as illustrated in Listing 5-3.

Listing 5-3. *Connecting to an Oracle Database by Using Instant Client*

```
C:\Documents and Settings\anyuser>set PATH=%PATH%;C:\Program Files\➥
instantclient_11_1

C:\Documents and Settings\anyuser>set TNS_ADMIN=C:\Program Files\➥
instantclient_11_1

C:\Documents and Settings\anyuser>sqlplus system@ORCL

SQL*Plus: Release 11.1.0.6.0 - Production on Sun Nov 9 11:40:31 2008

Copyright (c) 1982, 2007, Oracle.  All rights reserved.

Enter password:

Connected to:
Oracle Database 11g Enterprise Edition Release 11.1.0.6.0 - Production
With the Partitioning, OLAP, Data Mining and Real Application Testing options

SQL> SET linesize 84
SQL> SELECT instance_name, host_name
  2    FROM v$instance;

INSTANCE_NAME    HOST_NAME
---------------- -----------------------------------------------------------------
orcl             IGGY

SQL> exit
Disconnected from Oracle Database 11g Enterprise Edition Release 11.1.0.6.0 -➥
Production
With the Partitioning, OLAP, Data Mining and Real Application Testing options
```

SQL Developer

Another form of client installation that is worth mentioning is SQL Developer—a Java-based GUI tool that is useful to application developers as well as database administrators. It is a client installation in its own right and does not depend on other client software such as the Instant Client.

Installation of SQL Developer is painless:

1. Use your OTN account to download the necessary zipped files from Oracle Technology Network and unzip the contents into a directory of choice.

2. Click on the `sqldeveloper.exe` program and provide the details of the target database, as shown in Figure 5-1. Click Connect.

3. As illustrated in Figure 5-2, you can browse through the database by using the navigation panel on the left of the SQL Developer screen or submit SQL commands.

A GUI tool such as SQL Developer is much easier to use than a command-line tool such as SQL*Plus, but it cannot be used in conjunction with batch programs such as those used by Windows. You will see some examples of SQL Developer's use in Chapter 9.

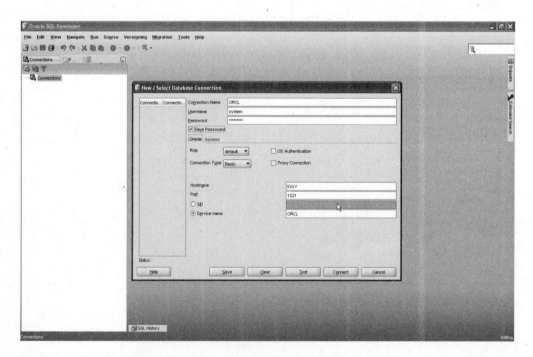

Figure 5-1. *Connecting to a database using SQL Developer*

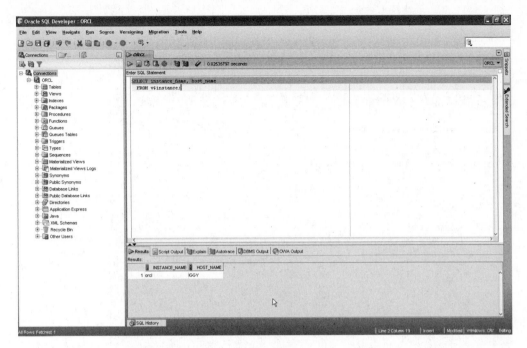

Figure 5-2. *Browsing through a database and submitting SQL commands using SQL Developer*

Server Installations

A *server installation* refers to the software that needs to be installed on the host computer of a database. If you're not using advanced Oracle architectures such as RAC or Automatic Storage Management (ASM), creating a server installation is a simple task, especially in a Windows environment. The steps are as follows:

1. Download the zip file containing the software from Oracle Technology Network and unzip it into a staging directory.

2. Navigate to the staging directory and click on `setup.exe` to start OUI. You are presented with the screen seen in Figure 5-3. Note the value of Oracle Home chosen by OUI; this will the home directory of the Oracle software. Deselect the checkbox option to create a starter database and click Next.

3. OUI then checks the prerequisites for the installation, as seen in Figure 5-4. Click Next.

4. OUI displays the summary seen in Figure 5-5. Click Next.

5. OUI begins installing the Oracle software; this takes a fairly long time. The progress screen shown in Figure 5-6 continuously displays the progress of the installation. When the installation is complete, OUI displays a success message, as illustrated in Figure 5-7. Click Exit.

On a Windows computer, you can perform the preceding steps by using any account with administrative privileges. However, I recommend that you create a special account called *oracle* for the purpose; this is the standard in non-Windows environments.

Figure 5-3. *Welcome screen of Oracle Universal Installer*

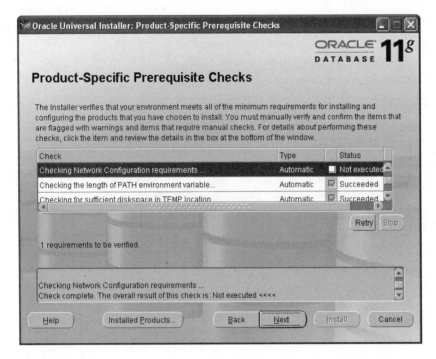

Figure 5-4. *Prerequisite checks conducted by Oracle Universal Installer*

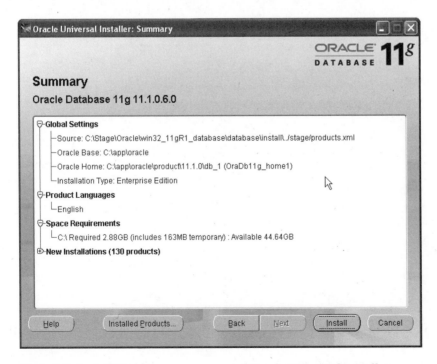

Figure 5-5. *Installation summary screen of Oracle Universal Installer*

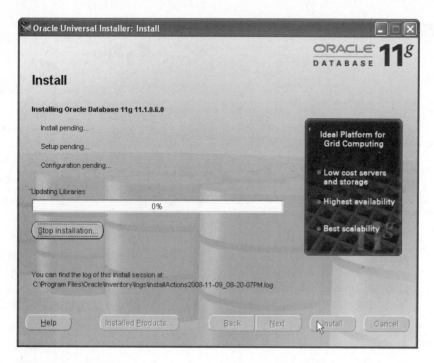

Figure 5-6. *Installation progress screen of Oracle Universal Installer*

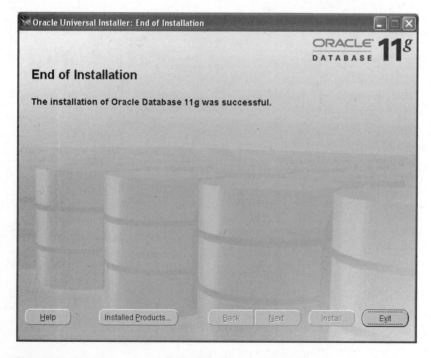

Figure 5-7. *Success message of Oracle Universal Installer*

Oracle Database Examples

Oracle provides a wealth of examples and demos that you can install on your computer for learning purposes. The steps are as follows:

1. Download the zip file containing the examples from Oracle Technology Network and unzip it into a staging directory.

2. Navigate to the staging directory and click on setup.exe to start OUI. OUI displays a welcome screen. Click Next.

3. Specify the Oracle Home into which the examples should be installed. Click Next.

4. OUI checks that all prerequisites are satisfied. Click Next.

5. OUI displays a summary screen. Click Install.

6. OUI begins installing the examples and demos. When the installation is complete, OUI displays a success message. Click Exit.

Perl

Perl is a modern open-source cross-platform programming language. You should ask a system administrator to install the Perl software on the host computer of your database because Oracle Enterprise Manager uses Perl scripts to monitor the database and perform corrective actions. You can download a Windows Installer package containing Perl for Windows from http://www.activeperl.com; simply double-click on it to begin the installation process on your laptop. Binaries for other platforms can be found at http://www.perl.org.

As illustrated in Listing 5-4, use the command perl -v to confirm that the Perl software is installed on the host computer of your database.

Listing 5-4. *Confirming That the Perl Software Is Installed on the Host Computer of the Database*

```
C:\Documents and Settings\oracle>perl -v

This is perl, v5.10.0 built for MSWin32-x86-multi-thread
(with 5 registered patches, see perl -V for more detail)

Copyright 1987-2007, Larry Wall

Binary build 1004 [287188] provided by ActiveState http://www.ActiveState.com
```

```
Built Sep  3 2008 13:16:37
```

Perl may be copied only under the terms of either the Artistic License or the
GNU General Public License, which may be found in the Perl 5 source kit.

Complete documentation for Perl, including FAQ lists, should be found on
this system using "man perl" or "perldoc perl". If you have access to the
Internet, point your browser at http://www.perl.org/, the Perl Home Page.

Summary

Here are some of the key points touched on in this chapter:

- Oracle makes its software and its reference manuals available for download without any artificial restrictions such as license keys and limited trials. Oracle's motto is *free to download, free to learn, unlimited evaluation time.* All you need is an Oracle Technology Network (OTN) account, available free of charge at http://www.oracle.com/technology/index.html.

- A *client installation* refers to the software that needs to be installed on every machine from which a connection to the database is initiated. This could be a user's laptop or an *application server.*

- Oracle provides the most essential software in a bundle called an *instant client*; you simply copy a few files to a directory of choice.

- SQL Developer is a Java-based GUI tool that is useful to application developers and database administrators. It is a client installation in its own right and does not depend on other client software such as the Instant Client.

- A *server installation* refers to the software that needs to be installed on the host computer of a database.

- Perl is a modern, open source, cross-platform programming language. The Perl software should be installed on the host computer of your database because Oracle Enterprise Manager uses Perl scripts to monitor the database and perform corrective actions.

Exercises

- Using the Perl language, write and execute a simple Perl program to display the greeting "hello, world" on your screen. This will prove that the Perl software is correctly installed on your laptop.[2]

Further Reading

Oracle Corporation. *Oracle Database 11*g *Quick Installation Guide for Microsoft Windows.* Oracle Corporation, 2007. A slim 14-page document covering the most common installation scenarios. Searchable or downloadable free of charge at `http://tahiti. oracle.com` or `http://www.oracle.com/technology/documentation/index.html`.

---

2. The "hello, world" exercise is a computer programming tradition that was introduced in *The C Programming Language* by Brian Kernighan and Dennis Ritchie (Prentice Hall, 1978).

CHAPTER 6

■ ■ ■

Database Creation

Who verily knows and who can here declare it, whence it was born and whence comes this creation?
The Gods are later than this world's production. Who knows then whence it first came into being?
He, the first origin of this creation, whether he formed it all or did not form it,
Whose eye controls this world in highest heaven, he verily knows it, or perhaps he knows not.

—*The Hymns of the Rigveda* by Ralph T. H. Griffith
(E. J. Lazarus and Co., Benares, 1897)

Oracle makes the process of creating a database as easy as eating pie—a database can be created from scratch in a few minutes to an hour, depending on its complexity. Mogens Norgaard, the CEO of a Danish company called Miracle A/S, recorded one of his employees, Morten Egan, clad in a straitjacket and creating a database in about thirty minutes by typing on his keyboard with his *nose!*

The reason for this demonstration was that a service provider had quoted fifty hours of labor to create a database. When viewers of the video protested that Egan had only created a very simple database, Norgaard recorded a video of Egan creating a more complex database in less than an hour, once again clad in a straitjacket and typing on the keyboard with his nose. In the same video, a fourteen-year-old intern named Daniel Christensen demonstrated that he, too, was capable of creating an Oracle database; he did it in twenty-six minutes.

To find both videos, search the YouTube catalog for the phrase "Unconventional Oracle Installation." Here are the opening remarks from the second video:

Norgaard: Mr. Egan, we've had some flak from our first "Nosejob" video. People say it's not a very serious way to show what [the service provider] was actually asked to do. Is that correct?

Egan: No, that is not correct. The thing that [the service provider] was asked to do was to install the database. The job of actually finding out how the database should be installed, what options should be in there, what parameters should be set, was done by me beforehand, and that took a month. So the paper that [the service provider] got to do the job was: install the database, change these two parameters, click Finish.

I had made an entire list of what to do; so it was basically a next-next-next installation type and I think the criticism is based on that. Well, the difficult thing is not to install the database, and that's correct; it's not difficult to install the database. The thing that takes time is the precursor thing where you think about how it should be set up and after you install the database where you say: OK, how do I design this thing for the application?

The only thing that [the service provider] was asked to do was the tiny part of installing the database because we did not have access to the machines, the only reason why [the service provider] was asked to do this. And I gave them a piece of paper with basically eight steps and listed the two parameters that need to be changed. And that was it.

Next-Next-Next; Click Finish

In this chapter, I'll first discuss the "Next-Next-Next; click Finish" method of creating a database. I'll then briefly discuss some tasks that you should consider performing after you create a database; specifically, installing the RDA and Statspack tools and disabling database features that have not been licensed. Finally, I'll introduce the manual method of database creation and some basic administrative tasks.

The simplest way of creating a database is to use the Database Creation Assistant (DBCA) program. If this is the first database you are creating on your computer, you first have to use the Net Configuration Assistant (NetCA) to configure a *listener*, an important process that comes into play when users start a database session. On the Windows platform, you will find DBCA and NetCA in the Oracle program group that was created when you installed the Oracle software. On Unix computers, you have to use the dbca and netca executables in the $ORACLE_HOME/bin folder and point the DISPLAY variable to any available X-server such as Xvnc.

Configuring a Listener

The process of configuring a listener is extremely simple and is described in the following steps:

1. Choose Listener Configuration on the welcome screen shown in Figure 6-1 and click the Next button.

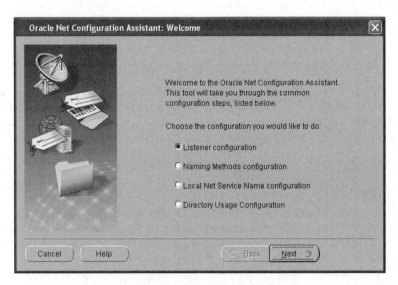

Figure 6-1. *Oracle Net Configuration Assistant: Welcome*

2. Choose Add on the Listener Configuration, Listener screen shown in Figure 6-2 and click Next.

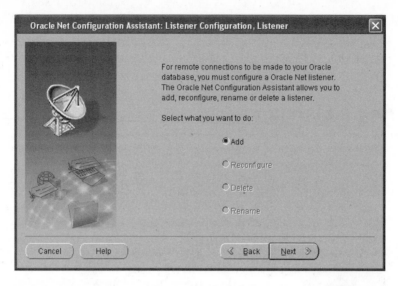

Figure 6-2. *Oracle Net Configuration Assistant: Listener Configuration, Listener*

3. Enter a listener name—for example, LISTENER—on the Listener Configuration, Listener Name screen shown in Figure 6-3 and click Next.

Figure 6-3. *Oracle Net Configuration Assistant: Listener Configuration, Listener Name*

4. Choose which network protocols should be used on the Listener Configuration, Select Protocols screen shown in Figure 6-4—TCP is the most common choice—and click Next.

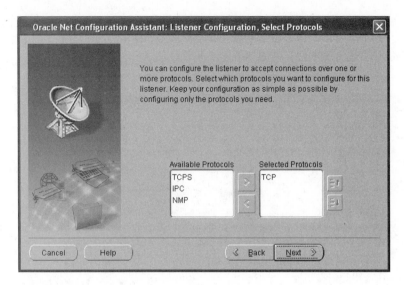

Figure 6-4. *Oracle Net Configuration Assistant: Listener Configuration, Select Protocols*

5. Choose a network port for the listener on the Listener Configuration, TCP/IP Protocols screen shown in Figure 6-5—1521 is the most common choice—and click Next.

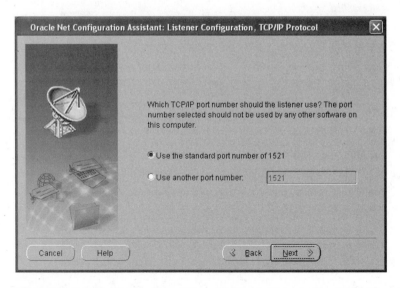

Figure 6-5. *Oracle Net Configuration Assistant: Listener Configuration, TCP/IP Protocol*

6. Select No from the Listener Configuration: More Listeners? screen shown in Figure 6-6 and click Next. It should only take a few seconds to configure and start the listener. Oracle then displays the success message shown in Figure 6-7.

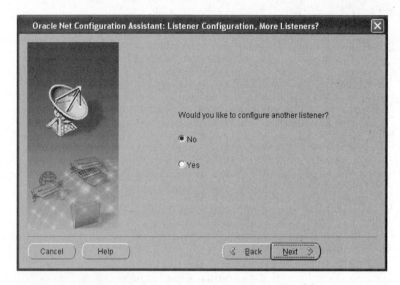

Figure 6-6. *Oracle Net Configuration Assistant: Listener Configuration, More Listeners?*

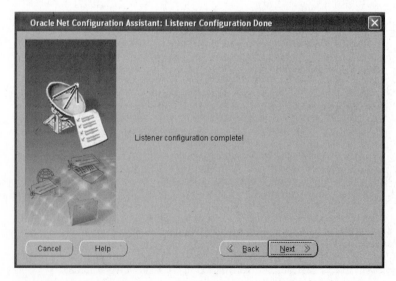

Figure 6-7. *Oracle Net Configuration Assistant: Listener Configuration Done*

To check that a listener has been created and started, you can use the lsnrctl status command, which will display output similar to that shown in Listing 6-1. Because you have not created a database yet, Oracle reports that the listener supports no services; this is expected.

Listing 6-1. *Sample Output of the* `lsnrctl status` *Command*

```
C:\Documents and Settings\oracle>lsnrctl status

LSNRCTL for 32-bit Windows: Version 11.1.0.6.0 - Production on 28-DEC-2008 21:09:53

Copyright (c) 1991, 2007, Oracle.  All rights reserved.

Connecting to (DESCRIPTION=(ADDRESS=(PROTOCOL=TCP)(HOST=localhost)(PORT=1521)))
STATUS of the LISTENER
------------------------
Alias                     LISTENER
Version                   TNSLSNR for 32-bit Windows: Version 11.1.0.6.0 -
Production
Start Date                27-DEC-2008 19:15:00
Uptime                    1 days 1 hr. 54 min. 59 sec
Trace Level               off
Security                  ON: Local OS Authentication
SNMP                      OFF
Listener Parameter File   C:\app\oracle\product\11.1.0\db_1\network\admin\listener.o
ra
Listener Log File         c:\app\oracle\diag\tnslsnr\hp6910\listener\alert\log.xml
Listening Endpoints Summary...
  (DESCRIPTION=(ADDRESS=(PROTOCOL=tcp)(HOST=hp6910)(PORT=1521)))
  (DESCRIPTION=(ADDRESS=(PROTOCOL=ipc)(PIPENAME=\\.\pipe\EXTPROC1521ipc)))
The listener supports no services
The command completed successfully
```

Creating and Configuring a Database

DBCA streamlines the process of creating and configuring a database and ensures that no steps are forgotten. The use of *database templates* speeds up and standardizes the database creation process. Of course, creating and configuring a database necessarily requires that we create and configure an instance to handle the work. The entire process is described in the following sections.

The Welcome Screen

As the welcome screen indicates, DBCA can be used to create a database, reconfigure an existing database, delete a database, and manage database templates. A *database template* is a copy of all the settings that were used to create a previous database. I recommend that you save the settings of every database that you create; this makes it easy to create another database with the same settings. Another good idea is to create an organizational standard and use it for all your databases. For convenience, Oracle provides three database templates, but they are not suitable for anything more than a starter database—for example, redo logs are not mirrored—and some customization is necessary.

Click the Next button on the welcome screen to go to Step 1: Operations.

■**Tip** Every DBCA screen sports a Help button which you can use to display information on how to use the screen.

Step 1: Operations

Figure 6-8 shows the screen for Step 1: Operations. Here you select the operation that you want to perform. The only option that needs a little explanation is Configure Automatic Storage Management. Automatic Storage Management (ASM) is an advanced Oracle technology for disk management. It replaces traditional *volume managers* and is most useful in high-end systems with hundreds of disks; it is also typically used in a Real Application Clusters (RAC) configuration. I will not be discussing ASM in this book; more information on this topic can be found in the references listed at the end of this chapter.

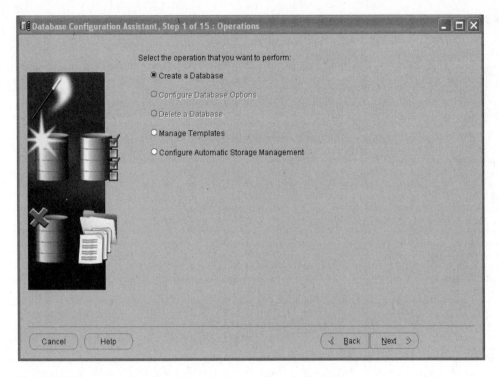

Figure 6-8. *Database Configuration Assistant, Step 1: Operations*

Select Create a Database and click Next to go to Step 2: Database Templates.

Step 2: Database Templates

Figure 6-9 shows the screen for Step 2: Database Templates. This screen lists the available templates, which specify *initialization parameters* and other choices that you make when creating a database. The use of templates is a very good practice; standardization usually improves the quality and maintainability of databases. Oracle provides three default templates: General Purpose or Transaction Processing, Custom Database, and Data Warehouse. It is tempting to choose the general-purpose template, since it is first in the list and the name indicates that it will suit most purposes. However, note that this template—along with the data warehouse template—is pre-seeded; that is, it includes pre-created data files. Pre-seeded templates are less customizable but allow databases to be created very quickly. Unfortunately, as you'll see in Table 6-1 later in this chapter, the pre-created data files are loaded with a great deal of optional software. You will probably never need most of these options, even though the installer refers to them as "common options." In the Exercises section, you will be asked to create your own pre-seeded template with just the software you need and with certain desirable settings.

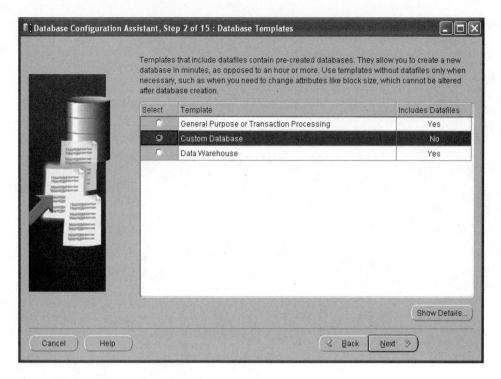

Figure 6-9. *Step 2: Database Templates*

For the purpose of this exercise, choose the General Purpose or Transaction Processing template. Click the Show Details button and examine the details of the template; in the screens that follow, you will be given the opportunity to modify some of the settings listed in the template. Then click Next to go to Step 3: Database Identification.

Step 3: Database Identification

Figure 6-10 shows the screen for Step 3: Database Identification. In this step, you choose a *database* name and an *instance* name. As explained in Chapter 4, the database is the collection of files on disk, while the instance is the collection of operating system processes that use the database. A database can be used by multiple instances; such a database is called a Real Application Clusters (RAC) database. Chapter 4 discusses RAC; more information about it can be found in the references listed at the end of this chapter. When creating a non-RAC database, it is conventional to choose the same value—for example, ORCL—for the database name and instance name. The instances in a RAC database are typically numbered serially; for example, ORCL1, ORCL2, and so on.

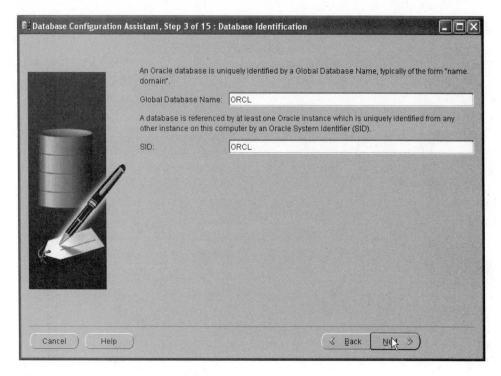

Figure 6-10. *Step 3: Database Identification*

Choose a database name and instance name and click Next to go to Step 4: Management Options.

Step 4: Management Options

Figure 6-11 shows the screen for Step 4: Management Options. In this step, you configure Enterprise Manager, the user-friendly GUI tool provided by Oracle for database administration. Its primary component is Database Control, which is used to manage a single database; a more advanced option called Grid Control can be used to manage all the databases in the enterprise from a single console. A major attraction of Database Control and Grid Control is that they are web applications and can be accessed using any Internet browser. Another major attraction is that they can monitor the databases and can send e-mail notifications and pager notifications when problems are detected.

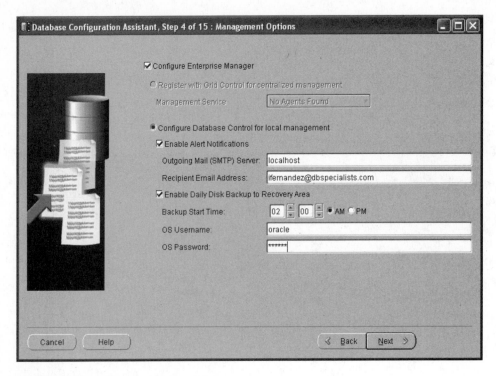

Figure 6-11. *Step 4: Management Options*

The Grid Control options will be grayed out unless a *management agent* has previously been installed on your computer. For this exercise, select Configure Database Control for Local Management.

Next, provide the name of a mail server that will process outgoing e-mail messages. You can ask a system administrator in your organization for this information. If your laptop is not directly connected to the organizational network, you can use tools such as Putty or SecureCRT to create a tunnel between your laptop and a mail server.

To accept the default backup scheme—described in Chapter 12—check the box that says Enable Daily Disk Backup to Recovery Area and provide an operating system account name and password that Oracle can use for the purpose.

Finally, click Next to go to Step 5: Database Credentials.

Step 5: Database Credentials

Figure 6-12 shows the screen for Step 5: Database Credentials. In this step, you choose passwords for the four most important administrative accounts in the database: SYS, SYSTEM, DBSNMP, and SYSMAN. The SYS account owns the core tables in the Oracle data dictionary, while the SYSTEM account owns administrative views and other components of Oracle's management infrastructure. The DBSNMP and SYSMAN views are used by Enterprise

Manager. There are a number of other administrative accounts, but they are all locked out when the database is created and should be enabled on an as-needed basis only.

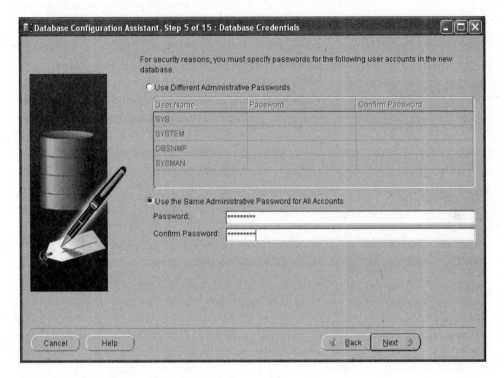

Figure 6-12. *Step 5: Database Credentials*

You can elect to use the same password for all four accounts. Use a password that meets the complexity requirements of your organization's security policy but is fairly easy to remember. After you have finished entering passwords, click Next to go to Step 6: Storage Options.

Step 6: Storage Options

Figure 6-13 shows the screen for Step 6: Storage Options. Here you select a storage method for database files. Most databases use traditional *file systems* for file storage. Automatic Storage Management (ASM) is an advanced Oracle technology for disk management—it replaces traditional *volume managers* and is most useful in high-end systems with hundreds or thousands of disks. More information on ASM can be found in the references listed at the end of this chapter. It is also possible to use *raw devices* to gain a performance advantage; this was a popular strategy at one time but is no longer in favor because it introduces complexity and increases the chances that database administrators will make mistakes with catastrophic consequences.

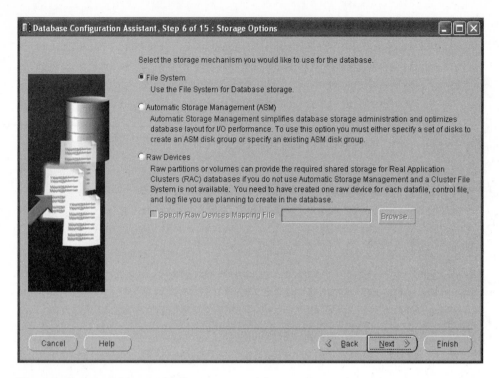

Figure 6-13. *Step 6: Storage Options*

Select File System and click Next to go to Step 7: Database File Locations.

Step 7: Database File Locations

Figure 6-14 shows the screen for Step 7: Database File Locations. A number of data files are automatically created by DBCA; you can let DBCA decide their names and locations or you can specify a name and location for each data file yourself. If you let Oracle choose, it constructs names and locations from the values of variables such as ORACLE_BASE, ORACLE_HOME, DB_NAME, and SID. Click the File Location Variables button to review these values; ORACLE_HOME is the location of the Oracle software, ORACLE_BASE is the parent directory of ORACLE_HOME, DB_NAME is the name of the database, and SID is the name of the instance. If you wish, you may alter the names and locations of individual files later, in Step 13: Database Storage.

One of the options you can choose on this screen is Oracle-Managed Files. This option was introduced in Oracle 9*i* in an effort to reduce the need to create and manage data files for tablespaces; it is no longer popular.

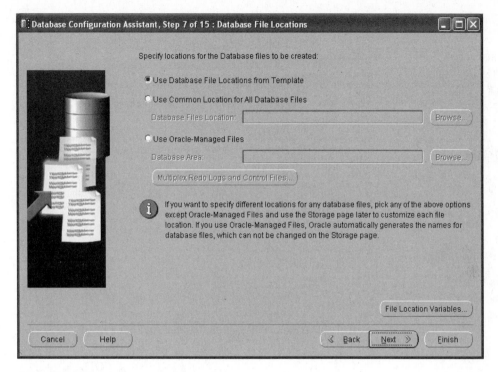

Figure 6-14. *Step 7: Database File Locations*

Select Use Database File Locations from Template and click the Next button to go to Step 8: Recovery Configuration.

Step 8: Recovery Configuration

Figure 6-15 shows the screen for Step 8: Recovery Configuration. In this step, you specify whether to use a common area called the *flash recovery area* to store backups created with Recovery Manager (RMAN) and archived redo logs; this is the recommended practice. To increase safety, you should specify a location that is on a different file system than the one containing the database. You must also specify the maximum amount of space that Oracle may use for the purpose; this value depends on the size of the database, the backup scheme, and the expected volume of archived redo logs. The default value of 2048 MB (2 GB) is not adequate, even for a starter database. Change the value to 8192 MB (8 GB) for now; you can adjust it at a later date if it does not meet your needs.

On this screen, you also specify whether you would like redo logs to be archived; this too is the recommended practice. Remember that if you do not archive redo logs, you cannot make a backup copy of the database unless you first shut it down and, if the database ever requires recovery, you cannot recover any changes made to the database after the latest backup.

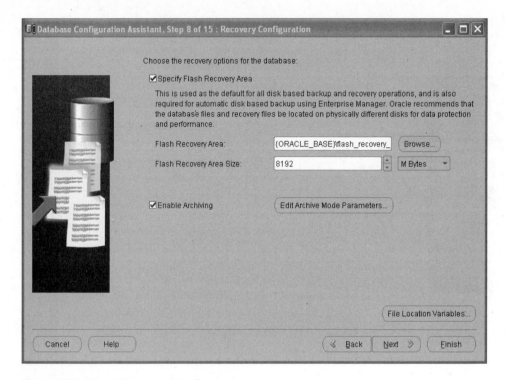

Figure 6-15. *Step 8: Recovery Configuration*

Select Specify Flash Recovery Area and Enable Archiving. Click the Edit Archive Mode Parameters button to review the settings relating to archiving; then click Next to go to Step 9: Database Content.

Step 9: Database Content

Figure 6-16 shows the screen for Step 9: Database Content. Because earlier in this example we chose a template that included data files, the only options DBCA provides in this screen are to install a number of *sample schemas* for instructional purposes and to run scripts of your choice after the database has been created.

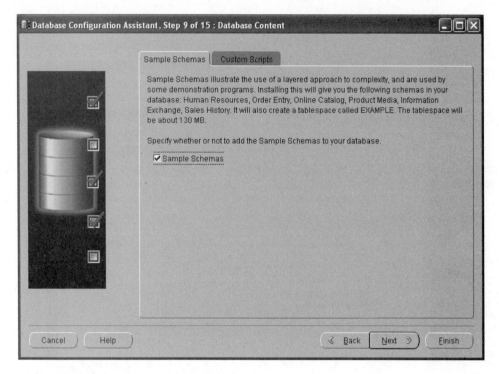

Figure 6-16. *Step 9: Database Content*

Select Sample Schemas; then click the Next button to go to Step 10: Initialization Parameters.

Step 10: Initialization Parameters

Figure 6-17 shows the screen for Step 10: Initialization Parameters. This screen packs a lot of options into four tabs: Memory, Sizing, Character Sets, and Connection Mode. In the Memory tab, you specify how much computer memory you are willing to devote to the Oracle database. The simplest option is to choose a single number and leave it to Oracle to manage it appropriately; this is called *automatic memory management.* Alternatively, you can explicitly specify how much memory Oracle should use for each purpose; for example, the shared pool and the buffer cache.

In the Sizing tab, you specify the maximum number of simultaneous connections to the database that can be expected and the default block size of the database. In our example, the block size is set to 8192 bytes (8 KB) and cannot be changed (because the template that we are using includes pre-created data files containing blocks of this size).

In the Character Sets tab, you specify character sets that accommodate the languages spoken by your users; an example is WE8MSWIN1252 which supports West European languages. Please refer to *Oracle Database 11g Globalization Support Guide* if you need to support other languages.

In the Connection Mode tab, you choose between dedicated server mode and shared server mode; these were discussed in Chapter 4.

You can click the All Initialization Parameters button if you would like to modify initialization parameters that are not presented on this screen.

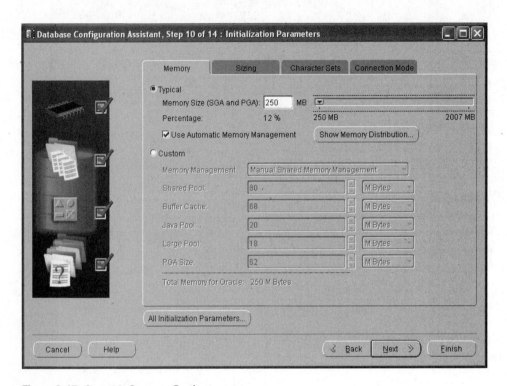

Figure 6-17. *Step 10: Storage Options*

Once you are satisfied with your choices, click Next to go to Step 11: Security Settings.

Step 11: Security Settings

Figure 6-18 shows the screen for Step 11: Security Settings. In this step, you can choose to accept the latest Oracle security recommendations; this is the recommended practice. These settings include enabling auditing of sensitive operations—such as creating and dropping users—and certain security settings such as locking accounts if the number of failed login attempts exceeds a threshold.

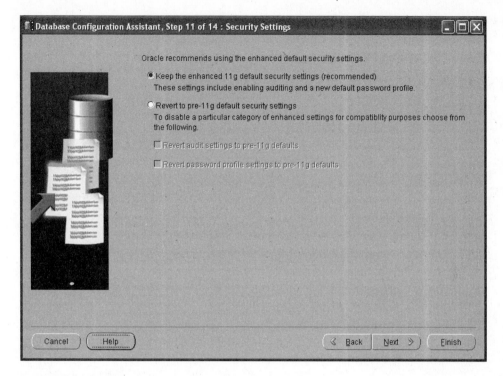

Figure 6-18. *Step 11: Security Settings*

Select Keep the Enhanced 11*g* Default Security Settings and click Next to go to Step 12: Automatic Maintenance Tasks.

Step 12: Automatic Maintenance Tasks

Figure 6-19 shows the screen for Step 12: Automatic Maintenance Tasks. Oracle Database 10*g* introduced automatic maintenance tasks such as collection of statistical information for the user of the query optimizer. In this screen, you can enable these automatic tasks; this is the recommended practice.

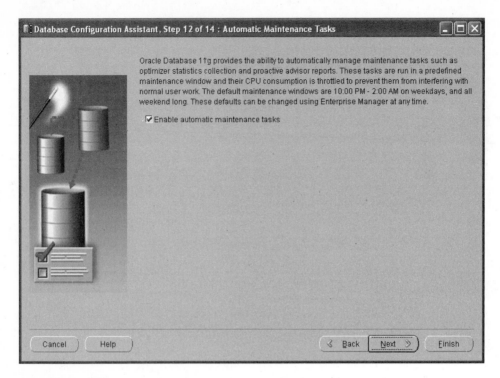

Figure 6-19. *Step 12: Automatic Maintenance Tasks*

Select Enable Automatic Maintenance Tasks and click Next to go to Step 13: Database Storage.

Step 13: Database Storage

Figure 6-20 shows the screen for Step 13: Database Storage. From this screen, you can add or remove tablespaces, data files, control files, and redo log files, or you can modify their names, locations, and sizes. However, you cannot add or remove tablespaces and data files, or change the sizes of data files, if you are using a template that contains pre-created data files. Notice that the templates provided by Oracle do not provide for mirroring of the redo log files; you should correct this by creating a mirror for each redo log in the flash recovery area. The templates also place all control files in the database area; you should correct this by placing one of them in the flash recovery area.

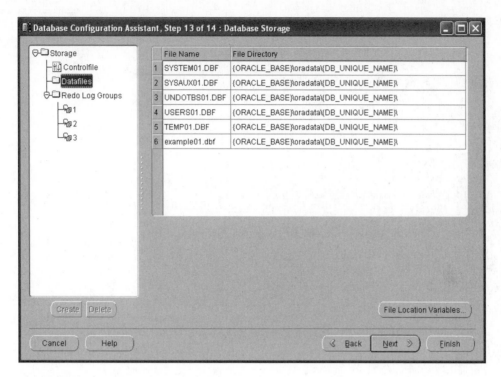

Figure 6-20. *Step 13: Database Storage*

Review the names and locations of the various categories of files and click the Next button to go to Step 14: Creation Options.

Step 14: Creation Options

Figure 6-21 shows the screen for Step 14: Creation Options. This is the final screen before DBCA starts creating the database. Remember to save your work as a template, *even if you did not make any changes to the default template*. Saving your work as a template keeps a record of your work; it also allows you to create other databases using the same settings. In the interest of further documenting your work, you should also select the option that generates database creation scripts—these are the scripts that DBCA runs behind the scenes to create the database.

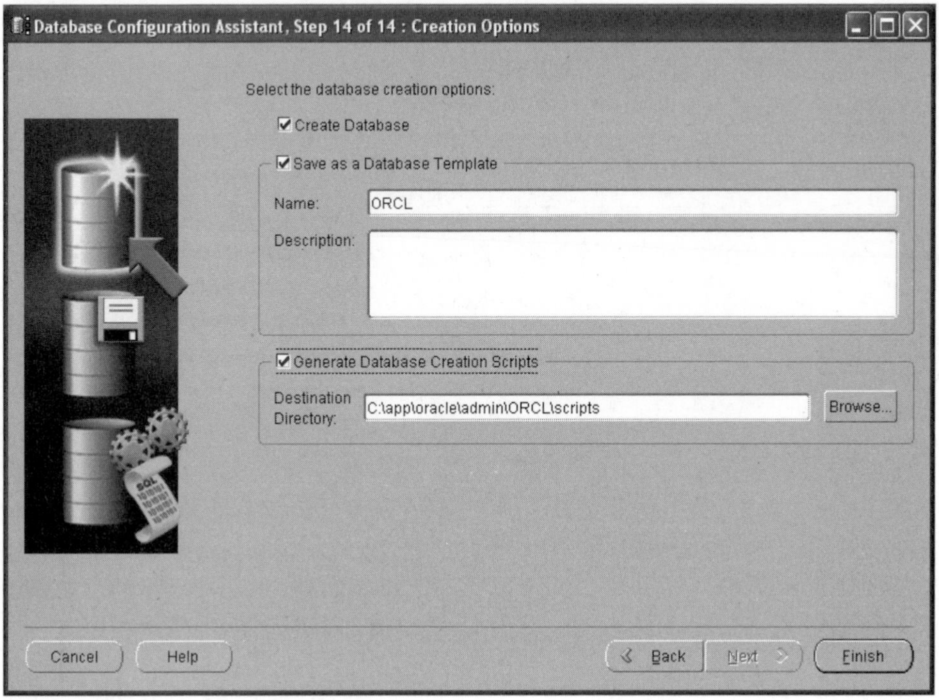

Figure 6-21. *Step 14: Creation Options*

Select Create Database, Save as a Database Template, and Generate Database Creation Scripts; then click Finish to instruct DBCA to create the database.

Confirmation Screen

Before creating the database, DBCA displays a confirmation screen that lists all the options you have selected. Click the Save as an HTML File button to generate a report. Let us review all the choices we made.

Common Options

Because we chose a template that included data files, Oracle did not allow us to pick and choose optional components for installation. Table 6-1 shows which options will be installed. DBCA refers to them as "common options," but you will probably never need most of them.

Table 6-1. *Common Options*

Option	Selected
Oracle JVM	True
Oracle Text	True
Oracle XML DB	True
Oracle Multimedia	True
Oracle OLAP	True
Oracle Spatial	True
Oracle Ultra Search	True
Oracle Label Security	False
Sample Schemas	True
Enterprise Manager Repository	True
Oracle Application Express	True
Oracle Warehouse Builder	True
Oracle Database Vault	False
Oracle Database Extensions for .NET	False

Initialization Parameters

Oracle databases have hundreds of initialization parameters, most of which have default values. Table 6-2 lists the few parameters that were set by DBCA.

Table 6-2. *Initialization Parameters*

Name	Value
audit_file_dest	{ORACLE_BASE}\admin\{DB_UNIQUE_NAME}\adump
audit_trail	db
compatible	11.1.0.0.0
control_files	{ORACLE_BASE}\oradata\{DB_UNIQUE_NAME}\control01.ctl, {ORACLE_BASE}\oradata\{DB_UNIQUE_NAME}\control02.ctl, {ORACLE_BASE}\oradata\{DB_UNIQUE_NAME}\control03.ctl
db_block_size	8 KB
db_name	ORCL
db_recovery_file_dest	{ORACLE_BASE}\flash_recovery_area
db_recovery_file_dest_size	8192 MB
diagnostic_dest	{ORACLE_BASE}
dispatchers	(PROTOCOL=TCP) (SERVICE={SID}XDB)

(continued)

Table 6-2. *Continued*

Name	Value
log_archive_format	ARC%S_%R.%T
memory_target	250 MB
open_cursors	300
processes	150
remote_login_passwordfile	EXCLUSIVE
undo_tablespace	UNDOTBS1

Data Files

All the data files listed in Table 6-3 were included in the template; we could have changed their names and locations if we had wished to do so.

Table 6-3. *Data Files*

Name	Tablespace	Size (MB)
{ORACLE_BASE}\oradata\{DB_UNIQUE_NAME}\SYSTEM01.DBF	SYSTEM	680
{ORACLE_BASE}\oradata\{DB_UNIQUE_NAME}\SYSAUX01.DBF	SYSAUX	540
{ORACLE_BASE}\oradata\{DB_UNIQUE_NAME}\UNDOTBS01.DBF	UNDOTBS1	25
{ORACLE_BASE}\oradata\{DB_UNIQUE_NAME}\USERS01.DBF	USERS	5
{ORACLE_BASE}\oradata\{DB_UNIQUE_NAME}\TEMP01.DBF	TEMP	20
{ORACLE_BASE}\oradata\{DB_UNIQUE_NAME}\example01.dbf	EXAMPLE	130

Control Files

Table 6-4 shows the control files that will be created by DBCA. It is conventional to triply mirror the control file because it is critical. However, at least one mirror copy should be placed in a different location for extra safety—this is not automatically performed by DBCA.

Table 6-4. *Control Files*

Name
{ORACLE_BASE}\oradata\{DB_UNIQUE_NAME}\control01.ctl
{ORACLE_BASE}\oradata\{DB_UNIQUE_NAME}\control02.ctl
{ORACLE_BASE}\oradata\{DB_UNIQUE_NAME}\control03.ctl

Redo Log Groups

Table 6-5 shows the redo log groups that will be created by DBCA. It is conventional to create at least three redo log groups; high-volume environments need even more. Mirroring the redo log files is recommended—DBCA does not do this automatically. Also, the sizes chosen by DBCA are fairly low.

Table 6-5. *Redo Log Groups*

Group	Size (KB)
1	51200
2	51200
3	51200

Success Messages

The creation process is particularly speedy if you use a template that includes pre-created data files. Once the database is created, DBCA displays success messages similar to the one in Figure 6-22. Of particular interest is the Database Control URL, which you will need in order to use Enterprise Manager to administer the database.

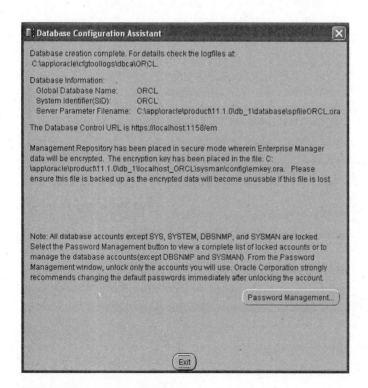

Figure 6-22. *Success Messages*

Post-Creation Tasks

You should consider performing the following tasks every time you've created a new database:

- You should disable access to any *management packs* that you have not licensed. You can do this from the Management Pack Access screen in Enterprise Manager, accessible via the Setup screen. You need to set the CONTROL_MANAGEMENT_PACK_ACCESS initialization parameter to NONE in order to disable access to Diagnostics Pack and Tuning Pack; you can do this from the Initialization Parameters screen, accessible via the Server screen.

- Unless you are using Enterprise Edition and have licensed Diagnostics Pack, you should consider installing Statspack, which is a free tool for performance analysis. Installation is quick and painless; simply run the spcreate.sql and spauto.sql scripts found in the ORACLE_HOME\rdbms\admin directory. Information on installing and using Statspack can be found in spdoc.txt in the same directory. We will discuss the use of Statspack in Chapter 16.

- You should consider installing the RDA tool, which is provided by Oracle Support to collect all the information about a database and its host system that might aid in the diagnosis of a problem. Oracle Support typically asks that you use this tool and send the collected data to Oracle whenever you request help in solving a problem. Although it was created to aid in diagnosing problems, it is of great help in exploring and documenting database configurations. Complete instructions for installing RDA can be found in Metalink note 314422.1: *Remote Diagnostic Agent (RDA) 4—Getting Started*. Metalink is the Oracle knowledge base and, you will need a valid Oracle support contract in order to gain access to it.

Other Methods of Database Creation

DBCA is a user-friendly tool for creating a database, but behind the scenes, it uses operating-system commands and SQL*Plus commands to do its work. You can use those same commands to create a database manually. The centerpiece is the CREATE DATABASE command, which is rich in options. In Listing 6-2, we create a functional database with a few simple commands and then destroy it, all in the space of a few minutes; the oradim utility is used to create and drop the corresponding Windows service. Complete instructions for creating a database with the CREATE DATABASE command can be found in *Oracle Database 11g Administrator's Guide*.

Listing 6-2. *Creating a Functional Database with a Few Simple Commands*

```
C:\Documents and Settings\oracle>oradim.exe -new -sid TEST
Instance created.

C:\Documents and Settings\oracle>type initTEST.ora
db_name=TEST
C:\Documents and Settings\oracle>set ORACLE_SID=TEST

C:\Documents and Settings\oracle>sqlplus "/ as sysdba"

SQL*Plus: Release 11.1.0.6.0 - Production on Mon Dec 29 01:56:21 2008

Copyright (c) 1982, 2007, Oracle.  All rights reserved.

Connected to an idle instance.

SQL> startup nomount pfile=initTEST.ora
ORACLE instance started.

Total System Global Area  150667264 bytes
Fixed Size                  1331740 bytes
Variable Size              92278244 bytes
Database Buffers           50331648 bytes
Redo Buffers                6725632 bytes
SQL> create database;

Database created.

SQL> select ts#, name from v$tablespace;

     TS# NAME
---------- ------------------------------
       0 SYSTEM
       1 SYSAUX
       2 SYS_UNDOTS

SQL> column name format a60
SQL> select ts#, name from v$datafile;
```

```
     TS# NAME
---------- ------------------------------------------------------------
         0 C:\APP\ORACLE\PRODUCT\11.1.0\DB_1\DATABASE\DBS1TEST.ORA
         1 C:\APP\ORACLE\PRODUCT\11.1.0\DB_1\DATABASE\SYX1TEST.ORA
         2 C:\APP\ORACLE\PRODUCT\11.1.0\DB_1\DATABASE\UND1TEST.ORA

SQL> column member format a60
SQL> select group#, member from v$logfile;

    GROUP# MEMBER
---------- ------------------------------------------------------------
         1 C:\APP\ORACLE\PRODUCT\11.1.0\DB_1\DATABASE\LOG1TEST.ORA
         2 C:\APP\ORACLE\PRODUCT\11.1.0\DB_1\DATABASE\LOG2TEST.ORA

SQL> column name format a60
SQL> select name from v$controlfile;

NAME
------------------------------------------------------------
C:\APP\ORACLE\PRODUCT\11.1.0\DB_1\DATABASE\CTL1TEST.ORA

SQL> shutdown immediate;
Database closed.
Database dismounted.
ORACLE instance shut down.
SQL> startup mount exclusive restrict pfile=initTEST.ora
ORACLE instance started.

Total System Global Area  150667264 bytes
Fixed Size                  1331740 bytes
Variable Size              92278244 bytes
Database Buffers           50331648 bytes
Redo Buffers                6725632 bytes
Database mounted.
SQL> drop database;

Database dropped.

Disconnected from Oracle Database 11g Enterprise Edition Release 11.1.0.6.0 -
Production
With the Partitioning, OLAP, Data Mining and Real Application Testing options
SQL> exit
```

```
C:\Documents and Settings\oracle>oradim.exe -delete -sid TEST
Instance deleted.
```

DBCA can also be used in command-line mode. In this mode you invoke DBCA from the operating system prompt and specify a *response file* that contains your directives. Information on response files can be found in any of the Oracle Database 11*g* installation guides.

Basic Database Administration Tasks

The most basic database administration tasks are stopping and starting Oracle database components—the listener, the instance, and Database Control—and changing initialization parameters; these are demonstrated in Listing 6-3. In a Windows environment, Oracle database components are typically managed using Windows *services* and are automatically stopped or started when the server is stopped or started. However, they can also be started from the command line, as is typical in Unix environments.

Listing 6-3 demonstrates the use of the lsnrctl and emctl utilities to manage the listener and Database Control, respectively. The PATH variable needs to include the location of the Oracle executables, and an Oracle instance must be specified by the ORACLE_SID variable. Note that in a Windows environment, the Oracle instance is typically started automatically when the corresponding service is started. However, for the purpose of this example, I modified the service so that this does not happen automatically. This allows you to see how to manage the instance using the sqlplus utility.

Initialization parameters can be changed using the ALTER SYSTEM command. However, not all parameters can be changed while the instance is running. In such cases the change can only be made to the *spfile*; that is, the parameter file. The changes will take effect when the instance is restarted.

Listing 6-3. *Performing Basic Database Administration Tasks*

```
C:\Documents and Settings\oracle>echo %PATH%
C:\Perl\site\bin;C:\Perl\bin;C:\app\oracle\product\11.1.0\db_1\bin;C:\WINDOWS\system
32;C:\WINDOWS;C:\WINDOWS\System32\Wbem

C:\Documents and Settings\oracle>set ORACLE_SID=ORCL
```

```
C:\Documents and Settings\oracle>lsnrctl start LISTENER

LSNRCTL for 32-bit Windows: Version 11.1.0.6.0 - Production on 01-JAN-2009 23:55:31

Copyright (c) 1991, 2007, Oracle.  All rights reserved.

Starting tnslsnr: please wait...

TNSLSNR for 32-bit Windows: Version 11.1.0.6.0 - Production
System parameter file is C:\app\oracle\product\11.1.0\db_1\network\admin\listener.or
a
Log messages written to c:\app\oracle\diag\tnslsnr\hp6910\listener\alert\log.xml
Listening on: (DESCRIPTION=(ADDRESS=(PROTOCOL=tcp)(HOST=hp6910)(PORT=1521)))
Listening on: (DESCRIPTION=(ADDRESS=(PROTOCOL=ipc)(PIPENAME=\\.\pipe\EXTPROC1521ipc)
))

Connecting to (DESCRIPTION=(ADDRESS=(PROTOCOL=TCP)(HOST=hp6910)(PORT=1521)))
STATUS of the LISTENER
------------------------
Alias                     LISTENER
Version                   TNSLSNR for 32-bit Windows: Version 11.1.0.6.0 - Productio
n
Start Date                01-JAN-2009 23:55:35
Uptime                    0 days 0 hr. 0 min. 7 sec
Trace Level               off
Security                  ON: Local OS Authentication
SNMP                      OFF
Listener Parameter File   C:\app\oracle\product\11.1.0\db_1\network\admin\listener.o
ra
Listener Log File         c:\app\oracle\diag\tnslsnr\hp6910\listener\alert\log.xml
Listening Endpoints Summary...
  (DESCRIPTION=(ADDRESS=(PROTOCOL=tcp)(HOST=hp6910)(PORT=1521)))
  (DESCRIPTION=(ADDRESS=(PROTOCOL=ipc)(PIPENAME=\\.\pipe\EXTPROC1521ipc)))
The listener supports no services
The command completed successfully

C:\Documents and Settings\oracle>net start OracleServiceORCL
The OracleServiceORCL service is starting.
The OracleServiceORCL service was started successfully.
```

C:\Documents and Settings\oracle>**sqlplus sys as sysdba**

SQL*Plus: Release 11.1.0.6.0 - Production on Thu Jan 1 23:58:08 2009

Copyright (c) 1982, 2007, Oracle. All rights reserved.

Enter password:
Connected to an idle instance.

SQL> **startup**
ORACLE instance started.

Total System Global Area 263639040 bytes
Fixed Size   1332552 bytes
Variable Size   234883768 bytes
Database Buffers   20971520 bytes
Redo Buffers   6451200 bytes
Database mounted.
Database opened.
SQL> **show parameter control_management_pack_access;**

NAME   TYPE   VALUE
------------------------------------ ----------- ------------------------------
control_management_pack_access   string   DIAGNOSTIC+TUNING
SQL> **alter system set control_management_pack_access=NONE;**

System altered.

SQL> alter system set processes=200;
alter system set processes=200
                  *
ERROR at line 1:
ORA-02095: specified initialization parameter cannot be modified

SQL> **alter system set processes=200 scope=spfile;**

System altered.

SQL> exit
Disconnected from Oracle Database 11g Enterprise Edition Release 11.1.0.6.0 - Produc
tion
With the Partitioning, OLAP, Data Mining and Real Application Testing options

```
C:\Documents and Settings\oracle>emctl start dbconsole
Oracle Enterprise Manager 11g Database Control Release 11.1.0.6.0
Copyright (c) 1996, 2007 Oracle Corporation.  All rights reserved.
https://hp6910:1158/em/console/aboutApplication
Starting Oracle Enterprise Manager 11g Database Control ...The OracleDBConsoleORCL s
ervice is starting................
The OracleDBConsoleORCL service was started successfully.



C:\Documents and Settings\oracle>lsnrctl status LISTENER

LSNRCTL for 32-bit Windows: Version 11.1.0.6.0 - Production on 02-JAN-2009 00:09:57

Copyright (c) 1991, 2007, Oracle.  All rights reserved.

Connecting to (DESCRIPTION=(ADDRESS=(PROTOCOL=TCP)(HOST=hp6910)(PORT=1521)))
STATUS of the LISTENER
------------------------
Alias                     LISTENER
Version                   TNSLSNR for 32-bit Windows: Version 11.1.0.6.0 - Production
Start Date                01-JAN-2009 23:55:35
Uptime                    0 days 0 hr. 14 min. 23 sec
Trace Level               off
Security                  ON: Local OS Authentication
SNMP                      OFF
Listener Parameter File   C:\app\oracle\product\11.1.0\db_1\network\admin\listener.o
ra
Listener Log File         c:\app\oracle\diag\tnslsnr\hp6910\listener\alert\log.xml
Listening Endpoints Summary...
  (DESCRIPTION=(ADDRESS=(PROTOCOL=tcp)(HOST=hp6910)(PORT=1521)))
  (DESCRIPTION=(ADDRESS=(PROTOCOL=ipc)(PIPENAME=\\.\pipe\EXTPROC1521ipc)))
Services Summary...
Service "ORCLXDB" has 1 instance(s).
  Instance "orcl", status READY, has 1 handler(s) for this service...
Service "ORCL_XPT" has 1 instance(s).
  Instance "orcl", status READY, has 1 handler(s) for this service...
Service "orcl" has 1 instance(s).
  Instance "orcl", status READY, has 1 handler(s) for this service...
The command completed successfully
```

C:\Documents and Settings\oracle>**emctl status dbconsole**
Oracle Enterprise Manager 11g Database Control Release 11.1.0.6.0
Copyright (c) 1996, 2007 Oracle Corporation. All rights reserved.
https://hp6910:1158/em/console/aboutApplication
Oracle Enterprise Manager 11g is running.

Logs are generated in directory C:\app\oracle\product\11.1.0\db_1/hp6910_ORCL/sysman
/log

C:\Documents and Settings\oracle>**emctl stop dbconsole**
Oracle Enterprise Manager 11g Database Control Release 11.1.0.6.0
Copyright (c) 1996, 2007 Oracle Corporation. All rights reserved.
https://hp6910:1158/em/console/aboutApplication
The OracleDBConsoleORCL service is stopping............
The OracleDBConsoleORCL service was stopped successfully.

C:\Documents and Settings\oracle>**sqlplus sys as sysdba**

SQL*Plus: Release 11.1.0.6.0 - Production on Fri Jan 2 00:13:07 2009

Copyright (c) 1982, 2007, Oracle. All rights reserved.

Enter password:

Connected to:
Oracle Database 11g Enterprise Edition Release 11.1.0.6.0 - Production
With the Partitioning, OLAP, Data Mining and Real Application Testing options

SQL> **shutdown immediate;**
Database closed.
Database dismounted.
ORACLE instance shut down.
SQL> exit
Disconnected from Oracle Database 11g Enterprise Edition Release 11.1.0.6.0 - Produc
tion
With the Partitioning, OLAP, Data Mining and Real Application Testing options

```
C:\Documents and Settings\oracle>net stop OracleServiceORCL
The OracleServiceORCL service is stopping.
The OracleServiceORCL service was stopped successfully.


C:\Documents and Settings\oracle>lsnrctl stop LISTENER

LSNRCTL for 32-bit Windows: Version 11.1.0.6.0 - Production on 02-JAN-2009 00:14:02

Copyright (c) 1991, 2007, Oracle.  All rights reserved.

Connecting to (DESCRIPTION=(ADDRESS=(PROTOCOL=TCP)(HOST=hp6910)(PORT=1521)))
The command completed successfully
```

As will be discussed in Chapter 9, many database administration tasks can be performed using Database Control. The opening screen of Database Control is illustrated in Figure 6-23.

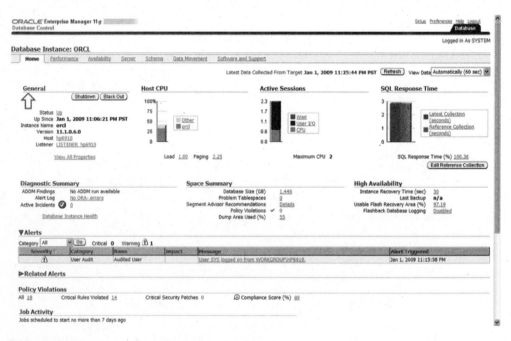

Figure 6–23. *Opening screen of Database Control*

Summary

Here is a short summary of the concepts touched upon in this chapter.

- NetCA can be used to configure a *listener*. DBCA can be used to create a database, reconfigure existing databases, delete a database, and manage database templates.

- A *database template* is a copy of all the settings that were used to create a previous database.

- Oracle provides three database templates: General Purpose or Transaction Processing, Custom Database, and Data Warehouse.

- Saving your work as a template allows you to review your work later; it also allows you to create other databases using the same settings.

- After creating a database, you should disable access to unlicensed management packs. If you do not have a license for Diagnostics Pack, you can install a free performance analysis tool called Statspack.

- RDA is a tool provided by Oracle Support to collect all the information about a database and its host system that might aid in the diagnosis of a problem. It is of great help in exploring and documenting database configurations.

- DBCA can also be used in command-line mode. In this mode you invoke DBCA from the operating system prompt and specify a *response file* that contains your directives.

- In a Windows environment, Oracle database components are typically managed using Windows services and are automatically stopped or started when the server is stopped or started. However, they can also be started from the command line, as is typical in Unix environments. The lsnrctl and emctl utilities can be used to manage the listener and Database Control, respectively. The sqlplus utility can be used to stop and start Oracle and change database settings.

Exercises

- Identify the Windows *services* that were created by NetCA and DBCA when you created a listener and database. Practice stopping and starting the listener and database using these services. Change the startup type to manual if you don't want these services to be started automatically when you reboot your computer.

- Create a database using the Custom Database template. Click the Help button on every screen and read the information provided. Select only those optional components that you plan to use, such as Sample Schemas and Enterprise Manager Repository. Identify the initialization parameters that have nondefault values and review the descriptions of these parameters in *Oracle Database 11g Reference*. Change the value of ARCHIVE_LAG_TARGET to 900 seconds. Increase the size of the redo log files to 100 MB, create a mirror copy of each redo log file in the flash recovery area, and add two additional redo log groups. Relocate one copy of the control file to the flash recovery area. Review the scripts generated by DBCA and the CREATE DATABASE statement in particular. Finally, use this newly created database to create a pre-seeded template that includes data files.

Further Reading

Oracle Corporation. *Oracle Database11g Reference*. Oracle Corporation, 2007. Describes the hundreds of Oracle initialization parameters. Freely searchable or downloadable free of charge at http://tahiti.oracle.com or http://www.oracle.com/technology/documentation/index.html.

Oracle Corporation. *Oracle Database 11g Administrator's Guide*. Oracle Corporation, 2007. Provides detailed instructions for creating and configuring an Oracle database. Freely searchable or downloadable free of charge at http://tahiti.oracle.com or http://www.oracle.com/technology/documentation/index.html.

Oracle Corporation. *Oracle Database 11g Globalization Support Guide*. Oracle Corporation, 2007. Explains how to choose a database character set. Freely searchable or downloadable free of charge at http://tahiti.oracle.com or http://www.oracle.com/technology/documentation/index.html.

Alapati, Sam. *Expert Oracle Database 11g Administration*. Apress, 2008. A useful reference for the intermediate to experienced DBA.

CHAPTER 7

■ ■ ■

Physical Database Design

In most people's vocabularies, design means veneer. It's interior decorating. It's the fabric of the curtains and the sofa. But to me, nothing could be further from the meaning of design. Design is the fundamental soul of a man-made creation that ends up expressing itself in successive outer layers of the product or service.

—Apple CEO Steve Jobs, interviewed in *Fortune* magazine; January 24, 2000

The two stages of database design are *logical* and *physical* design. Logical database design, also referred to as *data modeling*, is done first. It is the process of studying the workings of a business organization, constructing a set of tables to store the business data, and understanding the constraints on the data, the dependencies between the tables, and the business rules concerning the data. The logical database design process is conducted without reference to any specific database technology such as Oracle or Microsoft SQL Server, and a simple example can be found in *Oracle Database 11g Java Developer's Guide*. Tools such as Oracle Designer, CA ERwin Data Modeler, Embarcadero ER/Studio, and Toad Data Modeler can be used for the purpose. *Physical* database design follows logical database design. First, the logical model is mapped to the proprietary features of the chosen database technology. Security requirements, integrity requirements, and business rules are also implemented. Finally, we consider performance: the ability of the database engine to handle work requests efficiently. This typically involves the creation of *indexes* on the data, and Oracle Database provides a wealth of indexing mechanisms to choose from.

Performance considerations can come to the forefront at any time during the life of the database; new queries can be introduced at any time. Database administrators must therefore understand the mechanisms that can be used to improve performance.

Three broad categories of performance mechanisms are available for physical database design. *Indexes* can be used to quickly find the data. *Partitions* and *clusters* can be used to organize the data. Finally, *materialized views* and *denormalized tables* can be used to perform expensive operations like Joins ahead of time.

Indexes

An Oracle index is analogous to the index of words at the back of this book. For example, if you wanted to quickly locate information about indexes in this book, you would refer to the index at the back of this book, which would direct you to this page. Similarly, an Oracle index allows it to quickly locate a row of data that satisfies a query. Consider this query: SELECT * FROM employee WHERE last_name = 'FERNANDEZ'. If an index of last names was available, Oracle could quickly identify rows of data that satisfy the query. For each row of data in the table, this index would store the ROWID (address) of the row together with the value of LAST_NAME. In the absence of the index, Oracle would be forced to check every row of data in the table. Note that an index is tied to a single table; the following command creates an index of last names and gives it the name employee_i1:

```
CREATE INDEX employee_i1 ON employee(last_name)
```

Paradoxically, the use of an index does not always reduce the time taken to process a query. To understand why this might be so, suppose that we wanted to underline all lines in this book containing the word "the." A great many lines would qualify, and it would be faster to read the entire book, underlining as we went, instead of flipping back and forth between the index and the pages of the book. Now, consider the query SELECT * FROM employee WHERE hire_date > '1-Jan-1900'. It is very probable that a large percentage of data rows in the employee table will satisfy the query. Suppose that an index of hire dates is available. It would be faster to retrieve all rows of data in the quickest possible manner—that is, to scan the full table—than to flip back and forth from the index to the table. The decision to use an index is left to the query optimizer, which uses statistical information such as histograms to make its decisions.

More than one data item in a table might need to be indexed. However, a proliferation of indexes can negatively impact efficiency. To understand why, consider that Oracle must update all the relevant indexes whenever the data in a table is modified; for example, when a new row of data is inserted, Oracle must create a new index record in every single one of the indexes associated with the table. When a row of data is deleted, it must delete the corresponding index record from every index associated with the table. And, of course, indexes themselves require space within the database.

■**Tip** Use the MONITORING USAGE clause of the CREATE INDEX or ALTER INDEX commands to track whether your indexes are being used by the query optimizer.

Unique vs. Non-Unique Indexes

Sometimes, the collection of indexed values should not include duplicates. For example, no two employees should have the same employee ID number. You can use the UNIQUE clause of the CREATE INDEX command to enforce the uniqueness requirement, as in the following example:

```
CREATE UNIQUE INDEX employee_i1 ON employee(employee_ID)
```

Concatenated Indexes

Consider the following query, which retrieves all red cars registered in the state of California: SELECT * FROM automobile WHERE state = 'CA' and color = 'RED'. The query would probably benefit from an index of states or an index of colors, but an even more selective index would be an index of state and color *combinations*. The following command creates an index of state and color combinations and names it automobile_i1:

```
CREATE INDEX automobile_i1 ON automobile(state, color)
```

Oracle is capable of using the information in a concatenated index even if all relevant data items are not restricted in the SQL query. Instead of separate indexes, one of states and one of colors, let us suppose that a concatenated index has been created as in the previous paragraph. Also, suppose that the query specifies only the state or the color but not both. Oracle is capable of using the concatenated index even in such a case. For example, consider the query SELECT * FROM automobile WHERE state = 'CA'. In this case, it makes perfect sense to use the concatenated index described in the previous paragraph. Now consider the query SELECT * FROM automobile WHERE color = 'RED'. Because color is not the leading item in the concatenated index, it might appear at first sight that the concatenated index is not useful. However, Oracle can check the index 50 times, once for each state in the union, and thus identify rows satisfying both restrictions. It makes sense to do so because indexes are relatively compact objects, compared to tables. Also, database indexes are structured for easy lookup, just as the index of keywords at the back of this book is sorted in alphabetical order.

Function-Based Indexes

Indexes of the type we have considered so far are not as useful if the restrictions listed in the query include anything more complex than simple equality and inequality checks. For example, an index of salaries would not help if we are trying to identify employees for whom the *total* of salary and bonus is greater than a certain amount. Therefore, Oracle provides the ability to create indexes of the results of expressions. For example, the following command creates an index of the total of salary and bonus:

```
CREATE INDEX employee_i3 ON (salary + bonus)
```

Structure of an Index

Oracle indexes are structured for ease of use. To consider why structure is important, observe that the index of words at the back of this book would be far less useful if it were not sorted in alphabetical order. The typical Oracle index is a *balanced tree* or *b-tree*. The details are beyond the scope of this introductory text but suffice it to say that the indexing information is stored in the "leaves" of a balanced tree as illustrated in Figure 7-1.

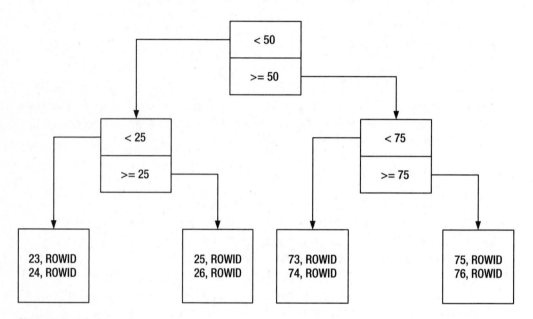

Figure 7-1. *A balanced tree*

What Indexes to Create?

Which indexes to create is a question that is not easily answered. The temptation is to create too many, but it is equally easy to forget to create any. Oracle will do the best it can with the available indexes, and powerful modern hardware can sometimes compensate for the lack of appropriate indexes. A commonly used rule is to create an index for every column that is restricted in a query. This may be too many, because the query optimizer bases the decision to use an index on the available statistical information about the table, and some indexes may never be used. Also, as I explained earlier, indexes must be modified whenever the data is modified and, therefore, indexes can slow down the database. However, there are some situations where indexes are not optional:

- Unique indexes are required to efficiently enforce the requirement of uniqueness; for example, no two employees can share a social security number. This is particularly true of any column or combination of columns designated as a *primary key*.

- Indexes should always be created on *foreign keys*. A foreign key is a column or set of columns that is required to map to the primary key of another table. Full table scans and table-level locks can result if a foreign key is not indexed.[1]

Oracle Database 11*g* provides several "advisors" that can generate recommendations for improving the performance of SQL queries; I will discuss them in detail in Chapter 17, which covers SQL tuning. Listing 7-1 provides an example of how the QUICK_TUNE procedure can be used to analyze an SQL statement and determine if additional indexes would improve performance. In this case, the QUICK_TUNE procedure recommends that a "function-based index" be created and even provides the necessary SQL commands to do so; you can replace the system-generated name for the index with a more meaningful name. Note that you need the ADVISOR privilege in order to use the QUICK_TUNE procedure.

Listing 7-1. *Using the QUICK_TUNE Procedure to Analyze an SQL Query and Determine if Additional Indexes Should Be Created to Improve Performance*

```
C:\Documents and Settings\IGNATIUS>sqlplus hr

SQL*Plus: Release 11.1.0.6.0 - Production on Sun Dec 30 10:47:20 2007

Copyright (c) 1982, 2007, Oracle.  All rights reserved.

Enter password:

Connected to:
Oracle Database 11g Enterprise Edition Release 11.1.0.6.0 - Production
With the Partitioning, OLAP, Data Mining and Real Application Testing options

SQL> EXEC DBMS_ADVISOR.QUICK_TUNE(DBMS_ADVISOR.SQLACCESS_ADVISOR, 'QUICK_TUNE',
'SELECT * FROM employees WHERE UPPER(last_name)=''DE HAAN''');

PL/SQL procedure successfully completed.
```

---

1. In *Expert One-On-One Oracle*, Tom Kyte says: "I sometimes wish I had a dollar for every time I was able to solve the insolvable hanging issue by simply running the query to detect un-indexed foreign keys and suggesting that we index the one causing the problem—I would be very rich." Tom provides the script in the book—it can also be found at http://asktom.oracle.com/tkyte/unindex/index.html.

```
SQL> SET LONG 100000
SQL> SET PAGESIZE 0
SQL> SET HEADING OFF
SQL> SELECT DBMS_ADVISOR.GET_TASK_SCRIPT('QUICK_TUNE') FROM dual;
Rem  SQL Access Advisor: Version 11.1.0.6.0 - Production
Rem
Rem  Username:        HR
Rem  Task:            QUICK_TUNE
Rem  Execution date:
Rem

CREATE INDEX "HR"."EMPLOYEES_IDX$$_00440000"
    ON "HR"."EMPLOYEES"
    (UPPER("LAST_NAME"))
    COMPUTE STATISTICS;

SQL> EXIT
Disconnected from Oracle Database 11g Enterprise Edition Release 11.1.0.6.0 - Pr
oduction
With the Partitioning, OLAP, Data Mining and Real Application Testing options
```

Index-Organized Tables

Ordinary Oracle tables are often referred to as *heaps* because the data they contain is not sorted in any way; separate structures—indexes—are needed in order to identify the records of interest efficiently. The *index-organized table* (*IOT*) is a single structure that unites a table and an index for its primary key. No separate index for the primary key is necessary, because the table itself is structured exactly as if it were an index for the primary key; all the non-key data is stored on the leaf blocks together with the key data. Indexes for other columns can be created in precisely the same way as indexes on ordinary tables.

Index-organized tables have a number of advantages. The union of table and primary key index in a single structure results in increased efficiency of retrieval operations. Certain maintenance operations (such as the MOVE operation) can be performed on them without invalidating all the indexes. Finally, index-organized tables can offer dramatic performance improvements if the primary key is composed of multiple data items and the leading item partitions the data in a natural way, for example, the store name in a table that contains sales data. The performance improvement comes from the physical clustering of related data that naturally results, the increased likelihood of finding the required data in the buffer cache, and the consequent reduction in disk activity.

Advanced Topics

Two advanced indexing methods are worth knowing about but are beyond the scope of this book: *bitmap* indexing and *reverse key* indexing. Information on those methods can be found in *Oracle Database 11g Concepts Manual* or the other references listed at the end of this chapter.

- An advanced type of index known as the *bitmap index* uses a single bit (0 or 1) to represent each row; a "bitmap" is generated for each distinct value contained in the indexed column.

- If the indexed column contains ever increasing values, Oracle will attempt to insert the index information into the same leaf block each time. This dramatically increases the frequency of splitting and balancing operations. The solution is to create a *reverse key* index.

Partitions

Because Oracle tables are stored as heaps, with no discernible internal organization, new rows of data are simply appended to the end of the table or anywhere else in the table there happens to be room. The strategy of using indexes to find the required rows of data quickly works well up to a point. But it begins to reveal its limitations as the amounts of data and the numbers of users approach the levels that we see in modern data warehouses and in online stores such as Amazon.com.

To understand the problem with heaps, imagine a history book containing facts like the following: "The Declaration of Independence was adopted by the Second Continental Congress on July 4, 1776." Suppose that these facts are not naturally organized into separate chapters for, say, individual countries but are randomly scattered throughout the book. We can still use the alphabetical index at the back of the book to discover facts about the United States relatively easily but, each time we retrieve a fact, we might have to visit a different page; this would obviously not be an efficient process.

A page of a book is analogous to a data block on a storage disk, and a chapter of related information in a book is analogous to an Oracle *partition*. Partitions divide data tables into separate storage pools; rows of data can be allocated to each storage pool using some criterion. Suppose we have a very large table of credit-card transactions, and they are randomly stored throughout the table without regard to date. To process the transactions completed in the last month, Oracle will have to retrieve more blocks of data from the storage disks than if transactions were stored with regard to date. The solution is to create a separate partition for each month. If a query spans partitions, Oracle need only visit the appropriate partitions; this is called *partition pruning*.

Oracle provides several methods of partitioning large tables, including list partitioning, range partitioning, and interval partitioning; the partitions can themselves be subpartitioned. Indexes can also be partitioned, and it makes a lot of sense to do so.

■**Tip** Partitioning is a separately licensed extra-cost option and must be purchased together with Oracle Enterprise Edition; it cannot be used with Oracle Standard Edition or with Oracle Express Edition.

Advantages of Partitioning

I have already alluded to the fact that partitioning might improve performance of SQL queries by reducing the number of data blocks that have to be retrieved from the storage disks, but this is not the only advantage; here are some others.

- A Join operation on two tables that are partitioned in the same manner can be parallelized. That is, Oracle can perform simultaneous Join operations, each one joining a partition of one table to the related partition in the other table and the results pooled. This technique is suitable when dealing with large data warehouses; it requires more computing power but can reduce the time required to process an SQL query.

- Partitions make it particularly easy to purge unneeded data. Dropping a partition can be a painless operation; deleting large numbers of records from an unpartitioned table is a resource-intensive operation.

- Making a backup copy of a large data warehouse is a time-consuming and resource-intensive operation. If the data in an old partition does not need to be modified and the partition is located in a dedicated tablespace, the tablespace can be put into read-only mode and one last backup copy of the tablespace can be created for archival purposes. From that point onward, the tablespace need not be included in backup copies.

- If an old partition cannot be removed from the database, an alternative is to move it to slower and cheaper storage; the faster and more expensive storage can be reserved for more current and frequently queried data.

- Maintenance operations can be performed on individual partitions without affecting the availability of the rest of the data in the rest of the table; for example, old partitions can be moved to cheaper storage without impacting the availability of the data in the rest of the table.

List Partitioning

In this form of partition, the refinancing criterion for each partition is a list of values. Consider a retail chain that has stores in three states. We might store sales data in a table created in the manner illustrated in Listing 7-2.

Listing 7-2. *Example of List Partitioning*

```
CREATE TABLE sales
(
    item# INTEGER,
    quantity INTEGER,
    store_name VARCHAR(30),
    state_code VARCHAR(2),
    sale_date DATE
)
PARTITION BY LIST (state_code)
(
    PARTITION california VALUES ('CA'),
    PARTITION oregon VALUES ('OR'),
    PARTITION washington VALUES ('WA')
);
```

Range Partitioning

In this form of partition, the refinancing criterion for each partition is a range of values. In the case described in the previous paragraph, we might alternatively store sales data in a table created in the manner illustrated in Listing 7-3.

Listing 7-3. *Example of Range Partitioning*

```
CREATE TABLE sales
(
    item# INTEGER,
    quantity INTEGER,
    store_name VARCHAR(30),
    state_code VARCHAR(2),
    sale_date DATE
)
PARTITION BY RANGE (sale_date)
(
    PARTITION olddata VALUES LESS THAN (TO_DATE('01-JAN-2008','DD-MON-YYYY')),
```

```
        PARTITION jan2008 VALUES LESS THAN (TO_DATE('01-FEB-2008','DD-MON-YYYY')),
        PARTITION feb2008 VALUES LESS THAN (TO_DATE('01-MAR-2008','DD-MON-YYYY')),
        PARTITION mar2008 VALUES LESS THAN (TO_DATE('01-APR-2008','DD-MON-YYYY')),
        PARTITION apr2008 VALUES LESS THAN (TO_DATE('01-MAY-2008','DD-MON-YYYY')),
        PARTITION may2008 VALUES LESS THAN (TO_DATE('01-JUN-2008','DD-MON-YYYY')),
        PARTITION jun2008 VALUES LESS THAN (TO_DATE('01-JUL-2008','DD-MON-YYYY')),
        PARTITION jul2008 VALUES LESS THAN (TO_DATE('01-AUG-2008','DD-MON-YYYY')),
        PARTITION aug2008 VALUES LESS THAN (TO_DATE('01-SEP-2008','DD-MON-YYYY')),
        PARTITION sep2008 VALUES LESS THAN (TO_DATE('01-OCT-2008','DD-MON-YYYY')),
        PARTITION oct2008 VALUES LESS THAN (TO_DATE('01-NOV-2008','DD-MON-YYYY')),
        PARTITION nov2008 VALUES LESS THAN (TO_DATE('01-DEC-2008','DD-MON-YYYY')),
        PARTITION dec2008 VALUES LESS THAN (TO_DATE('01-JAN-2009','DD-MON-YYYY'))
);
```

Interval Partitioning

One difficulty with partitioning by monotonically increasing data items such as dates is that new partitions have to be periodically added to the table; this can be accomplished using the ADD PARTITION clause of the ALTER TABLE command. Interval partitioning eliminates this difficulty by having Oracle automatically create new partitions as necessary. The example of the previous section can be rewritten as illustrated in Listing 7-4. Only one partition called olddata is initially created. New partitions are automatically created by Oracle as necessary when data is inserted into the table.

Listing 7-4. *Example of Interval Partitioning*

```
CREATE TABLE sales
(
    item# INTEGER,
    quantity INTEGER,
    store_name VARCHAR(30),
    state_code VARCHAR(2),
    sale_date DATE
)
PARTITION BY RANGE (sale_date)
INTERVAL(NUMTOYMINTERVAL(1, 'MONTH'))
(
    PARTITION olddata VALUES LESS THAN (TO_DATE('01-JAN-2008','DD-MON-YYYY'))
);
```

Hash Partitioning

Hash partitioning was useful before large RAID[2] arrays became commonplace; it can be used to *stripe* data across multiple disks in order to prevent the reading and writing speed of a single disk from becoming a performance bottleneck in OLTP[3] and other environments requiring very high levels of throughput. A *hashing function* (randomizing function) is applied to the data item used as the partitioning criterion in order to allocate new rows to partitions randomly. Listing 7-5 illustrates the use of this technique; the data is spread over four tablespaces, which are presumably located on separate disk drives.

Listing 7-5. *Example of Hash Partitioning*

```
CREATE TABLE sales
(
    item# INTEGER,
    quantity INTEGER,
    store_name VARCHAR(30),
    state_code VARCHAR(2),
    sale_date DATE
)
PARTITION BY HASH (sale_date)
PARTITIONS 4
STORE IN (data1, data2, data3, data4);
```

Reference Partitioning

Sometimes it makes sense to partition two or more tables using the same data item as the partitioning criterion *even though the tables do not share the data item.* As an example, consider the Orders and LineItems tables in the simple order management database described in *Oracle Database 11g Java Developer's Guide.* The two tables are linked by the purchase order number. It makes sense to partition the Orders table using the OrderDate data item. It would also make sense to partition the LineItems table using the same data item as the criterion *even though it is not part of the table.* This can be accomplished using *referential partitioning* as in Listing 7-6. Any number of tables can thus be partitioned using a common partitioning criterion that *appears in only one of the tables.*

---

2. Redundant Array of Inexpensive Disks

3. Online Transaction Processing

Listing 7-6. *Example of Reference Partitioning*

```
CREATE TABLE Orders
(
    PONo NUMBER(5),
    Custno NUMBER(3),
    OrderDate DATE,
    ShipDate DATE,
    ToStreet VARCHAR2(20),
    ToCity VARCHAR2(20),
    ToState CHAR(2),
    ToZip VARCHAR2(10),
    CONSTRAINT Orders_PK PRIMARY KEY (PONo),
    CONSTRAINT Orders_FK1 FOREIGN KEY (CustNo) REFERENCES Customers
)
PARTITION BY RANGE (OrderDate)
(
    PARTITION olddata VALUES LESS THAN (TO_DATE('01-JAN-2008','DD-MON-YYYY')),
    PARTITION jan2008 VALUES LESS THAN (TO_DATE('01-FEB-2008','DD-MON-YYYY')),
    PARTITION feb2008 VALUES LESS THAN (TO_DATE('01-MAR-2008','DD-MON-YYYY')),
    PARTITION mar2008 VALUES LESS THAN (TO_DATE('01-APR-2008','DD-MON-YYYY')),
    PARTITION apr2008 VALUES LESS THAN (TO_DATE('01-MAY-2008','DD-MON-YYYY')),
    PARTITION may2008 VALUES LESS THAN (TO_DATE('01-JUN-2008','DD-MON-YYYY')),
    PARTITION jun2008 VALUES LESS THAN (TO_DATE('01-JUL-2008','DD-MON-YYYY')),
    PARTITION jul2008 VALUES LESS THAN (TO_DATE('01-AUG-2008','DD-MON-YYYY')),
    PARTITION aug2008 VALUES LESS THAN (TO_DATE('01-SEP-2008','DD-MON-YYYY')),
    PARTITION sep2008 VALUES LESS THAN (TO_DATE('01-OCT-2008','DD-MON-YYYY')),
    PARTITION oct2008 VALUES LESS THAN (TO_DATE('01-NOV-2008','DD-MON-YYYY')),
    PARTITION nov2008 VALUES LESS THAN (TO_DATE('01-DEC-2008','DD-MON-YYYY')),
    PARTITION dec2008 VALUES LESS THAN (TO_DATE('01-JAN-2009','DD-MON-YYYY'))
);

CREATE TABLE LineItems
(
    LineNo NUMBER(2),
    PONo NUMBER(5) NOT NULL,
    StockNo NUMBER(4),
    Quantity NUMBER(2),
    Discount NUMBER(4,2),
    CONSTRAINT LineItems_PK PRIMARY KEY (LineNo, PONo),
    CONSTRAINT LineItems_FK1 FOREIGN KEY (PONo) REFERENCES Orders,
    CONSTRAINT LineItems_FK2 FOREIGN KEY (StockNo) REFERENCES StockItems
```

```
)
PARTITION BY REFERENCE (LineItems_FK1);
```

Composite Partitioning

Oracle offers the ability to further divide a partition into subpartitions using different criteria; this can make sense if a table is very large. In Listing 7-7, we first create one partition for each month (using the interval partitioning method) and then create subpartitions for each state.

Listing 7-7. *Example of List Partitioning*

```
CREATE TABLE sales
(
    item# INTEGER,
    quantity INTEGER,
    store_name VARCHAR(30),
    state_code VARCHAR(2),
    sale_date DATE
)
PARTITION BY RANGE (sale_date)
INTERVAL(NUMTOYMINTERVAL(1, 'MONTH'))
SUBPARTITION BY list (state_code)
(
    PARTITION olddata VALUES LESS THAN (TO_DATE('01-JAN-2008','DD-MON-YYYY'))
    (
        SUBPARTITION california VALUES ('CA'),
        SUBPARTITION oregon VALUES ('OR'),
        SUBPARTITION washington VALUES ('WA')
    )
);
```

Local and Global Indexes

Partitioning a table does not eliminate the need for any of its indexes. However, we must make a design choice for each index; indexes on partitioned tables can be either *local* or *global*. A local index is itself partitioned in exactly the same way as its table; one need only specify the LOCAL clause when creating the index to automatically create the necessary partitions for the use of the index. Local indexes are most suitable when the query specifies the partitioning criterion; they also promote *partition independence*; that is, they preserve our ability to perform maintenance operations on a partition without impacting the availability of the rest of the data in the table. Global indexes are most suitable when the query does not specify the partitioning criterion. A global index may or may not be partitioned and can even have a different partition scheme than its table.

Denormalization and Materialized Views

Denormalization is a technique that is used to improve the efficiency of Join operations. Consider the Orders and LineItems tables from the order management database described in *Oracle Database 11g Java Developer's Guide*. To avoid having to join these tables, we could replace them with a table that contains all the data items from both tables. This eliminates the need to join the two tables frequently, but it introduces its own set of problems. Observe that data items such as ToStreet, ToCity, ToState, and ToZip must now be duplicated if there is more than one line in an order; if any of these data items needs to be changed, multiple data rows will have to be updated. The duplication of data thus creates the possibility that mistakes will be made.

Materialized views can be used to avoid the problems created by denormalization. Instead of replacing the Orders and LineItems tables with a denormalized table, we could prejoin the tables and store the results in a structure called a *materialized view*, as illustrated in Listing 7-8.

Listing 7-8. *Example of a Materialized View*

```
CREATE MATERIALIZED VIEW Orders_LineItems
REFRESH ON COMMIT
ENABLE QUERY REWRITE
AS SELECT
    -- data items from the Orders table
    Orders.PONo,
    Orders.Custno,
    Orders.OrderDate,
    Orders.ShipDate,
    Orders.ToStreet,
    Orders.ToCity,
    Orders.ToState,
    Orders.ToZip,
    -- data items from the LineItems table
    LineItems.LineNo,
    LineItems.StockNo,
    LineItems.Quantity,
    LineItems.Discount
FROM Orders, LineItems
WHERE LineItems.PONo = Orders.PONo;
```

The data items from the Orders tables will still be duplicated, but the responsibility for accurate modifications to the materialized view rests with Oracle, which will modify the data in the materialized view whenever the data in the underlying tables is modified. For example, if the ToStreet data item of an order is modified, Oracle will modify all occurrences in the materialized view. Note that materialized views need to be indexed just like regular tables and can be partitioned if appropriate.

Materialized views can be directly referenced in SQL queries, but the same level of performance enhancement is obtained even if they are not directly referenced. Notice the ENABLE QUERY REWRITE clause in the command we used to create the Orders_LineItems materialized view; the optimizer silently *rewrites* queries and incorporates materialized views if possible.

Materialized view technology has many uses, for example, it can be used to aggregate information or to synchronize satellite databases. More information can be found in *Oracle Database 11g Concepts Manual* and *Oracle Database 11g Database Warehousing Guide*.

■**Tip** The SQL Access Advisor can be used to analyze a large workload and identify what materialized views should be created to improve database performance.

Clusters

In his book *Effective Oracle by Design* (Osborne Oracle Press, 2003), Tom Kyte quotes Steve Adams as saying: "If a schema has no IOTs or clusters, that is a good indication that no thought has been given to the matter of optimizing data access." While most people wouldn't agree with Steve's conclusion, it is true that most databases only use the simplest of table and index organizations—heap and b-tree respectively—and don't exploit the wealth of data access mechanisms provided by Oracle.[4]

Clusters improve the efficiency of the memory cache (and consequently of Join operations) because data from related tables can be stored in the *same* data blocks. Oracle itself uses the cluster mechanism to access some of the most important tables in the data dictionary; the C_OBJ# cluster includes 17 different tables including TAB$ (tables), COL$ (columns of tables), IND$ (indexes), and ICOL$ (columns of indexes). Oracle also uses the cluster mechanism in its spectacular TPC benchmarks; in one benchmark that was submitted in February 2007, an Oracle database achieved a throughput of more than four million transactions per minute.

Hash clusters provide quick access without the need for an index (if the value of the clustering key is specified in the SQL query). In Listing 7-9, we first *preallocate* space for

---

4. "Database independence" is sometimes offered as the reason not to use proprietary Oracle features. Surprisingly though, Oracle E-Business Suite does not exploit the cluster mechanism at all, even though it uses more than 20,000 tables.

a cluster called Orders_LineItems with 10,000 *hash buckets*, each of size 2 KB. When inserting a new data row in the cluster, Oracle will use a *hash function* to convert the cluster key (PONo in this case) into the address of a random hash bucket where it will store the row. When the row is retrieved later, all Oracle has to do is use the same hash function to locate the row.[5]

We use the cluster to store rows from the Orders table as well as the LineItems table, which means that related rows from the LineItems table will be stored in the same storage bucket *along with the corresponding row from the* Orders *table.* SQL queries that join the two tables and specify what value the PONo data item should have can now be expected to be very efficient.

Listing 7-9. *Example of a Cluster*

```
CREATE CLUSTER Orders_LineItems (PONo NUMBER(5))
HASHKEYS 10000 SIZE 2048;

CREATE TABLE Orders
(
    PONo NUMBER(5),
    Custno NUMBER(3),
    OrderDate DATE,
    ShipDate DATE,
    ToStreet VARCHAR2(20),
    ToCity VARCHAR2(20),
    ToState CHAR(2),
    ToZip VARCHAR2(10),
    CONSTRAINT Orders_PK PRIMARY KEY (PONo),
    CONSTRAINT Orders_FK1 FOREIGN KEY (CustNo) REFERENCES Customers
)
CLUSTER Orders_LineItems (PONo);

CREATE TABLE LineItems
(
    LineNo NUMBER(2),
    PONo NUMBER(5) NOT NULL,
    StockNo NUMBER(4),
    Quantity NUMBER(2),
    Discount NUMBER(4,2),
    CONSTRAINT LineItems_PK PRIMARY KEY (LineNo, PONo),
```

---

5. Hash clusters can suffer from the problems of "hash collisions" and "overflow chains" which might eventually cause their performance to degrade and require them to be rebuilt—you can also tweak the settings of the hashing function.

```
    CONSTRAINT LineItems_FK1 FOREIGN KEY (PONo) REFERENCES Orders,
    CONSTRAINT LineItems_FK2 FOREIGN KEY (StockNo) REFERENCES StockItems
)
CLUSTER Orders_LineItems (PONo);
```

Summary

Performance considerations can remain at the forefront throughout the life of the database; for example, new queries may be introduced at any time. Database administrators must therefore understand the mechanisms that can be used to improve performance. In this chapter, we provide an overview of these mechanisms. Here is a short summary of the concepts we touched upon in this chapter:

- The first stage in database design is called *logical database design* or *data modeling* and is conducted without reference to any specific database technology such as Oracle or Microsoft SQL Server.

- *Physical database design* follows logical database design. First, the logical model is mapped to the proprietary data types, language elements, and mechanisms provided by the chosen database technology. Next, security requirements are implemented using the various mechanisms provided by the technology, such as views. Finally, we consider performance—the ability of the database engine to handle work requests efficiently.

- The three broad categories of performance mechanisms are indexes to quickly find the data, partitions and clusters to organize the data, and *materialized views* and *denormalized tables* to perform expensive operations like joins ahead of time.

- An Oracle index is analogous to the index of words at the back of this book and allows Oracle to quickly locate a row of data that satisfies the restrictions of a query. However, indexes don't help much if a large percentage of rows in the table satisfy the restrictions of the query.

- A proliferation of indexes can negatively affect efficiency because Oracle must update all the relevant indexes whenever the data in a table is modified.

- Oracle indexes are structured for ease of use. The typical Oracle index is a *balanced tree* or *b-tree*.

- SQL Access Advisor can analyze an SQL query and determine if an additional index would improve performance.

- An *index-organized table* (IOT) is a single structure that unites a table and an index for its primary key.

- Partitions divide data tables into separate storage pools; rows of data can be allocated to each storage pool using some criterion. The partitioning methods provided by Oracle include list partitioning, range partitioning, interval partitioning, reference partitioning, hash partitioning, and composite partitioning.

- Indexes on partitioned tables can be local or global. A local index is itself partitioned in the same way as its table. Local indexes are most suitable when the query specifies the partitioning criterion; they also promote *partition independence*. Global indexes are most suitable when the query does not specify the partitioning criterion. A global index may or may not be partitioned and can even have a different partition scheme than its table.

- *Denormalized tables* and *materialized views* can be used to improve the efficiency of Join operations. Oracle automatically modifies the data in a materialized view whenever the data in the underlying tables is modified. The optimizer silently rewrites queries and incorporates materialized views if possible. Materialized views can also be used to aggregate information or to synchronize satellite databases.

- *Hash clusters* provide quick access without the need for an index (if the value of the clustering key is specified in the SQL query). They improve the efficiency of the memory cache (and consequently of Join operations) because data from related tables can be stored in the same data blocks.

Exercises

- Review the chapter titled "Java Stored Procedures Application Example" in the *Oracle Database 11g Java Developer's Guide*. Construct SQL language commands to create a suitable set of indexes on the `Customers`, `StockItems`, `Orders`, and `LineItems` tables.

- I suggested that you use the `MONITORING USAGE` clause of the `CREATE INDEX` or `ALTER INDEX` commands to track whether your indexes are being used by the query optimizer. Where is the information stored? Is it advisable to monitor usage continuously? How would you stop monitoring index usage?

- What alternatives could you suggest to the function-based index recommended by SQL Access Advisor in the `QUICK_TUNE` example in this chapter?

- I suggested that there were some situations where the use of indexes was not optional. Do indexes provide any advantage if the tables are very small?

- An index contains the address of the data in a table. Why are indexes on Index Organized Tables not invalidated if a DML operation causes rows to move?

- Can the data item used as the partitioning criterion ever be NULL?

- Create a partitioned table using one of the examples provided in this chapter. Create a local index on the table. Retrieve partitioning information about the table and index from the `USER_TAB_PARTITIONS` and `USER_IND_PARTITIONS` views.

- Construct SQL commands to create twelve partitions for the `Orders_LineItems` materialized view, one for each month of 2008.

Further Reading

Oracle Corporation. *Oracle Database 11g Concepts.* Oracle Corporation, 2007. The chapter titled "Schema Objects" provides an overview of indexes, partitioning, materialized views, and clusters. Searchable or downloadable free of charge at `http://www.oracle.com/technology/documentation/index.html`. Printed copies can also be purchased from Oracle's online store.

Oracle Corporation. *Oracle Database 11g VLDB and Partitioning Guide.* Oracle Corporation, 2007. Provides a very detailed discussion of partitioning. Searchable or downloadable free of charge at `http://www.oracle.com/technology/documentation/index.html`. Printed copies can also be purchased from Oracle's online store.

Oracle Corporation. *Oracle Database 11g SQL Language Reference Manual.* Oracle Corporation, 2007. Provides detailed information on all the commands necessary to create and modify indexes, index-organized tables, partitions, materialized views, and clusters. Searchable or downloadable free of charge at `http://www.oracle.com/technology/documentation/index.html`. Printed copies can also be purchased from Oracle's online store.

Kyte, Thomas. *Expert One-On-One Oracle.* Wrox Press, 2001. A long read at more than 1,200 pages, but it's worth every penny. The chapters titled "Database Tables" and "Database Indexes" cover the subject of table and index structures in considerable detail. The book was written when Oracle Database 8i was current—it is now out of print.

Kyte, Thomas. *Expert Oracle Database Architecture: 9i and 10g Programming Techniques and Solutions.* Apress, 2005. The successor book to *Expert One-On-One Oracle,* this has more detail and updated treatment in some areas, and some other material was omitted to keep the size manageable. The chapters titled "Database Tables" and "Database Indexes" are the ones relevant to our discussion. The complete text of *Expert One-On-One Oracle* is provided in an attached CD, so you get two books for the price of one.

Kyte, Thomas. *Effective Oracle by Design: Design and Build High-Performance Oracle Applications.* Osborne Oracle Press, 2003. More often than not, performance is an afterthought and Oracle's best performance features are not used. Tom's mantra is that the best performance results when performance issues are kept at the forefront during application and database, when Oracle performance features are exploited to the hilt, and when applications are properly instrumented. The chapter titled "Effective Schema Design" is relevant to our discussion.

■ ■ ■

CHAPTER 8

User Management and Data Loading

The woods are lovely, dark and deep.
But I have promises to keep,
And miles to go before I sleep,
And miles to go before I sleep.

Stopping by Woods on a Snowy Evening by Robert Frost

Your job does not end when you create a database; you still have to get the data into it and ensure that those who have a need to use it can do so. This chapter discusses how to control users and how to get large amounts of data in and out of databases. User management and data loading are two common chores performed by database administrators.

Schemas

Every object in a database is explicitly owned by a single owner and the owner of an object must explicitly authorize its use by somebody else. The collection of objects owned by a user is called a *schema*. To illustrate, Listing 8-1 shows a summary of the contents of the HR schema, one of the sample schemas that Oracle provides for educational purposes. Note that the terms *user, schema, schema owner,* and *account* are used interchangeably; for example, we may speak of either the HR user or the HR schema.

Listing 8-1. *Objects Commonly Found in Schemas*

```
SQL> CONNECT system
Enter password:
Connected.
SQL> SELECT    object_type,
  2            COUNT (*)
  3       FROM dba_objects
  4      WHERE owner = 'HR'
```

```
 5  GROUP BY object_type
 6  ORDER BY 2 DESC;

OBJECT_TYPE              COUNT(*)
------------------- ----------
INDEX                         19
TABLE                          7
SEQUENCE                       3
PROCEDURE                      2
TRIGGER                        2
VIEW                           1

6 rows selected.
```

The object types shown in Listing 8-1 are very common. *Tables* are the containers for our data; *indexes* help us find the data; *sequences* are continuously incrementing counters that generate unique identification numbers for data records; *procedures* are blocks of application logic that are stored within the database; *triggers* are specialized blocks of application logic that are triggered by specific events, such as a data record being added to a table; and *views* are "virtual tables" that can combine data from multiple tables.

Notice that we found the information we needed in DBA_OBJECTS. Coincidentally enough, Oracle manages the contents of a database using its own tables, indexes, sequences, procedures, triggers, and views; these are stored in the SYS schema. For example, DBA_OBJECTS is a *dictionary view* in the SYS schema. Listing 8-2 shows the contents of the SYS schema; notice the wide variety of object types.

Listing 8-2. *Objects Found in the SYS Schema*

```
SQL> CONNECT system
Enter password:
Connected.
SQL> SELECT   object_type,
  2           COUNT (*)
  3       FROM dba_objects
  4      WHERE owner = 'SYS'
  5  GROUP BY object_type
  6  ORDER BY 2 DESC;
```

```
OBJECT_TYPE           COUNT(*)
-------------------- ----------
JAVA CLASS              14736
VIEW                    2913
TYPE                    1110
TABLE                    712
INDEX                    710
JAVA RESOURCE            699
PACKAGE                  520
PACKAGE BODY             498
JAVA DATA                306
LIBRARY                  111
LOB                      100
TYPE BODY                 81
SEQUENCE                  80
FUNCTION                  67
PROCEDURE                 50
INDEX PARTITION           48
TABLE PARTITION           45
QUEUE                     15
OPERATOR                  15
TRIGGER                   13
RULE SET                  11
EVALUATION CONTEXT        10
CLUSTER                   10
SYNONYM                    9
DIRECTORY                  8
UNDEFINED                  6
CONTEXT                    5
CONSUMER GROUP             5
RULE                       4
JOB                        4
RESOURCE PLAN              3
PROGRAM                    3
WINDOW                     2
JOB CLASS                  2
SCHEDULE                   1
LOB PARTITION              1
WINDOW GROUP               1

37 rows selected.
```

■**Tip** Definitions of Oracle terms and links to the relevant sections of the reference manuals can be found in the Master Glossary available at `http://www.oracle.com/pls/db111/homepage`. Try using the master glossary to find the meanings of the terms you see in Listing 8-2.

Some of the objects in a schema, such as tables and indexes, represent blocks of storage; the others are actually definitions that are stored in tables. For example, DBA_OBJECTS is simply a definition stored in the VIEW$ table in the SYS schema. An object that represents blocks of storage is called a *segment*. Listing 8-3 shows that only a few of the object types displayed in Listing 8-2 actually represent blocks of storage; the others are only definitions stored in tables.

Listing 8-3. *Segment Types Found in the SYS Schema*

```
SQL> CONNECT system
Enter password:
Connected.
SQL> SELECT   segment_type,
  2           COUNT (*)
  3       FROM dba_segments
  4      WHERE owner = 'SYS'
  5   GROUP BY segment_type
  6   ORDER BY 2 DESC;

SEGMENT_TYPE        COUNT(*)
------------------ ----------
INDEX                    683
TABLE                    577
LOBINDEX                  98
LOBSEGMENT                98
INDEX PARTITION           48
TABLE PARTITION           45
TYPE2 UNDO                10
CLUSTER                   10
NESTED TABLE               4
ROLLBACK                   1
LOB PARTITION              1

11 rows selected.
```

More information about each type of object can be found in the appropriate dictionary view. As illustrated in Listing 8-4, a tremendous amount of information about tables can be found in DBA_TABLES. Coincidentally enough, a complete list of dictionary views can be found in a view called DICTIONARY; the actual SQL definitions of the views can be found in another view called DBA_VIEWS. You'll explore additional data dictionary views in the exercises at the end of this chapter, and I'll discuss the topic further in Chapter 9.

Listing 8-4. *Information about Tables in the* DBA_TABLES *View*

```
SQL> CONNECT system
Enter password:
Connected.
SQL> DESCRIBE DBA_TABLES;
 Name                                     Null?    Type
 ---------------------------------------- -------- ----------------------------
 OWNER                                    NOT NULL VARCHAR2(30)
 TABLE_NAME                               NOT NULL VARCHAR2(30)
 TABLESPACE_NAME                                   VARCHAR2(30)
 CLUSTER_NAME                                      VARCHAR2(30)
 IOT_NAME                                          VARCHAR2(30)
 STATUS                                            VARCHAR2(8)
 PCT_FREE                                          NUMBER
 PCT_USED                                          NUMBER
 INI_TRANS                                         NUMBER
 MAX_TRANS                                         NUMBER
 INITIAL_EXTENT                                    NUMBER
 NEXT_EXTENT                                       NUMBER
 MIN_EXTENTS                                       NUMBER
 MAX_EXTENTS                                       NUMBER
 PCT_INCREASE                                      NUMBER
 FREELISTS                                         NUMBER
 FREELIST_GROUPS                                   NUMBER
 LOGGING                                           VARCHAR2(3)
 BACKED_UP                                         VARCHAR2(1)
 NUM_ROWS                                          NUMBER
 BLOCKS                                            NUMBER
 EMPTY_BLOCKS                                      NUMBER
 AVG_SPACE                                         NUMBER
 CHAIN_CNT                                         NUMBER
 AVG_ROW_LEN                                       NUMBER
 AVG_SPACE_FREELIST_BLOCKS                         NUMBER
 NUM_FREELIST_BLOCKS                               NUMBER
```

DEGREE	VARCHAR2(10)
INSTANCES	VARCHAR2(10)
CACHE	VARCHAR2(5)
TABLE_LOCK	VARCHAR2(8)
SAMPLE_SIZE	NUMBER
LAST_ANALYZED	DATE
PARTITIONED	VARCHAR2(3)
IOT_TYPE	VARCHAR2(12)
TEMPORARY	VARCHAR2(1)
SECONDARY	VARCHAR2(1)
NESTED	VARCHAR2(3)
BUFFER_POOL	VARCHAR2(7)
ROW_MOVEMENT	VARCHAR2(8)
GLOBAL_STATS	VARCHAR2(3)
USER_STATS	VARCHAR2(3)
DURATION	VARCHAR2(15)
SKIP_CORRUPT	VARCHAR2(8)
MONITORING	VARCHAR2(3)
CLUSTER_OWNER	VARCHAR2(30)
DEPENDENCIES	VARCHAR2(8)
COMPRESSION	VARCHAR2(8)
COMPRESS_FOR	VARCHAR2(18)
DROPPED	VARCHAR2(3)
READ_ONLY	VARCHAR2(3)

Ordinary users don't have access to the dictionary views whose names begin with DBA_, because that would give them the ability to obtain information about other users. Instead, they have access to special sets of views whose names begin with USER_ and ALL_. The views whose names begin with USER_ show only those objects the current user actually owns. As illustrated in Listing 8-5, Oracle displays an error message when user hr tries to query the DBA_OBJECTS view. When user hr queries the USER_OBJECTS view instead, Oracle displays the same information that we saw in Listing 8-1. And, interestingly enough, when user hr queries the ALL_OBJECTS table, we see that it has access to tables in several other schemas.

Listing 8-5. *Querying the DBA_, USER_, and ALL_ Dictionary Views*

```
SQL> CONNECT hr
Enter password:
Connected.
SQL> SELECT   object_type,
  2           COUNT (*)
```

```
  3      FROM dba_objects
  4   GROUP BY object_type
  5   ORDER BY 2 DESC;
     FROM dba_objects
          *
ERROR at line 3:
ORA-00942: table or view does not exist

SQL> SELECT    object_type,
  2            COUNT (*)
  3       FROM user_objects
  4   GROUP BY object_type
  5   ORDER BY 2 DESC;


OBJECT_TYPE           COUNT(*)
------------------- ----------
INDEX                       19
TABLE                        7
SEQUENCE                     3
PROCEDURE                    2
TRIGGER                      2
VIEW                         1

6 rows selected.

SQL> SELECT    owner,
  2            object_type,
  3            COUNT (*)
  4       FROM all_objects
  5     WHERE object_type = 'TABLE'
  6   GROUP BY owner,
  7            object_type
  8   ORDER BY 3 DESC;


OWNER                           OBJECT_TYPE           COUNT(*)
------------------------------- ------------------- ----------
MDSYS                           TABLE                       47
SYS                             TABLE                       27
XDB                             TABLE                       18
WKSYS                           TABLE                       10
HR                              TABLE                        7
SYSTEM                          TABLE                        8
```

CTXSYS	TABLE	5
FLOWS_030000	TABLE	3
OLAPSYS	TABLE	2
EXFSYS	TABLE	1

```
10 rows selected.
```

■**Tip** Oracle provides five sample schemas for instructional purposes, including, for example, the Human Resources (hr) schema used in this chapter. They are described in *Oracle Database 11g Sample Schemas* and *Oracle Database 11g Examples Installation Guide*—both freely searchable and downloadable at http:// tahiti.oracle.com and at http://www.oracle.com/technology/documentation/index.html.

The scripts that create and populate the schemas should be installed when the Oracle software is installed, as discussed in Chapter 5. You can use the scripts as a template when creating scripts to populate your own database, for example, hr_cre.sql creates the tables in the hr schema, and hr_idx.sql creates indexes on the tables. The scripts are located in the ORACLE_HOME/demo/schema directory; the master script is mksample.sql. You can choose to have these schemas created and populated by Database Configuration Assistant (DBCA) when you create the database—as discussed in Chapter 6—or you can do it yourself using the instructions in *Oracle Database 11g Sample Schemas*.

User Management

As you might expect, nobody can store data in the database or retrieve data from it unless they are properly authorized to do so. The following sections explore the five commands required for user management: CREATE USER, ALTER USER, DROP USER, GRANT, and REVOKE. Only users with the appropriate privileges can execute these commands. For example, only a user with the Create User privilege can execute the CREATE USER command. You can perform user management tasks using the SYSTEM account.

Creating Users

The CREATE USER command is used to specify the alias by which the database knows a user; a typical convention is to use the first character of the user's first name and the first seven characters of the person's last name; for example, ifernand in the case of a user named Iggy Fernandez. Listing 8-6 shows a minimalist example of the CREATE USER command; the IDENTIFIED BY clause is used to specify the password that the user must specify to gain access to the database.

Listing 8-6. *Minimalist Form of the CREATE USER Command*

```
SQL> CONNECT system
Enter password:
Connected.
SQL> CREATE USER ifernand
  2  IDENTIFIED BY qazwsxedc;

User created.
```

The CREATE USER statement should typically specify a value for DEFAULT TABLESPACE—the tablespace where the user's tables and indexes are automatically placed if another tablespace is not explicitly specified—and TEMPORARY TABLESPACE—the tablespace used for sorting operations and other operations that require temporary space. However, if you do not specify values, DEFAULT TABLESPACE and TEMPORARY TABLESPACE are automatically set to the values listed in the DATABASE_PROPERTIES view. In this example, we also neglected to assign a value to the user's *profile*; this is automatically set to the value DEFAULT. Listing 8-7 shows some information from the DBA_USERS view; note especially the attributes of user ifernand.

Listing 8-7 is interesting also because it shows us just how many schemas are automatically created when the database is created. The creation date provides a clue as to the origin of these schemas; the creation date of August 30, 2005 tells me that those schemas were part of the database template that I used to create my database. The creation date of February 21, 2008 is the date when I installed the sample schemas in the database, soon after creating the database.

Listing 8-7. *Schema Attributes Stored in DBA_USERS*

```
SQL> CONNECT system
Enter password:
Connected.
SQL> COLUMN username format a20 heading "USER|NAME"
SQL> COLUMN created format a10 heading "CREATED"
SQL> COLUMN default_tablespace format a10 heading "DEFAULT|TABLESPACE"
SQL> COLUMN temporary_tablespace format a10 heading "TEMPORARY|TABLESPACE"
SQL> COLUMN profile format a20 heading "PROFILE"
SQL>
SQL> SELECT    username,
  2            created,
  3            default_tablespace,
  4            temporary_tablespace,
  5            PROFILE
```

```
 6      FROM dba_users
 7  ORDER BY created;
```

```
USER                            DEFAULT     TEMPORARY
NAME                 CREATED    TABLESPACE  TABLESPACE  PROFILE
-------------------- ---------- ----------  ----------  --------------------
SYS                  30-AUG-05  SYSTEM      TEMP        DEFAULT
SYSTEM               30-AUG-05  SYSTEM      TEMP        DEFAULT
OUTLN                30-AUG-05  SYSTEM      TEMP        DEFAULT
DIP                  30-AUG-05  USERS       TEMP        DEFAULT
TSMSYS               30-AUG-05  USERS       TEMP        DEFAULT
DBSNMP               30-AUG-05  SYSAUX      TEMP        MONITORING_PROFILE
WMSYS                30-AUG-05  SYSAUX      TEMP        DEFAULT
EXFSYS               30-AUG-05  SYSAUX      TEMP        DEFAULT
DMSYS                30-AUG-05  SYSAUX      TEMP        DEFAULT
CTXSYS               30-AUG-05  SYSAUX      TEMP        DEFAULT
XDB                  30-AUG-05  SYSAUX      TEMP        DEFAULT
ANONYMOUS            30-AUG-05  SYSAUX      TEMP        DEFAULT
ORDSYS               30-AUG-05  SYSAUX      TEMP        DEFAULT
SI_INFORMTN_SCHEMA   30-AUG-05  SYSAUX      TEMP        DEFAULT
ORDPLUGINS           30-AUG-05  SYSAUX      TEMP        DEFAULT
MDSYS                30-AUG-05  SYSAUX      TEMP        DEFAULT
OLAPSYS              30-AUG-05  SYSAUX      TEMP        DEFAULT
MDDATA               30-AUG-05  USERS       TEMP        DEFAULT
SYSMAN               30-AUG-05  SYSAUX      TEMP        DEFAULT
MGMT_VIEW            30-AUG-05  SYSTEM      TEMP        DEFAULT
SCOTT                30-AUG-05  USERS       TEMP        DEFAULT
HR                   21-FEB-08  USERS       TEMP        DEFAULT
OE                   21-FEB-08  USERS       TEMP        DEFAULT
SH                   21-FEB-08  USERS       TEMP        DEFAULT
IX                   21-FEB-08  USERS       TEMP        DEFAULT
PM                   21-FEB-08  USERS       TEMP        DEFAULT
BI                   21-FEB-08  USERS       TEMP        DEFAULT
IFERNAND             27-APR-08  USERS       TEMP        DEFAULT

28 rows selected.
```

The user's *profile* specifies a number of behaviors and quotas that apply to the user. For example, IDLE_TIME specifies the length of time after which an idle session is automatically disconnected in order to conserve system resources, and CPU_PER_SESSION specifies the maximum number of CPU cycles that any single session may utilize; a detailed description of these behaviors and quotas can be found in the CREATE PROFILE section of the *Oracle Database 11g SQL Language Reference*. You can customize the default profile using the ALTER PROFILE command, and you can create custom profiles using the CREATE PROFILE command. Listing 8-8 shows the definition of the DEFAULT profile.

Listing 8-8. *Definition of the DEFAULT Profile*

```
SQL> CONNECT system
Enter password:
Connected.
SQL> COLUMN resource_type format a15 heading "RESOURCE TYPE"
SQL> COLUMN resource_name format a30 heading "RESOURCE NAME"
SQL> COLUMN limit format a15 heading "LIMIT"
SQL> SELECT    resource_type,
  2            resource_name,
  3            LIMIT
  4        FROM dba_profiles
  5      WHERE PROFILE = 'DEFAULT'
  6  ORDER BY resource_type, resource_name;

RESOURCE TYPE    RESOURCE NAME                    LIMIT
---------------  -------------------------------  ---------------
KERNEL           COMPOSITE_LIMIT                  UNLIMITED
KERNEL           CONNECT_TIME                     UNLIMITED
KERNEL           CPU_PER_CALL                     UNLIMITED
KERNEL           CPU_PER_SESSION                  UNLIMITED
KERNEL           IDLE_TIME                        UNLIMITED
KERNEL           LOGICAL_READS_PER_CALL           UNLIMITED
KERNEL           LOGICAL_READS_PER_SESSION        UNLIMITED
KERNEL           PRIVATE_SGA                      UNLIMITED
KERNEL           SESSIONS_PER_USER                UNLIMITED
PASSWORD         FAILED_LOGIN_ATTEMPTS            10
PASSWORD         PASSWORD_GRACE_TIME              UNLIMITED
PASSWORD         PASSWORD_LIFE_TIME               UNLIMITED
PASSWORD         PASSWORD_LOCK_TIME               UNLIMITED
PASSWORD         PASSWORD_REUSE_MAX               UNLIMITED
PASSWORD         PASSWORD_REUSE_TIME              UNLIMITED
PASSWORD         PASSWORD_VERIFY_FUNCTION         NULL

16 rows selected.
```

Giving Permissions to Users

Oracle gives us tight control over what users are permitted to do; the GRANT command is the main tool for the purpose. User ifernand may be known to Oracle but he won't be able to start an interactive session; here's what happens when he tries to do so:

```
SQL> CONNECT ifernand
Enter password:
ERROR:
ORA-01045: user IFERNAND lacks CREATE SESSION privilege; logon denied
```

To give the database administrator more flexibility in managing users, the ability to start a session is not automatically available to database users, even if they own objects in the database. The ability to start a session can be granted when necessary, and revoking a user's ability to start a session does not remove any objects owned by the user. Let's give user ifernand the ability to start a session:

```
SQL> CONNECT system
Enter password:
Connected.
SQL> GRANT CREATE SESSION TO ifernand;

Grant succeeded.
```

User ifernand is now able to connect, but Oracle does not let him create any tables:

```
SQL> CONNECT ifernand
Enter password:
Connected.
SQL> CREATE TABLE TEST AS
  2  SELECT * FROM DUAL;
SELECT * FROM DUAL
          *
ERROR at line 2:
ORA-01031: insufficient privileges
```

We must explicitly give user ifernand permission to create tables; this is done with the GRANT command. Here's an example:

```
SQL> CONNECT system
Enter password:
Connected.
SQL> GRANT CREATE TABLE TO ifernand;

Grant succeeded.
```

User ifernand encounters another problem when he tries to create a table; he does not have a quota of space in any tablespace:

```
SQL> CONNECT ifernand
Enter password:
Connected.
SQL> CREATE TABLE TEST AS
  2  SELECT * FROM DUAL;
SELECT * FROM DUAL
              *
ERROR at line 2:
ORA-01950: no privileges on tablespace 'USERS'
```

We must explicitly give user ifernand a quota of space in at least one tablespace; this is done with the ALTER USER command:

```
SQL> CONNECT system
Enter password:
Connected.
SQL> ALTER USER ifernand QUOTA 128 m ON users;

User altered.
```

User ifernand will now be able to create a table in his default tablespace, USERS, but not in any other tablespace. Here's what happens when he tries to create a table in another tablespace:

```
SQL> CONNECT ifernand
Enter password:
Connected.
SQL> CREATE TABLE TEST (dummy VARCHAR2(1))
  2  STORAGE (INITIAL 128 m)
  3  TABLESPACE example;
CREATE TABLE TEST (dummy VARCHAR2(1))
*
ERROR at line 1:
ORA-01950: no privileges on tablespace 'EXAMPLE'
```

As shown next, user ifernand will only succeed in creating tables in the USERS tablespace. If he does not explicitly specify a tablespace when creating a table (or index), it is automatically created in the USERS tablespace, because that is his default tablespace.

```
SQL> CONNECT ifernand
Enter password:
Connected.
SQL> CREATE TABLE TEST (dummy VARCHAR2(1))
  2  STORAGE (INITIAL 128 m);

Table created.

SQL> SELECT tablespace_name
  2    FROM user_segments
  3   WHERE segment_name = 'TEST';

TABLESPACE_NAME
------------------------------
USERS
```

Once user ifernand exhausts his quota of space, his tables will not be able to grow any more and he will be not be able to create new tables (or indexes):

```
SQL> CONNECT ifernand
Enter password:
Connected.
SQL> ALTER TABLE TEST ALLOCATE EXTENT (SIZE 64 k);
ALTER TABLE TEST ALLOCATE EXTENT (SIZE 64 k)
*
ERROR at line 1:
ORA-01536: space quota exceeded for tablespace 'USERS'

SQL> CREATE INDEX test_i1 ON TEST(dummy);
CREATE INDEX test_i1 ON TEST(dummy)
                        *
ERROR at line 1:
ORA-01536: space quota exceeded for tablespace 'USERS'

SQL> SELECT tablespace_name,
  2         BYTES / 1048576 AS mb
  3    FROM user_ts_quotas;

TABLESPACE_NAME                        MB
------------------------------ ----------
USERS                                 128
```

Note that other users will not be able to retrieve or modify the contents of tables owned by user `ifernand` unless he explicitly gives them the necessary privileges. Listing 8-9 shows some examples of granting *table privileges* to users—the word `PUBLIC` denotes all users of the database.

Listing 8-9. *Granting Table Privileges to Users*

```
SQL> CONNECT ifernand
Enter password:
Connected.
SQL> GRANT SELECT ON TEST TO PUBLIC;

Grant succeeded.

SQL> GRANT INSERT ON TEST TO hr;

Grant succeeded.

SQL> GRANT UPDATE ON TEST TO clerical_role;

Grant succeeded.
```

TABLE, SYSTEM, AND ROLE PRIVILEGES

A recurring theme in this chapter's discussion has been that Oracle gives us the ability to control tightly what users are permitted to do. *Object privileges* are privileges to perform operations on objects; examples include `SELECT`, `INSERT`, `UPDATE`, and `DELETE` privileges on tables. *System privileges* are privileges that do not apply to specific objects; examples are `CREATE SESSION` and `CREATE TABLE`. *Roles* are collections of privileges that are created for convenience; all the privileges in a collection can be assigned to a user with a single command. For example, if you want to give a user the ability to perform database administration functions, you could give the `DBA` role to him or her—it includes such privileges as `CREATE USER` and `DROP USER`.

The permissions granted to each user of the database are tracked in the `dba_sys_privs`, `dba_role_privs`, and `dba_tab_privs` views; here are their definitions:

```
SQL> CONNECT system
Enter password:
Connected.
```

```
SQL> DESCRIBE dba_sys_privs
 Name                                       Null?     Type
 ---------------------------------------    --------  ---------------------------
 GRANTEE                                    NOT NULL  VARCHAR2(30)
 PRIVILEGE                                  NOT NULL  VARCHAR2(40)
 ADMIN_OPTION                                         VARCHAR2(3)


SQL> DESCRIBE dba_role_privs
 Name                                       Null?     Type
 ---------------------------------------    --------  ---------------------------
 GRANTEE                                              VARCHAR2(30)
 GRANTED_ROLE                               NOT NULL  VARCHAR2(30)
 ADMIN_OPTION                                         VARCHAR2(3)
 DEFAULT_ROLE                                         VARCHAR2(3)


SQL> DESCRIBE dba_tab_privs
 Name                                       Null?     Type
 ---------------------------------------    --------  ---------------------------
 GRANTEE                                    NOT NULL  VARCHAR2(30)
 OWNER                                      NOT NULL  VARCHAR2(30)
 TABLE_NAME                                 NOT NULL  VARCHAR2(30)
 GRANTOR                                    NOT NULL  VARCHAR2(30)
 PRIVILEGE                                  NOT NULL  VARCHAR2(40)
 GRANTABLE                                            VARCHAR2(3)
 HIERARCHY                                            VARCHAR2(3)
```

You will explore these views in the exercises at the end of this chapter, where you will be asked to audit the privileges of users.

Revoking Permissions Granted to Users

The REVOKE command can be used to revoke a privilege granted by a GRANT command. In Listing 8-10, user ifernand is revoking the privileges on the table test that he previously granted to various users. In the exercises at the end of this chapter, you will be asked to review the permissions granted to PUBLIC and revoke those that pose a security risk.

Listing 8-10. *Revoking Table Privileges from Users*

```
SQL> CONNECT ifernand
Enter password:
Connected.
```

```
SQL> REVOKE SELECT ON test FROM PUBLIC;

Revoke succeeded.

SQL> REVOKE INSERT ON test FROM hr;

Revoke succeeded.

SQL> REVOKE INSERT ON test FROM clerical_role;

Revoke succeeded.
```

Modifying User Attributes

The ALTER USER command can be used to change any of the attributes that can be specified by the CREATE USER command. One very common use of the command is to change a user's password; this particular use is not restricted to database administrators—users can use the ALTER USER command to change their own passwords, as shown in Listing 8-11. As we saw in the previous section, ALTER USER can also be used to give users a quota of space in a tablespace.

Listing 8-11. *Changing One's Own Password*

```
SQL> CONNECT ifernand
Enter password:
Connected.
SQL> ALTER USER ifernand IDENTIFIED BY t0ps3cr3t;

User altered.
```

Removing Users

The final command in the suite of user management commands is DROP USER; it removes all trace of the user from the database. As shown in Listing 8-12, if the user has created any objects with the database, then either those objects must first be removed manually or the CASCADE option must be specified when using the DROP USER command. CASCADE automatically removes all objects owned by the user being removed from the database.

Listing 8-12. *Dropping a User*

```
SQL> CONNECT system
Enter password:
Connected.
SQL> DROP USER ifernand;
DROP USER ifernand
*
ERROR at line 1:
ORA-01922: CASCADE must be specified to drop 'IFERNAND'

SQL> SELECT object_type,
  2          object_name
  3    FROM dba_objects
  4   WHERE owner = 'IFERNAND';

OBJECT_TYPE         OBJECT_NAME
------------------- ------------------------------
TABLE               TEST

SQL> DROP USER ifernand CASCADE;

User dropped.

SQL> SELECT object_type,
  2          object_name
  3    FROM dba_objects
  4   WHERE owner = 'IFERNAND';

no rows selected
```

Data Loading

Any user with the requisite privileges can insert data into tables, but database administrators are routinely called upon to help with bulk loading of data; this typically happens when a new software application is deployed, but it can happen on a routine basis in *data marts* and *data warehouses*. The simplest way to load data is to use scripts containing INSERT commands—one INSERT command per row—but this approach is only useful for small amounts of data. The sections that follow discuss some of the tools and techniques provided by Oracle for data loading.

The Export and Import Utilities

The exp and imp utilities—used for exporting data out of and importing data into a database, respectively—were once the workhorses of the Oracle world. The *data pump* utilities, which were introduced in Oracle Database 10g, have more features but also have the drawback of using PL/SQL routines for reading and writing and, as a result, can only read and create server-side files. On the other hand, the exp and imp utilities read and create client-side files such as those located on a user's laptop. The use of *named pipes* to transfer data from one database to another database without creating an intermediate file is not possible with the data pump utilities.[1] Also, the data pump utilities do not work with magnetic tapes and standby databases. As a result of limitations like these, the exp and imp utilities have not been fully supplanted by the new utilities. I discuss them here for completeness even though their use is now expressly discouraged by Oracle.[2]

The exp and imp utilities are rich in features; you can list them with the help=y clause. Listing 8-13 shows the features of the exp utility—the imp utility has very similar features.

Listing 8-13. *Features of the exp Utility*

```
C:\Documents and Settings\IGNATIUS>exp help=y

Export: Release 11.1.0.6.0 - Production on Sat Nov 15 18:15:45 2008

Copyright (c) 1982, 2007, Oracle.  All rights reserved.

You can let Export prompt you for parameters by entering the EXP
command followed by your username/password:

    Example: EXP SCOTT/TIGER

Or, you can control how Export runs by entering the EXP command followed
by various arguments. To specify parameters, you use keywords:

    Format:  EXP KEYWORD=value or KEYWORD=(value1,value2,...,valueN)
```

---

1. Metalink notes 30528.1 and 1018477.6 discuss the use of named pipes with the exp and imp utilities.

2. The following language appears in *Oracle Database 11g Utilities*: "Original export is desupported for general use as of Oracle Database 11g. The only supported use of Original Export in 11g is backward migration of XMLType data to a database version 10g release 2 (10.2) or earlier. Therefore, Oracle recommends that you use the new Data Pump Export and Import utilities, except in the following situations which require Original Export and Import:

    You want to import files that were created using the original Export utility (exp).

    You want to export files that will be imported using the original Import utility (imp). An example of this would be if you wanted to export data from Oracle Database 10g and then import it into an earlier database release."

```
Example: EXP SCOTT/TIGER GRANTS=Y TABLES=(EMP,DEPT,MGR)
         or TABLES=(T1:P1,T1:P2), if T1 is partitioned table
```

USERID must be the first parameter on the command line.

Keyword	Description (Default)	Keyword	Description (Default)
USERID	username/password	FULL	export entire file (N)
BUFFER	size of data buffer	OWNER	list of owner usernames
FILE	output files (EXPDAT.DMP)	TABLES	list of table names
COMPRESS	import into one extent (Y)	RECORDLENGTH	length of IO record
GRANTS	export grants (Y)	INCTYPE	incremental export type
INDEXES	export indexes (Y)	RECORD	track incr. export (Y)
DIRECT	direct path (N)	TRIGGERS	export triggers (Y)
LOG	log file of screen output	STATISTICS	analyze objects (ESTIMATE)
ROWS	export data rows (Y)	PARFILE	parameter filename
CONSISTENT	cross-table consistency(N)	CONSTRAINTS	export constraints (Y)

```
OBJECT_CONSISTENT      transaction set to read only during object export (N)
FEEDBACK               display progress every x rows (0)
FILESIZE               maximum size of each dump file
FLASHBACK_SCN          SCN used to set session snapshot back to
FLASHBACK_TIME         time used to get the SCN closest to the specified time
QUERY                  select clause used to export a subset of a table
RESUMABLE              suspend when a space related error is encountered(N)
RESUMABLE_NAME         text string used to identify resumable statement
RESUMABLE_TIMEOUT      wait time for RESUMABLE
TTS_FULL_CHECK         perform full or partial dependency check for TTS
TABLESPACES            list of tablespaces to export
TRANSPORT_TABLESPACE   export transportable tablespace metadata (N)
TEMPLATE               template name which invokes iAS mode export
```

Export terminated successfully without warnings.

Listing 8-14 shows an example of the use of the exp utility. We export the contents of the hr sample schema into a file called hr.dmp; we use the consistent=y clause to ensure that all the contents of the file accurately represent a single point in time.

Listing 8-14. *Using the exp Utility*

```
C:\Documents and Settings\IGNATIUS>exp hr file=hr.dmp consistent=y
tables=(countries,departments,employees,jobs,job_history,locations,regions)

Export: Release 11.1.0.6.0 - Production on Sun May 4 09:24:28 2008

Copyright (c) 1982, 2007, Oracle.  All rights reserved.

Password:

Connected to: Oracle Database 11g Enterprise Edition Release 11.1.0.6.0 - Production
With the Partitioning, OLAP, Data Mining and Real Application Testing options
Export done in WE8MSWIN1252 character set and AL16UTF16 NCHAR character set

About to export specified tables via Conventional Path ...
. . exporting table                    COUNTRIES          25 rows exported
. . exporting table                  DEPARTMENTS          27 rows exported
. . exporting table                    EMPLOYEES         107 rows exported
. . exporting table                         JOBS          19 rows exported
. . exporting table                  JOB_HISTORY          10 rows exported
. . exporting table                    LOCATIONS          23 rows exported
. . exporting table                      REGIONS           4 rows exported
Export terminated successfully without warnings.
```

Next, let's import the data into another schema using the `imp` utility, as illustrated in Listing 8-15; we can take advantage of the `fromuser` and `touser` clauses. Notice the warnings produced by the utility; it reports compilation errors for two triggers. This is because, in the absence of an explicit prohibition, the `exp` utility exported not only the data but also the definitions of indexes, constraints, triggers, and grants associated with the tables as well as the table and index statistics; the triggers on the `employee` table refer to stored procedures that do not exist in the destination schema.

Listing 8-15. *Using the imp Utility*

```
C:\Documents and Settings\IGNATIUS>imp ifernand file=hr.dmp fromuser=hr
touser=ifernand
tables=(countries,departments,employees,jobs,job_history,locations,regions)

Import: Release 11.1.0.6.0 - Production on Sun May 4 09:26:15 2008

Copyright (c) 1982, 2007, Oracle.  All rights reserved.
```

```
Password:

Connected to: Oracle Database 11g Enterprise Edition Release 11.1.0.6.0 - Production
With the Partitioning, OLAP, Data Mining and Real Application Testing options

Export file created by EXPORT:V11.01.00 via conventional path

Warning: the objects were exported by HR, not by you

import done in WE8MSWIN1252 character set and AL16UTF16 NCHAR character set
. importing HR's objects into IFERNAND
. . importing table                     "COUNTRIES"          25 rows imported
. . importing table                   "DEPARTMENTS"          27 rows imported
. . importing table                     "EMPLOYEES"         107 rows imported
. . importing table                          "JOBS"          19 rows imported
. . importing table                   "JOB_HISTORY"          10 rows imported
. . importing table                     "LOCATIONS"          23 rows imported
. . importing table                       "REGIONS"           4 rows imported
IMP-00041: Warning: object created with compilation warnings
 "CREATE TRIGGER "IFERNAND".secure_employees"
 "  BEFORE INSERT OR UPDATE OR DELETE ON employees"
 "BEGIN"
 "  secure_dml;"
 "END secure_employees;"
IMP-00041: Warning: object created with compilation warnings
 "CREATE TRIGGER "IFERNAND".update_job_history"
 "  AFTER UPDATE OF job_id, department_id ON employees"
 "  FOR EACH ROW"
 "BEGIN"
 "  add_job_history(:old.employee_id, :old.hire_date, sysdate,"
 "                :old.job_id, :old.department_id);"
 "END;"
About to enable constraints...
Import terminated successfully with warnings.
```

The Data Pump Utilities

The expdp (Data Pump Export) and impdp (Data Pump Import) utilities were introduced in Oracle Database 10g with support for parallelism, compression, and encryption, among other things. They were intended to supplant the exp and imp utilities but could not do so completely, for the reasons I have already stated. The invocation syntax for expdp and impdp is fairly similar to that for the exp and imp utilities; you can use the help=y clause to list their features.

Listing 8-16 illustrates use the expdp and impdp utilities to export and import the same tables that are referenced in Listing 8-14 and Listing 8-15. Notice the reference to a special directory called data_pump_dir and how intervention by the database administrator becomes necessary to give users permission to use this directory.

Listing 8-16. *Using the expdp and impdp Utilities*

```
C:\Documents and Settings\IGNATIUS>expdp hr directory=data_pump_dir dumpfile=hr.dmp
flashback_time="to_timestamp(sysdate)"
tables=(countries,departments,employees,jobs,job_history,locations,regions)


Export: Release 11.1.0.6.0 - Production on Sunday, 04 May, 2008 10:27:47


Copyright (c) 2003, 2007, Oracle.  All rights reserved.
Password:


Connected to: Oracle Database 11g Enterprise Edition Release 11.1.0.6.0 - Production
With the Partitioning, OLAP, Data Mining and Real Application Testing options
ORA-39002: invalid operation
ORA-39070: Unable to open the log file.
ORA-39087: directory name DATA_PUMP_DIR is invalid


C:\Documents and Settings\IGNATIUS>sqlplus system

SQL*Plus: Release 11.1.0.6.0 - Production on Sun May 4 10:34:42 2008

Copyright (c) 1982, 2007, Oracle.  All rights reserved.

Enter password:

Connected to:
Oracle Database 11g Enterprise Edition Release 11.1.0.6.0 - Production
With the Partitioning, OLAP, Data Mining and Real Application Testing options

SQL> grant read, write on directory data_pump_dir to hr;

Grant succeeded.

SQL> exit
Disconnected from Oracle Database 11g Enterprise Edition Release 11.1.0.6.0 -
```

Production
With the Partitioning, OLAP, Data Mining and Real Application Testing options

C:\Documents and Settings\IGNATIUS>**expdp hr directory=data_pump_dir dumpfile=hr.dmp**
flashback_time="to_timestamp(sysdate)"
tables=(countries,departments,employees,jobs,job_history,locations,regions)

Export: Release 11.1.0.6.0 - Production on Sunday, 04 May, 2008 10:43:41

Copyright (c) 2003, 2007, Oracle. All rights reserved.
Password:

Connected to: Oracle Database 11g Enterprise Edition Release 11.1.0.6.0 - Production
With the Partitioning, OLAP, Data Mining and Real Application Testing options
Starting "HR"."SYS_EXPORT_TABLE_01": hr/******** directory=data_pump_dir
dumpfile=hr/********.dmp flashback_time=to_timestamp(sysdate)
tables=(countries,departments,employees,jobs,job_history,locations,regions)
Estimate in progress using BLOCKS method...
Processing object type TABLE_EXPORT/TABLE/TABLE_DATA
Total estimation using BLOCKS method: 448 KB
Processing object type TABLE_EXPORT/TABLE/TABLE
Processing object type TABLE_EXPORT/TABLE/GRANT/OWNER_GRANT/OBJECT_GRANT
Processing object type TABLE_EXPORT/TABLE/INDEX/INDEX
Processing object type TABLE_EXPORT/TABLE/CONSTRAINT/CONSTRAINT
Processing object type TABLE_EXPORT/TABLE/INDEX/STATISTICS/INDEX_STATISTICS
Processing object type TABLE_EXPORT/TABLE/COMMENT
Processing object type TABLE_EXPORT/TABLE/CONSTRAINT/REF_CONSTRAINT
Processing object type TABLE_EXPORT/TABLE/TRIGGER
Processing object type TABLE_EXPORT/TABLE/STATISTICS/TABLE_STATISTICS
. . exported "HR"."COUNTRIES"   6.375 KB   25 rows
. . exported "HR"."DEPARTMENTS"   7.015 KB   27 rows
. . exported "HR"."EMPLOYEES"   16.80 KB   107 rows
. . exported "HR"."JOBS"   6.984 KB   19 rows
. . exported "HR"."JOB_HISTORY"   7.054 KB   10 rows
. . exported "HR"."LOCATIONS"   8.273 KB   23 rows
. . exported "HR"."REGIONS"   5.484 KB   4 rows
Master table "HR"."SYS_EXPORT_TABLE_01" successfully loaded/unloaded
****
Dump file set for HR.SYS_EXPORT_TABLE_01 is:
  C:\APP\IGNATIUS\ADMIN\TRAINING\DPDUMP\HR.DMP
Job "HR"."SYS_EXPORT_TABLE_01" successfully completed at 10:44:19

```
C:\Documents and Settings\IGNATIUS>impdp ifernand directory=data_pump_dir
dumpfile=hr.dmp remap_schema=hr:ifernand
tables=(countries,departments,employees,jobs,job_history,locations,regions)


Import: Release 11.1.0.6.0 - Production on Sunday, 04 May, 2008 10:49:44


Copyright (c) 2003, 2007, Oracle.  All rights reserved.
Password:


Connected to: Oracle Database 11g Enterprise Edition Release 11.1.0.6.0 - Production
With the Partitioning, OLAP, Data Mining and Real Application Testing options
ORA-39002: invalid operation
ORA-39070: Unable to open the log file.
ORA-39087: directory name DATA_PUMP_DIR is invalid


C:\Documents and Settings\IGNATIUS>sqlplus system


SQL*Plus: Release 11.1.0.6.0 - Production on Sun May 4 10:49:53 2008


Copyright (c) 1982, 2007, Oracle.  All rights reserved.


Enter password:


Connected to:
Oracle Database 11g Enterprise Edition Release 11.1.0.6.0 - Production
With the Partitioning, OLAP, Data Mining and Real Application Testing options


SQL> grant read, write on directory data_pump_dir to ifernand;


Grant succeeded.


SQL> exit
Disconnected from Oracle Database 11g Enterprise Edition Release 11.1.0.6.0 -
Production
With the Partitioning, OLAP, Data Mining and Real Application Testing options


C:\Documents and Settings\IGNATIUS>impdp ifernand directory=data_pump_dir
dumpfile=hr.dmp remap_schema=hr:ifernand
tables=(countries,departments,employees,jobs,job_history,locations,regions)


Import: Release 11.1.0.6.0 - Production on Sunday, 04 May, 2008 10:50:45
```

Copyright (c) 2003, 2007, Oracle. All rights reserved.
Password:

Connected to: Oracle Database 11g Enterprise Edition Release 11.1.0.6.0 - Production
With the Partitioning, OLAP, Data Mining and Real Application Testing options
Master table ifernand."SYS_IMPORT_TABLE_01" successfully loaded/unloaded
Starting ifernand."SYS_IMPORT_TABLE_01": ifernand/******** directory=data_pump_dir
dumpfile=hr.dmp remap_schema=hr:ifernand/********
tables=(countries,departments,employees,jobs,job_history,locations,regions)
Processing object type TABLE_EXPORT/TABLE/TABLE
Processing object type TABLE_EXPORT/TABLE/TABLE_DATA
. . imported ifernand."COUNTRIES"   6.375 KB   25 rows
. . imported ifernand."DEPARTMENTS"   7.015 KB   27 rows
. . imported ifernand."EMPLOYEES"   16.80 KB   107 rows
. . imported ifernand."JOBS"   6.984 KB   19 rows
. . imported ifernand."JOB_HISTORY"   7.054 KB   10 rows
. . imported ifernand."LOCATIONS"   8.273 KB   23 rows
. . imported ifernand."REGIONS"   5.484 KB   4 rows
Processing object type TABLE_EXPORT/TABLE/GRANT/OWNER_GRANT/OBJECT_GRANT
Processing object type TABLE_EXPORT/TABLE/INDEX/INDEX
Processing object type TABLE_EXPORT/TABLE/CONSTRAINT/CONSTRAINT
Processing object type TABLE_EXPORT/TABLE/INDEX/STATISTICS/INDEX_STATISTICS
Processing object type TABLE_EXPORT/TABLE/COMMENT
Processing object type TABLE_EXPORT/TABLE/CONSTRAINT/REF_CONSTRAINT
Processing object type TABLE_EXPORT/TABLE/TRIGGER
ORA-39082: Object type TRIGGER:ifernand."SECURE_EMPLOYEES" created with compilation
warnings
ORA-39082: Object type TRIGGER:ifernand."SECURE_EMPLOYEES" created with compilation
warnings
ORA-39082: Object type TRIGGER:ifernand."UPDATE_JOB_HISTORY" created with
compilation warnings
ORA-39082: Object type TRIGGER:ifernand."UPDATE_JOB_HISTORY" created with
compilation warnings
Processing object type TABLE_EXPORT/TABLE/STATISTICS/TABLE_STATISTICS
Job ifernand."SYS_IMPORT_TABLE_01" completed with 4 error(s) at 10:50:55

SQL*Loader

The SQL*Loader utility (sqlldr) is used to import data from sources located in other Oracle
databases; it is similar to the DB2 load utility and the SQL Server bcp utility. It imports data
from one or more data files whose structure is described in a SQL*Loader *control file*.

SQL*Loader offers tremendous flexibility in dealing with data files. For example:

- Fixed-length data items and variable-length (delimited) data items are both supported.

- Header records can be skipped.

- Bad records can be discarded.

- Data items from multiple lines can be combined.

- Data items can be selectively imported.

- Data records can be selectively imported.

- Data items from the same row of data can be inserted into multiple tables.

Listing 8-17 shows the contents of a simple SQL*Loader control file that describes how to load three columns of information from a *comma delimited file* into a table. The INFILE * clause indicates that there is no separate data file or *infile*; that is, the data is part of the control file itself.

Listing 8-17. *A Simple SQL*Loader Control File*

```
LOAD DATA
INFILE *
INTO TABLE DEPT
FIELDS TERMINATED BY ',' OPTIONALLY ENCLOSED BY '"'
(DEPTNO, DNAME, LOC)
BEGINDATA
12,RESEARCH,"SARATOGA"
10,"ACCOUNTING",CLEVELAND
11,"ART",SALEM
13,FINANCE,"BOSTON"
21,"SALES",PHILA.
22,"SALES",ROCHESTER
42,"INT'L","SAN FRAN"
```

This control file belongs to the first in a series of 11 case studies included with the Oracle software; the control files (ulcase*.ctl) and data files (ulcase*.dat) can be found in the ORACLE_HOME\rdbms\demo directory. SQL scripts for creating the necessary tables are also provided (ulcase*.sql). Complete instructions for testing the examples can be found in the comments section of each control file; they are also discussed in Chapter 6 of *Oracle Database 11g Utilities*, available at http://tahiti.oracle.com or http://www.oracle.com/technology/documentation/index.html. Listing 8-18 shows the results of performing the first case study.

Listing 8-18. *A Sample SQL*Loader Session*

```
C:\app\IGNATIUS\product\11.1.0\db_1\RDBMS\demo>sqlldr USERID=scott
CONTROL=ulcase1.ctl LOG=ulcase1.log
Password:

SQL*Loader: Release 11.1.0.6.0 - Production on Mon Nov 17 07:20:58 2008

Copyright (c) 1982, 2007, Oracle.  All rights reserved.

Commit point reached - logical record count 7

C:\app\IGNATIUS\product\11.1.0\db_1\RDBMS\demo>type ulcase1.log

SQL*Loader: Release 11.1.0.6.0 - Production on Mon Nov 17 07:20:58 2008

Copyright (c) 1982, 2007, Oracle.  All rights reserved.

Control File:   ulcase1.ctl
Data File:      ulcase1.ctl
  Bad File:     ulcase1.bad
  Discard File:  none specified

 (Allow all discards)

Number to load: ALL
Number to skip: 0
Errors allowed: 50
Bind array:     64 rows, maximum of 256000 bytes
Continuation:    none specified
Path used:      Conventional

Table DEPT, loaded from every logical record.
Insert option in effect for this table: INSERT

    Column Name                    Position   Len  Term Encl Datatype
------------------------------ ---------- ----- ---- ---- --------------------
DEPTNO                             FIRST     *   ,   0(") CHARACTER
DNAME                              NEXT      *   ,   0(") CHARACTER
LOC                                NEXT      *   ,   0(") CHARACTER
```

Table DEPT:

7 Rows successfully loaded.

0 Rows not loaded due to data errors.

0 Rows not loaded because all WHEN clauses were failed.

0 Rows not loaded because all fields were null.

Space allocated for bind array: 49536 bytes(64 rows)
Read   buffer bytes: 1048576

Total logical records skipped: 0
Total logical records read: 7
Total logical records rejected: 0
Total logical records discarded: 0

Run began on Mon Nov 17 07:20:58 2008
Run ended on Mon Nov 17 07:21:00 2008

Elapsed time was: 00:00:01.84
CPU time was: 00:00:00.02

■**Tip** Oracle does not provide a "SQL*Unloader" utility to complement the SQL*Loader utility—this is possibly the longest-standing gap in the Oracle Database product suite. Tom Kyte provides four different solutions at http://asktom.oracle.com/tkyte/flat/.

Summary

Here are some of the key points we touched upon in this chapter:

- Every object in a database is explicitly owned by a single owner, and the owner of an object must explicitly authorize its use by anybody else. The collection of objects owned by a user is called a *schema*. Oracle manages the contents of a database using its own tables, indexes, sequences, procedures, triggers, and views; these are stored in the SYS schema.

- The four commands required for user management are CREATE USER, ALTER USER, DROP USER, GRANT, and REVOKE commands.

- Object privileges are privileges to perform operations on objects; examples include SELECT, INSERT, UPDATE, and DELETE privileges on tables. System privileges are privileges that do not apply to specific objects; examples are CREATE SESSION and CREATE TABLE. Roles are collections of privileges that are created for convenience; all the privileges in a collection can be assigned to a user with a single command.

- The exp and imp utilities used to be the workhorses of the Oracle world; they are used to transfer data from one Oracle database to another. They are not as sophisticated as the "data pump" utilities introduced in Oracle Database 10g but their advantage is that they can work with client-side files, named pipes, magnetic tapes, and standby databases.

- The expdp (Data Pump Export) and impdp (Data Pump Import) utilities were introduced in Oracle Database 10g with support for parallelism, compression, and encryption among other things.

- The SQL*Loader utility is used to import data from sources in other Oracle databases; it is similar to the DB2 load utility and the SQL Server bcp utility. A complementary "SQL*Unloader" utility is not available.

Exercises

- In Chapter 6, we used the OLTP template to create a training database. Several sample schemas were automatically installed by the template. Drop the entire HR schema using the command DROP USER hr CASCADE and reinstall it using the scripts in ORACLE_HOME\demo\schema\human_resources. The main script is hr_main.sql. For more information, refer to *Oracle Database 11g Sample Schemas*.

- A list of suggested security policies can be found in *Oracle Database 10g Enterprise Manager Policy Reference Manual*.[3] Some of them have to do with access to dictionary tables, dictionary views, and powerful PL/SQL routines; others have to do with password management. Some of these policies are violated in the databases created by Database Configuration Assistant. Audit your database using the data dictionary views and correct the security violations that you find.

- Locate the SQL*Loader examples in the ORACLE_HOME\rdbms\demo directory. Review each example and load the data into your database. For more information, refer to *Oracle Database 11g Utilities*.

---

3. An updated version for Oracle Database 11g was not available when this book was written.

Further Reading

Oracle Corporation. *Oracle Database 11g Administrator's Guide.* Oracle Corporation, 2007. This is the most important book in every database administrator's library; Chapter 6 covers user management. It is freely searchable or downloadable at `http://tahiti.oracle.com` or `http://www.oracle.com/technology/documentation/index.html`.

Oracle Corporation. *Oracle Database Utilities 11g.* Oracle Corporation, 2007. Covers the `exp`, `imp`, `expdp`, `impdp`, and `sqlldr` utilities. It is freely searchable or downloadable at `http://tahiti.oracle.com` or `http://www.oracle.com/technology/documentation/index.html`.

Oracle Corporation. *Oracle Database 11g Sample Schemas.* Oracle Corporation, 2007. Covers the Human Resources (HR), Order Entry (OE), Online Catalog (OC), Information Exchange (IX), Product Media (PM), and Sales History (SH) sample schemas provided by Oracle. It is freely searchable or downloadable at `http://tahiti.oracle.com` or `http://www.oracle.com/technology/documentation/index.html`.

Oracle Corporation. *Oracle Database 10g Enterprise Manager Policy Reference Manual.* Oracle Corporation, 2005. It is freely searchable or downloadable at `http://tahiti.oracle.com` or `http://www.oracle.com/technology/documentation/index.html`. Among other things, this book contains a list of suggested security policies dealing with password management and with access to data dictionary information and powerful PL/SQL routines. An updated version for Oracle Database 11g was not available when this book was written.

Alapati, Sam. *Expert Oracle Database 11g Administration.* Apress, 2008. A useful reference for the intermediate to experienced DBA.

PART III

Database Support

CHAPTER 9

■ ■ ■

Taking Control

Then felt I like some watcher of the skies
When a new planet swims into his ken;
Or like stout Cortez, when with eagle eyes
He stared at the Pacific—and all his men
Look'd at each other with a wild surmise—
Silent, upon a peak in Darien.

—On First Looking into Chapman's Homer by John Keats

If you are going to be responsible for a database, you need to know what it contains and how it is being used. Which are the biggest tables? How are the data files, control files, and log files laid out? How many people have database accounts? How many people use the database at a time? Your first action when you acquire responsibility for a database should be to thoroughly explore it. Form-based tools such as Enterprise Manager, SQL Developer, and Remote Diagnostic Agent make it easy to explore the database.

Form-based tools also simplify the task of database administration. A long time ago in my career, I remember a manager looking on as I fixed a database problem. It took quite a while for me to get everything right because the only tool I had was the SQL*Plus command-line tool and I was constructing SQL commands on the fly to fix the problem. A workman is as good as his tools. The manager was not very impressed.

As illustrated in Listing 9-1, I suggest that you create an account with DBA privileges for your personal use so that you are not tempted to use the SYS or SYSTEM account while browsing or while performing chores. There are certainly times when you will have to use one of these accounts, but you should be able to do most of your daily work with your own account. This helps prevent unnecessary objects from being created in the SYS and SYSTEM schemas.

Listing 9-1. *Creating an Account with DBA Privileges*

```
SQL> CONNECT system
Enter password:
Connected.
SQL> CREATE USER ifernand
  2   IDENTIFIED BY change_immediately
  3   PASSWORD EXPIRE;

User created.

SQL> GRANT DBA TO ifernand;

Grant succeeded.

SQL> CONNECT ifernand
Enter password:
ERROR:
ORA-28001: the password has expired

Changing password for ifernand
New password:
Retype new password:
Password changed
Connected.
```

Enterprise Manager

Enterprise Manager comes in two flavors: Database Control and Grid Control. Both of them are web-based tools. Database Control is used to manage a single database, while Grid Control is used to manage multiple databases. Database Control is automatically installed when you create a database. I use the terms *Enterprise Manager* and *Database Control* interchangeably in the rest of this chapter.

As discussed in Chapter 6, Database Control can be installed by the Database Configuration Assistant if you so choose—this is the recommended method.

Database Control is typically started when the database is started. You can determine the starting URL by using the emctl utility. As illustrated in Listing 9-2, you can also use the emctl utility to manually start or stop Enterprise Manager.

Listing 9-2. *Starting Enterprise Manager*

```
C:\Documents and Settings\IGNATIUS>set ORACLE_SID=TRAINING

C:\Documents and Settings\IGNATIUS>emctl status dbconsole
Oracle Enterprise Manager 11g Database Control Release 11.1.0.6.0
Copyright (c) 1996, 2007 Oracle Corporation.  All rights reserved.
https://IGGY:5500/em/console/aboutApplication
Oracle Enterprise Manager 11g is not running.

C:\Documents and Settings\IGNATIUS>emctl start dbconsole
Oracle Enterprise Manager 11g Database Control Release 11.1.0.6.0
Copyright (c) 1996, 2007 Oracle Corporation.  All rights reserved.
https://IGGY:5500/em/console/aboutApplication
Starting Oracle Enterprise Manager 11g Database Control ...The
OracleDBConsoleTRAINING service is starting.............................
The OracleDBConsoleTRAINING service was started successfully.
```

You can accomplish most DBA tasks—from mundane tasks such as password resets and creating indexes (illustrated in Figure 9-1 and Figure 9-2) to complex tasks such as backup and recovery (discussed in Chapter 12 and Chapter 13)—by using Enterprise Manager instead of command-line tools such as SQL*Plus. The starting point for most of these tasks can be found in the Availability, Server, and Schema tabs of the Enterprise Manager home page. Performing database administration tasks becomes a matter of completing a form and clicking an Apply button or an OK button.

■**Tip** Before clicking the Apply or OK buttons on any task screen, click the Show SQL button to review the SQL statements that Oracle will use to perform the task. This is a great way to learn new SQL commands.

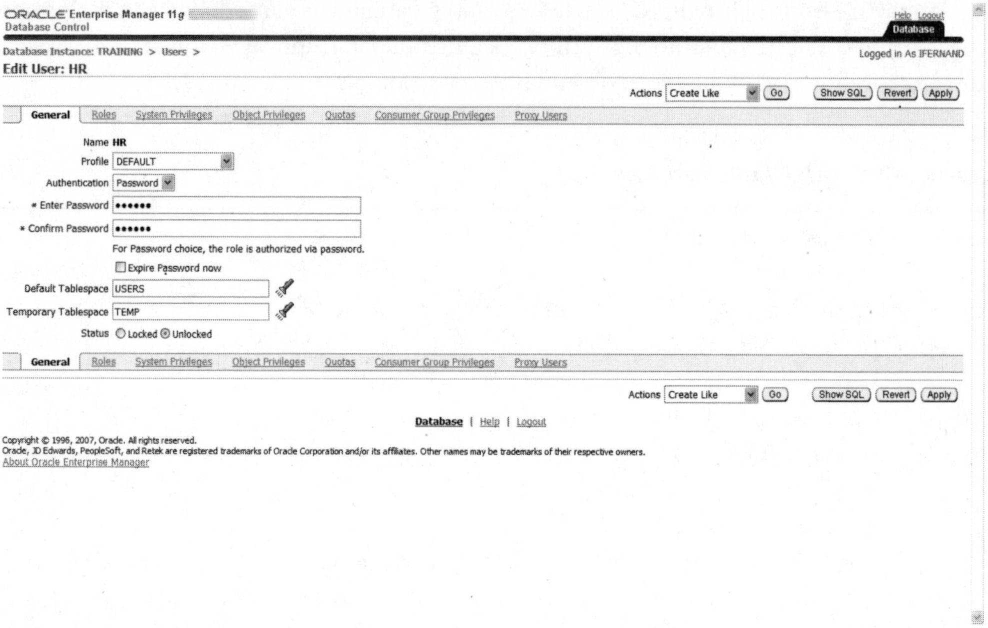

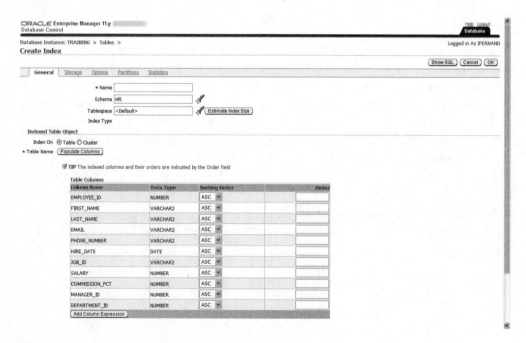

Figure 9-1. *Performing password resets by using Enterprise Manager*

Figure 9-2. *Creating indexes by using Enterprise Manager*

Unfortunately, a vast amount of Enterprise Manager functionality is available only if you have licensed the appropriate *management pack*. The list of management packs includes the Change Management Pack, Configuration Management Pack, Diagnostics Pack, Provisioning Pack, and Tuning Pack. I won't discuss any of the functionality of the management packs in this book because most organizations don't have the required licenses. Note that you must first license Enterprise Edition before you can license any of these packs; more information can be found in *Oracle Database 11g Licensing Information*.

More information about Enterprise Manager can be found in the references listed in the "Further Reading" section at the end of this chapter. In the "Exercises" section, you will be asked to use Enterprise Manager to answer several questions about your database.

SQL Developer

We discussed the installation of SQL Developer in Chapter 5. Until a few years ago, Oracle was very weak in the area of tools for software developers, but this changed with the release of SQL Developer. This Java-based tool for the Windows platform can be downloaded from the Oracle Technology Network (http://otn.oracle.com). The direct link is www.oracle.com/technology/software/products/sql/index.html.

SQL Developer is primarily a tool for software developers, but database administrators will find it extremely useful. Figure 9-3 and Figure 9-4 show common uses—examining the structure of a table and checking the execution plan for a query. Notice how easy it is to browse through collections of different types of objects by using the object tree in the left pane and the tabs in the right pane. The SQL tab in particular is very interesting; it displays SQL commands for creating the object. These SQL commands can be used as a template for creating a similar object.

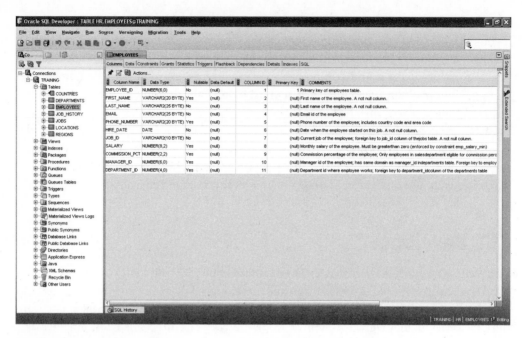

Figure 9-3. *Examining the structure of a table by using SQL Developer*

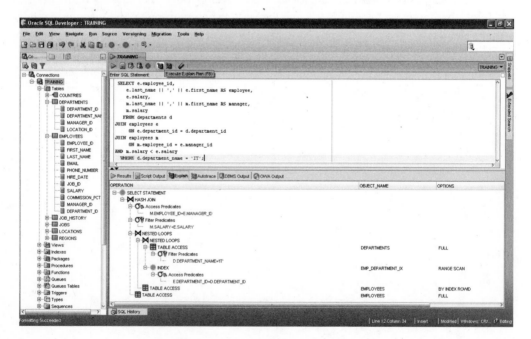

Figure 9-4. *Checking the execution plan of a query by using SQL Developer*

SQL Developer can also be used to perform some typical database administration tasks such as identifying and terminating blocking sessions.[1] In Figure 9-5, you can see that session 128 has been blocked by session 125 for 2,500 seconds. In Figure 9-6, you can see that session 125 is idle. It is waiting for a "SQL*Net message from client," and you can decide to terminate the session.

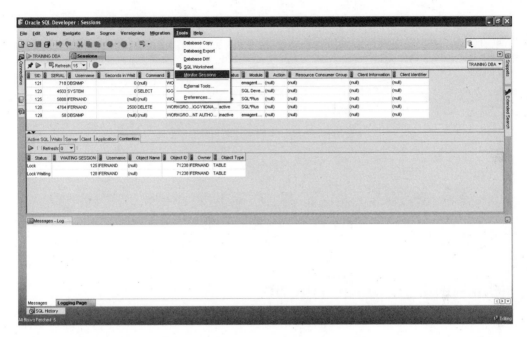

Figure 9-5. *Identifying a blocking session by using SQL Developer*

1. You cannot use Enterprise Manager to identify and terminate blocking sessions unless you have a license for the Diagnostics Pack.

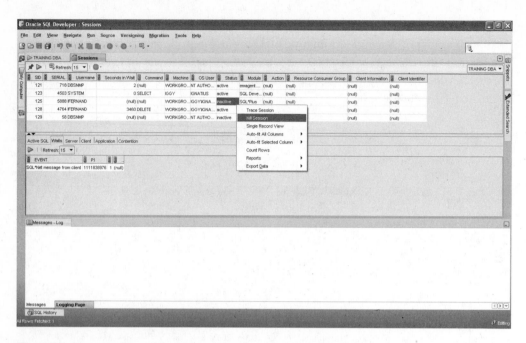

Figure 9-6. *Terminating a blocking session by using SQL Developer*

Remote Diagnostic Agent

We discussed the installation of Remote Diagnostic Agent (RDA) in Chapter 6. This tool is provided by Oracle Support to collect all the information about a database and its host system that might aid in the diagnosis of a problem. Oracle Support typically asks that you use this tool and send the collected data to Oracle whenever you request help in solving a problem. Although it was created to aid in the diagnosis of a problem, it is of great help in exploring and documenting database configurations.

RDA organizes the information it gathers into an HTML framework for easy viewing; the starting URL is RDA_start.htm. This is a wonderful way to document all aspects of a system. Figure 9-7 shows an example of system information collected by RDA, and Figure 9-8 shows an example of database information.

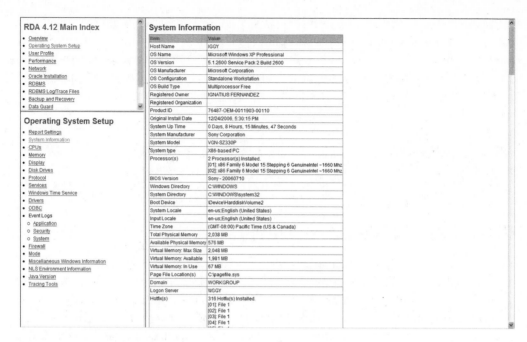

Figure 9-7. *System information collected by Remote Diagnostic Agent*

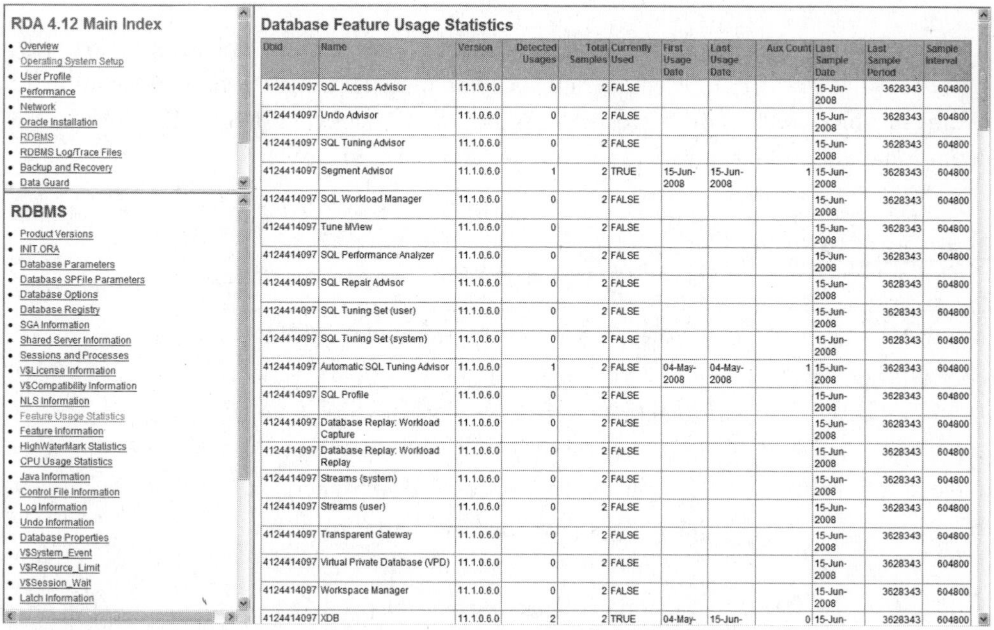

Figure 9-8. *Database information collected by Remote Diagnostic Agent*

Figure 9-8 is particularly interesting because it shows usage information of different Oracle features. You can use this information to check whether your organization is suitably licensed for the features it is using—for example, the use of Active Session History (ASH), Automatic Workload Repository (AWR), and Automatic Database Diagnostic Monitor (ADDM) require a license for the Diagnostics Pack.

■**Tip** RDA is a wonderful way to instantly create documentation about a database system. You can use RDA on all the databases in your organization and tie them together with a simple HTML framework.

Dictionary Tables and Views

Not surprisingly, Oracle stores database *metadata*—data about data—in tables, just as in the case of user data. This collection of tables is owned by the user sys and is called the *data dictionary*. An example is the ts$ table, which stores information about all tables in the database. However, the information in these tables is kept very condensed for efficiency, and Oracle therefore provides a large number of views that are more suitable for querying. If you have DBA privileges, you will be able to query these views; an example is the dba_tablespaces view, also owned by sys. Familiarity with these views is the hallmark of a competent database administrator.

Table 9-1 lists a few of the better-known views. A complete list can be found in *Oracle Database 11g Reference* along with detailed explanations. Listing 9-3 shows the columns of the ts$ table as well as the corresponding dba_tablespaces view. It also shows the actual definition of the dba_tablespaces view as listed in the dba_views view.

Table 9-1. *Well-Known Dictionary Views*

Name	Description
dba_users	Information about all users of the database
dba_tablespaces	Descriptions of each tablespace
dba_data_files	Descriptions of each data file in each tablespace
dba_indexes	Descriptions of each index in the database
dba_ind_columns	Descriptions of each column of each index
dba_tables	Descriptions of each table in the database
dba_tab_columns	Descriptions of each column of each table
dba_views	Descriptions of each view in the database

Listing 9-3. *A Sample Data Dictionary Table and View*

```
SQL> DESCRIBE sys.ts$
 Name                                      Null?    Type
 ----------------------------------------- -------- ----------------------------
 TS#                                       NOT NULL NUMBER
 NAME                                      NOT NULL VARCHAR2(30)
 OWNER#                                    NOT NULL NUMBER
 ONLINE$                                   NOT NULL NUMBER
 CONTENTS$                                 NOT NULL NUMBER
 UNDOFILE#                                          NUMBER
 UNDOBLOCK#                                         NUMBER
 BLOCKSIZE                                 NOT NULL NUMBER
 INC#                                      NOT NULL NUMBER
 SCNWRP                                             NUMBER
 SCNBAS                                             NUMBER
 DFLMINEXT                                 NOT NULL NUMBER
 DFLMAXEXT                                 NOT NULL NUMBER
 DFLINIT                                   NOT NULL NUMBER
 DFLINCR                                   NOT NULL NUMBER
 DFLMINLEN                                 NOT NULL NUMBER
 DFLEXTPCT                                 NOT NULL NUMBER
 DFLOGGING                                 NOT NULL NUMBER
 AFFSTRENGTH                               NOT NULL NUMBER
 BITMAPPED                                 NOT NULL NUMBER
 PLUGGED                                   NOT NULL NUMBER
 DIRECTALLOWED                             NOT NULL NUMBER
 FLAGS                                     NOT NULL NUMBER
 PITRSCNWRP                                         NUMBER
 PITRSCNBAS                                         NUMBER
 OWNERINSTANCE                                      VARCHAR2(30)
 BACKUPOWNER                                        VARCHAR2(30)
 GROUPNAME                                          VARCHAR2(30)
 SPARE1                                             NUMBER
 SPARE2                                             NUMBER
 SPARE3                                             VARCHAR2(1000)
 SPARE4                                             DATE
```

```
SQL> DESCRIBE sys.dba_tablespaces
 Name                                    Null?    Type
 --------------------------------------- -------- ----------------------------
 TABLESPACE_NAME                         NOT NULL VARCHAR2(30)
 BLOCK_SIZE                              NOT NULL NUMBER
 INITIAL_EXTENT                                   NUMBER
 NEXT_EXTENT                                      NUMBER
 MIN_EXTENTS                             NOT NULL NUMBER
 MAX_EXTENTS                                      NUMBER
 MAX_SIZE                                         NUMBER
 PCT_INCREASE                                     NUMBER
 MIN_EXTLEN                                       NUMBER
 STATUS                                           VARCHAR2(9)
 CONTENTS                                         VARCHAR2(9)
 LOGGING                                          VARCHAR2(9)
 FORCE_LOGGING                                    VARCHAR2(3)
 EXTENT_MANAGEMENT                                VARCHAR2(10)
 ALLOCATION_TYPE                                  VARCHAR2(9)
 PLUGGED_IN                                       VARCHAR2(3)
 SEGMENT_SPACE_MANAGEMENT                         VARCHAR2(6)
 DEF_TAB_COMPRESSION                              VARCHAR2(8)
 RETENTION                                        VARCHAR2(11)
 BIGFILE                                          VARCHAR2(3)
 PREDICATE_EVALUATION                             VARCHAR2(7)
 ENCRYPTED                                        VARCHAR2(3)
 COMPRESS_FOR                                     VARCHAR2(18)

SQL> SET LONG 10000
SQL> SELECT text
  2    FROM SYS.dba_views
  3   WHERE owner = 'SYS'
  4     AND view_name = 'DBA_TABLESPACES';

TEXT
--------------------------------------------------------------------------------
select ts.name, ts.blocksize, ts.blocksize * ts.dflinit,
        decode(bitand(ts.flags, 3), 1, to_number(NULL),
             ts.blocksize * ts.dflincr),
        ts.dflminext,
        decode(ts.contents$, 1, to_number(NULL), ts.dflmaxext),
        decode(bitand(ts.flags, 4096), 4096, ts.affstrength, NULL),
        decode(bitand(ts.flags, 3), 1, to_number(NULL), ts.dflextpct),
```

```
            ts.blocksize * ts.dflminlen,
            decode(ts.online$, 1, 'ONLINE', 2, 'OFFLINE',
                   4, 'READ ONLY', 'UNDEFINED'),
            decode(ts.contents$, 0, (decode(bitand(ts.flags, 16), 16, 'UNDO',
                   'PERMANENT')), 1, 'TEMPORARY'),
            decode(bitand(ts.dflogging, 1), 0, 'NOLOGGING', 1, 'LOGGING'),
            decode(bitand(ts.dflogging, 2), 0, 'NO', 2, 'YES'),
            decode(ts.bitmapped, 0, 'DICTIONARY', 'LOCAL'),
            decode(bitand(ts.flags, 3), 0, 'USER', 1, 'SYSTEM', 2, 'UNIFORM',
                   'UNDEFINED'),
            decode(ts.plugged, 0, 'NO', 'YES'),
            decode(bitand(ts.flags,32), 32,'AUTO', 'MANUAL'),
            decode(bitand(ts.flags,64), 64,'ENABLED', 'DISABLED'),
            decode(bitand(ts.flags,16), 16, (decode(bitand(ts.flags, 512), 512,
                   'GUARANTEE', 'NOGUARANTEE')), 'NOT APPLY'),
            decode(bitand(ts.flags,256), 256, 'YES', 'NO'),
            decode(tsattr.storattr, 1, 'STORAGE', 'HOST'),
            decode(bitand(ts.flags,16384), 16384, 'YES', 'NO'),
            decode(bitand(ts.flags,64), 0, null,
                   decode(bitand(ts.flags,65536), 65536,'FOR ALL OPERATIONS',
                   'DIRECT LOAD ONLY'))
from sys.ts$ ts, sys.x$kcfistsa tsattr
where ts.online$ != 3
and bitand(flags,2048) != 2048
and ts.ts# = tsattr.tsid
```

These views are typically queried by monitoring tools. For example, the query shown in Listing 9-4 displays the names of tablespaces that are more than 90 percent full.

Listing 9-4. *Querying the Data Dictionary*

```
COLUMN free_percentage format 990.00

WITH total_space AS
    (SELECT   tablespace_name,
              SUM (CASE
                     WHEN autoextensible = 'YES'
                        THEN maxbytes
                     ELSE BYTES
                   END) AS total_space
       FROM dba_data_files
     GROUP BY tablespace_name),
```

```
    used_space AS
    (SELECT   tablespace_name,
              SUM (BYTES) AS used_space
        FROM dba_segments
     GROUP BY tablespace_name)
SELECT tablespace_name,
       100 - (fs.used_space / ts.total_space) * 100 AS free_percentage
  FROM total_space ts NATURAL JOIN used_space fs
 WHERE 100 - (fs.used_space / ts.total_space) * 100 < 10;
```

■**Tip** A complete list of data dictionary views can be found in a data dictionary view called `DICTIONARY`.

Third-Party Tools

Several third-party tools are widely used; examples are Toad and DBArtisan. I particularly like DBArtisan because it allows access to multiple database technologies—Oracle, SQL Server, DB2, and MySQL—from a single console. Figure 9-9 illustrates the use of Toad to examine the structure of a table. Note the similarity with the corresponding screen of SQL Developer that you saw in Figure 9-3.

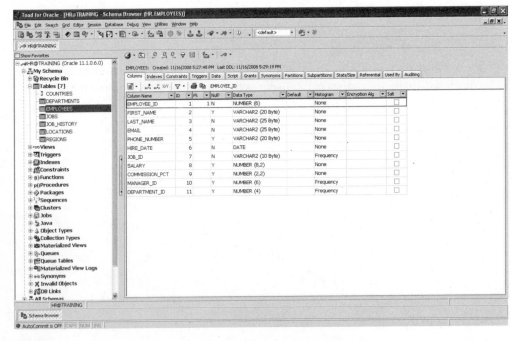

Figure 9-9. *Examining the structure of a table by using Toad*

Summary

Here are some of the key points touched on in this chapter:

- Enterprise Manager comes in two flavors: Database Control and Grid Control. Both are web-based tools. Database Control is used to manage a single database, whereas Grid Control is used to manage multiple databases. You can accomplish most DBA tasks—from mundane tasks such as password resets and creating indexes, to complex tasks such as backup and recovery—by using Enterprise Manager instead of command-line tools such as SQL*Plus.

- SQL Developer is primarily a tool for software developers, but database administrators will find it very useful. Common uses are examining the structure of a table and checking the execution plan for a query. It can also be used to perform some typical database administration tasks such as identifying and terminating blocking sessions.

- Remote Diagnostic Agent (RDA) is a tool provided by Oracle Support to collect information about a database and its host system. RDA organizes the information it gathers into an HTML framework for easy viewing; it is a wonderful way to document all aspects of a database system.

- Oracle stores database metadata—data about data—in tables, just as in the case of user data. This collection of tables is called the data dictionary. The information in the data dictionary tables is very cryptic and condensed for maximum efficiency during database operation. The data dictionary views are provided to make the information more comprehensible to the database administrator.

Exercises

- Use any of the tools described in this chapter to answer the following questions about your database:

  - Which is the largest table in the database and who owns it?

  - How many redo log groups have been created? Are the logs mirrored?

  - Which tables do not have indexes?

  - How many control files are being used? Where are they located?

  - What was the largest number of simultaneous sessions (high water mark)?

  - Do the data files have fixed sizes or do they expand automatically to accommodate more data?

- Use Oracle Enterprise Manager to perform the following tasks:

    - Reset the password of the hr user.

    - Create an index on the hire_date column of the employees table.

Further Reading

Oracle Corporation. *Note 314422.1: Remote Diagnostic Agent (RDA) 4—Getting Started.* You will need a MetaLink account in order to download this document from the Oracle knowledge base.

Oracle Corporation. *Note 330363.1: Remote Diagnostic Agent (RDA) 4—FAQ.* You will need a MetaLink account in order to download this document from the Oracle knowledge base.

Oracle Corporation. *Oracle Database 11g 2 Day DBA.* Oracle Corporation, 2007. Emphasizes the use of Enterprise Manager for common DBA tasks. Searchable or downloadable free of charge at http://tahiti.oracle.com or http://www.oracle.com/technology/documentation/index.html.

Oracle Corporation. *Oracle Database 11g Licensing Information.* Oracle Corporation, 2007. Explains which features of Enterprise Manager require special licenses. Searchable or downloadable free of charge at http://tahiti.oracle.com or http://www.oracle.com/technology/documentation/index.html.

Oracle Corporation. *Oracle Database 11g Reference.* Oracle Corporation, 2007. Explains which features of Enterprise Manager require special licenses. Searchable or downloadable free of charge at http://tahiti.oracle.com or http://www.oracle.com/technology/documentation/index.html.

Alapati, Sam. *Expert Oracle Database 11g Administration.* Apress, 2008. A very good one-volume desktop reference for the intermediate to experienced DBA.

Hotka, Dan. *Oracle SQL Developer Handbook.* McGraw-Hill, 2006. This book fills a need because Oracle does not provide a reference manual for SQL Developer.

CHAPTER 10

■ ■ ■

Monitoring

BEHOLD, the fool saith, "Put not all thine eggs in the one basket"—which is but a manner of saying, "Scatter your money and your attention;" but the wise man saith, "Put all your eggs in the one basket and—WATCH THAT BASKET."—Pudd'nhead Wilson's Calendar.

—*The Tragedy of Pudd'nhead Wilson* by Mark Twain

When I was growing up, I was sometimes awoken at night by the sound of a walking stick tapping on the ground—it was the night watchman patrolling the neighborhood. He would have had a better chance of surprising any burglars if he'd crept up on them quietly, but I never questioned why he advertised his presence so loudly. Armed only with a walking stick, he would have had to rely on strong lungs to wake up the neighborhood if he saw any burglars, so perhaps it was best to advertise his presence and hope that burglars would flee when they heard him coming. Nevertheless, the sound of his stick was comforting—it was good to know that someone trustworthy was watching the neighborhood while we slept.

The database administrator is responsible for watching the database. If something goes wrong with the database that could have been prevented, there is nobody else to blame. Database availability, changes, security, growth, backups, workload, performance, and capacity are some of the areas that should be monitored. Luckily, Oracle offers many tools for database monitoring. Enterprise Manager puts the information at our fingertips and can send out e-mail messages when things go wrong. Oracle also maintains all sorts of totals and counts that keep track of database workload, performance, and capacity. All that remains is to create regular *snapshots* of these numbers—this is automatically done by tools such as *STATSPACK* and *Automatic Workload Repository* (AWR). This *time-series* data can be manipulated with SQL queries and turned into graphs.[1]

---

1. As I state several time in this book, STATSPACK is a free tool, whereas AWR requires a license not only for Enterprise Edition but also for Diagnostics Pack. You saw how to enable STATSPACK snapshots in Chapter 6.

Monitoring Database Availability

The database administrator must continuously monitor the availability of the database and take the necessary action to restore service. The best source of information is the alert log, which contains error messages as well as alert messages; a sample is shown in Listing 10-1.

Listing 10-1. *An Extract from the Alert Log*

```
Sun Sep 07 15:19:41 2008
Starting ORACLE instance (normal)
LICENSE_MAX_SESSION = 0
LICENSE_SESSIONS_WARNING = 0
Picked latch-free SCN scheme 2
Using LOG_ARCHIVE_DEST_1 parameter default value as
C:\app\IGNATIUS\product\11.1.0\db_1\RDBMS
Using LOG_ARCHIVE_DEST_10 parameter default value as USE_DB_RECOVERY_FILE_DEST
Autotune of undo retention is turned on.
IMODE=BR
ILAT =18
LICENSE_MAX_USERS = 0
SYS auditing is disabled
Starting up ORACLE RDBMS Version: 11.1.0.6.0.
Using parameter settings in server-side spfile
C:\APP\IGNATIUS\PRODUCT\11.1.0\DB_1\DATABASE\SPFILEORCL.ORA
System parameters with non-default values:
  processes               = 150
  memory_target           = 256M
  control_files           = "C:\APP\IGNATIUS\ORADATA\ORCL\CONTROL01.CTL"
  control_files           = "C:\APP\IGNATIUS\ORADATA\ORCL\CONTROL02.CTL"
  control_files           = "C:\APP\IGNATIUS\ORADATA\ORCL\CONTROL03.CTL"
  db_block_size           = 8192
  compatible              = "11.1.0.0.0"
  db_recovery_file_dest   = "C:\app\IGNATIUS\flash_recovery_area"
  db_recovery_file_dest_size= 10G
  undo_tablespace         = "UNDOTBS1"
  remote_login_passwordfile= "EXCLUSIVE"
  db_domain               = ""
  dispatchers             = "(PROTOCOL=TCP) (SERVICE=ORCLXDB)"
  audit_file_dest         = "C:\APP\IGNATIUS\ADMIN\ORCL\ADUMP"
  audit_trail             = "DB"
  db_name                 = "ORCL"
```

```
open_cursors            = 300
diagnostic_dest         = "C:\APP\IGNATIUS"
```

■Tip List the contents of the V$DIAG_INFO view and look for the row containing the words Diag Trace—this gives you the location of the alert log. The name of the alert log will be alert_SID.log, where SID is the name of your database instance.

Fortunately, there is no need to stay glued to a computer the whole day, reviewing the alert log. When properly configured, both flavors of Enterprise Manager—Database Control and Grid Control—monitor the database and send e-mail messages whenever problems are detected.

Step-by-step instructions for configuring the monitoring capability can be found in *Oracle Database 11g 2 Day DBA*—the setup screens can be accessed using the *Metrics and Policy Settings* and *All Metrics* links in the Related Links section at the bottom of the Home page and the *Setup* and *Preferences* links at the top-right corner of the Home page.

■Tip Minimal monitoring is automatically configured by Database Configuration Assistant (DBCA) if the option is accepted when the database is created.

E-mail alerts can be sent to as many people as necessary. Different database administrators can elect to receive different subsets of the alerts. It is also possible to create *notification schedules* for cases when responsibilities rotate among the members of a team. E-mail alerts can be generated in two flavors—a *long format* and a *short format*. The short format is suitable for sending alerts about critical problems to pagers and cell phones. Listing 10-2 shows an example of the long format, and Listing 10-3 shows an example of the short format.

Listing 10-2. *Long-Format Alert*

```
EM Alert: Critical: ORCL - Session 161 is blocking 2 other sessions
From:  Enterprise Manager (iggyfernandez@gmail.com)
Sent: Tue 11/04/08 9:03 AM
To:  iggy_fernandez@hotmail.com


Target Name=ORCL
Target Type=Database Instance
Host=IGGY
```

```
Metric=Blocking Session Count
Blocking Session ID=SID: 161 Serial#: 1
Timestamp=Nov 4, 2008 9:02:51 AM PST
Severity=Critical
Message=Session 161 is blocking 2 other sessions
Notification Rule Name=Database Availability and Critical States
Notification Rule Owner=SYSMAN
```

Listing 10-3. *Short Format Alert*

```
EM:Critical:ORCL
From:  Enterprise Manager (iggyfernandez@gmail.com)
Sent: Wed 11/05/08 7:26 AM
To:  iggy_fernandez@hotmail.com

Failed to connect to database instance: ORA-12505: TNS:listener does not currently
know of SID given in connect descriptor (DBD ERROR: O..
```

It is possible to customize and extend the alerting capabilities of Enterprise Manager. If the option is licensed, new types of alerts can be created; for example, an alert could be generated if a batch job continues running past a defined maintenance window. Corrective action can be taken automatically if needed; for example, a job that continues running outside a defined maintenance window can be killed automatically or an incident record can be created in an incident management system.

■**Caution** The alert log contains informational messages in addition to error messages. Even if the database is being monitored by Enterprise Manager, the database administrator should periodically review the alert log.

Monitoring Changes

The database administrator can monitor changes to database objects using the Oracle auditing facilities. For example, the AUDIT TABLE and AUDIT ALTER TABLE commands enable auditing of changes to tables. The list of audited actions is contained in DBA_STMT_AUDIT_OPTS. If the database initialization parameter AUDIT_TRAIL is set to db_extended, Oracle also records the SQL statement associated with the action. As illustrated in Listing 10-4, the information can be found in the DBA_AUDIT_OBJECT view.

Listing 10-4. *Monitoring the History of Modifications to Tables and Other Objects*

```
SQL> SELECT    TIMESTAMP,
  2            action_name,
  3            sql_text
  4      FROM  dba_audit_object
  5     WHERE  owner = 'IFERNANDEZ'
  6   ORDER BY TIMESTAMP;


TIMESTAMP          ACTION_NAME      SQL_TEXT
---------------    ---------------  -------------------------------------------------
08/11/02 10:54:49  CREATE TABLE     CREATE TABLE mydual AS SELECT * FROM dual
08/11/02 10:54:57  ALTER TABLE      ALTER TABLE mydual ADD (dummy2 INTEGER)
08/11/02 10:55:28  DROP TABLE       DROP TABLE mydual
```

I will have more to say on the subject of auditing in Chapter 14 and, in particular, on the location and sizing of the audit trail.

Monitoring Security

The database administrator can use the Oracle auditing facilities to monitor database usage. The AUDIT CREATE SESSION command causes all connections and disconnections to be recorded. Of particular interest for security purposes are the USERHOST, TERMINAL, and OS_USERNAME values in the DBA_AUDIT_SESSION view. These tell us where a connection originated; unusual values might indicate unauthorized intrusions. For example, when I checked the database on my laptop, I found what appeared to be connections that originated from another computer called ST-ADC\STAHC13. This alarmed me and I checked the TIMESTAMP and LOGOFF_TIME values in DBA_AUDIT_SESSION; fortunately, they predated the creation of the database, which meant that the mysterious audit records were in the database template used by Database Configuration Assistant (DBCA) when the database was created. The results of my investigation can be seen in Listing 10-5.

Listing 10-5. *Monitoring the History of Connections and Disconnections*

```
SQL> SELECT    userhost,
  2            os_username,
  3            username,
  4            COUNT (*)
  5      FROM  dba_audit_session
  6   GROUP BY userhost,
  7            os_username,
```

```
 8           username
 9  ORDER BY userhost,
10           os_username,
11           username;
```

USERHOST	OS_USERNAME	USERNAME	COUNT(*)
IGGY	IGNATIUS	PERFSTAT3	2
IGGY	IGNATIUS	SYSMAN	7
IGGY	IGNATIUS	SYSTEM	5
IGGY	SYSTEM	DBSNMP	22
IGGY	SYSTEM	IGNATIUS	1
IGGY	SYSTEM	SYSMAN	182
IGGY	SYSTEM	SYSTEM	46
ST-ADC\STAHC13	aime	CTXSYS	3
ST-ADC\STAHC13	aime	SCOTT	1
ST-ADC\STAHC13	aime	SYSTEM	6
ST-ADC\STAHC13	aime	WKSYS	1
WORKGROUP\IGGY	IGGY\IGNATIUS	BI	1
WORKGROUP\IGGY	IGGY\IGNATIUS	DBSNMP	1
WORKGROUP\IGGY	IGGY\IGNATIUS	HR	15
WORKGROUP\IGGY	IGGY\IGNATIUS	IFERNANDEZ	66
WORKGROUP\IGGY	IGGY\IGNATIUS	OE	4
WORKGROUP\IGGY	IGGY\IGNATIUS	PERFSTAT	10
WORKGROUP\IGGY	IGGY\IGNATIUS	SH	2
WORKGROUP\IGGY	IGGY\IGNATIUS	START_JOB	1
WORKGROUP\IGGY	IGGY\IGNATIUS	STOP_JOB	1
WORKGROUP\IGGY	IGGY\IGNATIUS	SYS	1
WORKGROUP\IGGY	IGGY\IGNATIUS	SYSMAN	8
WORKGROUP\IGGY	IGGY\IGNATIUS	SYSTEM	5
WORKGROUP\IGGY	NT AUTHORITY\SYSTEM	DBSNMP	628

```
SQL> SELECT TIMESTAMP AS logon_time,
  2           logoff_time
  3    FROM dba_audit_session
  4    WHERE os_username = 'aime';
```

```
LOGON_TIME          LOGOFF_TIME
------------------  -------------------
2007/10/15 07:27:38
2007/10/15 07:27:39
2007/10/15 07:27:41 2007/10/15 07:27:41
2007/10/15 07:27:41
2007/10/15 07:27:42
2007/10/15 07:27:44 2007/10/15 07:27:44
2007/10/15 07:36:27
2007/10/15 07:36:29 2007/10/15 07:36:30
2007/10/15 07:36:31 2007/10/15 07:36:31
2007/10/15 07:56:09 2007/10/15 07:56:52
2007/10/15 08:36:01 2007/10/15 08:36:01
```

You should also check the security settings of the database. Here are two of the most important questions to ask:

- Is there a password policy that forces users to change their passwords at regular intervals? Is password complexity enforced? Is an account automatically locked if there are too many failed login attempts? (The answers can be found in the DBA_ PROFILES view.)

- Which users have DBA privileges? (The answer can be found in the DBA_ROLE_PRIVS view.)

Monitoring Backups

Oracle provides a utility called Recovery Manager (RMAN) for database backups and recovery. One of the advantages of RMAN is that it maintains detailed history information. You can use RMAN commands such as list backup to review the history of backups. You can issue commands such as report need backup and report unrecoverable to determine whether fresh backups are needed. You can also obtain a report of backups on the View Backup Report page of Enterprise Manager.

The use of RMAN for backups and recovery is discussed in Chapters 12 and 13, respectively.

Monitoring Growth

As illustrated in Listing 10-6, you can use the information in the DBA_DATA_FILES view to monitor the size of your database; the query shows the size in megabytes of each tablespace in your database.

Listing 10-6. *Using the* `DBA_DATA_FILES` *View to Monitor the Size of the Database*

```
SELECT   tablespace_name,
         SUM (BYTES) / 1048576 AS mb
    FROM dba_data_files
GROUP BY tablespace_name
ORDER BY tablespace_name;
```

You can incorporate the query in Listing 10-6 into a batch report with the SQL*Plus command-line tool, or you can execute it interactively with SQL Developer. Alternatively, as illustrated in Figure 10-1, Enterprise Manager offers a visual representation of space usage.

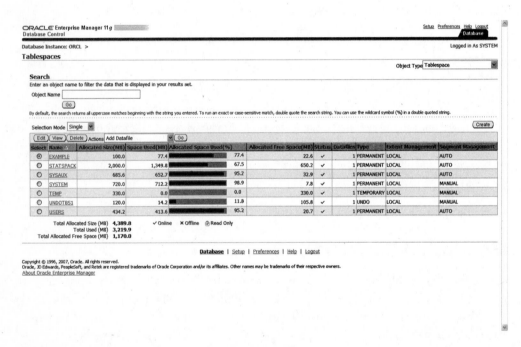

Figure 10-1. *Database size report in Enterprise Manager*

Table sizes can be monitored using the `DBA_SEGMENTS` view. The query in Listing 10-7 displays table sizes in megabytes; it uses the `RANK` function to limit the list to the ten biggest tables.

Listing 10-7. *Using* DBA_SEGMENTS *to Determine the Ten Biggest Tables*

```
WITH ranked_information AS

    (SELECT owner,
            segment_name,
            BYTES / 1048576 AS mb,
            RANK () OVER (ORDER BY BYTES DESC) AS RANK
       FROM dba_segments
      WHERE segment_type = 'TABLE')

SELECT   RANK,
         owner,
         segment_name,
         mb
    FROM ranked_information
   WHERE RANK <= 10

ORDER BY RANK;
```

In some cases, it is also useful to monitor the number of rows in specific tables; this is efficiently accomplished by checking the NUM_ROWS value in the DBA_TABLES view. NUM_ROWS is an approximate value that is updated when optimizer statistics are collected. If accurate counts are required, you can use the computationally expensive SELECT COUNT(*) command instead. Historical data is not automatically stored by Oracle; you will have to develop your own method of capturing and storing this information. You could, for example, create a special table in which to store periodic snapshots of the number of rows in specific tables that are of interest to you.

Monitoring Workload

It is very important to understand the database workload. Most databases have a distinctive workload profile. If you've regularly checked your database workload profile, you will be able to detect deviations and trends.

■**Tip** Regular and distinct patterns in the workload profile indicate database stability.

The V$SYSSTAT view keeps track of hundreds of different aspects of the database workload, such as logons, executions, commits, logical reads, physical reads, redo size, and the like. These metrics—with a few notable exceptions such as *logons current* and *opened cursors current*—are cumulative, which means that their values increase during the lifetime of the database. *Snapshots* of the information in the V$SYSSTAT view are available in the STATS$SYSSTAT table (in the case of STATSPACK) and in the DBA_HIST_SYSSTAT view (in the case of AWR); they are described in Listing 10-8. The SNAP_ID (snapshot ID) and DBID (database ID) values are used to identify snapshots—they link to the STATS$SNAPSHOT table and the DBA_HIST_SNAPSHOT view, which contain details such as the time when the snapshot was created.

Listing 10-8. *Tables and Views for Monitoring the Database Workload*

```
SQL> DESCRIBE v$sysstat;
 Name                                      Null?    Type
 ----------------------------------------- -------- --------------------
 STATISTIC#                                         NUMBER
 NAME                                               VARCHAR2(64)
 CLASS                                              NUMBER
 VALUE                                              NUMBER
 STAT_ID                                            NUMBER


SQL> DESCRIBE stats$sysstat;
 Name                                      Null?    Type
 ----------------------------------------- -------- ----------------------------
 SNAP_ID                                   NOT NULL NUMBER
 DBID                                      NOT NULL NUMBER
 INSTANCE_NUMBER                           NOT NULL NUMBER
 STATISTIC#                                NOT NULL NUMBER
 NAME                                      NOT NULL VARCHAR2(64)
 VALUE                                              NUMBER


SQL> DESCRIBE dba_hist_sysstat
 Name                                      Null?    Type
 ----------------------------------------- -------- ----------------------------
 SNAP_ID                                   NOT NULL NUMBER
 DBID                                      NOT NULL NUMBER
 INSTANCE_NUMBER                           NOT NULL NUMBER
 STAT_ID                                   NOT NULL NUMBER
 STAT_NAME                                 NOT NULL VARCHAR2(64)
 VALUE                                              NUMBER
```

The Excel graph shown in Figure 10-2 was generated using the data produced by the SQL query shown in Listing 10-9. The graph shows a distinct pattern, indicating database stability. The PIVOT operator is used to produce new columns and the LAG analytic function is used to operate on data in different rows. The use of subquery factoring breaks the query into logical pieces and makes it readable.

Listing 10-9. *SQL Query to List Logical Reads per Second and Physical Reads per Second for a One-Week Period*

```
WITH

    -- Pivot the data in the STATS$SYSSTAT table
    -- Create separate columns for physical reads and logical reads

    pivoted_data AS

    (SELECT *
       FROM (SELECT snap_id,
                    NAME,
                    VALUE
               FROM stats$sysstat)
            PIVOT (SUM(value)
              FOR name IN ('physical reads' AS physical_reads,
                           'session logical reads' AS logical_reads))),

    deltas AS

    -- Use the LAG analytic function to determine the amount of increase

    (SELECT snap_id,

            snap_time,

            snap_time
              - LAG (snap_time)
                  OVER (PARTITION BY startup_time
                        ORDER BY snap_id)
              AS duration,

            physical_reads
              - LAG (physical_reads)
                  OVER (PARTITION BY startup_time
```

```
                   ORDER BY snap_id)
          AS physical_reads,

      logical_reads
        - LAG (logical_reads)
           OVER (PARTITION BY startup_time
                 ORDER BY snap_id)
        AS logical_reads

    FROM pivoted_data NATURAL JOIN stats$snapshot)

SELECT   snap_id,
         to_char(snap_time, 'yyyy/mm/dd hh24:mi') as snap_time,
         physical_reads / duration / (24 * 60 * 60) as physical_reads_per_second,
         logical_reads / duration / (24 * 60 * 60) AS logical_reads_per_second
    FROM deltas

ORDER BY snap_id;
```

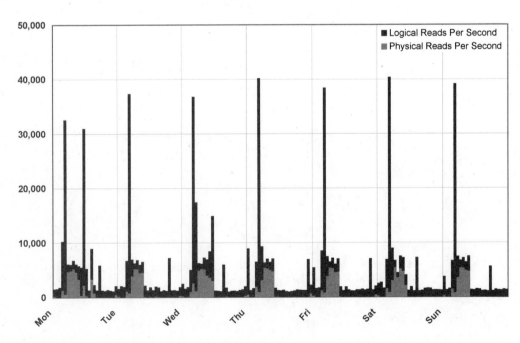

DATABASE WORKLOAD

Figure 10-2. *Excel graph of logical reads and physical reads produced using the time-series data in the* STATS$SYSSTAT *table*

Monitoring Performance

Be sure to monitor the performance of important queries. The V$SQLAREA view records execution statistics such as executions, CPU time, elapsed time, logical reads, and physical reads for each SQL statement cached in the *library cache*—it is therefore a source of workload information as well as performance information. Snapshots of the information in the V$SQLAREA view are available in the STATS$SQL_SUMMARY table (in the case of STATSPACK) and in the DBA_HIST_SQLSTAT view (in the case of AWR). The SQL statement in Listing 10-10 retrieves the average execution times of each of two SQL queries of choice in successive time periods; the query can easily be modified to include additional queries that are critical to application performance. Notice the use of the LAST_VALUE analytic function to interpolate missing values.

Listing 10-10. *SQL Query to List the Average Elapsed Times for Two SQL Queries of Choice*

```
WITH pivoted_data AS

    -- Pivot the data in STATS$SQL_SUMMARY using two values of the SQL ID column.
    -- q1 and q2 refer to the two values of interest in the SQL ID column.
    -- Create new columns representing the total elapsed time and the number of
    -- executions of each of the two queries.
    -- The newly created columns are named as follows:
    --   q1_elapsed_time
    --   q1_executions
    --   q2_elapsed_time
    --   q2_executions

    (SELECT *
       FROM (SELECT snap_id,
                    sql_id,
                    elapsed_time,
                    executions
               FROM stats$sql_summary)
            PIVOT (SUM(elapsed_time) AS elapsed_time,
                   SUM(executions) AS executions
              FOR sql_id IN ('&&1' AS q1,
                             '&&2' AS q2))),

    interpolated_data AS
```

```
-- Interpolate any missing values using the LAST_VALUE analytic function.
-- Use the last non-null value after the database was started.
-- The STATS$SNAPSHOT view tells us when the database was started.

(SELECT snap_id,

        snap_time,

        startup_time,

        LAST_VALUE (q1_elapsed_time IGNORE NULLS)
          OVER (PARTITION BY startup_time
                ORDER BY snap_id
                ROWS BETWEEN UNBOUNDED PRECEDING AND CURRENT ROW)
          AS q1_elapsed_time_i,

        LAST_VALUE (q1_executions IGNORE NULLS)
          OVER (PARTITION BY startup_time
                ORDER BY snap_id
                ROWS BETWEEN UNBOUNDED PRECEDING AND CURRENT ROW)
          AS q1_executions_i,

        LAST_VALUE (q2_elapsed_time IGNORE NULLS)
          OVER (PARTITION BY startup_time
                ORDER BY snap_id
                ROWS BETWEEN UNBOUNDED PRECEDING AND CURRENT ROW)
          AS q2_elapsed_time_i,

        LAST_VALUE (q2_executions IGNORE NULLS)
          OVER (PARTITION BY startup_time
                ORDER BY snap_id
                ROWS BETWEEN UNBOUNDED PRECEDING AND CURRENT ROW)
          AS q2_executions_i

  FROM pivoted_data NATURAL JOIN stats$snapshot),

deltas AS

-- Use the LAG analytic function to determine the amount of increase.

(SELECT snap_id,
```

```
          snap_time,

          q1_elapsed_time_i
            - LAG (q1_elapsed_time_i)
                OVER (PARTITION BY startup_time
                        ORDER BY snap_id)
            AS q1_elapsed_time_d,

          q1_executions_i
            - LAG (q1_executions_i)
                OVER (PARTITION BY startup_time
                        ORDER BY snap_id)
            AS q1_executions_d,

          q2_elapsed_time_i
            - LAG (q2_elapsed_time_i)
                OVER (PARTITION BY startup_time
                        ORDER BY snap_id)
            AS q2_elapsed_time_d,

          q2_executions_i
            - LAG (q2_executions_i)
                OVER (PARTITION BY startup_time
                        ORDER BY snap_id)
            AS q2_executions_d

     FROM interpolated_data)

-- Print the number of executions and average execution time for each time period.
-- Convert microseconds to seconds when printing the average execution time.
-- Don't print any negative values.

SELECT   snap_id,

         TO_CHAR (snap_time, 'yyyy/mm/dd hh24:mi') AS snap_time,

         CASE
           WHEN q1_elapsed_time_d > 0 AND q1_executions_d > 0
             THEN q1_executions_d
         END AS q1_executions_d,
```

```
      CASE
        WHEN q1_elapsed_time_d > 0 AND q1_executions_d > 0
          THEN q1_elapsed_time_d / q1_executions_d / 1000000
      END AS q1_elapsed_time_a,

      CASE
        WHEN q2_elapsed_time_d > 0 AND q2_executions_d > 0
          THEN q2_executions_d
      END AS q2_executions_d,

      CASE
        WHEN q2_elapsed_time_d > 0 AND q2_executions_d > 0
          THEN q2_elapsed_time_d / q2_executions_d / 1000000
      END AS q2_elapsed_time_a

  FROM deltas

ORDER BY snap_id;
```

Monitoring Capacity

The V$OSSTAT view offers cumulative values for operating system metrics such as CPU usage. Snapshots of the information in the V$OSSTAT view are available in the STATS$OSSTAT table (in the case of STATSPACK) and in the DBA_HIST_OSSTAT view (in the case of AWR); they are described in Listing 10-11. The SQL statement in Listing 10-12 computes the CPU utilization percentage for each time period.

Listing 10-11. *Tables and Views for Monitoring Database Capacity*

```
SQL> DESCRIBE v$osstat;
 Name                                      Null?    Type
 ----------------------------------------- -------- ----------------------------
 STAT_NAME                                          VARCHAR2(64)
 VALUE                                              NUMBER
 OSSTAT_ID                                          NUMBER
 COMMENTS                                           VARCHAR2(64)
 CUMULATIVE                                         VARCHAR2(3)
```

```
SQL> DESCRIBE stats$osstat
Name                                      Null?     Type
----------------------------------------- -------- ----------------------------
SNAP_ID                                   NOT NULL NUMBER
DBID                                      NOT NULL NUMBER
INSTANCE_NUMBER                           NOT NULL NUMBER
OSSTAT_ID                                 NOT NULL NUMBER
VALUE                                              NUMBER


SQL> DESCRIBE dba_hist_osstat
Name                                      Null?     Type
----------------------------------------- -------- ----------------------------
SNAP_ID                                   NOT NULL NUMBER
DBID                                      NOT NULL NUMBER
INSTANCE_NUMBER                           NOT NULL NUMBER
STAT_ID                                   NOT NULL NUMBER
STAT_NAME                                 NOT NULL VARCHAR2(64)
VALUE                                              NUMBER
```

Listing 10-12. *SQL Query to Compute the CPU Utilization Percentage*

```
WITH

    pivoted_data AS

    -- Pivot the data in the STATS$OSSTAT table.
    -- Create separate columns for total idle time and total busy time

    (SELECT *
       FROM (SELECT snap_id,
                    osstat_id,
                    VALUE
               FROM stats$osstat)
            PIVOT (SUM(value)
              FOR osstat_id IN (1 AS idle_time,
                                2 AS busy_time))),

    deltas AS

    -- Use the LAG analytic function to determine the amount of increase
```

```
    (SELECT snap_id,

           snap_time,

           idle_time
             - LAG (idle_time)
                 OVER (PARTITION BY startup_time
                     ORDER BY snap_id)
             AS idle_time,

           busy_time
             - LAG (busy_time)
                 OVER (PARTITION BY startup_time
                     ORDER BY snap_id)
             AS busy_time

      FROM pivoted_data NATURAL JOIN stats$snapshot)

SELECT    snap_id,
          to_char(snap_time, 'yyyy/mm/dd hh24:mi') as snap_time,
          busy_time / (idle_time + busy_time) AS cpu_utilization_p
    FROM deltas

ORDER BY snap_id;
```

■**Tip** If you have licensed the System Monitoring Plug-In for Hosts, Enterprise Manager can track disk and CPU utilization and alert you when thresholds are breached.

Third-Party Tools

Many organizations use third-party tools for enterprise-wide monitoring. Examples include Patrol from BMC, Tivoli from IBM, and OpenView from HP. Open-source tools such as Nagios are also a popular choice. An enterprise-wide tool that is agnostic to database and server technologies will have more breadth than Oracle Enterprise Manager but not as much depth. However, Enterprise Manager is constrained by the number of extra-cost options that must be separately licensed—they include Provisioning Pack, Database Change Management Pack, Database Tuning Pack, Database Configuration Pack, Database Diagnostics Pack, System Monitoring Plug-in for Hosts, and so on.

    If you join a team of database administrators, you should ask your colleagues for information about the monitoring tools being used in your organization.

Summary

Here is a short summary of the concepts touched upon in this chapter:

- Database availability, changes, security, growth, backups, workload, performance, and capacity are some of the areas that should be monitored by the database administrator.

- The *alert log* contains error messages and informational messages. The location of the alert log is listed in the V$DIAG_INFO view. The name of the alert log will be alert_*SID*.log, where *SID* is the name of your database instance.

- Enterprise Manager monitors the database and sends e-mail messages when problems are detected.

- The database administrator can monitor changes to database objects using the Oracle auditing facilities. For example, the AUDIT TABLE and AUDIT ALTER TABLE commands enable auditing of changes to tables.

- The AUDIT CREATE SESSION command causes all connections and disconnections to be recorded.

- Recovery Manager (RMAN) maintains detailed history information about backups. RMAN commands such as list backup, report need backup, and report unrecoverable can be used to review backups. Enterprise Manager can also be used to review backups.

- The database size can be monitored using DBA_DATA_FILES; table size can be monitored using DBA_SEGMENTS.

- Oracle maintains a large number of totals and counts that keep track of database workload, performance, and capacity. STATSPACK and AWR create regular snapshots of these numbers—this time-series data can be manipulated with SQL queries and turned into graphs. The V$SESSTAT view keeps track of hundreds of different aspects of the database workload, such as logons, executions, commits, logical reads, physical reads, redo size, and so on. The V$SQLAREA view records execution statistics such as executions, CPU time, elapsed time, logical reads, and physical reads for each SQL statement cached in the library cache. The V$OSSTAT view offers cumulative values of operating system metrics such as CPU usage.

Exercises

- Review the discussion of user management in Chapter 8. Also review the definitions of the DBA_ROLE_PRIVS and DBA_PROFILES views in *Oracle Database 11g Reference*—available at http://tahiti.oracle.com or http://www.oracle.com/technology/documentation/index.html. Answer the following questions: Which database users have DBA authority? Is there a password policy that forces database users to change their passwords at regular intervals? Is password complexity enforced? Is an account automatically locked if there are too many failed login attempts?

- Develop a system that tracks database growth and table growth. Create history tables to capture the information contained in the DBA_DATA_FILES and DBA_SEGMENTS views. Write SQL queries that report daily, weekly, and monthly growth.

- Modify the STATSPACK queries in this chapter for use with the corresponding AWR views: DBA_HIST_SNAPSHOT, DBA_HIST_SYSSTAT, DBA_HIST_SQLSTAT, and DBA_HIST_OSSTAT. The definitions of the AWR views can be found in *Oracle Database 11g Reference*—available at http://tahiti.oracle.com or http://www.oracle.com/technology/documentation/index.html.

Further Reading

Oracle Corporation. *Oracle Database 11g 2 Day DBA*. Oracle Corporation, 2007. Freely searchable or downloadable free of charge at http://tahiti.oracle.com or http://www.oracle.com/technology/documentation/index.html. Chapter 10, "Monitoring and Tuning the Database" contains step-by-step instructions for configuring the monitoring features of Enterprise Manager.

Oracle Corporation. *Oracle Database 10g Enterprise Manager Advanced Configuration*. Oracle Corporation, 2007. Freely searchable or downloadable free of charge at http://tahiti.oracle.com or http://www.oracle.com/technology/documentation/index.html. At the time of writing, the 11g version of this manual was not yet available.

Oracle Corporation. *Oracle Database 10g Enterprise Manager Licensing Information*. Oracle Corporation, 2007. Freely searchable or downloadable free of charge at http://tahiti.oracle.com or http://www.oracle.com/technology/documentation/index.html. At the time of writing, the 11g version of this manual was not yet available. It lists all the extra-charge options.

Oracle Corporation. *Oracle Database 11g Data Warehousing Guide.* Oracle Corporation, 2007. Freely searchable or downloadable free of charge at `http://tahiti.oracle.com` or `http://www.oracle.com/technology/documentation/index.html`. Chapter 21, "SQL for Analysis and Reporting," discusses *analytic functions* and the `PIVOT` operator, which were used extensively in the code samples in this chapter.

Alapati, Sam. *Expert Oracle Database 11g Administration.* Apress, 2008. A useful reference for the intermediate to experienced database administrator.

CHAPTER 11

Fixing Problems

Rise and shine, sleepy Joe
There are places to go
There are windows to clean on the way
You've got nothing to lose
But a shine on your shoes
Do the best things you can every day

—Composed by John Carter and Russell Alquist and recorded by Herman's Hermits
(free.napster.com/search/results.html?query=herman's+hermits&type=artist)

To state the obvious, fixing problems is the part of the database administrator's job that takes precedence over everything else. In his best-selling book, *The 7 Habits of Highly Effective People*, Stephen Covey explains that our activities can be divided among four quadrants depending on their urgency and importance. Figure 11-1 illustrates these quadrants.

Restoring service when the database crashes is an example of an activity that is both important *and* urgent. Determining the root cause of the database crash is important but not as urgent. The loud ringing of your cell phone demands your immediate attention but is rarely more important than the task at hand. And, of course, watching the latest sensational video on YouTube is unimportant and not urgent.

We tend to spend most of our time in the quadrant of activities that are important and urgent. However, the ideal place to spend time is the quadrant of activities that are important but *not* urgent, for example, keeping records, identifying the root causes of incidents and eliminating them, updating documentation, automating common tasks, and so forth.

In this chapter, you will watch a real-life problem as it progresses from detection to resolution. You will learn a five-step systematic approach to problem-fixing and the difference between *incident management* and *problem management*. I will cover the variety of Internet resources that are available to you, introduce an Oracle knowledge base called MetaLink, and explain how to get technical support from Oracle Corporation. Finally, I will discuss a few common problems.

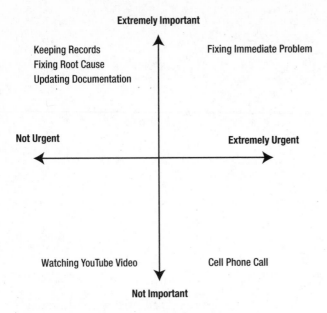

Extremely Important

Keeping Records
Fixing Root Cause
Updating Documentation

Fixing Immediate Problem

Not Urgent   **Extremely Urgent**

Watching YouTube Video   Cell Phone Call

Not Important

Figure 11-1. *Classifying activities into four quadrants*

Systematic Five-Step Problem-Solving Method

In his book *The Art and Science of Oracle Performance Tuning*, Christopher Lawson describes a systematic five-step method for solving a performance-tuning problem. The method applies to any problem, not just to a performance problem. Oracle Database versions and software tools may change, but the five steps always remain the same. A problem may be simple and require only a few minutes of your time or it may be tremendously complex and require weeks, but the five steps always remain the same:

1. *Define* the problem. This requires patient listening, skillful questioning, and even careful observation. "Is the database having a problem?" is a question, not a problem statement. "The users are complaining" is a poorly defined problem statement. "I cannot connect to the database" is very precise. Ask the user for the history of the problem. Ask what previous efforts have been made to solve the problem. Ask what changed recently in the environment, for example, software or hardware upgrades. Ask whether all users are affected or only some. Ask whether the problem occurs at specific times of the day or week. Ask whether all parts of the application are equally affected or just parts. *Avoid confusing the problem with the solution—for example, "The problem is that we need to reboot the server."* A good way to end this phase is with a reproducible test case or with one or more Oracle error codes.

2. *Investigate* the problem and collect as much pertinent evidence as possible. A good place to start is the Oracle alert log.

3. *Analyze* the data collected in the second step and isolate the cause of the performance problem. This is often the most challenging part of the performance-tuning exercise. If the root cause is not found, you can go back to the second step to continue your investigation of the problem or to the first step to refine the definition of the problem.

4. *Solve* the problem by creating a solution that addresses the cause of the problem. Solutions are not always obvious and, therefore, this part of the exercise might require a great deal of ingenuity and creativity.

5. *Implement* the solution in a safe and controlled manner. An appropriate level of testing should be conducted in a suitable testing environment. Necessary approvals should be obtained, and the organization's change management procedures should be followed. *Before* and *after* measurements should be obtained in the case of performance problems. If the *after* measurements indicate that the problem is not fixed, you can return to step 2 and continue your investigation of the problem.

The flowchart in Figure 11-2 illustrates the problem-solving work flow.

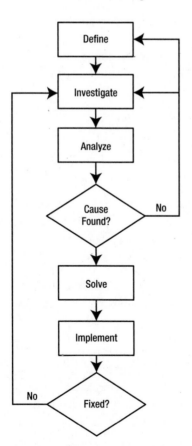

Figure 11-2. *Systematic five-step problem-solving method*

The Book We All Want and Best Practices for Problem Management

The book we all want is a book that has a clear description of every Oracle problem and step-by-step instructions for fixing them. That book will never be written. There are just too many problems that can occur. Problems can have multiple solutions. The solution may depend on *your particular circumstances*. In many cases, it is not even clear what the problem really is. The best you can do is to use best practices for problem management. Here are my suggestions:

- *Fix problems proactively*: Monitoring your database and preventing problems is better than fixing problems—for example, add space to a database before it fills up completely and jobs begin to fail.

- *Find the root cause of problems*: After the problem has been fixed, look for the underlying root cause—for example, find out why the database is growing and how much space will be needed over the medium term.

- *Use good tools*: A worker is only as good as his tools. The more tools you have, the better you will be equipped to solve a problem. Commonly used tools include Oracle-supplied tools such as Enterprise Manager and SQL Developer and third-party tools such as Toad from Quest Software and DBArtisan from Embarcadero Technologies.

- *Use standard operating procedures (SOPs)*: The two obvious advantages of standard operating procedures are consistency and efficiency, but there are many others. We will return to the subject of standard operating procedures in Chapter 15.

- *Document the database environment*: Remote Diagnostic Agent (RDA), introduced in Chapter 9, is a simple tool that you can use to document your environment. An RDA collection collects all the information about the database and operating system into one compact package that is very useful in solving problems.

- *Ask for help*: There are several online forums that can help you solve a problem. If you have an Oracle support contract, you can escalate a problem to an Oracle engineer. We will return to this subject later in this chapter.

- *Keep work records*: The most important thing to do is to keep work records. When a problem reoccurs, it helps to have access to the details of prior occurrences. Every environment is prone to certain problems—for example, Oracle Database 10.1.0.3 is affected by a bug that causes the nightly statistics gathering job GATHER_STATS_JOB to fail—the characteristic error code is ORA-00904.

■Note An IT organization without work records is like a dentist's office without dental records. Work records are one of the ten deliverables of the database administration role listed in Chapter 15.

Figure 11-3, courtesy of Database Specialists, proves the value of work records in solving chronic problems.

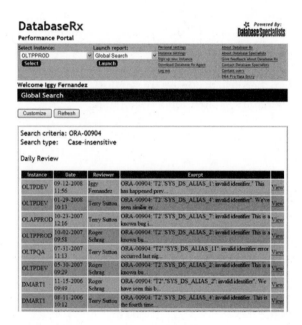

Figure 11-3. *Searching work records*

Real-Life Example—Unresponsive Listener

Here are the transcripts—with some editing to preserve confidentiality—of several instant messaging conversations between a DBA and another member of the IT staff. The problem puzzles the DBA the first time but is fixed very quickly the second time it occurs.

Define the Problem

A member of the IT staff tells the DBA that the database "seems to be locked up." This phase ends when the DBA is able to reproduce the problem—he cannot connect to the database from the reporting server. The DBA now has a clear definition of the problem.

```
User: help. our oracle database server seems to be locked up
User: if I do sql
User: it says cannot connect. I cannot connect from reporting server
DBA: ok let me try that
DBA: ok i cannot connect either
```

Investigate and Analyze the Problem

The DBA now begins looking for information that may shed light on the problem. The first thing he does is check the alert log. He finds that the database is healthy, and he is able to connect to it without going through the listener, that is, using a local session on the database server itself. This phase ends when he discovers that there are two listeners. This is apparently the cause of the problem, because the timestamp of the last good entry in the alert log coincides with the time when the second listener was started.

```
DBA: no errors in alert log
DBA: cpu and load average good check
DBA: without the @ i can connect
DBA: this tells me that the database is OK
DBA: connections to port 1521 are failing
User: listener ?
DBA: trying telnet localhost 1521 to find out if there is connectivity to the port
DBA: hmmmm there is
DBA: $ telnet localhost 1521
Trying 127.0.0.1...
Connected to localhost.localdomain (127.0.0.1).
Escape character is '^]'.
DBA: that is the behaviour i expect
DBA: can you try it from the reporting server
DBA: telnet should produce the same output
DBA: i.e. it should connect
User: ok. one sec
DBA: i.e. it should "connect" but not quite
DBA: i.e. it should detect somebody listening
DBA: but obviously there is no telnet daemon there
DBA: and it will hang
User: it hangs
DBA: same output as above
DBA: ok ...
DBA: the last connection recorded in tail
/local/service/oracle/product/10.2.0/db/network/log/listener.log
```

on the db server was at 14:17

DBA: it is now 15:05

DBA: 09-JUN-2007 14:17:47 *
(CONNECT_DATA=(SID=devdb)(CID=(PROGRAM=)(HOST=__jdbc__)(USER) *
(ADDRESS=(PROTOCOL=tcp)(HOST=127.0.0.1)(PORT=5009)) * establish * proddb * 0 09-JUN-
2007 14:17:47 * (CONNECT_DATA=(SID=devdb)(CID=(PROGRAM=)(HOST=__jdbc__)(USER) *
(ADDRESS=(PROTOCOL=tcp)(HOST=127.0.0.1)(PORT=5010)) * establish * proddb * 0

DBA: definitely a problem with the listener

DBA: but ....

DBA: my guess is that somehow the database server cannot talk to the world

DBA: the way it works is that ...

DBA: all traffic flows throught the 1521 port

DBA: both inbound and outbound

DBA: for all sessions

DBA: there is one unix process servicing each client process

DBA: but everybody talks over the 1521 port

DBA: looks like the report server can reach the 1521 port

DBA: but perhaps the db cannot talk back

DBA: aah i have it

DBA: $ ps -ef |grep lsnr

oracle 19832 1 0 Mar31 ? 00:05:40
/local/service/oracle/product/10.2.0/db/bin/tnslsnr LISTENER -inherit

oracle 19987 19832 0 14:17 ? 00:00:00
/local/service/oracle/product/10.2.0/db/bin/tnslsnr LISTENER -inherit

DBA: look carefully

DBA: two listeners

DBA: one at 14:17

DBA: the second process is the child of the first

Solve the Problem and Implement the Solution

Having determined that the second listener is the problem, the DBA first tries to shut down the listeners gracefully. When that fails, he uses the Unix kill command. The situation returns to normal as soon as the second listener is terminated. The DBA promises to research what caused the second listener to be started and why nobody was able to connect to the database as a result.

User: can we restart the listener

DBA: let me try

DBA: i cannot stop it the normal way

DBA: because the normal way involves conecting to it

DBA: lsnrctl hangs
User: aaah
DBA: $ lsnrctl status

LSNRCTL for Linux: Version 10.2.0.1.0 - Production on 09-JUN-2007 15:18:28

Copyright (c) 1991, 2005, Oracle. All rights reserved.

Connecting to (DESCRIPTION=(ADDRESS=(PROTOCOL=TCP)(HOST=127.0.0.1)(PORT=1521)))
DBA: hangs at that point
User: ok. makes sense. something is locked up in that process. may be one of the threads
DBA: ok killing both
User: yeah.
DBA: woo hoo
DBA: i killed the second process
DBA: i can connect now
DBA: SQL*Plus: Release 10.2.0.1.0 - Production on Wed Jun 9 15:21:32 2007

Copyright (c) 1982, 2005, Oracle. All rights reserved.

Connected to:
Oracle Database 10g Release 10.2.0.1.0 - Production

SQL> quit
Disconnected from Oracle Database 10g Release 10.2.0.1.0 - Production
DBA: it was failing before
DBA: check on the report server
User: yeah. it works fine now
User: great.
DBA: thanks ... two heads are better than one
User: I agree. It's good to know what happened. great. thanks.
DBA: i;ll do some research
DBA: on the phrase "two listeners"
User: ok. cool. gotta go. bye
DBA: l8r

One Week Later

When the problem occurred again, very little diagnosis and resolution time was required.

```
User: hi, the oracle server seems to have died last night. can you check. tks
DBA: really?
DBA: that's really bad
User: it was running level 0 backup y'day and I thought because of that queries were
timing out. but looks like it's hosed.
DBA: checking now
User: thank you!
DBA: it may be the same problem that we saw a week ago
DBA: dev
DBA: checking
DBA: yes ... two listeners
DBA: nobody can attach
User: hmmm
DBA: problem cleared
User: tks.
```

Opportunities for Improvement

The database administrator in this example has considerable Oracle experience and good problem-solving skills, but there are nevertheless several opportunities for improvement:

- The problem was reported to the DBA by a member of the IT staff, well after the problem started. There were no monitoring mechanisms in place to automatically alert the database administrator about the loss of service.

- There was no further investigation after the first incident. The problem had been fixed, but the root cause had not been determined. In this case, the listener log file contained many occurrences of the following message: `WARNING: Subscription for node down event still pending`. This would have been a good place to start the investigation.

Incident Management vs. Problem Management

An *incident* is a single occurrence of a problem. Incident management and problem management are therefore separate aspects of IT management. *Incident management* is concerned with restoring service as rapidly as possible. *Problem management* is concerned with permanently fixing defects so the incidents are not repeated.

In the real-life example in the preceding section, the organization gets high marks for incident management but low marks for problem management. Problem management is facilitated by record keeping—tools such as BMC Remedy Service Desk can be used for this purpose. Knowledge of the event was confined to the database administrator and the member of the IT staff who contacted him. Records were not kept, the incident was forgotten, and a second service outage occurred a week later.

Internet Resources

The Internet is a treasure trove of information that can help you in solving a problem. For example, user groups such as the Northern California Oracle Users Group (`http://www.nocoug.org`) have made vast collections of electronic presentations and white papers available on their web pages. Often a simple Google search will bring up an answer, but many specialized resources also are available:

- Online Oracle documentation

- Online forums

- Oracle Technology Network

- Ask Tom web site

- Usenet

- Oracle-L mailing list

The highest quality resource is of course the online Oracle documentation, which is shown in Figure 11-4. This documentation is freely viewable, searchable, and downloadable at `http://www.oracle.com/technology/documentation`.[1] Click the View Library link of any documentation set to get to the corresponding search page. Documentation for older versions of Oracle software going back to Oracle 7 is available here. If you need to be able to work offline, you can download as much documentation as you need.

■**Tip** Download the documentation you need to your desktop or laptop so you can browse the documentation while offline. Downloading the documentation to your computer is particularly advisable if you prefer the PDF versions. Because of the documents' large size, it is more efficient to browse through them while offline.

---

1. A subset of Oracle documentation is available at `http://tahiti.oracle.com`.

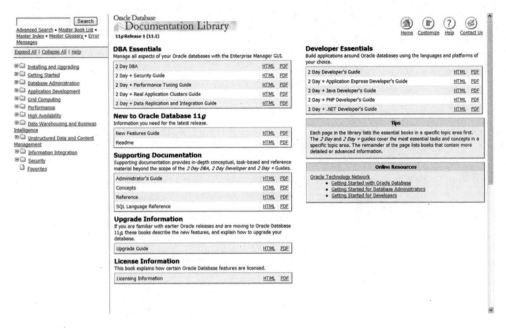

Figure 11-4. *Online Oracle documentation*

You also can ask questions on the Oracle forums (http://forums.oracle.com), shown in Figure 11-5. Many Oracle experts donate a lot of time answering questions posted here.

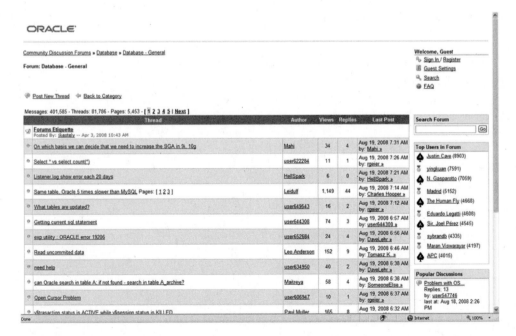

Figure 11-5. *The Oracle forums*

The Oracle Technology Network (http://otn.oracle.com) is an Oracle-sponsored site filled with useful resources including articles, sample code, and tutorials. It also contains links to the Oracle documentation and Oracle forums. Figure 11-6 shows the Oracle Technology Network.

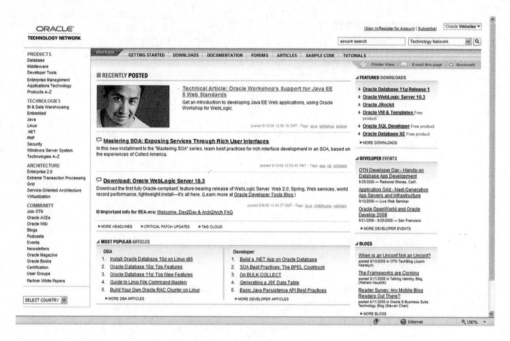

Figure 11-6. *The Oracle Technology Network*

Oracle author Tom Kyte has been answering Oracle questions for many years. His web site, Ask Tom, is now at http://asktom.oracle.com, as shown in Figure 11-7. He'll answer your question if he hasn't already answered a similar question before and if the answer would be of wide interest.

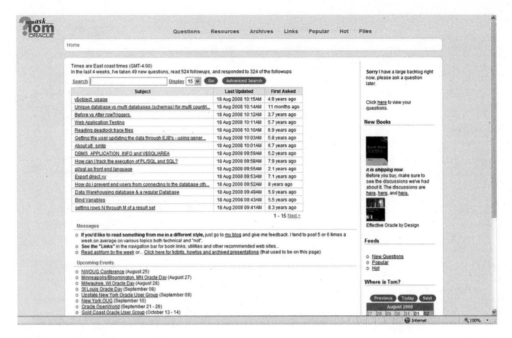

Figure 11-7. *The Ask Tom web site*

Another good place to ask questions is the Usenet newsgroup `comp.databases.oracle. server`, shown in Figure 11-8. Many Oracle experts donate a lot of time answering questions posted here. Most Internet service providers provide access to newsgroups, but you can also use a Google account to ask questions. A vast archive of past questions is hosted by Google (`http://groups.google.com`).

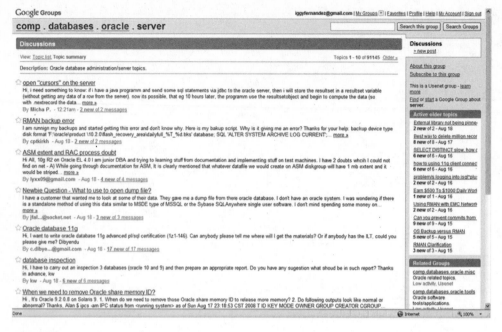

Figure 11-8. *The* `comp.databases.oracle.server` *Usenet group*

If you've exhausted other alternatives, consider asking your question to the subscribers of the Oracle-L mailing list. To ask a question, send an e-mail message to `oracle-l@freelists.org`. To subscribe or unsubscribe, send an e-mail message to `oracle-l-requests@freelists.org` with the word *subscribe* or *unsubscribe* in the subject line.

Working with Oracle Support

You can search the Oracle knowledge base (MetaLink) and obtain technical support from Oracle Support if you are paying annual support fees to Oracle and have a valid Customer Support Identifier (CSI). The support fees are typically 22 percent of the cost of your Oracle licenses. If you choose to forgo Oracle support, you will not be entitled to any patches (fixes for software bugs) or upgrades. The web page of Oracle Support is `http://metalink.oracle.com`, shown in Figure 11-9. The tabs on the page indicate the range of things that you can do here—for example, read the headlines, search the knowledge base, request service, download patches, participate in forums, and so forth.

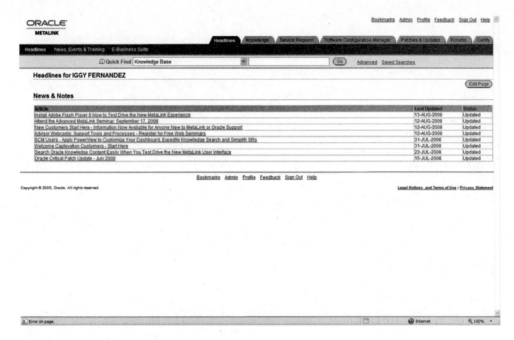

Figure 11-9. *Working with Oracle Support*

If you cannot find the answer in the Oracle knowledge base (Figure 11-10), you can create a service request (Figure 11-11). The priority of the service request and the corresponding service-level commitment depend on the impact to your organization. For instance, a production outage is classified as Severity 1 and is given the highest level of attention.

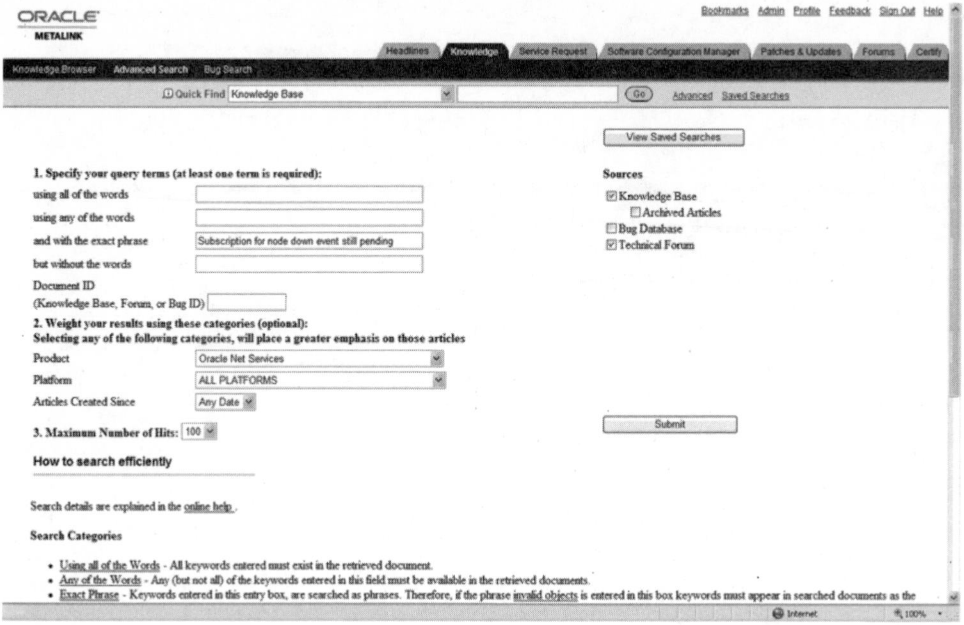

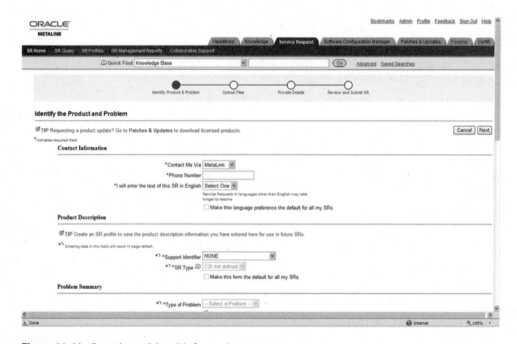

Figure 11-10. *Searching the MetaLink knowledge base*

Figure 11-11. *Creating a MetaLink service request*

Remote Diagnostic Agent (RDA)

We touched on RDA collections in Chapter 9. An RDA collection, shown in Figure 11-12, collects all the information about the database and operating system into one compact package that can be attached to a service request. The RDA collection eliminates the need for Oracle engineers to ask questions about the database environment and shortens the time required for problem resolution.

■**Tip** An RDA collection is a great problem-solving tool and facilitates collaboration among DBAs. A best practice for Oracle database administration is to install the RDA utility in every database environment to avoid losing time when faced with a severe problem that requires vendor support. Periodic RDA collections also serve as a record of changes to the database environment.

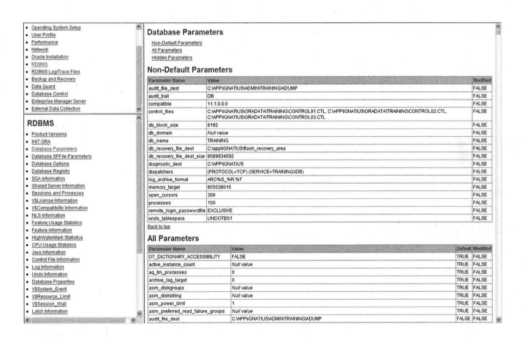

Figure 11-12. *An RDA collection*

Automatic Diagnostic Repository (ADR)

Beginning with Oracle Database 11*g*, the history of Oracle errors is stored in a directory structure called the Automatic Diagnostic Repository (ADR). Oracle provides a tool called adrci (ADR Command Interpreter) to query the ADR and to create packages containing diagnostic information. These packages can be attached to service requests. You will see an example of the use of adrci later in this chapter.

Error Codes

With a few exceptions such as locking problems, the most important symptom of a problem is the error code. These error codes are all listed in *Oracle Database 11g Error Messages*[2]—part of the Oracle documentation set—and there are literally tens of thousands of them. Here is a simple example featuring the very first Oracle error in the book, ORA-00001; the user is trying to insert a record that already exists:

```
C:\Documents and Settings\IGNATIUS>set ORACLE_SID=ORCL

C:\Documents and Settings\IGNATIUS>sqlplus ifernandez

SQL*Plus: Release 11.1.0.6.0 - Production on Sun Aug 24 04:52:44 2008

Copyright (c) 1982, 2007, Oracle.  All rights reserved.

Enter password:

Connected to:
Oracle Database 11g Enterprise Edition Release 11.1.0.6.0 - Production
With the Partitioning, OLAP, Data Mining and Real Application Testing options

SQL> INSERT INTO hr.employees
  2     SELECT *
  3        FROM hr.employees;
INSERT INTO hr.employees
*
ERROR at line 1:
ORA-00001: unique constraint (HR.EMP_EMAIL_UK) violated


SQL> exit
Disconnected from Oracle Database 11g Enterprise Edition Release 11.1.0.6.0 -
Production
With the Partitioning, OLAP, Data Mining and Real Application Testing options
```

■**Tip** When investigating a problem, the best question to ask is "What is the Oracle error code?" Sometimes applications mask the error code, and this hinders the investigation into a problem.

---

2. Searchable or downloadable free of charge at http://tahiti.oracle.com or at http://www.oracle.com/technology/documentation.

A very limited amount of advice about each Oracle error code is provided in *Oracle Database 11g Error Messages*. Here is what we find in the case of ORA-00001:

```
ORA-00001: unique constraint (string.string) violated
Cause: An UPDATE or INSERT statement attempted to insert a duplicate key. For
Trusted Oracle configured in DBMS MAC mode, you may see this message if a duplicate
entry exists at a different level.
Action: Either remove the unique restriction or do not insert the key.
```

■**Tip** Oracle supplies the `oerr` utility for Unix platforms; it displays the text of an error message as well as the cause and action. To display the text associated with ORA-00001, simply type `oerr ora 1`. This utility is not available for Windows, but Yong Huang has written a Windows version that is available at `yong321.` `freeshell.org/freeware/Windowsoerr.html`.

Notice that an Oracle error code has two parts: a facility code and a five-digit number, separated by a hyphen. Leading zeros are often omitted—for example, ORA-00600 and ORA-600 refer to the same error. Here is an example of an error message produced by the Recovery Manager (RMAN) tool:

```
RMAN-06171: not connected to target database
Cause: A command was issued but no connection to the target database has been
established.
Action: Issue a CONNECT TARGET command to connect to the target database.
```

You must learn to identify which Oracle error codes indicate problems with the infrastructure supported by the database administrator and which codes indicate errors made by a user or problems with an application. For example, Table 11-1 lists the standard named exceptions that are part of the PL/SQL programming language—they indicate problems with the application in question.

Table 11-1. *Named Exceptions in PL/SQL*

Name	Error Code
ACCESS_INTO_NULL	ORA-06530
COLLECTION_IS_NULL	ORA-06531
CURSOR_ALREADY_OPEN	ORA-06511
DUP_VAL_ON_INDEX	ORA-00001
INVALID_CURSOR	ORA-01001
INVALID_NUMBER	ORA-01722

(continued)

Table 11-1. *Continued.*

Name	Error Code
LOGIN_DENIED	ORA-01017
NO_DATA_FOUND	ORA-01403
NOT_LOGGED_ON	ORA-01012
PROGRAM_ERROR	ORA-06501
ROWTYPE_MISMATCH	ORA-06504
SELF_IS_NULL	ORA-30625
STORAGE_ERROR	ORA-06500
SUBSCRIPT_BEYOND_COUNT	ORA-06533
SUBSCRIPT_OUTSIDE_LIMIT	ORA-06532
SYS_INVALID_ROWID	ORA-01410
TIMEOUT_ON_RESOURCE	ORA-00051
TOO_MANY_ROWS	ORA-01422
VALUE_ERROR	ORA-06502
ZERO_DIVIDE	ORA-01476

■**Tip** Errors reported in the Oracle alert log usually represent infrastructure errors. A good example is
ORA-01653: Unable to extend table HR.EMPLOYEES by 1024 in tablespace EXAMPLE.

Four Errors

I have enough space to discuss only a few errors. I selected the following four errors for
discussion because they are common and frequently misunderstood.

ORA-01555: Snapshot Too Old

Here is the minimal explanation of the ORA-01555 error that you will find in *Oracle Database 11g Error Messages*:

```
ORA-01555: Snapshot too old; rollback segment number string with name "string" too
small
Cause: rollback records needed by a reader for consistent read are overwritten by
other writers
Action: If in Automatic Undo Management mode, increase undo_retention setting.
Otherwise, use larger rollback segments
```

Consider a query that begins at 9 a.m. and completes at 10 a.m. Suppose that the query is counting the number of records in a very large table and suppose that the table is very active—that is, records are constantly being inserted into the table. Suppose that Oracle's answer to the query is ten billion records. Does the answer indicate the number of records at 9 a.m., at 10 a.m., or at some intermediate time in between those times?

If we were working with other database technologies such as IBM's DB2 or Informix, Microsoft's SQL Server, or Sybase, the answer would be 10 a.m. because the query would not complete until it had locked all the records in the table; it would wait for all insert, update, and delete operations to complete and it would block others from starting. In other words, readers block writers, and writers block readers. With Oracle, on the other hand, readers do *not* block writers, and writers do *not* block readers. Instead, Oracle determines what the answer to the query would have been at the instant the query *started*, that is, at 9 a.m.; this manner of operation is called *read consistency*.[3] Read consistency extends to a single query by default or can extend to an entire transaction. For example, the entire contents of a database can be exported by using read-consistent mode to ensure that there are no conflicts or inconsistencies in the data.

To ensure read consistency, Oracle must construct a snapshot of the database at the time the query or transaction started. If the required data has changed since the query started, Oracle must obtain a prior version of the data from the rollback segments. However, the rollback segments are a shared resource, and the information they contain may be overwritten if other transactions need the space. Therefore, Oracle may not be able to construct the snapshot—that is, the snapshot may be *too old to be reconstructed*.

Prior to Oracle 9*i*, the number and size of rollback segments was left to the database administrator. Beginning with Oracle 9*i*, this task should be entrusted to Oracle by changing the value of the UNDO_MANAGEMENT setting to AUTO. If the Snapshot too old error occurs, increase the value of the UNDO_RETENTION setting and ensure, through trial and error, that the tablespace specified by the UNDO_TABLESPACE setting is big enough, adding data files or increasing the size of data files as necessary. The default value of the UNDO_RETENTION setting is 900 seconds (15 minutes); a large value such as 14,400 (4 hours) may be more appropriate, depending on the circumstances, but must be supported by an undo tablespace that is large enough. Note that the Snapshot too old error can never be completely avoided because it is always possible for queries to take so long that the available resources are exhausted. Also, transactions that modify the data typically take precedence over transactions that read the data—that is, the modified transactions will overwrite the information in the rollback segments if space is short, irrespective of the value of the UNDO_RETENTION setting. This can be prevented by imposing a *retention guarantee* on the undo tablespace by using the ALTER TABLESPACE command. More care than usual must be taken to ensure that the undo tablespace is adequately sized if a retention guarantee is in effect.

---

3. SQL Server offers read consistency beginning with SQL Server 2005. However, it is not the default manner of operation.

ORA-00060: Deadlock Detected

Once again, we see only a minimal explanation in *Oracle Database 11g Error Messages*:

```
ORA-00060: deadlock detected while waiting for resource
Cause: Transactions deadlocked one another while waiting for resources.
Action: Look at the trace file to see the transactions and resources involved. Retry
if necessary.
```

This error is frequently encountered but is one of the least understood Oracle errors. A *deadlock* is a situation in which two transactions interfere with each other; each is waiting for a lock on a resource locked by the other. *The correct thing for the application to do when this error is received is to issue the* ROLLBACK *command and retry the transaction.*

Create two tables, PARENT and CHILD, related to each other by a referential constraint (foreign key), and populate them with data by using the following commands:

```
CREATE TABLE parent (
  parent_ID INTEGER NOT NULL,
  CONSTRAINT parent_PK PRIMARY KEY (parent_id)
);

CREATE TABLE child (
  child_ID INTEGER NOT NULL,
  parent_ID INTEGER NOT NULL,
  CONSTRAINT child_PK PRIMARY KEY (child_id),
  CONSTRAINT child_FK FOREIGN KEY (parent_ID) references parent
);

INSERT INTO parent (parent_ID) values (1);
INSERT INTO parent (parent_ID) values (2);
INSERT INTO child (child_ID, parent_ID) values (1,1);
INSERT INTO child (child_ID, parent_ID) values (2,2);
```

Suppose that two users try to delete the data from the CHILD table, but each deletes records in a different order. At step 3 in the following example, user A will be blocked because user B has already locked the requested record. User B will be blocked in turn at step 4, and a deadlock results. To resolve the deadlock, Oracle picks either user A or user B as a victim, and any effects of the last command issued by the victim are rolled back. To allow the other user to proceed, the victim must then issue the ROLLBACK command to release any other locks it still holds—it can then retry its transaction:

```
/* Step 1: User A */ DELETE FROM child WHERE child_ID=1;

/* Step 2: User B */ DELETE FROM child WHERE child_ID=2;
```

```
/* Step 3: User A */ DELETE FROM child WHERE child_ID=1;

/* Step 4: User B */ DELETE FROM child WHERE child_ID=2;
```

In the preceding example, two users are modifying the *same* data. Deadlock also occurs in the next example, *even though the users are modifying different data.* At step 3, user A will be blocked because Oracle needs to verify the absence of child records before deleting a parent record. In the absence of an index on the child_ID column of the Child table, Oracle attempts to lock the entire Child table and is prevented from doing so because user A has a lock on one of the records in the table. User B is blocked in turn at step 4, and a deadlock results:

```
/* Step 1: User A */ DELETE FROM child WHERE child_ID=1;

/* Step 2: User B */ DELETE FROM child WHERE child_ID=2;

/* Step 3: User A */ DELETE FROM parent WHERE parent_ID=1;

/* Step 4: User B */ DELETE FROM parent WHERE parent_ID=2;
```

Defects in database design such as un-indexed foreign keys can increase the frequency of deadlocks, but deadlocks can happen any time more than one user is using the database. All database programs must anticipate the possibility and take the appropriate action when a deadlock happens—that is, *issue the* ROLLBACK *command and retry the transaction.*

ORA-00600: Internal Error Code

Oracle reports an ORA-00600 error in the alert log whenever it encounters an unexpected condition—the frequent cause is an Oracle bug—and stops processing the SQL statement it was processing at the time. Here is the verbiage from *Oracle Database 11g Error Messages*:

```
ORA-00600: internal error code, arguments: [string], [string], [string], [string],
[string], [string], [string], [string]
Cause: This is the generic internal error number for Oracle program exceptions. This
indicated that a process encountered an exceptional condition.
Action: Report as a bug - the first argument is the internal error number.
```

■**Caution** ORA-00600 errors should *always* be investigated, and the DBA should confirm that the error was not triggered by a corrupted data block.

Here is an example of an ORA-00600 incident, from detection to diagnosis. The following code will produce an ORA-00600 error in Oracle Database 11.1.0.6. Notice that an ORA-00600 error has a number of arguments, each enclosed in square brackets. The first such argument is the most important and is used to further classify the error.

```
C:\Documents and Settings\IGNATIUS>sqlplus ifernandez

SQL*Plus: Release 11.1.0.6.0 - Production on Sun Aug 17 06:53:23 2008

Copyright (c) 1982, 2007, Oracle.  All rights reserved.

Enter password:

Connected to:
Oracle Database 11g Enterprise Edition Release 11.1.0.6.0 - Production
With the Partitioning, OLAP, Data Mining and Real Application Testing options

SQL> CREATE OR REPLACE FUNCTION xml_decode (i_xml_string IN VARCHAR2)
  2      RETURN VARCHAR2
  3  IS
  4  BEGIN
  5      RETURN DBMS_XMLGEN.CONVERT (i_xml_string, DBMS_XMLGEN.entity_decode);
  6  END;
  7  /

Function created.

SQL> SELECT xml_decode
  2             ('The owl & the pussycat went to sea'
  3             ) AS decoded_xml
  4      FROM DUAL;
SELECT xml_decode
       *
ERROR at line 1:
ORA-00600: internal error code, arguments: [qmxtcCtxConvertString], [44], [44],
[], [], [], [], []
ORA-06512: at "SYS.DBMS_XMLGEN", line 19
ORA-06512: at "SYS.DBMS_XMLGEN", line 295
ORA-06512: at "IFERNANDEZ.XML_DECODE", line 5
```

The first thing to do is to check the Oracle alert log. If you've forgotten where it is, you can check the value of the BACKGROUND_DUMP_DEST setting:

```
SQL> SHOW parameter background_dump_dest;

NAME                                 TYPE          VALUE
------------------------------------ ------------- ------------------------------
background_dump_dest                 string        c:\app\ignatius\diag\rdbms\orc
                                                   l\orcl\trace
```

Here is what was seen in the Oracle alert log. The alert log indicated that full details would be found in a trace file:

```
Sun Aug 17 06:55:42 2008
Errors in file c:\app\ignatius\diag\rdbms\orcl\orcl\trace\orcl_ora_2300.trc
(incident=93862):
ORA-00600: internal error code, arguments: [qmxtcCtxConvertString], [44], [44], [],
[], [], [], []
Incident details in:
c:\app\ignatius\diag\rdbms\orcl\orcl\incident\incdir_93862\orcl_ora_2300_i93862.trc
Sun Aug 17 06:55:47 2008
Trace dumping is performing id=[cdmp_20080817065547]
Sun Aug 17 06:55:49 2008
Sweep Incident[93862]: completed
```

Here are the first few lines from the trace file mentioned in the alert log. This file lists the SQL statement that resulted in the ORA-00600 error and the call stack. The *call stack* is the nested sequence of C-language routines invoked by the Oracle server process that handled the query.

```
Dump file
c:\app\ignatius\diag\rdbms\orcl\orcl\incident\incdir_93862\orcl_ora_2300_i93862.trc
Oracle Database 11g Enterprise Edition Release 11.1.0.6.0 - Production
With the Partitioning, OLAP, Data Mining and Real Application Testing options
Windows XP Version V5.1 Service Pack 2
CPU                  : 2 - type 586
Process Affinity     : 0x00000000
Memory (Avail/Total): Ph:188M/2037M, Ph+PgF:1550M/3930M, VA:1223M/2047M
Instance name: orcl
Redo thread mounted by this instance: 1
Oracle process number: 31
Windows thread id: 2300, image: ORACLE.EXE (SHAD)
```

```
*** 2008-08-17 06:55:42.615
*** SESSION ID:(128.5) 2008-08-17 06:55:42.615
*** CLIENT ID:() 2008-08-17 06:55:42.615
*** SERVICE NAME:(SYS$USERS) 2008-08-17 06:55:42.615
*** MODULE NAME:(SQL*Plus) 2008-08-17 06:55:42.615
*** ACTION NAME:() 2008-08-17 06:55:42.615


Dump continued from file:
c:\app\ignatius\diag\rdbms\orcl\orcl\trace\orcl_ora_2300.trc
ORA-00600: internal error code, arguments: [qmxtcCtxConvertString], [44], [44], [],
[], [], [], []


========= Dump for incident 93862 (ORA 600 [qmxtcCtxConvertString]) ========


*** 2008-08-17 06:55:42.615
----- Current SQL Statement for this session (sql_id=14vkwj71tm4jp) -----
SELECT xml_decode
            ('The owl & the pussycat went to sea'
            ) AS decoded_xml
  FROM DUAL
----- PL/SQL Stack -----
----- PL/SQL Call Stack -----
  object       line  object
  handle     number  name
27BFA604         19  package body SYS.DBMS_XMLGEN
27BFA604        295  package body SYS.DBMS_XMLGEN
29636544          5  function IFERNANDEZ.XML_DECODE


----- Call Stack Trace -----
calling               call    entry                argument values in hex
location              type    point                (? means dubious value)
-------------------   ------  -------------------  ----------------------------
_skdstdst()+114       CALLrel _kgdsdst()+0         30336A14 2
_ksedst1()+91         CALLrel _skdstdst()+0
_ksedst()+50          CALLrel _ksedst1()+0         0 1
_dbkedDefDump()+298   CALLrel _ksedst()+0          0
5
_ksedmp()+40          CALLrel _dbkedDefDump()+0    3 2
_ksfdmp()+21          CALLrel _ksedmp()+0          3EB
```

Next, we use the `adrci` tool and create a package of information that can be sent to Oracle Support. The specific command is `ips` (Incident Packaging Service). Notice that ADR differentiates between a problem and an incident:

```
C:\Documents and Settings\IGNATIUS>adrci

ADRCI: Release 11.1.0.6.0 - Beta on Sun Aug 17 07:39:41 2008

Copyright (c) 1982, 2007, Oracle.  All rights reserved.

ADR base = "c:\app\ignatius"
adrci> set homepath diag\rdbms\orcl\orcl
adrci> show problem

ADR Home = c:\app\ignatius\diag\rdbms\orcl\orcl:
*************************************************************************
PROBLEM_ID           PROBLEM_KEY
LAST_INCIDENT        LASTINC_TIME
-------------------- -----------------------------------------------------------
-------------------- ----------------------------------------
4                    ORA 600 [qmxtcCtxConvertString]
93862                2008-08-17 06:55:42.568000 -07:00
3                    ORA 7445 [PC:0x7C9106C3]
44589                2007-11-28 15:41:50.468000 -08:00
2                    ORA 1578
36156                2007-11-27 08:58:14.531000 -08:00
1                    ORA 7445 [PC:0x7C911F6C]
9769                 2007-11-20 06:53:33.843000 -08:00
4 rows fetched

adrci> ips create package incident 93862
Created package 1 based on incident id 93862, correlation level typical
adrci> ips generate package 1 in c:\temp
Generated package 1 in file c:\temp\ORA600qmx_20080817074039_COM_1.zip, mode
complete
adrci> exit
```

An alternative to creating a service request is to research the problem ourselves by using the MetaLink knowledge base. Specifically, we have to use a search tool called the ORA-00600 Troubleshooter, shown in Figure 11-13. We have to provide the first argument of the ORA-00600 error that we encountered and the first 15 lines of the call stack.

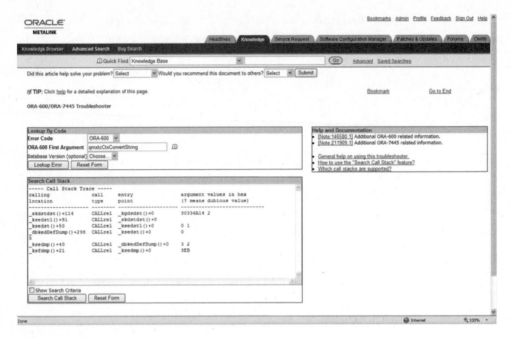

Figure 11-13. *Using the ORA-600 Troubleshooter*

When we click the Lookup Error button, Oracle shows us a research note discussing our particular error, as shown in Figure 11-14. We see that the error was caused by an Oracle bug.

Finally, we can click the link to the bug description, shown in Figure 11-15. We see that the problem has been fixed in Oracle Database 11.1.0.7.

Figure 11-14. *A MetaLink research note*

Figure 11-15. *A MetaLink bug report*

ORA-07445: Exception Encountered

An ORA-07445 error causes the instant termination of the Oracle server process that was handling the query being processed at the time. This sort of error occurs when an Oracle server process attempts to perform an illegal operation such as reading an area of memory that is not allocated to it—the operating system detects the illegal operation and forces the Oracle server process to shut itself down. ORA-00600 and ORA-7445 errors should be handled in the exact same way.

Summary

Here is a short summary of the concepts touched on in this chapter:

- Our activities can be divided among four quadrants depending on their urgency and importance. The ideal place to spend time is the quadrant of activities that are important but not urgent—for example, keeping records, identifying the root causes of incidents and eliminating them, updating documentation, and automating common tasks.

- The first step in solving a problem is to *define* the problem. The second step is to *investigate* the problem. The third step is to *analyze* the data. The fourth step is to *solve* the problem. The last step is to *implement* the solution in a safe and controlled manner.

- Best practices for problem management include fixing problems proactively, finding the root cause of problems, using good tools, using standard operating procedures, using RDA collections, and keeping work records.

- An *incident* is a single occurrence of a problem. *Incident management* is concerned with restoring service as rapidly as possible. *Problem management* is concerned with permanently fixing defects so the incidents are not repeated.

- High-quality Internet resources include the Oracle documentation site, Oracle Technology Network, the online forums, Ask Tom, the Usenet newsgroup `comp.databases.oracle.server`, and the Oracle-L mailing list.

- If you have purchased an Oracle support contract, you can search the Oracle knowledge base MetaLink and escalate problems to the Oracle Support team.

- The history of Oracle errors is stored in a directory structure called the Automatic Diagnostic Repository (ADR). Oracle provides a tool called `adrci` (ADR Command Interpreter) to query the ADR and to create packages containing diagnostic information to send to the Oracle Support team.

- An Oracle error code has two parts: a facility code and a five digit number, separated by a hyphen. The DBA must learn to identify which Oracle error codes indicate problems with the database infrastructure and which codes indicate errors made by a user or a problem with an application. The named exceptions defined by PL/SQL are examples of error codes that indicate problems in the application, not in the database infrastructure.

- An ORA-01555: Snapshot too old error message means that the query has taken so long that the undo information required to re-create the required read-consistent snapshot of the database has been overwritten by other transactions—that is, the snapshot is too old to be reconstructed.

- An ORA-00060: Deadlock detected error message means that Oracle detected that two transactions are blocking each other and picked one of them as a victim. The appropriate action that the victim must take is to issue the ROLLBACK command and retry its transaction.

- An ORA-00600: Internal error code error message indicates that Oracle encountered an unexpected condition and stopped processing the query in question. ORA-00600 errors should always be investigated, and the DBA should confirm that they were not triggered by corrupted data blocks.

- An ORA-07445: Exception encountered error message means that the Oracle server process attempted to perform an illegal operation and was forced to terminate itself by the operating system.

Exercises

- Review the listener problem that was the subject of the IM conversations printed in this chapter. Use any of the resources listed in this chapter to determine the root cause of the problem and find the permanent fix.

- Reproduce one of the deadlock examples in your database. Check whether any messages are recorded in the alert log. Check whether a trace file is produced and review it. What happens if the victim simply retries its last SQL command instead of issuing the ROLLBACK command and retrying its entire transaction?

- Stop after step 3 of one of the deadlock examples. Session A is now blocked by session B, but Oracle cannot take any action because this is not yet a deadlock scenario. Use a GUI tool such as SQL Developer, Enterprise Manager, Toad, or DBArtisan to identify the blocking process and terminate it.

- In what kind of problem scenarios might users not receive any error messages?

- The users are complaining that their application is behaving sluggishly. How would you check the database environment for signs of trouble?

- Categorize the following errors into user errors and infrastructure errors. What should be done to fix each of them?

```
ORA-01017: invalid username/password; logon denied
ORA-00923: FROM keyword not found where expected
ORA-01653: unable to extend table HR.EMPLOYEES by 128 in tablespace EXAMPLE
ORA-12154: TNS:could not resolve the connect identifier specified
ORA-12541: TNS:no listener
ORA-12514: TNS:listener does not currently know of service requested in
connect descriptor
```

- What defect, if any, do you observe in the following PL/SQL code segment?

```
WHEN OTHERS THEN  -- handles all other errors
    dbms_output.put_line('Some other kind of error occurred.');
```

- Review the ORA-00600 example discussed in this chapter. Is it caused by an Oracle defect or a shortcoming in the application? What value should be passed to the CONVERT function (instead of ENTITY_DECODE) to avoid the problem?

Further Reading

Alapati, Sam. *Expert Oracle Database 11g Administration.* Apress, 2008. A useful reference for the intermediate to experienced DBA.

Lawson, Christopher. *The Art and Science of Oracle Performance Tuning.* Apress, 2003. This book has not been updated for Oracle Database 10g and 11g, but the 5-step method it teaches is as valid today as it was when the book was written. I highly recommend it.

CHAPTER 12

■ ■ ■

Backups

As to our Conduct in the Affair of Extinguishing Fires, tho' we do not want Hands or Good-Will, yet we seem to want Order and Method, and therefore I believe I cannot do better than to offer for our Imitation, the Example of a City in a Neighbouring Province. There is, as I am well inform'd, a Club or Society of active Men belonging to each Fire Engine; whose Business is to attend all Fires with it whenever they happen; and to work it once a Quarter, and see it kept in order.

—Benjamin Franklin, in an anonymous letter to the *Pennsylvania Gazette* (of which he was the editor), following a disastrous fire in Philadelphia in the 18th century

American national hero Benjamin Franklin often wrote anonymous letters to the *Pennsylvania Gazette*, a prominent newspaper that he himself owned and edited. In one such letter he coined the famous phrase "an ounce of prevention is worth a pound of cure" and, in addition to making several suggestions for the prevention of fires, he suggested that Philadelphia imitate his native Boston in establishing fire stations and employing firefighters; not only should all efforts be made to prevent fires but the city should be adequately prepared to handle the next inevitable fire.

Backups are to a database what fire stations and fire fighters are to a city; we may protect the database against damage the best we can, but we must be prepared if the database ever gets damaged, through user or operator error or hardware failure, and needs to be repaired. A backup is a snapshot of a database or a part of a database; if the database is damaged, the damaged parts can be repaired using the backups. Archived logs can be used in conjunction with backups to replay transactions that changed data after the backup was performed. This chapter describes how to create various kinds of backups; the next chapter describes how to use them to repair databases. The impatient reader may note that a backup can be created with two simple words: BACKUP DATABASE but, as the leading mind of the European renaissance, Leonardo da Vinci, said: "*Those who are in love with practice without knowledge are like the sailor who gets into a ship without rudder or compass and who never can be certain whether he is going. Practice must always be founded on sound theory.*"

Why Do You Need Backups?

Oracle guru Tom Kyte likes to say that "*Why* is probably the right answer." "*Why do you need backups?*" is a wise question because consideration of the answer will dictate your backup strategy; it might even determine whether you need backups at all. Backups consume resources: disk space, tapes, CPU cycles, IO bandwidth, network bandwidth, tape drive bandwidth, operator time, and so on. None of those are free. The necessary hardware and software are not free, either. Consider, for example, the following scenarios"

- A new version of the application is to be deployed, and many objects in the database will be modified. The developers have requested that a backup be created just before the new version is deployed. However, you might be able to recover the database using previous backups and archived redo logs, and a new backup may not be necessary. Also, you can use Oracle "flashback" technology to recover the database without using backups at all. If the database is very large but only a small portion will be affected by the new deployment, an alternative might be to duplicate the tables that will be affected, using CREATE TABLE AS commands— the original data can be restored from the duplicate tables if the deployment is unsuccessful.

- Consider a "reporting database" that only contains *materialized views*[1] that reflect the data in other databases. If the materialized views become damaged, they can be completely refreshed using the original data. The entire database could be re-created from scripts. In this scenario, one does not need good *backups*; one just needs good *scripts.*

- I once managed a database named "Flatline" that was used to store archived data that had been deleted from the transactional databases but needed to be retained for an extended period for legal reasons. New data was only loaded into the database once a month. Obviously, it needed backups only once a month.

- Oracle provides *read-only tablespaces* for archived data. These don't need as many backups as the rest of the database.

An appropriate backup strategy is one that meets the needs of the business while remaining cost-effective. A different strategy might be needed for each database in the enterprise, the goal being to "provide cost-effective stewardship of the IT assets and

---

1. A *materialized view* is an SQL statement that has been precomputed, or materialized. These views are typically used to *pre-join* tables in the interest of computational efficiency. Their contents are typically not as accurate as the contents of the tables referenced in the SQL expression, but they are useful in situations such as month-end reporting where the most recent data is not required. Another typical use is to store a local copy of data from a remote database.

resources used in providing IT services."[2] Mission-critical databases such as those used in e-commerce have the most demanding requirements. The requirement for a mission-critical e-commerce database might be to "make backups without impacting database performance and quickly recover from failures." Such a requirement typically dictates the use of advanced hardware and software, with all the associated cost. For example, advanced options such as parallel backup, parallel recovery, single-block recovery, and "database flashback" are only available with the Enterprise Edition of Oracle Database 11g.

Horror Stories

All of the following stories are true, based on personal experience—mine.

A deployment of a new version of a business application was unsuccessful, and the database administrator was asked to undo the changes made to the database by recovering the database from the previous night's backups and the redo logs. He discovered that the backup script that was scheduled to run every night had been failing for three months; its defect was that it did not send an alert to the database administrator when it failed in its task. Luckily the redo logs were being copied to a file server and none of the archived redo logs had been deleted. The database administrator restored the database from the last good backup and started applying the redo logs to recover the missing transactions. Even the tiniest damage to any of the archived redo logs would have abruptly terminated the recovery operation but, luckily, none of the redo logs were damaged.

■**Tip** Implement a script that checks whether the database has been successfully backed up. This script should be *separate* from the backup script. Also consider daily and weekly reports listing backup successes and failures for all databases in the enterprise—such reports are also useful for tracking how data volumes and backup times are growing.

A new database administrator was creating a new database and was told by a system administrator that the system administration team handled all aspects of backup. The database administrator took him at his word but unfortunately, this particular server had been built using a new standard; the database administration team was responsible for backups, not the system administration team. This mission-critical database was used for a whole year before and then decommissioned. It had never been backed up.

---

2. This is the goal of financial management, as stated in the IT Service Management (ITSM) literature. I'll discuss ITSM in Chapter 15.

> **Tip** Backups should be tested periodically. A recovery test should be conducted before a database is put to use.

A database administrator had disabled an automated backup script one night because it would conflict with a deployment of a new version of a business application. The deployment failed and the database in question was successfully restored to its previous state using the previous night's backup and redo logs. However, the database administrator forgot to re-enable the automated backup script. One month later, there was another application deployment, which also failed. This time, the database could not be restored and the data had to be manually re-created.

It happened to me—it could happen to you!

Types of Backup

It bears repeating that an appropriate backup strategy is one that meets the needs of the business while remaining cost-effective. You have many choices to make; I'll describe some of them here.

Tape Backups vs. Disk Backups

The two main storage choices are tape and disk. Each choice has advantages and disadvantages. It is generally accepted that disk backups are not a substitute for tape backups. A common practice is to make backup copies on disk when possible and have them copied to tape in a separate operation.

Advantages and Disadvantages of Tape Backups

On the plus side, tapes are relatively cheap compared to disks, which means that multiple backups can be retained without too much expense; multiple backups obviously offer extra protection. Tapes are also more reliable than disks; disks are electromechanical devices and therefore more prone to failure. Also, tapes are serial-access devices and can achieve very high sustained reading and writing speeds.

On the minus side, the process of retrieving a single file from tapes is slower than with disks because the serial nature of tapes requires that the entire preceding portions be read first. Also, tapes are usually not kept online; they are typically ejected from the tape drive and may even be sent offsite for storage in secure fireproof facilities—for this reason they may not be readily available in an emergency. A database administrator working remotely might not be able to initiate database recovery without the assistance of "remote hands" to perform actions like inserting tapes into a tape drive. Also, tape backup management is itself a specialized IT activity; the database administrator may need assistance from IT personnel with the required knowledge.

In general, tapes are faster in serial-access situations, such as copying large numbers of files to a blank tape. They are slower in random-access situations, such as retrieving one file from tape.

Advantages and Disadvantages of Disk Backups

On the plus side, backup and recovery can be initiated by the database administrator without "remote hands" assistance and without requiring specialized knowledge of the tape backup technology that is being used.

On the minus side, disks are relatively expensive compared to tape, which means that the available capacity is usually much more limited and there may not be enough space available to create a backup copy of the database, let alone multiple backups.

Full Backups vs. Partial Backups

Backups require the use of computer resources such as storage disks and storage tapes as well as memory, CPU cycles, and network bandwidth. They must therefore be scheduled so as not to interfere with normal database operations; typically, they are scheduled for nights and weekends. If the database is very large, we may not have the time and resources to create a backup of the entire database in a single operation; instead, we might spread the activity over the course of a week and create a backup of just a portion of the database every night. Also, some portions of the database may be designated as *read-only*, and it is not necessary to create multiple backups of this data.

Level 0 Backups vs. Level 1 Backups

A full backup is also called a *level 0* backup. This is a backup containing every data block. A *level 1* backup is one that contains only those data blocks that have changed since the level 0 backup. A level 1 backup is also called an *incremental* backup. A level 0 backup might be created on weekends when there is plenty of time available, and a level 1 backup might be created every night when there is less time available. A feature called *block change tracking* can be used to avoid having to examine every block; the changed blocks are listed in the *block change tracking file*.

Physical Backups vs. Logical Backups

The term *physical backup* refers to exact copies of data blocks and data files produced by a tool such as Recovery Manager (RMAN). The term *logical backup* refers to a structured copy of the data in the tables such as is produced by Data Pump Export or a `CREATE TABLE AS SELECT` command.

A logical backup can be much smaller than the corresponding physical backup because there is typically much unused space within the data blocks and the data files and because the database contains index data in addition to table data. However, logical backups cannot be used to restore the database; they can only be used to re-create the *data* within an otherwise functional database.

If the database (or part of it) is restored from physical backups, then the redo logs can be used to recover all modifications to the data made since the physical backup was initiated. If a logical backup is used to re-create data, any modifications to the data made after the logical backup was initiated are lost.

Consistent Backups vs. Inconsistent Backups

Many databases are used around-the-clock; if the data in the database is being modified while the backup is being created, the backup might contain internal consistencies because each data block in the database is visited just once during a backup operation and any subsequent changes to the block will not be captured. The only way to guarantee a consistent backup is to make the database unavailable and prevent changes during the backup operation. However, inconsistent physical backups are very useful because the information contained in the redo log files can be used to fix any inconsistencies in such backups.

Hot vs. Cold Backups

Hot backups (also called *online backups*) are backups that are created while the database (or relevant portion thereof) is accessible by users and can be modified while the backup is underway. *Cold backups* (also called *offline backups*) are backups that are created while the database (or relevant portion thereof) is inaccessible and cannot be modified while the backup is underway.

Hot backup and *online backup* are generally considered synonymous with *inconsistent backup*, while *cold backup* and *offline backup* are considered synonymous with *consistent backup*. However, if the database was not shut down gracefully, a cold backup also may contain inconsistencies. And it is possible to make a consistent *logical* backup of the database while the database is online. Finally note that an online backup of a portion of the database that cannot be modified (for example, a "read-only" table space) is guaranteed to be consistent.

Oracle-Managed Backups vs. User-Managed Backups

Backups created using Recovery Manager (RMAN) are called *Oracle-managed backups* and backups created by other methods are called *user-managed backups*. For example, Network Appliance provides an advanced technology that can be used to create snapshots of the largest databases in seconds or minutes by recording only the *addresses* of the blocks in the database instead of the *data* contained in the blocks—a copy of a block is only made if the data in one of these blocks is subsequently changed.

Advantages of Oracle-Managed Backups

Backups created using Recovery Manager have many advantages:

- Arguably, the biggest advantage of Recovery Manager is the ease of use. The entire database can be backed up with the simple words BACKUP DATABASE.

- Another great advantage of Recovery Manager is that it stores history data. The history data is needed during recovery operations, but it can be queried by the database administrator at any time; a typical use is to verify that the database has been backed up.

- Recovery Manager offers features that are not available anywhere else. Examples are incremental backups, detection of corrupted blocks, and recovery of single blocks.

Advantages of User-Managed Backups

Some types of user-managed backups offer great advantages. For example, snapshot technology has the advantage of lightning speed of both backup and recovery. Making a backup of a file is lightning fast because it only requires that the addresses of blocks be recorded, not the data contained in the blocks—recovery of a file is also lightning fast because it only requires that one list of block addresses be switched with another. The best of both worlds is achieved when snapshots are registered in the Recovery Manager repository—this allows Recovery Manager to use the snapshots for database recovery.

Practical Demonstration: Physical Backups

Here is a practical demonstration of the use of RMAN to create a backup copy of the database. As you will see, this can be accomplished with a few short commands. First we give NLS_DATE_FORMAT an appropriate value—it controls the format in which dates are displayed. When we invoke RMAN, it displays version information and gives us a command prompt:

```
C:\Documents and Settings\IGNATIUS>set ORACLE_SID=ORCL

C:\Documents and Settings\IGNATIUS>set NLS_DATE_FORMAT=YYYY/MM/DD HH24:MI

C:\Documents and Settings\IGNATIUS>rman

Recovery Manager: Release 11.1.0.6.0 - Production on Sun Sep 7 15:18:48 2008

Copyright (c) 1982, 2007, Oracle.  All rights reserved.
```

Next we establish a command session with the database using the command CONNECT TARGET. RMAN displays the database name (ORCL in this case) and the *DBID*, a unique numeric identifier used to distinguish between databases with the same name:

```
RMAN> CONNECT TARGET;

connected to target database: ORCL (DBID=1192595344)
```

All that remains is to instruct RMAN to make a backup copy of the database. RMAN first tells us that information about the backup will be stored in the control file of the database instead of a separate *recovery catalog*, a separate Oracle database dedicated to storing information about database backups. RMAN then opens a "channel" to the backup location but then runs into a problem. RMAN cannot make backup copies of the files, because they are in NOARCHIVELOG mode and the database is still open for access:

```
RMAN> BACKUP DATABASE;

Starting backup at 2008/09/07 15:19
using target database control file instead of recovery catalog
allocated channel: ORA_DISK_1
channel ORA_DISK_1: SID=137 device type=DISK
channel ORA_DISK_1: starting full datafile backup set
channel ORA_DISK_1: specifying datafile(s) in backup set
RMAN-03009: failure of backup command on ORA_DISK_1 channel at 09/07/2008 15:19:06
ORA-19602: cannot backup or copy active file in NOARCHIVELOG mode
continuing other job steps, job failed will not be re-run
```

■**Note** If the database is open for access while a backup copy is being created, the data may change during the backup operation. The backup copy will therefore not be an accurate snapshot of the database; that is, it will be inconsistent; the information in the redo logs can be used to reverse any changes made during the course of the backup.

RMAN proceeds to make a backup copy of the control file and the parameter file (spfile)—this is automatically done after every BACKUP DATABASE command:

```
channel ORA_DISK_1: starting full datafile backup set
channel ORA_DISK_1: specifying datafile(s) in backup set
including current control file in backup set
including current SPFILE in backup set
channel ORA_DISK_1: starting piece 1 at 2008/09/07 15:19
channel ORA_DISK_1: finished piece 1 at 2008/09/07 15:19
piece handle=C:\APP\IGNATIUS\FLASH_RECOVERY_AREA\ORCL\BACKUPSET\2008_09_07\O1_MF_NCS
NF_TAG20080907T151905_4D8NTXW2_.BKP tag=TAG20080907T151905 comment=NONE
channel ORA_DISK_1: backup set complete, elapsed time: 00:00:03
RMAN-00571: ===========================================================
RMAN-00569: =============== ERROR MESSAGE STACK FOLLOWS ===============
RMAN-00571: ===========================================================

RMAN-03009: failure of backup command on ORA_DISK_1 channel at 09/07/2008 15:19:06
ORA-19602: cannot backup or copy active file in NOARCHIVELOG mode
```

Before we can make a backup copy of the database, we will have to prevent the data from being changed during the backup operation. We first shut down the database and then *mount* it without opening it for access:

```
RMAN> SHUTDOWN IMMEDIATE;

database closed
database dismounted
Oracle instance shut down

RMAN> STARTUP MOUNT;

connected to target database (not started)
Oracle instance started
database mounted

Total System Global Area    267825152 bytes

Fixed Size                    1332584 bytes
Variable Size               209717912 bytes
Database Buffers             50331648 bytes
Redo Buffers                  6443008 bytes
```

We then issue the backup instruction again and, this time, RMAN is able to make backup copies of each data file. The backup operation creates two *backup sets*. The first set contains backup copies of the data files, and the second contains a backup copy of the control file and the parameter file. A backup set consists of *pieces*; each piece is a file that contains data blocks from one or more files. The RMAN dialog looks like this:

```
RMAN> BACKUP DATABASE;

Starting backup at 2008/09/07 15:19
allocated channel: ORA_DISK_1
channel ORA_DISK_1: SID=154 device type=DISK
channel ORA_DISK_1: starting full datafile backup set
channel ORA_DISK_1: specifying datafile(s) in backup set
input datafile file number=00001 name=C:\APP\IGNATIUS\ORADATA\ORCL\SYSTEM01.DBF
input datafile file number=00002 name=C:\APP\IGNATIUS\ORADATA\ORCL\SYSAUX01.DBF
input datafile file number=00005 name=C:\APP\IGNATIUS\ORADATA\ORCL\EXAMPLE01.DBF
input datafile file number=00003 name=C:\APP\IGNATIUS\ORADATA\ORCL\UNDOTBS01.DBF
input datafile file number=00004 name=C:\APP\IGNATIUS\ORADATA\ORCL\USERS01.DBF
channel ORA_DISK_1: starting piece 1 at 2008/09/07 15:19
channel ORA_DISK_1: finished piece 1 at 2008/09/07 15:22
piece handle=C:\APP\IGNATIUS\FLASH_RECOVERY_AREA\ORCL\BACKUPSET\2008_09_07\01_MF_NNN
DF_TAG20080907T151954_4D8NWCXK_.BKP tag=TAG20080907T151954 comment=NONE
channel ORA_DISK_1: backup set complete, elapsed time: 00:02:36
channel ORA_DISK_1: starting full datafile backup set
channel ORA_DISK_1: specifying datafile(s) in backup set
including current control file in backup set
including current SPFILE in backup set
channel ORA_DISK_1: starting piece 1 at 2008/09/07 15:22
channel ORA_DISK_1: finished piece 1 at 2008/09/07 15:22
piece handle=C:\APP\IGNATIUS\FLASH_RECOVERY_AREA\ORCL\BACKUPSET\2008_09_07\01_MF_NCS
NF_TAG20080907T151954_4D801BQ5_.BKP tag=TAG20080907T151954 comment=NONE
channel ORA_DISK_1: backup set complete, elapsed time: 00:00:03
Finished backup at 2008/09/07 15:22
```

We can ask RMAN to summarize the results of the backup operation with the LIST BACKUP command. For example, let us ask RMAN to summarize the results of all backups created in the last 5 minutes. Notice that the backup pieces have been created in the "flash recovery area"—the total size of the backup is a little over 1 GB:

```
RMAN> LIST BACKUP OF DATABASE COMPLETED AFTER 'SYSDATE - 5/(24*60)';

List of Backup Sets
===================


BS Key  Type LV Size       Device Type Elapsed Time Completion Time
------- ---- -- ---------- ----------- ------------ ----------------
2       Full    1.04G      DISK        00:02:32     2008/09/07 15:22
        BP Key: 2   Status: AVAILABLE  Compressed: NO  Tag: TAG20080907T151954
        Piece Name: C:\APP\IGNATIUS\FLASH_RECOVERY_AREA\ORCL\BACKUPSET\2008_09_07\O1
_MF_NNNDF_TAG20080907T151954_4D8NWCXK_.BKP
  List of Datafiles in backup set 2
  File LV Type Ckp SCN    Ckp Time          Name
  ---- -- ---- ---------- ---------------- ----
  1       Full 946006     2008/09/07 15:19 C:\APP\IGNATIUS\ORADATA\ORCL\SYSTEM01.DBF
  2       Full 946006     2008/09/07 15:19 C:\APP\IGNATIUS\ORADATA\ORCL\SYSAUX01.DBF
  3       Full 946006     2008/09/07 15:19 C:\APP\IGNATIUS\ORADATA\ORCL\UNDOTBS01.DB
F
  4       Full 946006     2008/09/07 15:19 C:\APP\IGNATIUS\ORADATA\ORCL\USERS01.DBF
  5       Full 946006     2008/09/07 15:19 C:\APP\IGNATIUS\ORADATA\ORCL\EXAMPLE01.DB
F
```

All that is left to do before terminating the RMAN session is to make the database accessible once again.

```
RMAN> ALTER DATABASE OPEN;

database opened

RMAN> EXIT;

Recovery Manager complete.
```

Before moving on, let's put the database into ARCHIVELOG mode, so that we can create backup copies of the database even while it is being used and its data is subject to change. We need to issue the ALTER DATABASE ARCHIVELOG while the database is "mounted" but not opened for access.

```
C:\Documents and Settings\IGNATIUS>sqlplus / as sysdba

SQL*Plus: Release 11.1.0.6.0 - Production on Sun Sep 7 15:24:14 2008

Copyright (c) 1982, 2007, Oracle.  All rights reserved.

Connected to:
Oracle Database 11g Enterprise Edition Release 11.1.0.6.0 - Production
With the Partitioning, OLAP, Data Mining and Real Application Testing options

SQL> SHUTDOWN IMMEDIATE;
Database closed.
Database dismounted.
ORACLE instance shut down.
SQL> STARTUP MOUNT;
ORACLE instance started.

Total System Global Area  267825152 bytes
Fixed Size                  1332584 bytes
Variable Size             209717912 bytes
Database Buffers           50331648 bytes
Redo Buffers                6443008 bytes
Database mounted.
SQL> ALTER SYSTEM SET log_archive_dest_1="LOCATION=USE_DB_RECOVERY_FILE_DEST";

System altered.

SQL> ALTER DATABASE ARCHIVELOG;

Database altered.

SQL> ALTER DATABASE OPEN;

Database altered.
```

To check our work, let us manually close the current redo log and switch to the next one. V$ARCHIVED_LOG will tell us if a copy of the redo log file was created; we see that the redo log was copied to the flash recovery area.

```
SQL> ALTER SYSTEM SWITCH LOGFILE;
```

System altered.

```
SQL> SELECT NAME FROM V$ARCHIVED_LOG;
```

NAME

C:\APP\IGNATIUS\FLASH_RECOVERY_AREA\ORCL\ARCHIVELOG\2008_09_07\01_MF_1_4_4D808HO
7_.ARC

```
SQL> EXIT;
```
Disconnected from Oracle Database 11g Enterprise Edition Release 11.1.0.6.0 - Produc
tion
With the Partitioning, OLAP, Data Mining and Real Application Testing options

Practical Demonstration: Logical Backups

The Data Pump Export tool is very powerful and flexible—it has features such as parallel unloading and the ability to select precise subsets of data. Let us export the data from the HR schema, one of the sample schemas that were created for us by the Database Configuration Assistant. Notice the use of the flashback_time qualifier; it ensures that any changes made to the data while the export is in progress are not copied. Notice also the size of this backup; it is significantly smaller than the physical backup we performed earlier.

```
C:\Documents and Settings\IGNATIUS>expdp userid=\"/ as sysdba\" schemas=hr flashback
_time=\"to_timestamp(to_char(sysdate,'dd-mm-yyyy hh24:mi:ss'),'dd-mm-yyyy hh24:mi:ss
')\"
```

Export: Release 11.1.0.6.0 - Production on Sunday, 07 September, 2008 16:07:00

Copyright (c) 2003, 2007, Oracle. All rights reserved.

Connected to: Oracle Database 11g Enterprise Edition Release 11.1.0.6.0 - Production
With the Partitioning, OLAP, Data Mining and Real Application Testing options
Starting "SYS"."SYS_EXPORT_SCHEMA_02": userid="/******** AS SYSDBA" schemas=hr flas
hback_time="to_timestamp(to_char(sysdate,'dd-mm-yyyy hh24:mi:ss'),'dd-mm-yyyy hh24:m
i:ss')"

```
Estimate in progress using BLOCKS method...
Processing object type SCHEMA_EXPORT/TABLE/TABLE_DATA
Total estimation using BLOCKS method: 448 KB
Processing object type SCHEMA_EXPORT/USER
Processing object type SCHEMA_EXPORT/SYSTEM_GRANT
Processing object type SCHEMA_EXPORT/ROLE_GRANT
Processing object type SCHEMA_EXPORT/DEFAULT_ROLE
Processing object type SCHEMA_EXPORT/PRE_SCHEMA/PROCACT_SCHEMA
Processing object type SCHEMA_EXPORT/SEQUENCE/SEQUENCE
Processing object type SCHEMA_EXPORT/TABLE/TABLE
Processing object type SCHEMA_EXPORT/TABLE/GRANT/OWNER_GRANT/OBJECT_GRANT
Processing object type SCHEMA_EXPORT/TABLE/INDEX/INDEX
Processing object type SCHEMA_EXPORT/TABLE/CONSTRAINT/CONSTRAINT
Processing object type SCHEMA_EXPORT/TABLE/INDEX/STATISTICS/INDEX_STATISTICS
Processing object type SCHEMA_EXPORT/TABLE/COMMENT
Processing object type SCHEMA_EXPORT/PROCEDURE/PROCEDURE
Processing object type SCHEMA_EXPORT/PROCEDURE/ALTER_PROCEDURE
Processing object type SCHEMA_EXPORT/VIEW/VIEW
Processing object type SCHEMA_EXPORT/TABLE/CONSTRAINT/REF_CONSTRAINT
Processing object type SCHEMA_EXPORT/TABLE/TRIGGER
Processing object type SCHEMA_EXPORT/TABLE/STATISTICS/TABLE_STATISTICS
Processing object type SCHEMA_EXPORT/POST_SCHEMA/PROCACT_SCHEMA
. . exported "HR"."COUNTRIES"                 6.375 KB      25 rows
. . exported "HR"."DEPARTMENTS"               7.015 KB      27 rows
. . exported "HR"."EMPLOYEES"                 16.80 KB     107 rows
. . exported "HR"."JOBS"                      6.984 KB      19 rows
. . exported "HR"."JOB_HISTORY"              7.054 KB      10 rows
. . exported "HR"."LOCATIONS"                 8.273 KB      23 rows
. . exported "HR"."REGIONS"                   5.484 KB       4 rows
Master table "SYS"."SYS_EXPORT_SCHEMA_02" successfully loaded/unloaded
******************************************************************************
Dump file set for SYS.SYS_EXPORT_SCHEMA_02 is:
  C:\APP\IGNATIUS\ADMIN\ORCL\DPDUMP\EXPDAT.DMP
Job "SYS"."SYS_EXPORT_SCHEMA_02" successfully completed at 16:09:43


C:\Documents and Settings\IGNATIUS>dir C:\APP\IGNATIUS\ADMIN\ORCL\DPDUMP\EXPDAT.DMP
 Volume in drive C has no label.
 Volume Serial Number is 58A6-3CDF


 Directory of C:\APP\IGNATIUS\ADMIN\ORCL\DPDUMP


09/07/2008  04:09 PM           417,792 EXPDAT.DMP
```

```
1 File(s)        417,792 bytes
0 Dir(s)  21,337,731,072 bytes free
```

A concise list of Data Pump Export options can be obtained using the command `expdp help=y`. Some useful options are COMPRESSION, CONTENT, DIRECTORY, DUMPFILE, FILESIZE, FLASHBACK_TIME, FULL, PARALLEL, PARFILE, SCHEMAS, TABLES, and TABLESPACES.

Common RMAN Commands

The RMAN commands that you will most frequently encounter (in addition to BACKUP) are LIST, REPORT, CROSSCHECK, DELETE, SHOW, and CONFIGURE; Table 12-1 provides some examples. For a complete description of these and other commands, please refer to the Oracle Database 11*g* reference manuals.

Table 12-1. *Common RMAN commands*

Command	Purpose
LIST BACKUP OF DATABASE SUMMARY	Produces a summary of all backups recorded in the control file (and recovery catalog if one is being used).
LIST BACKUP OF DATABASE COMPLETED AFTER 'SYSDATE - 1'	Produces a detailed listing of all backups completed over the course of the last 24 hours.
CROSSCHECK BACKUP	Checks if all the pieces of the backups recorded in the control file are still on disk and have not been inadvertently removed. Backup pieces that can no longer be located are designated as "expired."
DELETE EXPIRED BACKUP	Removes information about a backup from the control file (or recovery catalog if one is being used) if the backup pieces cannot be found on disk.
REPORT OBSOLETE	Produces a list of backups that are older than the retention policy that is in effect. The SHOW RETENTION POLICY command can be used to determine which retention policy is in effect.
DELETE FORCE NOPROMPT OBSOLETE	Removes information about a backup from the control file (or recovery catalog if one is being used) if the backup is older than the retention policy in effect. The backup pieces are also removed from disk. The FORCE qualifier instructs RMAN not to complain about missing backup pieces. The NOPROMPT qualifier instructs RMAN not to prompt for confirmation before beginning the delete operation.
DELETE ARCHIVELOG ALL COMPLETED BEFORE 'SYSDATE - 7'	Deletes archived redo logs older than seven days.
SHOW ALL	Lists all the RMAN configuration parameters.
CONFIGURE CONTROLFILE AUTOBACKUP ON	Instructs Oracle to make a backup copy of the control file automatically whenever a new data file is added to the database.

Listing 12-1 demonstrates the use of these commands; we put all the commands into a *command file* called rman.rcv. We also set the NLS_DATE_FORMAT environment variable to force RMAN to print the time of each operation, not just the date.

Listing 12-1. *Common RMAN Commands*

```
C:\Documents and Settings\IGNATIUS>type rman.rcv
SET ECHO ON;
CONNECT TARGET;
LIST BACKUP OF DATABASE SUMMARY;
LIST BACKUP OF DATABASE COMPLETED AFTER 'SYSDATE - 1';
CROSSCHECK BACKUP;
DELETE EXPIRED BACKUP;
REPORT OBSOLETE;
DELETE FORCE NOPROMPT OBSOLETE;
REPORT UNRECOVERABLE DATABASE;
DELETE ARCHIVELOG ALL COMPLETED BEFORE 'SYSDATE - 7';
SHOW ALL;
CONFIGURE CONTROLFILE AUTOBACKUP ON;
EXIT;

C:\Documents and Settings\IGNATIUS>set NLS_DATE_FORMAT=YYYY/MM/DD HH24:MI

C:\Documents and Settings\IGNATIUS>rman <rman.rcv

Recovery Manager: Release 11.1.0.6.0 - Production on Sun Sep 7 16:50:18 2008

Copyright (c) 1982, 2007, Oracle.  All rights reserved.

RMAN>
echo set on

RMAN> CONNECT TARGET;
connected to target database: ORCL (DBID=1192595344)

RMAN> LIST BACKUP OF DATABASE SUMMARY;
using target database control file instead of recovery catalog
```

```
List of Backups
===============
Key      TY LV S Device Type Completion Time  #Pieces #Copies Compressed Tag
-------  -- -- - ----------- ---------------- ------- ------- ---------- ---
2        B  F  A DISK        2008/09/07 15:22 1       1       NO         TAG20080907T
151954
```

RMAN> **LIST BACKUP OF DATABASE COMPLETED AFTER 'SYSDATE - 1';**

```
List of Backup Sets
===================

BS Key  Type LV Size       Device Type Elapsed Time Completion Time
------- ---- -- ---------- ----------- ------------ ----------------
2       Full    1.04G      DISK        00:02:32     2008/09/07 15:22
        BP Key: 2   Status: AVAILABLE  Compressed: NO  Tag: TAG20080907T151954
        Piece Name: C:\APP\IGNATIUS\FLASH_RECOVERY_AREA\ORCL\BACKUPSET\2008_09_07\01
_MF_NNNDF_TAG20080907T151954_4D8NWCXK_.BKP
  List of Datafiles in backup set 2
  File LV Type Ckp SCN    Ckp Time         Name
  ---- -- ---- ---------- ---------------- ----
  1       Full 946006     2008/09/07 15:19 C:\APP\IGNATIUS\ORADATA\ORCL\SYSTEM01.DBF
  2       Full 946006     2008/09/07 15:19 C:\APP\IGNATIUS\ORADATA\ORCL\SYSAUX01.DBF
  3       Full 946006     2008/09/07 15:19 C:\APP\IGNATIUS\ORADATA\ORCL\UNDOTBS01.DB
F
  4       Full 946006     2008/09/07 15:19 C:\APP\IGNATIUS\ORADATA\ORCL\USERS01.DBF
  5       Full 946006     2008/09/07 15:19 C:\APP\IGNATIUS\ORADATA\ORCL\EXAMPLE01.DB
F
```

RMAN> **CROSSCHECK BACKUP;**
```
allocated channel: ORA_DISK_1
channel ORA_DISK_1: SID=170 device type=DISK
crosschecked backup piece: found to be 'AVAILABLE'
backup piece handle=C:\APP\IGNATIUS\FLASH_RECOVERY_AREA\ORCL\BACKUPSET\2008_09_07\01
_MF_NCSNF_TAG20080907T151905_4D8NTXW2_.BKP RECID=1 STAMP=664816749
crosschecked backup piece: found to be 'AVAILABLE'
backup piece handle=C:\APP\IGNATIUS\FLASH_RECOVERY_AREA\ORCL\BACKUPSET\2008_09_07\01
```

_MF_NNNDF_TAG20080907T151954_4D8NWCXK_.BKP RECID=2 STAMP=664816795
crosschecked backup piece: found to be 'AVAILABLE'
backup piece handle=C:\APP\IGNATIUS\FLASH_RECOVERY_AREA\ORCL\BACKUPSET\2008_09_07\01
_MF_NCSNF_TAG20080907T151954_4D801BQ5_.BKP RECID=3 STAMP=664816954
Crosschecked 3 objects

RMAN> **DELETE EXPIRED BACKUP;**
using channel ORA_DISK_1

RMAN> **REPORT OBSOLETE;**
RMAN retention policy will be applied to the command
RMAN retention policy is set to redundancy 1
Report of obsolete backups and copies
Type   Key   Completion Time   Filename/Handle
-------------------- ------ ------------------ --------------------
Backup Set   1   2008/09/07 15:19
   Backup Piece   1   2008/09/07 15:19   C:\APP\IGNATIUS\FLASH_RECOVERY_AREA\O
RCL\BACKUPSET\2008_09_07\01_MF_NCSNF_TAG20080907T151905_4D8NTXW2_.BKP

RMAN> **DELETE FORCE NOPROMPT OBSOLETE;**
RMAN retention policy will be applied to the command
RMAN retention policy is set to redundancy 1
using channel ORA_DISK_1
Deleting the following obsolete backups and copies:
Type   Key   Completion Time   Filename/Handle
-------------------- ------ ------------------ --------------------
Backup Set   1   2008/09/07 15:19
   Backup Piece   1   2008/09/07 15:19   C:\APP\IGNATIUS\FLASH_RECOVERY_AREA\O
RCL\BACKUPSET\2008_09_07\01_MF_NCSNF_TAG20080907T151905_4D8NTXW2_.BKP
deleted backup piece
backup piece handle=C:\APP\IGNATIUS\FLASH_RECOVERY_AREA\ORCL\BACKUPSET\2008_09_07\01
_MF_NCSNF_TAG20080907T151905_4D8NTXW2_.BKP RECID=1 STAMP=664816749
Deleted 1 objects

RMAN> **REPORT UNRECOVERABLE DATABASE;**
Report of files that need backup due to unrecoverable operations
File Type of Backup Required Name
---- ---------------------- ------------------------------------

```
RMAN> DELETE ARCHIVELOG ALL COMPLETED BEFORE 'SYSDATE - 7';
released channel: ORA_DISK_1
allocated channel: ORA_DISK_1
channel ORA_DISK_1: SID=170 device type=DISK

RMAN> SHOW ALL;
RMAN configuration parameters for database with db_unique_name ORCL are:
CONFIGURE RETENTION POLICY TO REDUNDANCY 1; # default
CONFIGURE BACKUP OPTIMIZATION OFF; # default
CONFIGURE DEFAULT DEVICE TYPE TO DISK; # default
CONFIGURE CONTROLFILE AUTOBACKUP OFF; # default
CONFIGURE CONTROLFILE AUTOBACKUP FORMAT FOR DEVICE TYPE DISK TO '%F'; # default
CONFIGURE DEVICE TYPE DISK PARALLELISM 1 BACKUP TYPE TO BACKUPSET; # default
CONFIGURE DATAFILE BACKUP COPIES FOR DEVICE TYPE DISK TO 1; # default
CONFIGURE ARCHIVELOG BACKUP COPIES FOR DEVICE TYPE DISK TO 1; # default
CONFIGURE MAXSETSIZE TO UNLIMITED; # default
CONFIGURE ENCRYPTION FOR DATABASE OFF; # default
CONFIGURE ENCRYPTION ALGORITHM 'AES128'; # default
CONFIGURE COMPRESSION ALGORITHM 'BZIP2'; # default
CONFIGURE ARCHIVELOG DELETION POLICY TO NONE; # default
CONFIGURE SNAPSHOT CONTROLFILE NAME TO 'C:\APP\IGNATIUS\PRODUCT\11.1.0\DB_1\DATABASE
\SNCFORCL.ORA'; # default

RMAN> CONFIGURE CONTROLFILE AUTOBACKUP ON;
new RMAN configuration parameters:
CONFIGURE CONTROLFILE AUTOBACKUP ON;
new RMAN configuration parameters are successfully stored

RMAN> EXIT;

Recovery Manager complete.
```

The "Easy" Button

Oracle provides an "easy" button for backups. If you create the database using Database Configuration Assistant (DBCA), you have the option of accepting a default backup scheme—the scheduling will be handled by Oracle's internal scheduler. If you do not enable backups when the database is created, you can use Enterprise Manager later to do so, as shown in Figure 12-1, Figure 12-2, and Figure 12-3. The default Oracle backup scheme, which is fine for all small databases and many bigger ones, is as follows:

- On day 1, a level 0 backup is performed in the form of an *image copy* of each data file. An image copy of a file is the same size as the file of which it is a copy.

- Beginning on day 2, a level 1 backup (that is, an incremental backup) is performed every day. Remember that a level 1 backup contains only those data blocks that have changed since the last level 0 backup.

- Beginning on day 3, the *previous* day's incremental backup is merged with the image copies.

This recovery scheme provides the ability to recover the database to any point after the last *two* backups.

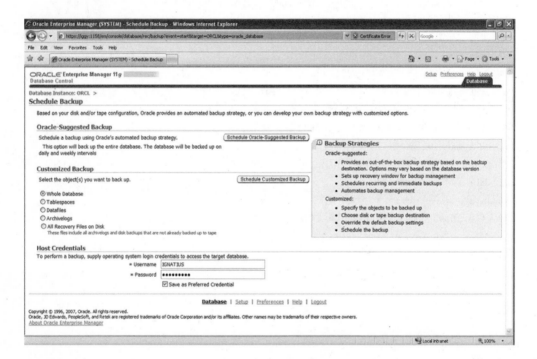

Figure 12-1. *Using Enterprise Manager to schedule backups*

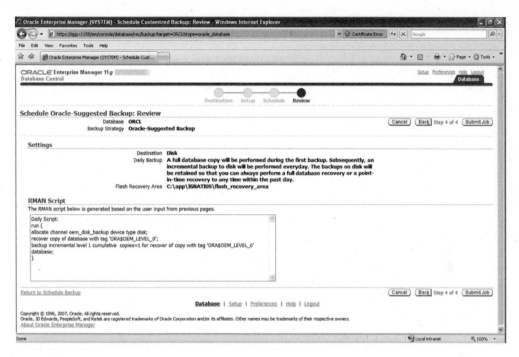

Figure 12-2. *RMAN script for the backup scheme suggested by Oracle*

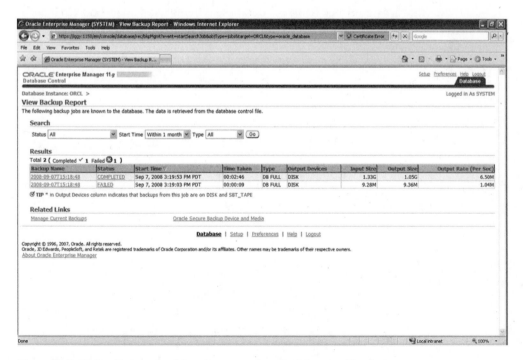

Figure 12-3. *Using Enterprise Manager to review the history of backups*

Summary

Here is a short summary of the concepts we touched upon in this chapter.

- A backup is a snapshot of a database or a part of a database; if the database is damaged, the damaged parts can be repaired using the backups. Archived logs can be used in conjunction with backups to replay transactions that changed data after the backup was performed.

- An appropriate backup strategy is one that meets the needs of the business while remaining cost-effective.

- A common practice is to make backup copies on disk when possible and have them copied to tape in a separate operation.

- Backups require a lot of computer resources and are therefore typically scheduled at nights and on weekends when other activity is at a minimum. If the database is very large, we may not have the time and resources to create a backup of the entire database in a single operation.

- Incremental backups can be used to conserve computer resources; we copy only those data blocks which have changed since the last backup.

- Backups that are performed while the database is being used might contain inconsistencies. The information in the redo log files can be used to eliminate the inconsistencies.

- Physical backups are copies of whole database blocks. Logical backups are copies of the data records themselves.

- Recovery Manager (RMAN) is usually the tool of choice for creating physical backups. Data Pump Export can be used for creating logical backups.

- If the database is created using DBCA, you can choose to accept the Oracle-suggested backup scheme and schedule backups immediately. You can also use Enterprise Manager later to schedule backups.

Exercises

- Practice all the RMAN commands listed in this chapter on your learning database. Use the LIST, REPORT, CROSSCHECK, DELETE, SHOW, and CONFIGURE commands. Make a consistent physical backup, and then make an inconsistent physical backup. Review the history of your backups using Enterprise Manager.

- Refer to the Recovery Manager documentation and find out how to make *compressed* backups.

- Make a consistent *logical* backup of one of the sample schemas in your learning database using Data Pump Export. Can the history of logical backups be reviewed using Enterprise Manager?

- Review the Data Pump Export documentation and determine the meaning of the following options: `COMPRESSION`, `CONTENT`, `DIRECTORY`, `DUMPFILE`, `FILESIZE`, `FLASH-BACK_TIME`, `FULL`, `PARALLEL`, `PARFILE`, `SCHEMAS`, `TABLES`, and `TABLESPACES`.

- Use `CREATE TABLE AS SELECT` (CTAS) commands to make logical backups of a few tables in the HR sample schema.

- Using Enterprise Manager, schedule a daily backup of your test database with the Oracle-suggested backup method. Then find out how this backup is scheduled. You will have to use the online forums and other internet resources to find the answer because the answer is not contained in the official Oracle documentation.

- Schedule a daily backup of your learning database without using Enterprise Manager. Put all the necessary commands into a command script called backup.rcv. Test the script using the command `rman <backup.rcv >backup.log`. Use the `at` command in Windows or the `crontab` command in Unix to schedule the backup.

- Ask a database administrator in your company for information on the company's backup strategy. Discuss hardware, software, configuration, and scheduling.

Further Reading

Oracle Corporation. *Oracle Database 11g Backup and Recovery Reference*. Oracle Corporation, 2007. Contains syntax diagrams (railroad diagrams) for all RMAN commands. Authoritative and detailed but difficult to read. Searchable or downloadable free of charge at `http://www.oracle.com/technology/documentation`. Printed copies can be purchased from Oracle's online store.

Oracle Corporation. *Oracle Database 11g Backup and Recovery User's Guide*. Oracle Corporation, 2007. Required reading for serious students. Searchable or downloadable free of charge at `http://www.oracle.com/technology/documentation`. Printed copies can be purchased from Oracle's online store.

Oracle Corporation. *Oracle Database 11g Utilities*. Oracle Corporation, 2007. Describes
    Data Pump Export and Data Pump Import as well as the older export and import util-
    ities. Searchable or downloadable free of charge at http://www.oracle.com/technology/
    documentation. Printed copies can be purchased from Oracle's online store.

Darl Kuhn, Sam R. Alapati, and Arup Nanda. *RMAN Recipes for Oracle Database 11g:
    A Problem-Solution Approach*. Apress, 2007. Readers who tire of railroad diagrams
    might find the problem-solution approach refreshing.

CHAPTER 13

Recovery

These Officers, with the Men belonging to the Engine, at their Quarterly Meetings, discourse of Fires, of the Faults committed at some, the good Management in some Cases at others, and thus communicating their Thoughts and Experience they grow wise in the Thing, and know how to command and to execute in the best manner upon every Emergency.

—Benjamin Franklin, in a letter to the *Pennsylvania Gazette*, following a disastrous fire in Philadelphia in the 18th century

In the previous chapter, you learned how to make backup copies of the database. You will now turn your attention to repairing the database if it gets damaged. For the purposes of this chapter, you should assume the availability of backup copies made using Recovery Manager (RMAN) but you will discover that backup copies are not the only repair option available. You will also get acquainted with a powerful tool called Data Recovery Advisor (DRA), which greatly simplifies the database administrator's job.

Horror Stories

The following are true stories based on personal experiences.

Sometimes we make a mountain out of a molehill. Early in my career, in the days of Oracle 7, a few blocks of data in the company's most critical database were found to be corrupted. Any transaction that touched the affected blocks could not complete, but the database was otherwise functional. This was a large Enterprise Resource Planning (ERP) database that the business depended on for all aspects of its functioning, so the application administrators went into high gear. There were no disk backups because of the sheer size of the database, so the application administrators recalled the tapes from the offsite storage facility. They shut down the database at the end of the day and began restoring it from tapes, hoping to have the database ready for business the next day. However, three-quarters of the way into the restore operation, a defect was found in the tapes and the application administrators had to requisition the previous set of tapes from the offsite storage facility. The offsite storage facility was 100 miles away, and this necessitated a substantial delay.

After the database files were successfully restored from tape, the administrators began the task of recovering transactions from the archived redo log files; this took a huge amount of time. From start to finish, the restore and recovery operation took 48 hours instead of the original estimate of 12 hours, and the business lost two days of work. The mistake was using a one-size-fits-all repair strategy that did not take into consideration the amount of damage; it is not necessary to shut down and restore the entire database if only one data file is damaged. In Oracle Database 11g, it is even possible to repair individual blocks without affecting the availability of the rest of the database.

■**Tip** An appropriate repair strategy is one that is tailored to the situation and causes minimum downtime. Individual data files and data blocks can be repaired without impacting the rest of the database.

In my second story, which occurs more recently in my career, all the king's horses and all the king's men couldn't put Humpty Dumpty together again. The disks crashed, and a large data warehouse database became unusable. Unfortunately, the disk backups were being stored on the same disks as the database, and restoration from tapes was the only option. Needless to say, any archived redo logs that were not on tape were lost forever, which meant that a significant number of transactions could never be recovered. In a bad case of déjà vu, the first set of tapes was found to be defective, and restoration had to be started afresh using a second set of tapes. But that was not the end of the story; the database was still unusable even after all available redo logs had been applied. It turned out that data was regularly loaded in NOLOGGING mode; this means that redo information was not being recorded in the redo logs. Large parts of the database had to be re-created from other sources, and it was several weeks before it was fully functional again.

It happened to me—it could happen to you.

■**Tip** Issue the ALTER DATABASE FORCE LOGGING command to prevent users from using NOLOGGING mode without the knowledge of the database administrators.

Types of Recovery

There are several kinds of repair operations; I describe each in turn in this section.

Restore vs. Recover

These two terms are often used synonymously in everyday usage—for example, the title of this chapter is simply "Recovery," and the title of this section is "Types of Recovery." However, the words *restore* and *recover* have specialized technical meanings for the database administrator. The word *restore* refers to the operation of replacing a damaged or missing file such as a data file, control file, or archived redo log file from a backup copy. The word *recover* refers to the process of replaying transactions recorded in the redo logs and making the database usable again. Usually, the recovery process is preceded by the restore process. However, Oracle performs automatic recovery operations (a.k.a. *crash recovery*) if the database is restarted after an ungraceful shutdown such as a system crash.

Coincidentally enough, the two most important Recovery Manager commands for repairing a database are RESTORE and RECOVER—they are powerful commands with a rich set of options. Later in this chapter, you will see how DRA simplifies the database administrator's job.

Full Recovery vs. Partial Recovery

If one part of a database is damaged, the rest of the database usually continues to function. The most common examples are loss of a data file (except a data file from the SYSTEM tablespace) or corruption of a few blocks of data. It is usually possible to restore and recover the affected parts of the database without impacting the availability of the rest of the database.

■**Note** Single-block recovery is available only in the Enterprise Edition.

Complete Recovery vs. Incomplete Recovery

After the affected parts of the database are *restored* from the backup, the transactions in the redo log files must be *recovered*. Sometimes the recovery phase cannot be completed. For example, an archived redo log may be lost or damaged. Or we might intentionally wish to stop the recovery process at a point in time in the past; perhaps we wish to erase the effects of mistakes made by a user. You will hear the term RESETLOGS used in conjunction with an incomplete recovery, and the *incarnation number* of the database is incremented in such cases. Incomplete recovery is also referred to as *point-in-time recovery*.

Traditional vs. Flashback

Point-in-time recovery after user error can be very time-consuming when the database is large or when a large number of redo logs have to be processed. The Enterprise Edition of Oracle Database 11*g* offers the option to unwind transactions by using a special type of log called the *flashback log*. This can be orders of magnitude faster than traditional recovery but is limited by the amount of space reserved for the storage of flashback logs. Note that the flashback method of recovering a database cannot be used to recover from physical damage to the database such as corruption of data blocks.

Physical Recovery vs. Logical Recovery

All the methods of recovery that I have covered so far can be classified as *physical recovery* because they are not tailored to the affected data. An alternative to physical recovery following user error is *logical recovery*, which is tailored to the affected data. Here are some examples:

- If an index is corrupted, it can be dropped and re-created without compromising the data in the underlying table.

- If data is inadvertently deleted, it might be possible to reconstruct it from paper records.

- The Data Pump Import utility can be used to restore a table from a logical backup made by using that utility. This is illustrated in Listing 13-1.

Oracle Database 11*g* also offers a variety of methods for logical recovery based on the information contained in the undo segments. These methods are called flashback methods; I'll present more information about them later in this chapter.

Listing 13-1. *Logical Recovery of a Single Table by Using the Data Pump Import Utility*

```
C:\Documents and Settings\IGNATIUS>impdp userid=\"/ as sysdba\" dumpfile=expdat.dmp
tables=hr.employees table_exists_action=replace

Import: Release 11.1.0.6.0 - Production on Monday, 08 September, 2008 8:56:30

Copyright (c) 2003, 2007, Oracle.  All rights reserved.

Connected to: Oracle Database 11g Enterprise Edition Release 11.1.0.6.0 - Production
With the Partitioning, OLAP, Data Mining and Real Application Testing options
Master table "SYS"."SYS_IMPORT_TABLE_01" successfully loaded/unloaded
Starting "SYS"."SYS_IMPORT_TABLE_01":  userid="/******** AS SYSDBA" dumpfile=expdat.
dmp tables=hr.employees table_exists_action=replace
Processing object type SCHEMA_EXPORT/TABLE/TABLE
Processing object type SCHEMA_EXPORT/TABLE/TABLE_DATA
. . imported "HR"."EMPLOYEES"                        16.80 KB     107 rows
Processing object type SCHEMA_EXPORT/TABLE/GRANT/OWNER_GRANT/OBJECT_GRANT
Processing object type SCHEMA_EXPORT/TABLE/INDEX/INDEX
Processing object type SCHEMA_EXPORT/TABLE/CONSTRAINT/CONSTRAINT
Processing object type SCHEMA_EXPORT/TABLE/INDEX/STATISTICS/INDEX_STATISTICS
Processing object type SCHEMA_EXPORT/TABLE/COMMENT
Processing object type SCHEMA_EXPORT/TABLE/CONSTRAINT/REF_CONSTRAINT
Processing object type SCHEMA_EXPORT/TABLE/TRIGGER
```

```
Processing object type SCHEMA_EXPORT/TABLE/STATISTICS/TABLE_STATISTICS
Job "SYS"."SYS_IMPORT_TABLE_01" successfully completed at 08:56:48
```

Flashback Technology

The information contained in the undo segments can be used to reconstruct prior versions of the data. The amount of information available in the undo segments is governed by the size of the undo segments and by the UNDO_RETENTION setting. The default value of the UNDO_RETENTION setting is only 900 seconds (15 minutes)—you should increase it to a more appropriate value. Also make sure that the undo segments are fairly large.

Note The more advanced flashback features such as Flashback Transaction Query, Flashback Table, and Flashback Database are available only with the Enterprise Edition of Oracle Database 11*g*.

Flashback Query

If data in a table is inadvertently changed, the prior values of the data items can be obtained by using the undo segments, and suitable SQL statements can be constructed to correct the data, as in the following example.

First, let's increase the salary of employee 101 by $1,000:

```
SQL> UPDATE employees
  2     SET salary=salary + 1000
  3   WHERE employee_id = 101;

1 row updated.

SQL> SELECT salary
  2     FROM employees
  3   WHERE employee_id = 101;

    SALARY
----------
     18000

SQL> COMMIT;

Commit complete.
```

Next, let's determine what the employee's salary used to be, one hour ago. This is done with the use of the AS OF TIMESTAMP clause:

```
SQL> SELECT salary
  2    FROM employees AS OF TIMESTAMP SYSDATE - 1/24
  3   WHERE employee_id = 101;

    SALARY
----------
     17000
```

Next, let's formulate an update command to change the employee's salary back to the original value. Notice the use of the AS OF TIMESTAMP clause once again:

```
SQL> UPDATE employees
  2    SET salary = (SELECT salary
  3                    FROM employees AS OF TIMESTAMP SYSDATE - 1/24
  4                   WHERE employee_id = 101)
  5   WHERE employee_id = 101;

1 row updated.

SQL> COMMIT;

Commit complete.

SQL> SELECT salary
  2    FROM employees
  3   WHERE employee_id = 101;

    SALARY
----------
     17000
```

Flashback Versions

If a row of data is changed multiple times, the VERSIONS BETWEEN clause can be used to search for prior versions of the row in the undo segments. VERSIONS_STARTTIME and VERSIONS_XID are *pseudocolumns* that tell us when each version was created and which transaction created it. The absence of these values indicates the time prior to the window specified in the query. In the following example, you can see the original value of the employee's salary ($17,000), the transaction that changed the value to $18,000, and the transaction that reversed the change:

```
SQL> COLUMN versions_starttime FORMAT a32
SQL> SELECT versions_starttime,
  2           versions_xid,
  3           salary
  4      FROM employees VERSIONS BETWEEN TIMESTAMP SYSDATE - 1/24 AND SYSDATE
  5     WHERE employee_id = 101;

VERSIONS_STARTTIME                 VERSIONS_XID        SALARY
-------------------------------    ----------------    ----------
28-NOV-07 02.15.02 PM              05000F0031030000      17000
28-NOV-07 02.14.31 PM              09001000D4030000      18000
                                                         17000
```

Flashback Transaction

The SQL statements required to reverse changes can be automatically generated from the undo segments. For example, an INSERT statement can be reversed with a DELETE statement, and vice versa. All one needs to do is to select the necessary SQL statements from the flashback_transaction_query view—a DBA-level privilege called SELECT ANY TRANSACTION is required. The transaction identifier (XID) in the following example is the one obtained in the previous section:

```
SQL> SELECT undo_sql
  2      FROM flashback_transaction_query
  3     WHERE XID = '09001000D4030000';

UNDO_SQL
--------------------------------------------------------------------------------
update "HR"."EMPLOYEES" set "SALARY" = '17000' where ROWID = 'AAARAgAAFAAAABYABj
';
```

Flashback Table

All changes made to a table can be removed by using the FLASHBACK TABLE command if the information in the undo segments has not yet been overwritten by newer transactions. For example, suppose that we inadvertently increased the salary of all employees, as in the following example:

```
SQL> UPDATE employees
  2    · SET salary=salary + 1000;
```

```
107 rows updated.

SQL> COMMIT;

Commit complete.
```

Before we use the FLASHBACK TABLE command, we must give Oracle permission to restore rows to new locations if necessary. We do this using the ENABLE ROW MOVEMENT clause of the ALTER TABLE command; we can then issue the FLASHBACK TABLE command:

```
SQL> FLASHBACK TABLE employees TO TIMESTAMP SYSDATE - 1/24;
FLASHBACK TABLE employees TO TIMESTAMP SYSDATE - 1/24
                *
ERROR at line 1:
ORA-08189: cannot flashback the table because row movement is not enabled

SQL> ALTER TABLE employees ENABLE ROW MOVEMENT;

Table altered.

SQL> FLASHBACK TABLE employees TO TIMESTAMP SYSDATE - 1/24;

Flashback complete.
```

Flashback Drop

If an entire table is inadvertently deleted, it can be simply recovered from the Recycle Bin by using the FLASHBACK TABLE...TO BEFORE DROP command. Dropped tables remain in the Recycle Bin until they are explicitly purged by using the PURGE command:

```
SQL> CREATE TABLE employees_backup AS SELECT * FROM employees;

Table created.

SQL> SELECT COUNT (*)
  2    FROM employees_backup;

  COUNT(*)
----------
       107

SQL> DROP TABLE employees_backup;
```

Table dropped.

```
SQL> DESCRIBE user_recyclebin;
 Name                                     Null?    Type
 ---------------------------------------- -------- -----------------------------
 OBJECT_NAME                              NOT NULL VARCHAR2(30)
 ORIGINAL_NAME                                     VARCHAR2(32)
 OPERATION                                         VARCHAR2(9)
 TYPE                                              VARCHAR2(25)
 TS_NAME                                           VARCHAR2(30)
 CREATETIME                                        VARCHAR2(19)
 DROPTIME                                          VARCHAR2(19)
 DROPSCN                                           NUMBER
 PARTITION_NAME                                    VARCHAR2(32)
 CAN_UNDROP                                        VARCHAR2(3)
 CAN_PURGE                                         VARCHAR2(3)
 RELATED                                  NOT NULL NUMBER
 BASE_OBJECT                              NOT NULL NUMBER
 PURGE_OBJECT                             NOT NULL NUMBER
 SPACE                                             NUMBER

SQL> SELECT object_name,
  2          original_name
  3    FROM user_recyclebin;

OBJECT_NAME                      ORIGINAL_NAME
-------------------------------- --------------------------------
BIN$1ethyUzGQEW849KhDJOcJg==$0 EMPLOYEES_BACKUP
```

SQL> **FLASHBACK TABLE employees_backup TO BEFORE DROP;**

Flashback complete.

```
SQL> SELECT COUNT (*)
  2    FROM employees_backup;

  COUNT(*)
----------
       107
```

```
SQL> DROP TABLE employees_backup;

Table dropped.

SQL> PURGE user_recyclebin;

Recyclebin purged.

SQL> FLASHBACK TABLE employees_backup TO BEFORE DROP;
FLASHBACK TABLE employees_backup TO BEFORE DROP
*
ERROR at line 1:
ORA-38305: object not in RECYCLE BIN
```

Flashback Data Archive

This feature was introduced in Oracle Database 11*g*. An archive can be created to store all changes made to data rows during the lifetime of a table. The archive is not dependent on the undo segments and, consequently, its contents are not lost if the information in the undo segments is overwritten by new transactions. A complete discussion is outside the scope of this chapter.

Flashback Database

The biggest weapon in the armory of flashback features is the FLASHBACK DATABASE command. For example, let's suppose that major changes are being made to the database. You need to simply create a *restore point* by using the CREATE RESTORE POINT command. If the changes need to be tested and test data created before releasing the database to the users, you could simply create a second restore point. If the testing is successful, the test data can be completely erased by reverting to the second restore point, and the database can then be released to the users. If the testing is unsuccessful, you can simply revert to the first restore point to wipe out all traces of your changes.

The use of the FLASHBACK DATABASE command requires that the database be shut down and then brought into the MOUNT state. After the command has completed, the database must be opened with the RESETLOGS option. All this can be most simply accomplished from the User Directed Recovery section of the Perform Recovery page of Enterprise Manager, shown in Figure 13-1.

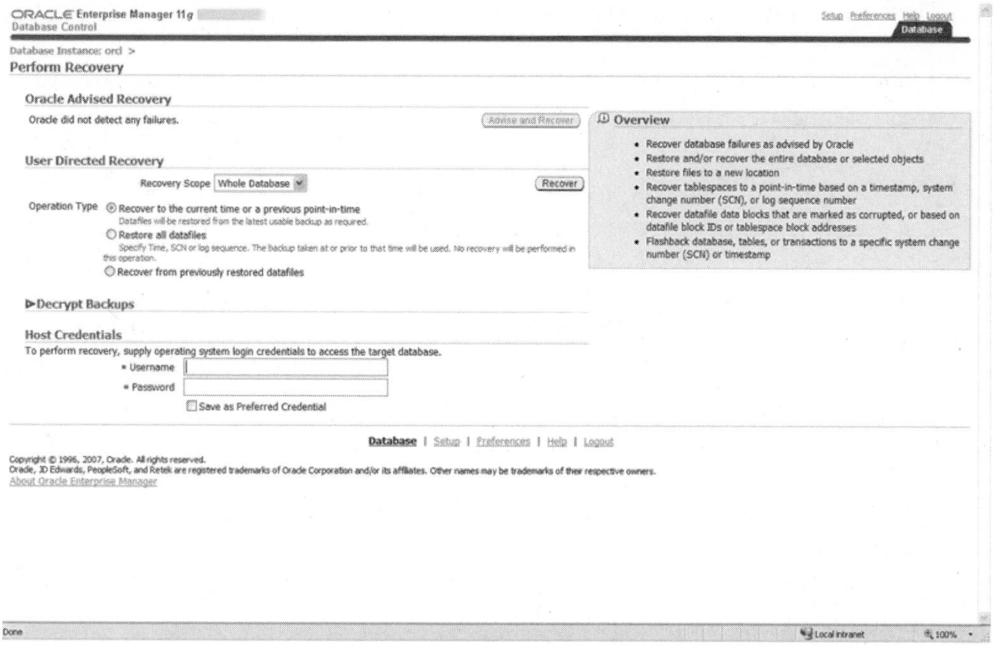

Figure 13-1. *Using Enterprise Manager for user-directed recovery*

Note that the Flashback Database technique depends on a special type of log file called a flashback log. The retention of information in flashback logs is governed by the Oracle parameter DB_FLASHBACK_RETENTION_TARGET. Also, the database administrator must explicitly enable logging by using the command ALTER DATABASE FLASHBACK ON before opening the database.

LogMiner

You can also recover prior versions of data from the archived redo logs by using a utility called LogMiner, as illustrated in Listing 13-2. LogMiner has the capability to construct *undo SQL* that you can use to selectively reverse changes to your data.

Listing 13-2. *Logical Recovery Using the LogMiner Utility*

```
SQL> EXECUTE DBMS_LOGMNR.add_logfile (logfilename => 'C:\APP\IGNATIUS\FLASH_RECOVERY
_AREA\ORCL\ARCHIVELOG\2008_09_20\O1_MF_1_77_4FBYS33F_.ARC', options => DBMS_LOGMNR.N
EW);
```

PL/SQL procedure successfully completed.

```
SQL> EXECUTE DBMS_LOGMNR.add_logfile (logfilename => 'C:\APP\IGNATIUS\FLASH_RECOVERY
_AREA\ORCL\ARCHIVELOG\2008_09_20\O1_MF_1_78_4FBYS6J3_.ARC', options => DBMS_LOGMNR.a
ddfile);
```

PL/SQL procedure successfully completed.

```
SQL> EXECUTE DBMS_LOGMNR.add_logfile (logfilename => 'C:\APP\IGNATIUS\FLASH_RECOVERY
_AREA\ORCL\ARCHIVELOG\2008_09_20\O1_MF_1_79_4FBYSOOH_.ARC', options => DBMS_LOGMNR.a
ddfile);
```

PL/SQL procedure successfully completed.

```
SQL> SELECT sql_undo
  2    FROM v$logmnr_contents
  3   WHERE seg_name = 'EMPLOYEES'
  4     AND ROWNUM < 5;

SQL_UNDO
--------------------------------------------------
update "HR"."EMPLOYEES"
  set
    "SALARY" = 2600
  where
    "SALARY" = 3250 and
    ROWID = 'AAARcwAAFAAAABUAAA';

update "HR"."EMPLOYEES"
  set
    "SALARY" = 2600
  where
    "SALARY" = 3250 and
    ROWID = 'AAARcwAAFAAAABUAAB';

update "HR"."EMPLOYEES"
  set
    "SALARY" = 4400
  where
    "SALARY" = 5500 and
    ROWID = 'AAARcwAAFAAAABUAAC';
```

```
update "HR"."EMPLOYEES"
  set
    "SALARY" = 13000
  where
    "SALARY" = 16250 and
    ROWID = 'AAARcwAAFAAAABUAAD';
```

Note that LogMiner works as advertised only if you have enabled *minimal supplemental logging*. According to the Oracle Database 11*g* documentation, this "ensures that LogMiner (and any products building on LogMiner technology) has sufficient information to support chained rows and various storage arrangements such as cluster tables and index-organized tables." The command that enables minimal supplemental logging is ALTER DATABASE ADD SUPPLEMENTAL LOG DATA.

A complete discussion of LogMiner can be found in Chapter 18 of *Oracle Database 11g Utilities*.

Data Recovery Advisor

Physical recovery usually requires the use of Recovery Manager. The two most powerful RMAN repair commands are simply RESTORE DATABASE and RECOVER DATABASE. The first command restores all data files from the last backup. The second command uses the redo logs and recovers all the changes made since the backup. But full database recovery using the RESTORE DATABASE and RECOVER DATABASE commands is not required in all cases. The most appropriate database strategy is one that is tailored to the situation, and RMAN provides a wide range of repair options that might overwhelm the beginner. However, Oracle Database 11*g* also provides a powerful tool called Data Recovery Advisor (DRA) that greatly simplifies the database administrator's job.

We demonstrate physical recovery by using DRA to repair corrupt blocks, the same situation described in my first horror story. In those days, Oracle did not offer the capability to repair individual blocks while the rest of the database was still being used, though it did offer the capability to repair individual files. Block recovery is the least invasive of all recovery operations, and DRA makes the process as easy as it is possible to imagine.

I decided to intentionally corrupt one of the data blocks in the Employees table in the sample HR schema, and the DBA_EXTENTS view gave me the information I needed to determine exactly which blocks to corrupt. I shut down the database and modified the file containing those blocks by using a binary editor. Then I started the database, and everything worked normally until I tried to list the contents of the table. SQL Developer then displayed the error dialog shown in Figure 13-2.

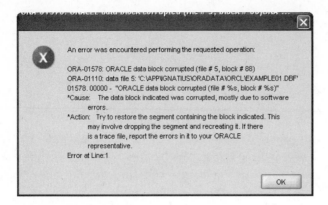

Figure 13-2. *SQL Developer error dialog*

The Oracle-recommended action was "Try to restore the segment containing the block indicated. This may involve dropping the segment and re-creating it. If there is a trace file, report the error in it to your Oracle representative." But DRA makes short work of the problem.

First, let's check whether any *other* blocks are also corrupted. That seems like the smart thing to do—if one block has somehow been corrupted, then other blocks might also have been corrupted, and we could fix all of them at the same time. We use the VALIDATE DATABASE command to check the entire database. (Note that checking the entire database may take a lot of time, and Recovery Manager does provide the ability to check individual data files.) Fortunately, we find that the only block that is corrupted is block 88 in the file EXAMPLE01.DBF:

```
C:\Documents and Settings\IGNATIUS>RMAN

Recovery Manager: Release 11.1.0.6.0 - Production on Tue Nov 20 12:55:09 2007

Copyright (c) 1982, 2007, Oracle.  All rights reserved.

RMAN> CONNECT TARGET;

connected to target database: ORCL (DBID=1166437381)

RMAN> VALIDATE DATABASE;

Starting validate at 20-NOV-07
using target database control file instead of recovery catalog
allocated channel: ORA_DISK_1
channel ORA_DISK_1: SID=140 device type=DISK
channel ORA_DISK_1: starting validation of datafile
```

```
channel ORA_DISK_1: specifying datafile(s) for validation
input datafile file number=00001 name=C:\APP\IGNATIUS\ORADATA\ORCL\SYSTEM01.DBF
input datafile file number=00002 name=C:\APP\IGNATIUS\ORADATA\ORCL\SYSAUX01.DBF
input datafile file number=00005 name=C:\APP\IGNATIUS\ORADATA\ORCL\EXAMPLE01.DBF
input datafile file number=00003 name=C:\APP\IGNATIUS\ORADATA\ORCL\UNDOTBS01.DBF
input datafile file number=00004 name=C:\APP\IGNATIUS\ORADATA\ORCL\USERS01.DBF
channel ORA_DISK_1: validation complete, elapsed time: 00:01:05
List of Datafiles
=================
File Status Marked Corrupt Empty Blocks Blocks Examined High SCN
---- ------ ------------- ------------ --------------- ----------
1   OK     0             11422        88320           1013319
  File Name: C:\APP\IGNATIUS\ORADATA\ORCL\SYSTEM01.DBF
  Block Type Blocks Failing Blocks Processed
  ---------- -------------- ----------------
  Data       0              63456
  Index      0              11155
  Other      0              2287

File Status Marked Corrupt Empty Blocks Blocks Examined High SCN
---- ------ ------------- ------------ --------------- ----------
2   OK     0             27908        75032           1013283
  File Name: C:\APP\IGNATIUS\ORADATA\ORCL\SYSAUX01.DBF
  Block Type Blocks Failing Blocks Processed
  ---------- -------------- ----------------
  Data       0              11040
  Index      0              9279
  Other      0              26805

File Status Marked Corrupt Empty Blocks Blocks Examined High SCN
---- ------ ------------- ------------ --------------- ----------
3   OK     0             0            9600            1013319
  File Name: C:\APP\IGNATIUS\ORADATA\ORCL\UNDOTBS01.DBF
  Block Type Blocks Failing Blocks Processed
  ---------- -------------- ----------------
  Data       0              0
  Index      0              0
  Other      0              9600
```

```
File Status Marked Corrupt Empty Blocks Blocks Examined High SCN
---- ------ -------------- ------------ ---------------- ----------
4    OK     0              366          640              1010771
     File Name: C:\APP\IGNATIUS\ORADATA\ORCL\USERS01.DBF
     Block Type Blocks Failing Blocks Processed
     ---------- -------------- ----------------
     Data       0              93
     Index      0              41
     Other      0              140


File Status Marked Corrupt Empty Blocks Blocks Examined High SCN
---- ------ -------------- ------------ ---------------- ----------
5    FAILED 0              1719         12800            1010926
     File Name: C:\APP\IGNATIUS\ORADATA\ORCL\EXAMPLE01.DBF
     Block Type Blocks Failing Blocks Processed
     ---------- -------------- ----------------
     Data       1              4406
     Index      0              1264
     Other      0              5411


validate found one or more corrupt blocks
See trace file c:\app\ignatius\diag\rdbms\orcl\orcl\trace\orcl_ora_300.trc for d
etails
channel ORA_DISK_1: starting validation of datafile
channel ORA_DISK_1: specifying datafile(s) for validation
including current control file for validation
including current SPFILE in backup set
channel ORA_DISK_1: validation complete, elapsed time: 00:00:01
List of Control File and SPFILE
=================================
File Type    Status Blocks Failing Blocks Examined
------------ ------ -------------- ----------------
SPFILE       OK     0              2
Control File OK     0              594
Finished validate at 20-NOV-07
```

We then issue the LIST FAILURE, ADVISE FAILURE, and REPAIR FAILURE commands in turn. The LIST FAILURE command simply tells us what we already know at this point—that the file EXAMPLE01.DBF contains a corrupted block:

```
RMAN> LIST FAILURE;

List of Database Failures
=========================


Failure ID Priority Status    Time Detected Summary
---------- -------- --------- ------------- -------
306        HIGH     OPEN      20-NOV-07     Datafile 5: 'C:\APP\IGNATIUS\ORADATA
\ORCL\EXAMPLE01.DBF' contains one or more corrupt blocks
```

Next we ask DRA to analyze the problem and recommend a course of action. If possible, DRA lists manual methods that can be used to recover from the problem. For example, a data file that has been inadvertently moved to a different directory can be restored to its previous location. In this case, there are no such alternatives, and DRA tells us that the only course is to restore the corrupted block from the backup copies of the database and redo any modifications made to the block since the backup copy was created. DRA automatically creates a RMAN script for the purpose, and the REPAIR FAILURE PREVIEW command lists the contents of the script:

```
RMAN> ADVISE FAILURE;

List of Database Failures
=========================


Failure ID Priority Status    Time Detected Summary
---------- -------- --------- ------------- -------
306        HIGH     OPEN      20-NOV-07     Datafile 5: 'C:\APP\IGNATIUS\ORADATA
\ORCL\EXAMPLE01.DBF' contains one or more corrupt blocks

analyzing automatic repair options; this may take some time
using channel ORA_DISK_1
analyzing automatic repair options complete

Mandatory Manual Actions
========================
no manual actions available

Optional Manual Actions
```

```
========================
no manual actions available

Automated Repair Options
========================
Option Repair Description
------ ------------------
1      Perform block media recovery of block 88 in file 5
  Strategy: The repair includes complete media recovery with no data loss
  Repair script: c:\app\ignatius\diag\rdbms\orcl\orcl\hm\reco_2286670653.hm
```

RMAN> **REPAIR FAILURE PREVIEW;**

```
Strategy: The repair includes complete media recovery with no data loss
Repair script: c:\app\ignatius\diag\rdbms\orcl\orcl\hm\reco_2286670653.hm

contents of repair script:
   # block media recovery
   recover datafile 5 block 88;
```

All that is left to do now is to execute the script created by DRA. This is done via the simple command REPAIR FAILURE. The NOPROMPT qualifier can be used if we don't want to be prompted for confirmation at various points during the process.

First the corrupted block is restored from the backup copies of the database:

RMAN> **REPAIR FAILURE NOPROMPT;**

```
Strategy: The repair includes complete media recovery with no data loss
Repair script: c:\app\ignatius\diag\rdbms\orcl\orcl\hm\reco_2286670653.hm

contents of repair script:
   # block media recovery
   recover datafile 5 block 88;
executing repair script

Starting recover at 20-NOV-07
using channel ORA_DISK_1
```

```
channel ORA_DISK_1: restoring block(s)
channel ORA_DISK_1: specifying block(s) to restore from backup set
restoring blocks of datafile 00005
channel ORA_DISK_1: reading from backup piece C:\APP\IGNATIUS\FLASH_RECOVERY_ARE
A\ORCL\BACKUPSET\2007_11_20\O1_MF_NNNDF_TAG20071120T072012_3N5YSKTV_.BKP
channel ORA_DISK_1: piece handle=C:\APP\IGNATIUS\FLASH_RECOVERY_AREA\ORCL\BACKUP
SET\2007_11_20\O1_MF_NNNDF_TAG20071120T072012_3N5YSKTV_.BKP tag=TAG20071120T0720
12
channel ORA_DISK_1: restored block(s) from backup piece 1
channel ORA_DISK_1: block restore complete, elapsed time: 00:00:07
```

Finally, any modifications made to the block since the backup copy was created are redone with the help of the redo logs:

```
starting media recovery

archived log for thread 1 with sequence 7 is already on disk as file C:\APP\IGNA
TIUS\FLASH_RECOVERY_AREA\ORCL\ARCHIVELOG\2007_11_20\O1_MF_1_7_3N6HBW5V_.ARC
archived log for thread 1 with sequence 8 is already on disk as file C:\APP\IGNA
TIUS\FLASH_RECOVERY_AREA\ORCL\ARCHIVELOG\2007_11_20\O1_MF_1_8_3N6J9JJ3_.ARC
archived log for thread 1 with sequence 9 is already on disk as file C:\APP\IGNA
TIUS\FLASH_RECOVERY_AREA\ORCL\ARCHIVELOG\2007_11_20\O1_MF_1_9_3N6LCORF_.ARC
archived log for thread 1 with sequence 10 is already on disk as file C:\APP\IGN
ATIUS\FLASH_RECOVERY_AREA\ORCL\ARCHIVELOG\2007_11_20\O1_MF_1_10_3N6LC22G_.ARC
archived log for thread 1 with sequence 11 is already on disk as file C:\APP\IGN
ATIUS\FLASH_RECOVERY_AREA\ORCL\ARCHIVELOG\2007_11_20\O1_MF_1_11_3N6LC5VT_.ARC
archived log for thread 1 with sequence 12 is already on disk as file C:\APP\IGN
ATIUS\FLASH_RECOVERY_AREA\ORCL\ARCHIVELOG\2007_11_20\O1_MF_1_12_3N6LC74D_.ARC
archived log for thread 1 with sequence 13 is already on disk as file C:\APP\IGN
ATIUS\FLASH_RECOVERY_AREA\ORCL\ARCHIVELOG\2007_11_20\O1_MF_1_13_3N6LC8KL_.ARC
media recovery complete, elapsed time: 00:00:05
Finished recover at 20-NOV-07
repair failure complete

RMAN> EXIT;

Recovery Manager complete.
```

Recovery Using Enterprise Manager

Enterprise Manager further simplifies the task of repairing a database; all you have to do is to click a few buttons. Click the Availability option on the Database page to display the Availability subpage shown in Figure 13-3.

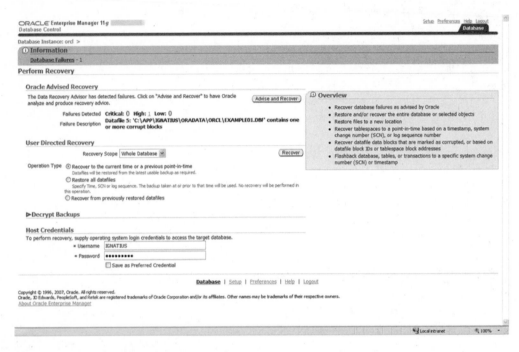

Figure 13-3. *Oracle-advised recovery—step 1*

The Oracle Advised Recovery section tells us that a data file with corrupt blocks has been found. Supply operating system login credentials in the Host Credentials section and click the Advise and Recover button. Enterprise Manager then displays the screen shown in Figure 13-4.

Select the failure that you want repaired; then click Advise. Enterprise Manager displays the screen shown in Figure 13-5.

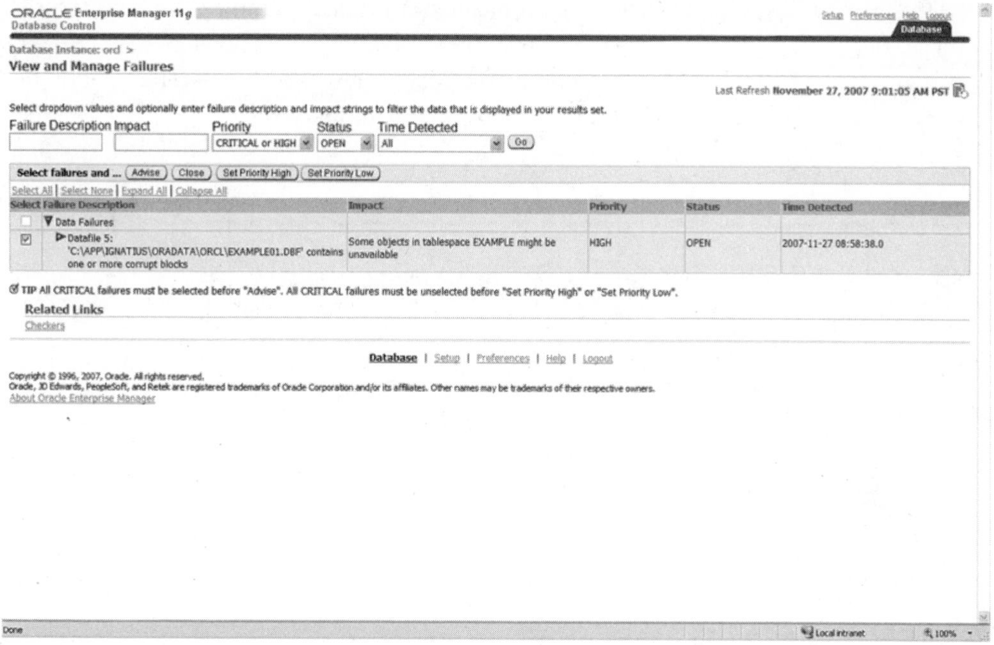

Figure 13-4. *Oracle-advised recovery—step 2*

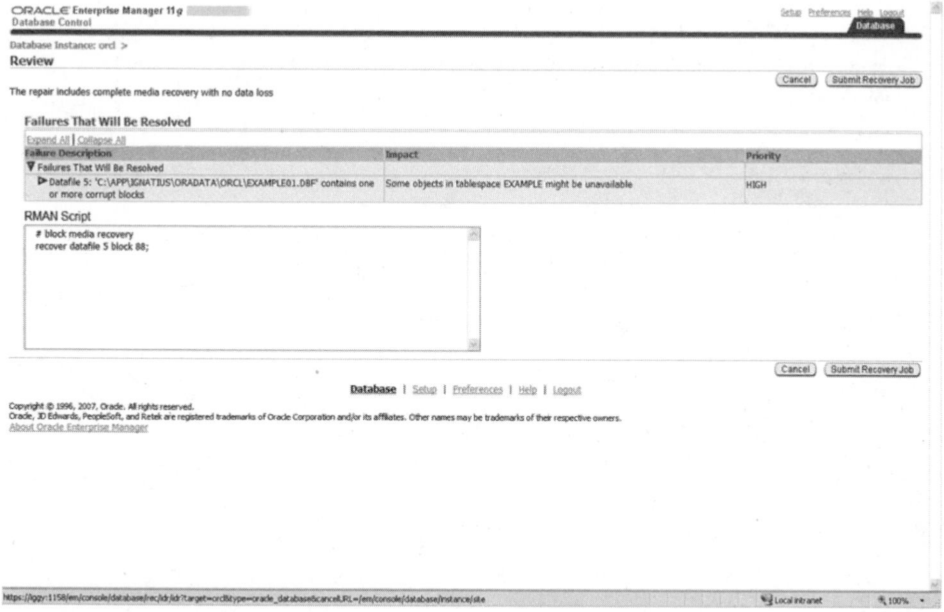

Figure 13-5. *Oracle-advised recovery—step 3*

Finally, click the Submit Recovery Job button to start the repair procedure. Enterprise Manager displays the screen shown in Figure 13-6.

After a while, click View Results and view the details of the successful repair operation. You should see a screen similar to the one shown in Figure 13-7.

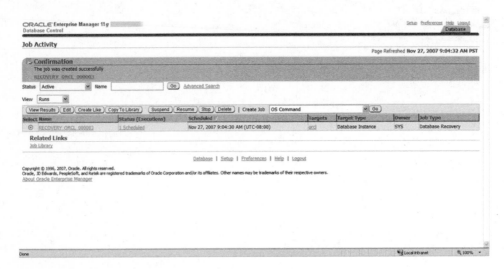

Figure 13-6. *Oracle-advised recovery—step 4*

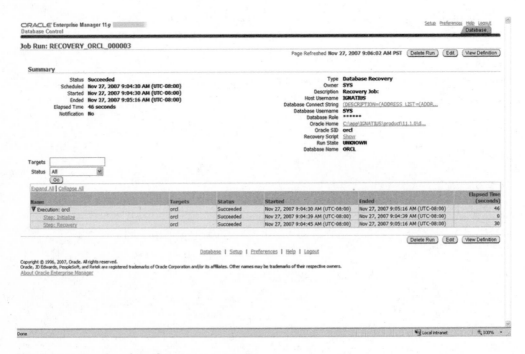

Figure 13-7. *Oracle-advised recovery—step 5*

Documentation and Testing

I'd like to conclude this introduction to the subject of recovery with a brief mention of testing. Not testing recovery procedures is a terrible mistake. A recovery test should always be performed before a new database is put to use. However, it is not feasible to perform periodic testing on a live database. The RMAN command DUPLICATE DATABASE can be used to verify the usability of backups without harming the live database. If the database is too large, you can exclude some tablespaces.

It is also important to document the recovery procedures. Chapter 15 covers the importance of standard operating procedures (SOPs). Database recovery is the most stressful task that a database administrator has to perform, and a SOP is exactly what you need to guide you through the situation.

Summary

Here is a short summary of the concepts touched on in this chapter:

- An appropriate repair strategy is one that is tailored to the situation and causes minimum downtime. Individual data files and data blocks can be repaired without impacting the rest of the database. Single-block recovery is available only with the Enterprise Edition.

- The Data Pump Import utility can be used to restore a table from a logical backup made using that utility.

- The word *restore* refers to the operation of replacing a damaged or missing file from a backup copy. The word *recover* refers to the process of relaying transactions recorded in the redo logs.

- A common reason for incomplete recovery is user error. It is the only option if the archived redo logs are damaged.

- Flashback techniques such as Flashback Query, Flashback Versions, Flashback Transaction, Flashback Table, and Flashback Drop can be used to reverse logical damage caused by user error. These techniques depend on the availability of the required information in the undo segments. The Flashback Archive technique can be used to record all changes made to data rows during the lifetime of a table.

- The Flashback Database technique can be used to easily recover from major changes or major damage to the database. This technique uses a special kind of log file called a flashback log.

- You can also recover prior versions of data from the archived redo logs by using LogMiner. Enable *supplemental minimal logging* to ensure that LogMiner has sufficient information to support chained rows and various storage arrangements such as cluster tables and index-organized tables.

- Data Recovery Advisor (DRA) completely simplifies the task of repairing a database. The commands LIST FAILURE, ADVISE FAILURE, and REPAIR FAILURE can be used to easily recovery from any failure. The task can also be performed by using Enterprise Manager.

- Not performing recovery testing is a critical mistake. The DUPLICATE DATABASE command can be used to verify the usability of backups without harming the live database. A standard operating procedure (SOP) for database recovery can be your guide to handling this most stressful of database administration tasks.

Exercises

- Shut down your learning database. Rename the USERS01.DBF file, and then try to open the database. Use Data Recovery Advisor to restore the missing file from backups and to recover transactions from the redo logs. Confirm that the database can now be opened for access.

- Flashback features such as Flashback Query, Flashback Versions, and Flashback Transaction depend on the availability of undo information in the undo segments. Information is lost if it is overwritten by newer transactions. Undo retention is governed by the UNDO_RETENTION parameter. Check the value of UNDO_RETENTION in your database. Find out how to increase the value. Add data files to the UNDO tablespace if you think it is not big enough to support this value. How would you determine how much space is enough? Refer to the Oracle documentation and find out how to *guarantee* the retention of undo information.

- The Flashback Database feature depends on a special kind of log file called a flashback log stored in the flash recovery area. The amount of information retained in the flashback logs is covered by the DB_FLASHBACK_RETENTION_TARGET parameter. Check the value of DB_FLASHBACK_RETENTION_TARGET in your database. Find out how to increase the value. Check the value of DB_RECOVERY_FILE_DEST—it will tell you the location of the flash recovery area, which is used to store backup copies as well as flashback logs. Check the size of the flash recovery area; is it big enough? Check the V$DATABASE view and determine whether logging of flashback information is enabled; if not, find out how to enable logging.

- Refer to Oracle Database 11*g* Licensing Information (available at `http://www.oracle.com/technology/documentation`) to determine which of the recovery methods discussed in this chapter are available only with the Enterprise Edition of Oracle Database 11*g*.

- Create a restore point by using the `CREATE RESTORE POINT` command. Modify the data in the `Employees` table in the `HR` schema. Shut down the database and bring it into the mounted state. Use the `FLASHBACK DATABASE` command to restore the database to the restore point. Open the database by using the `RESETLOGS` clause. Check the incarnation information in `V$DATABASE_INCARNATION`. Verify that the modifications you made to the `Employees` table have been reversed.

- Oracle by Example (OBE) is a collection of tutorials provided by Oracle on various subjects. Perform all the steps in the tutorial on backups and recovery—it is available at `http://www.oracle.com/technology/obe/11gr1_2day_dba/backup/backup.htm`. The tutorial assumes the use of a Unix platform, but adapting the commands to the Windows platform should be easy.

Further Reading

Oracle Corporation. *Oracle by Example*. This is an online series of tutorials and demonstrations with step-by-step instructions and screenshots. A tutorial on backups is available at `http://www.oracle.com/technology/obe/11gr1_2day_dba/backup/backup.htm`. The tutorial assumes the use of a Unix platform, but adapting the commands to the Windows platform is easy.

Oracle Corporation. *Oracle Database 11g Advanced Application Developer's Guide*. Oracle Corporation, 2007. Chapter 13, "Using Flashback Technology," is a good introduction to flashback features. Searchable or downloadable free of charge at `http://www.oracle.com/technology/documentation`. Printed copies can be purchased from Oracle's online store.

Oracle Corporation. *Oracle Database 11g Backup and Recovery Reference*. Oracle Corporation, 2007. Contains syntax diagrams (railroad diagrams) for all RMAN commands. Authoritative and detailed but difficult to read. Searchable or downloadable free of charge at `http://www.oracle.com/technology/documentation`. Printed copies can be purchased from Oracle's online store.

Oracle Corporation. *Oracle Database 11g Backup and Recovery User's Guide*. Oracle Corporation, 2007. Required reading for serious students. Searchable or downloadable free of charge at `http://www.oracle.com/technology/documentation`. Printed copies can be purchased from Oracle's online store.

Oracle Corporation. *Oracle Database 11*g *2 Day DBA*. Oracle Corporation, 2007. Chapter 9, "Performing Backup and Recovery," covers some of the material in this chapter including the use of Enterprise Manager to schedule backups. Searchable or downloadable free of charge at `http://www.oracle.com/technology/documentation`. Printed copies can be purchased from Oracle's online store.

Oracle Corporation. *Oracle Database 11*g *Utilities*. Oracle Corporation, 2007. Describes Data Pump Export and Data Pump Import as well as the older export and import utilities. Also describes the LogMiner utility. Searchable or downloadable free of charge at `http://www.oracle.com/technology/documentation`. Printed copies can be purchased from Oracle's online store.

Kuhn, Darl, and Sam R. Alapati and Arup Nanda. *RMAN Recipes for Oracle Database 11*g: *A Problem-Solution Approach*. Apress, 2007. Readers who tire of railroad diagrams might find the problem-solution approach refreshing.

∎ ∎ ∎

CHAPTER 14

Database Maintenance

"Sometimes," he added, "there is no harm in putting off a piece of work until another day. But when it is a matter of baobabs, that always means a catastrophe. I knew a planet that was inhabited by a lazy man. He neglected three little bushes . . ."

—*The Little Prince* by Antoine de Saint-Exupéry

In my first job as a database administrator, working for a Fortune 100 company, I managed only three databases, each no more than a hundred megabytes in size, and had ample time for database maintenance. I performed regular database maintenance procedures to keep the databases in peak operating condition, including data archiving and purging and rebuilding of tables and indexes. I also published graphs of database and application performance every week.

Gartner Research estimated in 2007 that the average amount of data managed by each database administrator is one terabyte. This allows very little time for database maintenance.

The Maintenance Plan

Here are the components of a simple maintenance plan—they should be automated as much as possible. The following sections of this chapter cover each component in detail.

- Regular backups are absolutely critical to the safety of the database. Backup logs should be reviewed frequently and a recovery exercise should be conducted at least once a year—more often if possible.

- The query optimizer relies on statistical information about the data. Statistics are automatically refreshed by Oracle every night, but some sites use a custom approach. Manual intervention may be occasionally needed.

- Data that is no longer needed should be archived and then purged from the database. Tables and indexes that contain a large amount of wasted space should be rebuilt to reclaim space.

- Log files should be reviewed regularly, daily if possible. Old log files should be removed.

- Disk capacity and system capacity should be reviewed regularly. Disk space should be proactively added to the database.

- User activities should be audited.

- Passwords should be changed regularly or when compromised. Unneeded accounts should be locked or removed.

- Patches should be applied to the database when necessary.

■**Caution** Index rebuilding and table defragmentation are often conducted without sufficient justification—the paper by Juan Loaiza and Bhaskar Himatsingka listed at the end of this chapter questions the need for these activities.

Backups

Backups are the most important aspect of database maintenance, but the honest truth is that most companies don't pay enough attention to them. Here are some best practices for backups; please refer to the chapters on backup and recovery for specific information on methods of backup (and recovery).

Generic Best Practices for Database Backups

The following practices apply to all database backups, not just Oracle backups.

- Establish a service level agreement (SLA) for backups and recovery. Clearly document the maximum amount of data loss that is permitted, backup retention policies, and how much time is allowed for database recovery.

- Document the backup methodology and have it formally reviewed. Publish the documentation to an audience that includes the database owner.

- Periodically test the recoverability of backups. Typically, this is done in a testing environment. A recovery test establishes how long it will take to recover the database.

- Be prepared to recover from user error, for example when a user inadvertently updates or deletes the wrong data. I presented several options in Chapter 13.

- Have a contingency plan that covers damage to the operating system or hardware—be prepared to move the database to another server.

- Ensure the safety of backups. The traditional method is to send backup tapes offline. Newer methods involve backups to a *backup appliance* over the network. A combination of *near-line* (disk) and *far-line* (tape or network) backups can be used. Near-line backups reduce the time needed for recovery, while far-line backups increase the safety of backups. The tape library should not be a single point of failure—ensure that data can be recovered even if the tape library is damaged.

- Retain multiple backups in case one set of backups is damaged.

- Backup scripts should incorporate error checking and an adequate amount of logging. The logs should be retained for an appropriate time. Notification of backup failures should be sent to the database administrators. Backup failures should be formally investigated.

- Reports of backup successes and failures, the amount of data backed up, and the time it took to perform backups should be generated and sent to an audience that includes the database administrators and the database owner.

- Changes to any aspect of backup procedures, whether temporary or permanent, should be performed under formal change control procedures.

Tip Don't forget to perform backups of databases used for development and testing.

Best Practices for Oracle Database Backups

The following practices apply specifically to Oracle database backups:

- Use Recovery Manager (RMAN) for backups. The advantages of RMAN are so numerous and valuable that it is hard to justify not using it. For example, RMAN checks data blocks for corruption while it is making a backup, single-block recovery is possible with RMAN, and so on.

Tip Backups performed using third-party software such as Network Appliance Snapshot can be integrated with RMAN.

- Prevent unlogged operations in databases that use ARCHIVELOG mode; use the ALTER DATABASE FORCE LOGGING command to do this.

- Back up all aspects of the database including the archived redo logs (for databases that use ARCHIVELOG mode), the control file, and the parameter file (spfile).

- Create logical backups (exports) to supplement physical backups. This creates a certain amount of protection from logical damage, such as data entry errors. Use a setting such as FLASHBACK_TIME to ensure the consistency of the exported data.

- Leverage Oracle's flashback features by increasing the value of UNDO_RETENTION from the default value of 15 minutes to a more appropriate value such as 24 hours. This allows recovery from logical damage without having to resort to physical backups.

- Databases that run in ARCHIVELOG mode should set LAG_ARCHIVE_TARGET to an appropriate value, such as 15 minutes, to control maximum data loss.

- Incorporate the use of techniques that check for data corruption. These include initialization parameters, such as DB_BLOCK_CHECKING, DB_BLOCK_CHECKSUM, and DB_LOST_WRITE_UPDATE, and commands that scan the database, such as VALIDATE DATABASE.

■Tip Oracle Database 11*g* introduced a single parameter called DB_ULTRA_SAFE that controls the values of DB_BLOCK_CHECKING, DB_BLOCK_CHECKSUM, and DB_LOST_WRITE_UPDATE.

Statistics

The query optimizer requires statistical information about the data such as the number of rows in each table, in order to generate efficient query plans; this information is collected using the procedures in the DBMS_STATS package. Beginning with Oracle Database 10*g*, statistical information about the data is refreshed automatically by a scheduled nightly job called GATHER_STATS_JOB; you are free to disable this job in favor of a custom approach. Oracle supplies a wide collection of procedures to collect and manage statistics including GATHER, DELETE, GET, SET, IMPORT, EXPORT, LOCK, UNLOCK, PUBLISH, and RESTORE procedures; a complete list of them follows, and details can be found in *Oracle Database PL/SQL Packages and Types Reference 11*g.

ALTER_STATS_HISTORY_RETENTION
CONVERT_RAW_VALUE
CONVERT_RAW_VALUE_NVARCHAR
CONVERT_RAW_VALUE_ROWID
COPY_TABLE_STATS
CREATE_EXTENDED_STATS
CREATE_STAT_TABLE
DELETE_COLUMN_STATS
DELETE_DATABASE_PREFS
DELETE_DATABASE_STATS
DELETE_DICTIONARY_STATS
DELETE_FIXED_OBJECTS_STATS
DELETE_INDEX_STATS
DELETE_PENDING_STATS
DELETE_SCHEMA_PREFS
DELETE_SCHEMA_STATS
DELETE_SYSTEM_STATS
DELETE_TABLE_PREFS
DELETE_TABLE_STATS
DIFF_TABLE_STATS_IN_HISTORY
DIFF_TABLE_STATS_IN_PENDING
DIFF_TABLE_STATS_IN_STATTAB
DROP_EXTENDED_STATS
DROP_STAT_TABLE
EXPORT_COLUMN_STATS
EXPORT_DATABASE_PREFS
EXPORT_DATABASE_STATS
EXPORT_DICTIONARY_STATS
EXPORT_FIXED_OBJECTS_STATS
EXPORT_INDEX_STATS
EXPORT_PENDING_STATS
EXPORT_SCHEMA_PREFS

EXPORT_SCHEMA_STATS
EXPORT_SYSTEM_STATS
EXPORT_TABLE_PREFS
EXPORT_TABLE_STATS
FLUSH_DATABASE_MONITORING_INFO
GATHER_DATABASE_STATS
GATHER_DICTIONARY_STATS
GATHER_FIXED_OBJECTS_STATS
GATHER_INDEX_STATS
GATHER_SCHEMA_STATS
GATHER_SYSTEM_STATS
GATHER_TABLE_STATS
GENERATE_STATS
GET_COLUMN_STATS
GET_INDEX_STATS
GET_PARAM
GET_STATS_HISTORY_AVAILABILITY
GET_STATS_HISTORY_RETENTION
GET_SYSTEM_STATS
GET_TABLE_STATS
IMPORT_COLUMN_STATS
IMPORT_DATABASE_PREFS
IMPORT_DATABASE_STATS
IMPORT_DICTIONARY_STATS
IMPORT_FIXED_OBJECTS_STATS
IMPORT_INDEX_STATS
IMPORT_SCHEMA_PREFS
IMPORT_SCHEMA_STATS
IMPORT_SYSTEM_STATS
IMPORT_TABLE_PREFS
IMPORT_TABLE_STATS

LOCK_PARTITION_STATS
LOCK_SCHEMA_STATS
LOCK_TABLE_STATS
PREPARE_COLUMN_VALUES
PREPARE_COLUMN_VALUES_NVARCHAR2
PREPARE_COLUMN_VALUES_ROWID
PUBLISH_PENDING_STATS
PURGE_STATS
RESET_GLOBAL_PREFS_DEFAULTS
RESET_PARAM_DEFAULTS
RESTORE_DICTIONARY_STATS
RESTORE_FIXED_OBJECTS_STATS
RESTORE_SCHEMA_STATS
RESTORE_SYSTEM_STATS
RESTORE_TABLE_STATS
SET_COLUMN_STATS
SET_DATABASE_PREFS
SET_GLOBAL_PREFS
SET_INDEX_STATS
SET_PARAM
SET_SCHEMA_PREFS
SET_SYSTEM_STATS
SET_TABLE_PREFS
SET_TABLE_STATS
SHOW_EXTENDED_STATS_NAME
UNLOCK_PARTITION_STATS
UNLOCK_SCHEMA_STATS
UNLOCK_TABLE_STATS
UPGRADE_STAT_TABLE

■**Caution** Small changes in statistics can sometimes produce big changes in query plans—not always for the better—and this problem can challenge even the most experienced database administrators. The LOCK and RESTORE procedures can be very useful in fixing problems caused by changes in statistics.

Archiving and Purging

Database performance commonly degrades as the database grows large. To keep the database performing optimally, you should remove unnecessary data from the database. In some cases, it may be necessary to save a copy of the data in a data archive, such as flat files, XML documents, or the like, before the data is purged from the database. The archiving phase also involves a special backup that is tagged with a high retention setting, such as seven years.

The freed space is automatically used by new data. Regular purging keeps the size of the database under control and helps keep performance stable. If a large amount of data is purged at a time, the sizes of the tables and indexes will not be commensurate with the amount of data they actually contain, and additional maintenance will be required to compact and shrink the bloated tables and indexes. This is discussed in the section on rebuilding tables and indexes.

The use of partitioning can completely eliminate the need for archiving, purging, and rebuilding. For example, a table can be divided into partitions in such a way that each month's data is inserted into a separate partition. Queries that require the most recent data perform optimally because the required data will be clustered in a relatively small number of data blocks instead of being randomly scattered throughout the table as happens when partitioning is not used. In the case of partitioned tables, purging the data requires only that a partition be dropped; this is a very quick operation. If the old partitions are in a separate tablespace, an alternative to purging is to convert the tablespaces to read-only mode and move them to cheap storage such as WORM drives or unmirrored SATA disks; this is a wonderful way to keep performance optimal without having to remove data. Even the overhead of backups can be kept under control; read-only tablespaces require to be backed up only one more time with a high retention setting and then no longer need to be backed up.

Caution Partitioning is a very expensive option that is only available with Enterprise Edition, and few sites have the required licenses. Don't fall into the trap of using the partitioning feature without first ensuring that you are licensed to use it.

Rebuilding

The size of a table does not change when records are deleted from it—the indexes associated with the table will not shrink in size either. The wasted space causes three problems:

- The gains that come from caching blocks of data in memory are reduced because fewer records are packed into each block.

- Additional space on disk will be required as the database grows.

- Backup and recovery will require more time, more space, and more computing resources.

The tables and indexes will have to be rebuilt to reclaim space—several methods are available for the purpose. Tables and indexes that have a lot of wasted space are automatically identified by the Automatic Segment Advisor, which runs automatically during the nightly maintenance window; sample results are shown in Figure 14-1.

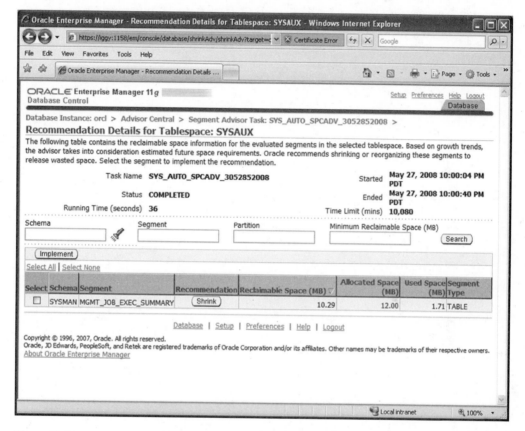

Figure 14-1. *Automatic Segment Advisor*

Alternatively, you can conduct your own investigation of wasted space, using the SPACE_USAGE procedure. Listing 14-1 shows a sample run; we see that 1161 blocks are empty.

Listing 14-1. *An Example of the SPACE_USAGE Procedure*

```
SQL> SET serveroutput on
SQL>
SQL> DECLARE
  2      l_full_blocks           NUMBER;
  3      l_fs1_blocks            NUMBER;
```

```
 4      l_fs2_blocks            NUMBER;
 5      l_fs3_blocks            NUMBER;
 6      l_fs4_blocks            NUMBER;
 7      l_unformatted_blocks    NUMBER;
 8      l_full_bytes            NUMBER;
 9      l_fs1_bytes             NUMBER;
10      l_fs2_bytes             NUMBER;
11      l_fs3_bytes             NUMBER;
12      l_fs4_bytes             NUMBER;
13      l_unformatted_bytes     NUMBER;
14   BEGIN
15      DBMS_SPACE.space_usage (segment_owner        => 'SYSMAN',
16                              segment_name         => 'MGMT_JOB_EXEC_SUMMARY',
17                              segment_type         => 'TABLE',
18                              full_blocks          => l_full_blocks,
19                              fs1_blocks           => l_fs1_blocks,
20                              fs2_blocks           => l_fs2_blocks,
21                              fs3_blocks           => l_fs3_blocks,
22                              fs4_blocks           => l_fs4_blocks,
23                              unformatted_blocks   => l_unformatted_blocks,
24                              full_bytes           => l_full_bytes,
25                              fs1_bytes            => l_fs1_bytes,
26                              fs2_bytes            => l_fs2_bytes,
27                              fs3_bytes            => l_fs3_bytes,
28                              fs4_bytes            => l_fs4_bytes,
29                              unformatted_bytes    => l_unformatted_bytes
30                              );
31      DBMS_OUTPUT.put_line ('Full blocks:' || l_full_blocks);
32      DBMS_OUTPUT.put_line ('Upto 25% free:' || l_fs1_blocks);
33      DBMS_OUTPUT.put_line ('Upto 50% free:' || l_fs2_blocks);
34      DBMS_OUTPUT.put_line ('Upto 75% free:' || l_fs3_blocks);
35      DBMS_OUTPUT.put_line ('Upto 100% free:' || l_fs4_blocks);
36      DBMS_OUTPUT.put_line ('Unformatted blocks:' || l_unformatted_blocks);
37   END;
38   /
Full blocks:294
Upto 25% free:0
Upto 50% free:2
Upto 75% free:1
Upto 100% free:1161
Unformatted blocks:46

PL/SQL procedure successfully completed.
```

Once you have identified tables and indexes that will benefit from compaction, you can reclaim the wasted space using the SHRINK SPACE command, as in Listing 14-2. Note that you will have to give Oracle permission explicitly to relocate rows, using the ENABLE ROW MOVEMENT command—Oracle does not do this automatically, so as not to affect any application that has taken advantage of row addresses (ROWIDs).

Listing 14-2. *An Example of the SHRINK SPACE Procedure*

```
SQL> ALTER TABLE sysman.mgmt_job_exec_summary
  2   ENABLE ROW MOVEMENT;

Table altered.

SQL> ALTER TABLE sysman.mgmt_job_exec_summary
  2   SHRINK SPACE;

Table altered.
```

Log File Maintenance

Log files of all kinds accumulate over time and can fill up the available space. For example, a *trace file* is created whenever certain errors occur, such as ORA-00060 (deadlock) and ORA-00600 (internal error). Listing 14-3 shows the first few lines from such a trace file.

Listing 14-3. *An Extract from a Trace File for an ORA-00060 Error*

```
Trace file c:\app\ignatius\diag\rdbms\orcl\orcl\trace\orcl_ora_5196.trc
Oracle Database 11g Enterprise Edition Release 11.1.0.6.0 - Production
With the Partitioning, OLAP, Data Mining and Real Application Testing options
Windows XP Version V5.1 Service Pack 2
CPU              : 2 - type 586
Process Affinity  : 0x00000000
Memory (Avail/Total): Ph:451M/2037M, Ph+PgF:2345M/3930M, VA:1243M/2047M
Instance name: orcl
Redo thread mounted by this instance: 1
Oracle process number: 7
Windows thread id: 5196, image: ORACLE.EXE (SHAD)


*** 2008-06-07 09:32:39.734
*** SESSION ID:(99.609) 2008-06-07 09:32:39.734
*** CLIENT ID:() 2008-06-07 09:32:39.734
```

```
*** SERVICE NAME:(SYS$USERS) 2008-06-07 09:32:39.734
*** MODULE NAME:(SQL*Plus) 2008-06-07 09:32:39.734
*** ACTION NAME:() 2008-06-07 09:32:39.734

*** 2008-06-07 09:32:39.734
DEADLOCK DETECTED ( ORA-00060 )

[Transaction Deadlock]

The following deadlock is not an ORACLE error. It is a
deadlock due to user error in the design of an application
or from issuing incorrect ad-hoc SQL. The following
information may aid in determining the deadlock:

Deadlock graph:
                    ---------Blocker(s)--------  ---------Waiter(s)---------
Resource Name       process session holds waits  process session holds waits
TM-00011bc5-00000000     7      99    SX   SSX      31     105    SX   SSX
TM-00011bc5-00000000    31     105    SX   SSX       7      99    SX   SSX


session 99: DID 0001-0007-000028EA    session 105: DID 0001-001F-00000041
session 105: DID 0001-001F-00000041   session 99: DID 0001-0007-000028EA

Rows waited on:
  Session 99: no row
  Session 105: no row

----- Information for the OTHER waiting sessions -----
Session 105:
  sid: 105 ser: 881 audsid: 349519 user: 88/IGGY flags: 0x45
  pid: 31 O/S info: user: SYSTEM, term: IGGY, ospid: 5112
    image: ORACLE.EXE (SHAD)
  client details:
    O/S info: user: IGGY\IGNATIUS, term: IGGY, ospid: 4548:6076
    machine: WORKGROUP\IGGY program: sqlplus.exe
    application name: SQL*Plus, hash value=3669949024
  Current SQL Statement:
  DELETE FROM PARENT WHERE ID=2


----- End of information for the OTHER waiting sessions -----
```

```
Information for THIS session:

----- Current SQL Statement for this session (sql_id=9vym32vjhdgzc) -----
DELETE FROM PARENT WHERE ID=1

=====================================================
```

The log files are organized into an Automatic Diagnostics Repository (ADR), whose location is controlled by the DIAGNOSTIC_DEST setting. Log files are automatically purged after 30 days—you can change the retention window using the SET CONTROL option of the adrci tool. You can also purge log files manually using the tool's PURGE command, as in Listing 14-4.

Listing 14-4. *Using the adrci Tool to Manage Log Files*

```
C:\Documents and Settings\IGNATIUS>adrci

ADRCI: Release 11.1.0.6.0 - Beta on Sat Jun 7 12:03:21 2008

Copyright (c) 1982, 2007, Oracle.  All rights reserved.

ADR base = "c:\app\ignatius"
adrci> show homepath
ADR Homes:
diag\clients\user_ignatius\host_2237066830_11
diag\clients\user_system\host_2237066830_11
diag\clients\user_unknown\host_411310321_11
diag\rdbms\orcl\orcl
diag\rdbms\test\test
diag\rdbms\training\training
diag\tnslsnr\iggy\listener
adrci> set homepath diag\rdbms\orcl\orcl
adrci> show tracefile
    diag\rdbms\orcl\orcl\trace\5_88_0_887612.BKD
    diag\rdbms\orcl\orcl\trace\alert_orcl.log
    diag\rdbms\orcl\orcl\trace\IOUG.tkprof
    diag\rdbms\orcl\orcl\trace\orcl_arc0_5608.trc
    diag\rdbms\orcl\orcl\trace\orcl_cjq0_960.trc
    diag\rdbms\orcl\orcl\trace\orcl_dbrm_4324.trc
    diag\rdbms\orcl\orcl\trace\orcl_fbda_3284.trc
    diag\rdbms\orcl\orcl\trace\orcl_m000_1408.trc
    diag\rdbms\orcl\orcl\trace\orcl_m000_1412.trc
```

```
        diag\rdbms\orcl\orcl\trace\orcl_m000_2468.trc
        diag\rdbms\orcl\orcl\trace\orcl_m000_4248.trc
        diag\rdbms\orcl\orcl\trace\orcl_m000_4636.trc
        diag\rdbms\orcl\orcl\trace\orcl_m000_5628.trc
        diag\rdbms\orcl\orcl\trace\orcl_m001_5736.trc
        diag\rdbms\orcl\orcl\trace\orcl_m004_1048.trc
        diag\rdbms\orcl\orcl\trace\orcl_m005_1904.trc
        diag\rdbms\orcl\orcl\trace\orcl_m008_4156.trc
        diag\rdbms\orcl\orcl\trace\orcl_mmnl_3148.trc
        diag\rdbms\orcl\orcl\trace\orcl_ora_5196.trc
        diag\rdbms\orcl\orcl\trace\orcl_reco_2512.trc
        diag\rdbms\orcl\orcl\trace\orcl_rvwr_1176.trc
        diag\rdbms\orcl\orcl\trace\orcl_smon_5724.trc
adrci> purge -age 60
adrci> show tracefile
        diag\rdbms\orcl\orcl\trace\5_88_0_887612.BKD
        diag\rdbms\orcl\orcl\trace\alert_orcl.log
        diag\rdbms\orcl\orcl\trace\IOUG.tkprof
        diag\rdbms\orcl\orcl\trace\orcl_dbrm_4324.trc
        diag\rdbms\orcl\orcl\trace\orcl_m000_2468.trc
        diag\rdbms\orcl\orcl\trace\orcl_ora_5196.trc
        diag\rdbms\orcl\orcl\trace\orcl_rvwr_1176.trc
adrci> exit
```

■**Tip** Trace files can be very large. The maximum size of a trace file is controlled by the max_dump_file_size initialization setting, whose default value is "unlimited." Consider changing the setting to a value that is appropriate for your environment.

Auditing

Oracle provides the ability to audit all aspects of database usage. Audit records can be stored in the AUD$ table owned by SYS or in files outside the database—this is controlled by the AUDIT_TRAIL and AUDIT_FILE_DEST settings. There are a number of useful views on the AUD$ table, the chief ones being DBA_AUDIT_TRAIL and DBA_AUDIT_SESSION. Listing 14-5 shows a sample of the data in the DBA_AUDIT_SESSION table.

Listing 14-5. *A Sample Listing of the Contents of the* DBA_AUDIT_SESSION *View*

```
SQL> SELECT    TIMESTAMP AS "LOGON",
  2            logoff_time AS "LOGOFF",
  3            logoff_lread AS "GETS",
  4            logoff_pread AS "READS",
  5            logoff_lwrite AS "WRITES",
  6            session_cpu AS "CPU"
  7       FROM dba_audit_session
  8      WHERE username = 'IGGY'
  9        AND logoff_time IS NOT NULL
 10   ORDER BY TIMESTAMP;
```

LOGON	LOGOFF	GETS	READS	WRITES	CPU
11/25 19:07	11/25 19:08	1187	11	364	32
11/25 19:08	11/25 19:16	2105	12	417	32
11/25 19:16	11/25 19:17	1138	3	431	20
11/25 19:18	11/25 19:18	849	0	356	24
11/25 19:18	11/25 19:19	1266	0	516	17
11/25 19:20	11/25 19:29	2655	0	1136	47
11/25 19:33	11/25 19:35	3894	6	1597	49
11/25 19:38	11/25 19:38	154	0	15	3
11/25 19:40	11/25 19:41	71	0	6	11
11/25 19:41	11/25 20:13	2778	10	1059	50
11/25 20:14	11/25 20:28	319540	1123	643	1011
11/28 11:30	11/28 11:30	383	13	6	5
05/26 11:31	05/26 20:10	2427	101	726	100
05/26 14:29	05/26 14:29	58	0	6	0
05/26 14:31	05/26 14:31	58	0	6	0
05/26 14:32	05/26 20:09	258	8	12	21
06/07 09:21	06/07 17:21	3049	114	732	83
06/07 09:32	06/07 17:21	274	15	49	3

```
18 rows selected.
```

When creating a database using DBCA, you can choose to enable auditing for logon and logoff events and certain privileged activities such as ALTER DATABASE and ALTER USER. A number of views can be used to determine which activities are being audited, the chief ones being DBA_STMT_AUDIT_OPTS (which SQL commands are being monitored) and DBA_OBJ_AUDIT_OPTS (which tables are being monitored). Listing 14-6 shows a sample of the data in the DBA_STMT_AUDIT_OPTS table.

Listing 14-6. *A Sample Listing of the Contents of the* DBA_STMT_AUDIT_OPTS *View*

```
SQL> SELECT    audit_option,
  2            CASE
  3               WHEN user_name IS NOT NULL
  4                  THEN user_name
  5               ELSE 'ALL USERS'
  6            END AS username
  7       FROM dba_stmt_audit_opts
  8  ORDER BY audit_option, user_name;


AUDIT_OPTION                             USERNAME
---------------------------------------- ------------------------------
ALTER ANY PROCEDURE                      ALL USERS
ALTER ANY TABLE                          ALL USERS
ALTER DATABASE                           ALL USERS
ALTER PROFILE                            ALL USERS
ALTER SYSTEM                             ALL USERS
ALTER USER                               ALL USERS
CREATE ANY JOB                           ALL USERS
CREATE ANY LIBRARY                       ALL USERS
CREATE ANY PROCEDURE                     ALL USERS
CREATE ANY TABLE                         ALL USERS
CREATE EXTERNAL JOB                      ALL USERS
CREATE PUBLIC DATABASE LINK              ALL USERS
CREATE SESSION                           ALL USERS
CREATE USER                              ALL USERS
DROP ANY PROCEDURE                       ALL USERS
DROP ANY TABLE                           ALL USERS
DROP PROFILE                             ALL USERS
DROP USER                                ALL USERS
EXEMPT ACCESS POLICY                     ALL USERS
GRANT ANY OBJECT PRIVILEGE               ALL USERS
GRANT ANY PRIVILEGE                      ALL USERS
GRANT ANY ROLE                           ALL USERS
ROLE                                     ALL USERS
SYSTEM AUDIT                             ALL USERS

24 rows selected.
```

Reviewing audit records regularly is a good practice. Note that Oracle does not delete old audit data automatically—that is the responsibility of the database administrator. You should consider archiving the data using the exp or expdp utilities before you delete it.

Tip The AUD$ table is placed in the SYSTEM tablespace when the database is created. The AUD$ table can grow very large, SO the SYSTEM tablespace is not a good location for it—it should be housed in a dedicated tablespace instead. Metalink notes 72460.1 *Moving AUD$ to Another Tablespace and Adding Triggers to AUD$* and *1019377.6 Script to move SYS.AUD$ table out of SYSTEM tablespace* discuss this issue.

User Management

The security of the database is the responsibility of the database administrator. Here are some simple security rules:

- Passwords should be changed regularly. This is controlled by the PASSWORD_LIFE_TIME, PASSWORD_REUSE_TIME, and PASSWORD_REUSE_MAX settings in the DEFAULT profile. Resist the temptation to relax or disable these settings.

- Shared passwords should be changed when an employee is relieved of his or her responsibilities or leaves the company. For example, database administrators typically share the passwords to the SYS and SYSTEM accounts. These passwords should be changed whenever a database administrator leaves the organizational group or the company.

- Users should be required to have strong passwords; this is not required by default. Execute the utlpwdmg.sql script from the SYS account to enforce the requirement.

- When a user's job responsibilities change, their database privileges should be changed appropriately. When a user leaves the organization, their account should be removed from the database.

Capacity Management

Regular capacity reviews are part of good database management. Database size and free space should be recorded at regular intervals—the required information can be found in the DBA_DATA_FILES and DBA_FREE_SPACE views, as shown in Listing 14-7. Database size and free space can also be checked using Enterprise Manager, as shown in Figure 14-2. Space should be proactively added to the database as necessary. Growth projections should be made and opportunities to reclaim disk space should be identified. Capacity management also refers to utilization of system resources such as CPU and memory. The information in the STATSPACK reports and tables can be used to track system utilization or you can develop a simple system that periodically captures system utilization metrics from the V$SYSSTAT table.

Listing 14-7. *Checking Database Size and Free Space*

```
SQL> SET linesize 80
SQL> SET pagesize 1000
SQL> COLUMN tablespace_name format a10
SQL> COLUMN file_name format a20
SQL>
SQL> SELECT    tablespace_name,
  2            file_name,
  3            file_id,
  4            BYTES / 1024 AS kb,
  5            autoextensible,
  6            increment_by * 8192 / 1024 AS next_kb,
  7            maxbytes / 1024 AS max_kb
  8       FROM dba_data_files
  9   ORDER BY tablespace_name,
 10            file_id;
```

TABLESPACE	FILE_NAME	FILE_ID	KB	AUT	NEXT_KB	MAX_KB
EXAMPLE	C:\APP\IGNATIUS\ORAD ATA\ORCL\EXAMPLE01.D BF	5	102400	YES	640	33554416
STATSPACK	C:\APP\IGNATIUS\ORAD ATA\ORCL\STATSPACK01 .DBF	6	2048000	NO	0	0
SYSAUX	C:\APP\IGNATIUS\ORAD ATA\ORCL\SYSAUX01.DB F	2	650944	YES	10240	33554416
SYSTEM	C:\APP\IGNATIUS\ORAD ATA\ORCL\SYSTEM01.DB F	1	727040	YES	10240	33554416
UNDOTBS1	C:\APP\IGNATIUS\ORAD ATA\ORCL\UNDOTBS01.D BF	3	122880	YES	5120	33554416

```
USERS       C:\APP\IGNATIUS\ORAD        4      5120 YES      1280    33554416
            ATA\ORCL\USERS01.DBF
```

6 rows selected.

```
SQL> SELECT   file_id,
  2             SUM (BYTES) / 1024 AS free_kb
  3       FROM dba_free_space
  4   GROUP BY file_id
  5   ORDER BY file_id;

   FILE_ID    FREE_KB
---------- ----------
         1       7424
         2      32320
         3     104128
         4       1984
         5      23168
         6     714944
```

6 rows selected.

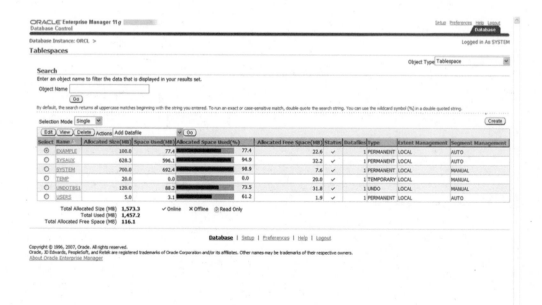

Figure 14-2. *Checking the database size and free space using Enterprise Manager*

Time Series

A *time series* is a sequence of measurements made at periodic intervals. The STATSPACK tables contain much time series data and can be used for capacity reviews. The STATSPACK tables STATS$OSSTAT, STATS$SYSSTAT, STATS$SYSTEM_EVENT and STATS$SYS_TIME_MODEL are of particular interest—they store snapshots of the dynamic performance views V$OSSTAT, V$SYSSTAT, V$SYSTEM_EVENT, and V$SYS_TIME_MODEL respectively. As illustrated in Listing 14-8, V$OSSTAT offers cumulative values of various operating system metrics such as CPU usage and STATS$OSSTAT contains snapshots of this data—the snapshots are identified by the SNAP_ID column.

Listing 14-8. *Comparison of Data in V$OSSTAT and STATS$OSSTAT*

```
SQL> SELECT stat_name, value FROM v$osstat;
```

STAT_NAME	VALUE
NUM_CPUS	2
IDLE_TIME	3769723
BUSY_TIME	668049
USER_TIME	463348
SYS_TIME	204701
AVG_IDLE_TIME	1884476
AVG_BUSY_TIME	333641
AVG_USER_TIME	231300
AVG_SYS_TIME	101963
RSRC_MGR_CPU_WAIT_TIME	1278
PHYSICAL_MEMORY_BYTES	2136969216
VM_IN_BYTES	1393717248
VM_OUT_BYTES	394657792

```
13 rows selected.

SQL> SELECT snap_id, osstat_id, value
  2    FROM stats$osstat
  3   WHERE snap_id IN (3000, 3001);
```

```
SNAP_ID  OSSTAT_ID      VALUE
-------- ---------- ----------
    3000          0          2
    3000          1  654407998
    3000          2   72816975
    3000          3   60092930
    3000          4   12053254
    3000          6     670791
    3000         14          0
    3000         15       1.25
    3000       1008      16396
    3001          0          2
    3001          1  655068971
    3001          2   72864457
    3001          3   60137335
    3001          4   12056331
    3001          6     670791
    3001         14          0
    3001         15 .309570313
    3001       1008     494964
```

18 rows selected.

The time series data in the STATSPACK tables can be manipulated with SQL queries into a format that is suitable for reports and graphs. First we use the PIVOT operator to create a two-dimensional table of the cumulative values (Listing 14-9). Then we use an analytic function called LAG to compute the difference between the values in successive rows (Listing 14-10). The CPU utilization graph seen in Figure 14-3 was generated using the data produced by the SQL query shown in Listing 14-11.

Listing 14-9. *Using the PIVOT Operator to Produce Two-Dimensional Tables*

```
SQL> COLUMN busy_time FORMAT 9999999990
SQL> COLUMN idle_time FORMAT 9999999990
SQL>
SQL> SELECT *
  2    FROM (SELECT snap_id, osstat_id, value FROM stats$osstat
  3           WHERE SNAP_ID IN (3000, 3001))
  4         PIVOT
  5         (SUM(value) FOR osstat_id IN (1 AS idle_time, 2 AS busy_time));
```

```
    SNAP_ID    IDLE_TIME    BUSY_TIME
---------- ----------- -----------
      3000   654407998    72816975
      3001   655068971    72864457
```

Listing 14-10. *Using Analytic Functions to Correlate Data in Different Rows*

```
SQL> COLUMN busy_time FORMAT 9999999990
SQL> COLUMN idle_time FORMAT 9999999990
SQL>
SQL> SELECT snap_id,
  2          idle_time - LAG (idle_time) OVER (ORDER BY snap_id) AS idle_time,
  3          busy_time - LAG (busy_time) OVER (ORDER BY snap_id) AS busy_time
  4     FROM (SELECT snap_id, osstat_id, value FROM stats$osstat
  5           WHERE SNAP_ID IN (3000, 3001))
  6           PIVOT
  7           (SUM(value) FOR osstat_id IN (1 AS idle_time, 2 AS busy_time));
```

```
    SNAP_ID    IDLE_TIME    BUSY_TIME
---------- ----------- -----------
      3000
      3001      660973       47482
```

Listing 14-11. *SQL Query to Compute CPU Utilization*

```
WITH osstat AS
    (SELECT snap_id,
            LAG (snap_id) OVER (ORDER BY snap_id) AS prev_snap_id,
            idle_time - LAG (idle_time) OVER (ORDER BY snap_id) AS idle_time,
            busy_time - LAG (busy_time) OVER (ORDER BY snap_id) AS busy_time
       FROM (SELECT snap_id, osstat_id, value FROM stats$osstat
             PIVOT
             (SUM(value) FOR osstat_id IN (1 AS idle_time, 2 AS busy_time)))
SELECT   s1.snap_time,
         o.busy_time / (o.idle_time + o.busy_time) AS cpu_utilization
    FROM osstat o,
         stats$snapshot s1,
         stats$snapshot s2
   WHERE s1.snap_id = o.snap_id
     AND s2.snap_id = o.prev_snap_id
     AND s2.startup_time = s1.startup_time
ORDER BY s1.snap_id;
```

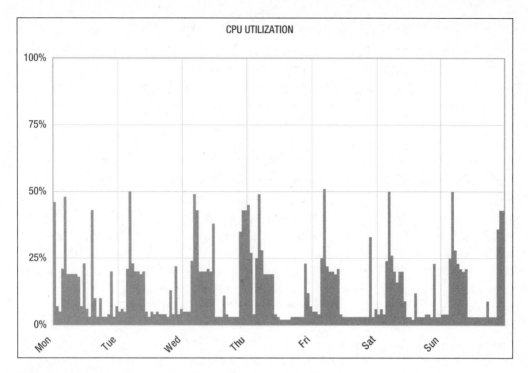

Figure 14-3. *CPU utilization graph produced from the data in the* STATS$OSSTAT *table*

There is a wealth of other useful data in the STATSPACK tables. For example, STATS$SYSSTAT offers cumulative values of Oracle metrics such as logical reads and physical reads, STATS$SYSTEM_EVENT reports the time spent waiting for I/O, locks, and other resources, and STATS$SYS_TIME_MODEL offers summary information such as the total of the elapsed times of all SQL queries processed by Oracle.

Patching

Oracle periodically releases fixes, known as *patches*, for software bugs. A *one-off patch* is a fix for an individual bug, while a *patchset* is a collection of numerous bug fixes. A *critical patch update* (CPU) is a collection of fixes for security-related bugs; Oracle releases one such CPU every quarter. A patchset has an Oracle database version string associated with it; for example, 10.2.0.4 is a patchset associated with Oracle 10*g* Release 2. By contrast, one-off patches and CPUs are identified by a single number; for example, 7210195 is the number of the July 2008 CPU. One-off patches, patches, and patchsets can be downloaded from the Patches & Updates section of the Metalink customer portal.

Some organizations adopt a policy of applying software patches and CPUs whenever they become available. Listing 14-12 is a typical notice regarding the availability of a new CPU that you will receive from Oracle if you have a support contract.

Listing 14-12. *Notification about a Critical Patch Update (CPU)*

```
July 15th, 2008

Oracle Critical Patch Update July 2008

Dear Oracle customer,

The Critical Patch Update for July 2008 was released on July 15, 2008. Oracle
strongly recommends applying the patches as soon as possible.

The Critical Patch Update Advisory is the starting point for relevant information.
It includes the list of products affected, pointers to obtain the patches, a summary
of the security vulnerabilities for each product suite, and links to other important
documents. Supported products that are not listed in the "Supported Products and
Components Affected" section of the advisory do not require new patches to be
applied.

Also, it is essential to review the Critical Patch Update supporting documentation
referenced in the Advisory before applying patches, as this is where you can find
important pertinent information.

The Critical Patch Update Advisory is available at the following location:

Oracle Technology Network:
http://www.oracle.com/technology/deploy/security/alerts.htm

The next four Critical Patch Update release dates are:

*  October 14, 2008
*  January 13, 2009
*  April 14, 2009
*  July 14, 2009

Sincerely, Oracle Security Alerts
```

The notification about a critical patch update directs readers to a web page where they can find more information. Once you have determined the specific patch number applicable to your operating system platform, you can download the CPU from the Patches & Updates section of the Metalink customer portal, as illustrated in Figure 14-4.

Figure 14-4. *Patches & Updates section of Metalink*

Critical path updates are applied using the opatch utility—complete instructions are provided together with the patch. The opatch lsinventory command can be used to determine which patches have been applied to your environment, as illustrated in Listing 14-13.

Listing 14-13. *Determining Which Patches Have Been Applied to an Oracle Environment*

```
C:\Documents and Settings\IGNATIUS>set ORACLE_HOME=C:\app\IGNATIUS\product\11.1.0\db
_1

C:\Documents and Settings\IGNATIUS>%ORACLE_HOME%\OPatch\opatch lsinventory
Invoking OPatch 11.1.0.6.0

Oracle Interim Patch Installer version 11.1.0.6.0
Copyright (c) 2007, Oracle Corporation.  All rights reserved.

Oracle Home        : C:\app\IGNATIUS\product\11.1.0\db_1
Central Inventory : C:\Program Files\Oracle\Inventory
   from             : n/a
OPatch version     : 11.1.0.6.0
OUI version        : 11.1.0.6.0
OUI location       : C:\app\IGNATIUS\product\11.1.0\db_1\oui
```

Log file location : C:\app\IGNATIUS\product\11.1.0\db_1\cfgtoollogs\opatch\opatch200
8-09-14_22-07-31PM.log

Lsinventory Output file location : C:\app\IGNATIUS\product\11.1.0\db_1\cfgtoollogs\o
patch\lsinv\lsinventory2008-09-14_22-07-31PM.txt

```
--------------------------------------------------------------------------------
Installed Top-level Products (3):

Oracle Client                                                    11.1.0.6.0
Oracle Database 11g                                             11.1.0.6.0
Oracle Database 11g Examples                                    11.1.0.6.0
There are 3 products installed in this Oracle Home.

Interim patches (1) :

Patch  7210195      : applied on Sun Sep 14 21:48:02 PDT 2008
   Created on 11 July 2008, 12:29:01 hrs US/Pacific
   Bugs fixed:
     7210195, 7225995, 7001236, 6870937, 7046502, 6972189, 6736527, 6263237
     6883418, 7156923, 7150477, 7009011, 6862429, 6945432, 6843252, 6896720
     6770913, 6368018, 6669705, 6973000, 6747927, 6834074, 7044721, 6899880
     6865809, 7009291, 6677798, 4703814, 6960195, 6874662, 5852921, 6612471
     6695139, 6809176, 5763576, 5941030, 6919510, 6684357, 6701400, 6431470
     6805242, 6867178, 6864063, 6867263, 6750049, 6376928, 6756089, 6342503
     6266400, 6751113, 6145570, 6417271, 6521934, 6408390, 6438892, 6367945
     6617137, 6530141, 6646866, 6744214, 6168363, 6647108, 6353873, 6412375
     6609623, 6636451, 6735167, 6438731, 6194582, 6400501, 6438752, 6769651

--------------------------------------------------------------------------------

OPatch succeeded.
```

Summary

Here is a short summary of the concepts we touched upon in this chapter.

- Database maintenance is required to keep the database in peak operating condition. Most aspects of database maintenance can be automated. Oracle performs some maintenance automatically, specifically the collection of statistics for the use of the query optimizer.

- Database backups are the most important responsibility of the database administrator. RMAN is the preferred tool for numerous reasons. Recovery testing is vital to validate the backup procedures.

- The query optimizer requires statistical information about the data—for example, the number of rows in each table—in order to generate efficient query plans; this information is collected using the collection of procedures in the DBMS_STATS package. Beginning with Oracle Database 10g, statistical information about the data is collected automatically by a scheduled nightly job; you are free to disable this job in favor of a custom approach.

- Archiving refers to the task of making a copy of old data in preparation for deleting it from the database.

- Purging refers to the task of deleting data that has already been archived.

- Rebuilding refers to the task of compacting tables and indexes from which large amounts of data have been purged.

- Log files and trace files are stored in the Automatic Diagnostics Repository (ADR) and managed using the adrci utility.

- Audit records should be periodically reviewed, archived, and purged.

- Passwords should be changed regularly, shared passwords should be changed when they are compromised, password complexity should be enforced, and accounts should be removed when the owners are relieved of their responsibilities or leave the company.

- The information in DBA_DATA_FILES and DBA_FREE_SPACE can be used to set up a simple system for management of disk capacity.

- The information in the STATSPACK tables STATS$OSSTAT, STATS$SYSSTAT, STATS$SYSTEM_EVENT can be used to produce graphs of system capacity.

Exercises

- Scan your database for corruption using the VALIDATE DATABASE command.

- Determine the start and end times of the "maintenance windows" in your database. Which maintenance jobs run during these windows?

- Temporarily disable auditing and move the AUD$ table to a dedicated tablespace.

- Develop a procedure to track the growth of tablespaces and free space. Use the information in the DBA_DATA_FILES and DBA_FREE_SPACE views. Capture the information once a week.

- Explain the "autoextensible" feature of data files. Is it enabled in your database? What are its advantages? What are its disadvantages?

- Develop a procedure to track the growth of the 20 biggest tables in your database. Use the information in the DBA_SEGMENTS view. Capture the information once a week.

- Using the data in the STATS$SYSSTAT table, create graphs of the following workload metrics: logical reads, physical reads, logical reads per transaction, and physical reads per transaction.

- Download the latest critical patch update and apply it to your database.

- Locate the alert log and listener log of your database. What do they contain? Create an automated process to manage their size.

Further Reading

Oracle Corporation. *Oracle Database 11g Backup and Recovery User's Guide.* Oracle Corporation, 2007. Freely searchable or downloadable free of charge at http://tahiti. oracle.com or http://www.oracle.com/technology/documentation/index.html.

Oracle Corporation. *Oracle Database 11g Performance Guide.* Oracle Corporation, 2007. Freely searchable or downloadable free of charge at http://tahiti.oracle.com or http://www.oracle.com/technology/documentation/index.html. Chapter 13 explains the need for statistics and how to manage them using the DBMS_STATS package.

Oracle Corporation. *Oracle Database 11g Security Guide.* Oracle Corporation, 2007. Freely searchable or downloadable free of charge at http://tahiti.oracle.com or http://www. oracle.com/technology/documentation/index.html. Includes discussions of auditing and user management.

Alapati, Sam. *Expert Oracle Database 11g Administration.* Apress, 2008. A useful reference for the intermediate and experienced database administrator.

Loaiza, Juan and Himatsingka, Bhaskar. *How to stop defragmenting and start living: the definitive word on fragmentation.* A milestone in the evolution of Oracle database administration practices. The Simple Algorithm for Fragmentation Elimination (SAFE) described in this paper was incorporated into Oracle 8*i*. Available on the Oracle Technology Network (OTN) web site http://otn.oracle.com.

CHAPTER 15

■■■

The Big Picture and the Ten Deliverables

And if you don't know Which *to Do*
Of all the things in front of you,
Then what you'll have when you are through
Is just a mess without a clue …

—Winnie the Pooh in *The Tao of Pooh* by Benjamin Hoff

What *are the deliverables of the database administration role? How likely is it that the deliverables will be completed if you cannot articulate what they are?* "Deliverables" are not the same as "current priorities," because priorities change from day to day; performance improvement may be your priority today, but it may not be your priority when performance returns to acceptable levels. Deliverables are not the same as "assigned tasks," either, because assigned tasks change from day to day; resetting passwords for forgetful users may be one of your assigned tasks today, but you may not have do it any more if, for example, your organization begins using self-service technology or single sign-on technology, or if the task is assigned to a Service Desk. An example of a deliverable is "*databases that meet the needs of the business*"—the deliverable does not change from day to day. If there is only one database administrator in the organization, then it is the individual's deliverable. If database administration is performed by a team, it is a *shared* deliverable.

This is the most important chapter in this book—I discuss the big IT picture and offer very specific guidance in the form of ten deliverables of the database administration role. Few, if any, other books address this topic.

If you take the lessons in this one chapter to heart, you can quickly become a better Oracle database administrator than you thought possible. *Competency in Oracle technology is only half of the challenge of being a database administrator.* If you had very little knowledge of Oracle technology but knew exactly "which" needed to be done, you could always find out how to do it—there is Google and there are online manuals aplenty. Too many Oracle database administrators don't know "which to do," and what they have when they are through is "just a mess without a clue."

An Instructive Job Interview

Early in my career, I interviewed for a "Programmer/Analyst" job at Hewlett-Packard. The manager who interviewed me gave me the following test. He explained that the problem was to produce a report containing sorted employee information and asked me to draw a flow chart explaining the approach I would use to solve the problem. He gave me some paper and left the room for half an hour. When he left, I wrote a COBOL program that sorted and printed a file of employee records. I prided myself on my programming skills and I was certain that the program would work correctly the first time.

When he came back, the manager read my program carefully and complimented me on my programming skills. Then he told me what I had missed. I had written a complete COBOL program but had completely ignored the Software Development Life Cycle: Initiation, System Concept Development, Planning, Requirements Analysis, Design, Development, Integration and Test, Implementation, Operations and Maintenance, and Disposition.[1]

In summary, I was a very good COBOL programmer but did not see the big software development picture.

Well, I did not get the job at Hewlett-Packard, but soon after that I got my first job as a database administrator—at Intel. Database administration became my career and, in time, I became the manager of a team of database administrators managing 1,000 databases for a large service provider. My technical skills were never stronger, but there seemed to be something missing. We were burned out from working 60 hours every week, we felt unappreciated, and we were constantly at loggerheads with other groups.

In time, I realized that technical knowledge was not enough. We needed to understand how all the pieces of IT fit together and how they interacted with each other. In other words, we needed to see the big picture.

---

1. A good introduction to the Systems Development Life Cycle can be found at http://www.usdoj.gov/jmd/irm/lifecycle/table.htm.

WHO IS A SENIOR DBA?

I have attended many interviews for Oracle DBA positions in my career and, with one exception, always found that the interviewers set great store on knowledge of Oracle syntax. A big problem is that the typical interviewer usually only asks questions about those Oracle features that he or she uses on the job and is most familiar with. Any candidate who has not used those Oracle features is then automatically eliminated.

Jeremiah Wilton was the first Oracle DBA at Amazon.com, joining the company when it was still a small startup and building the DBA team there. In an interview published in the journal of the Northern California Oracle Users Group (NoCOUG), I asked him the following question:

My daughter's piano teacher likes to say that practice makes permanent, not perfect. Just because I've been a database administrator a long time doesn't qualify me as a "senior" database administrator—or does it? Who is a "senior" database administrator? Do I need a college degree? Do I need to be a "syntax junkie?" Do I really need experience with Oracle Streams or ASM to claim the title?

In his reply, Jeremiah suggested that anybody with a few years of experience under their belt was entitled to call themselves a senior DBA, but he did not value years of experience and knowledge of Oracle syntax very much:

"To me, senior means that you have used a lot of Oracle's features, solved a lot of problems, and experienced a variety of production situations. Do these qualities necessarily mean that I will want to hire you? No.

Of far greater importance than seniority is a DBA's ability to solve problems in a deductive and logical manner, to synthesize creative solutions to problems, and to forge positive and constructive business relationships with colleagues and clients. For years at Amazon, we simply tried to hire extraordinarily smart people with a strong interest in working with Oracle and others. Some of Amazon's most senior DBAs started with little or no Oracle experience. I believe that the focus on experience in specific technologies and seniority causes employers to pay more and get less than they could when filling DBA positions."

How I Became a DBA

I became an Oracle DBA by accident. I was supporting another database technology when Big Bob, the Oracle DBA at my then employer, suddenly resigned. I was asked to take over because I had expressed an interest in becoming an Oracle DBA.

I created a documentation template and asked Bob to spend his remaining time documenting each database using the template. He protested that he did not have the time to provide so much detail and suggested that we meet for an hour or two.

At the meeting, Bob told me not to worry and that I was a smart kid and would soon learn my way around. We ran through the list of databases in about half an hour, spending less than a minute on each while I hastily scribbled notes.

But it wasn't Big Bob's fault at all, because documentation and record-keeping were not organizational priorities. When the time came for me to take over from him, Big Bob had little more for me than a few passwords, a firm handshake, and lots of good wishes.

THE IMPORTANCE OF COMMUNICATION

Which kind of database administrator would you want to maintain your database? One whose speech was sprinkled with incomprehensible Oracle terminology or one who communicated with you in language you understood? I mentioned previously that all the interviews that I attended during my job searches, with one single exception, focused on my knowledge of Oracle syntax. A U.S.-based provider of remote DBA services called Database Specialists uses a very unusual approach to interviewing Oracle DBA candidates. Questions about Oracle syntax are not asked. Instead, the interview focuses on the candidate's ability to communicate.

Database Specialists uses a systematic institutional approach to database administration, and the linchpin of the process is communication with its customers. A daily report on every database that is maintained by Database Specialists is sent to the appropriate distribution list. This is not a computer-generated report or graph but an actual memo from a live person. This gives customers visibility into database operations and reassures them that a systematic process of database administration is being followed, even if a memo might sometimes say only "No new issues at this time." All the daily reports are available online in a customer-accessible Internet portal, and they constitute a historical record of all the issues with the database. Here is an example—names and details have been changed to protect customer confidentiality:

```
From: Iggy Fernandez [mailto:ifernandez@dbspecialists.com]
Sent: Friday, February 29, 2008 10:11 AM
To: tsutton@ReallyBigCo.com; gsadler@ReallyBigCo.com;
Cc: archive@dbspecialists.com;
Subject: Daily Database Review for ReallyBigCo PRODDB

Our daily review of this instance has found the following:
```

    Pollux is now the primary database server and Castor is now the standby
database server. The reversal of roles was performed last night and the
transcript has been sent to Terry. I performed the switchover using the same
method used in the past by Gary, only changing the dates embedded in file names.

    Quoting Terry, the reason for the switchover was: "Having switched to the
standby, we are now using StorageTek instead of NetApp storage. We are working
on replacing the disks in the NetApp array with faster ones."

    The recent performance problems have two symptoms: much higher CPU
utilization than historical norms and continued degradation in I/O performance.
The current hypothesis for increased CPU utilization is that the increase is
correlated with the expansion of the amount of data and the number of users. The
cause of the degradation in I/O performance is under investigation by the system
administrators.

--Iggy

    When a DBA candidate is interviewed at Database Specialists, the focus is on the candidate's communication skills. The first exercise is to write a daily report of the sort just illustrated. The candidate is shown an extract from the Oracle alert log and asked to write a report discussing the Oracle errors listed in the extract. There is no expectation that the candidate has had previous experience with those errors, and the candidate is welcome to research the answers online; this mimics the approach used by real database administrators in real life. In fact, there may not be any "right" answer at all.

    The second exercise is a role-playing exercise that focuses on *verbal* communication. The exercise mimics a common event in the life of a database administrator—a critical problem that has high visibility and requires a number of participants. The candidate is given access to a lab system owned by Database Specialists and is asked to join a telephonic conference. To prepare for the exercise, the candidate is directed to a white paper—available on the Database Specialists web site—that discusses the problem-solving approaches that would be useful during the exercise. Participating on the conference call are members of the Database Specialists team, one of whom represents the customer while the rest represent other IT personnel such as system administrators. The customer describes the problem, and the candidate is expected to ask questions, diagnose, and solve the problem with the help of the other participants on the call. The problem is actually simulated in a lab database, and the candidate is expected to check the database and communicate the findings. The candidate is welcome to research the problem online, since there is no expectation that he or she has any experience with the specific problem that is being simulated.

    Why does this interviewing approach work for Database Specialists? It works because Database Specialists uses a systematic institutional approach to database administration, one in which communication skills are critical.

ITIL

The IT Information Library (ITIL), sponsored by the U.K. government, provides a conceptual overview of and detailed guidance about IT practice. It is a collaborative effort of many IT organizations—not an academic theory—and provides guidance that is independent of the hardware and software being used. The first version was issued in the late 1980s and it now is the international standard for IT practice. The discussion that follows is an adaptation of the framework and terminology presented in the ITIL literature.[2]

The Big Picture

As shown in Figure 15-1, everything starts with the business. The IT department provides IT services to the business. These services are managed using IT service management (ITSM) processes such as Service Level Management, Incident Management, and Change Management. The Infrastructure Management team manages the hardware and software that power the services required by the business—it is divided into a Design and Planning (D&P) team, a Deployment team, and an Operations team. The Application Management team designs and develops the software applications underlying the services used by the business. The ITSM team is the interface between the business and the Infrastructure Management team. In particular, the Service Desk is the single point of contact for all users of the services.

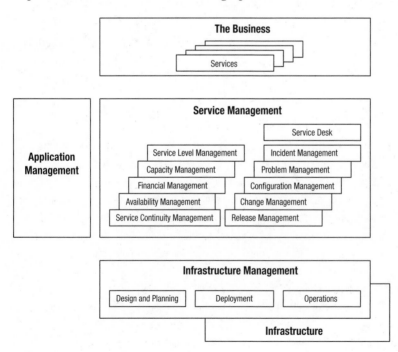

Figure 15-1. *The big picture*

---

2.   The descriptions and definitions used in this chapter are from ITIL Version 2.

The preceding is a very formal description of IT practice, and many companies don't have large IT teams. But IT principles don't change whether the IT team consists of a single employee or hundreds of employees. For example, service level expectations always exist, whether they are formally documented in a *Service Level Agreement* (SLA) or not.

■**Tip** The database administrator is part of the Operations team. This is an intuitively correct classification since the term "administrator" suggests the day-to-day maintenance of an operational database. However, persons with the title Database Administrator can often be found in the Deployment team and the Applications Management team—a testament to the multidisciplinary job descriptions found in the real world.

IT Service Management Processes

The ITSM team manages the services used by the business. It is the interface between the business and the Infrastructure Management team. The ITSM team uses the ten management processes described in the following sections. Note that the services *managed* by the ITSM team are actually *provided* by the Operations team. ITSM principles apply whether or not a company has a dedicated ITSM team. For example, a principle of change management is that all changes be properly authorized. Another change management principle is that records of changes are kept and documentation is kept up-to-date. Such principles don't change whether or not a company has a dedicated Change Manager. A database administrator should seek approval before making changes, keep records of changes, and update the documentation regardless.

Some of the processes of ITSM are strategic—Service Level Management, Financial Management, Capacity Management, Availability Management, and IT Continuity Management (also known as "Disaster Recovery"). Other branches are tactical—Incident Management, Problem Management, Configuration Management, Change Management, and Release Management. Formal definitions are provided in the following sections along with appropriate suggestions for the database administrator. The definitions are taken from *ITIL V2 Glossary v01* (Office of Government Commerce, 2006) and are reproduced with permission.[3] The highlighted terms in the definitions have their own formal definitions, and the serious student can find them in the same document.

---

3. ITIL ® is a Registered Trade Mark, and a Registered Community Trade Mark of the Office of Government Commerce, and is registered in the U.S. Patent and Trademark Office. ITIL Glossaries/Acronyms © Crown Copyright Office of Government Commerce. Reproduced with the permission of the Controller of HMSO and the Office of Government Commerce.

Service Level Management

Service Level Management (SLM) is *"the **Process** responsible for negotiating **Service Level Agreements**, and ensuring that these are met. SLM is responsible for ensuring that all **IT Service Management Processes**, **Operational Level Agreements**, and **Underpinning Contracts** are appropriate for the agreed **Service Level Targets**. SLM monitors and reports on **Service Levels**, and holds regular **Customer** reviews."*

The database administrator cannot meet the expectations of the business if he or she does not know what they are. These expectations usually center on availability and performance; for example, databases that are used by e-commerce applications typically have very high availability and performance requirements.

In the absence of clearly communicated expectations and measurable service levels, the job of database administration becomes a reactive exercise instead of the proactive exercise it should be—for example, performance tuning is conducted only after the business complains of poor performance.

Financial Management

Financial Management for IT Services is *"the **Process** responsible for managing an **IT Service Provider's Budgeting**, **Accounting** and **Charging** requirements."*

Oracle license payments can be a substantial part of the IT department's budget. At the time of writing, a license for Oracle Database Enterprise Edition for a single CPU costs $47,500 or more and depends on the number of cores in the CPU; a license for a 4-core Intel CPU costs $95,000. Many features such as partitioning are extra-cost options. Annual support costs are currently 22% of the base price, and development and "standby" databases must also be separately licensed.

Database administrators should understand Oracle's licensing policies and maintain an accurate inventory of installed software. Note that Oracle does not use "license keys" to unlock software and it is therefore easy to install inadvertently software that is not properly licensed, such as Enterprise Edition instead of Standard Edition. It should be particularly noted that many features are automatically installed as part of the installation process and cannot be deinstalled. Examples include Partitioning and the various Management Packs. Collector Jobs for Diagnostics Pack are automatically created and scheduled even though very few sites are licensed to use the feature. As described in Chapter 6, the database administrator must take explicit steps to deactivate the Management Packs after the database is created.

■**Tip** The `DBA_FEATURE_USAGE_STATISTICS` view shows which Oracle features are being used. This information should be regularly reviewed to ensure that unlicensed features are not being inadvertently used.

IT Service Continuity Management

IT Service Continuity Management (ITSCM) is *"the **Process** responsible for managing **Risks** that could seriously impact **IT Services**. ITSCM ensures that the **IT Service Provider** can always provide minimum agreed **Service Levels**, by reducing the **Risk** to an acceptable level and **Planning** for the **Recovery** of **IT Services**. ITSCM should be designed to support **Business Continuity Management**."*

IT Continuity Management is commonly referred to as "Disaster Recovery," and the database administrator must be prepared to re-create the database at an alternate location if a disaster should make the primary location unusable. This service is a subset of Business Continuity Management, which is responsible for all aspects of the business, including IT. The database administrator is responsible for databases only, and the three approaches that can be used are *hot standby, warm standby*, and *cold standby*. In the hot standby approach, an Oracle database is created on a server in the alternate location and is continuously synchronized with the primary database so that failover time can be kept to a minimum. In the warm standby approach, the hardware (including network components) is available at an alternate site but the database has to be re-created from backup tapes—this option is less expensive than the hot standby approach. In the cold standby approach, alternate facilities with power and cabling are identified but the hardware is only procured in the event of a disaster—this is the cheapest option.

Capacity Management

Capacity Management is *"the **Process** responsible for ensuring that the **Capacity** of **IT Services** and the **IT Infrastructure** is able to deliver agreed **Service Level Targets** in a **Cost Effective** and timely manner. Capacity Management considers all **Resources** required to deliver the IT Service, and plans for short, medium and long term **Business Requirements**."*

In the absence of systematic capacity management, database administration becomes a reactive exercise in which, for example, space is added to databases only when they are close to failure. A systematic approach requires that trends be monitored. This requires periodic checking of database size, free space within tablespaces, CPU utilization, disk utilization, network utilization, and similar parameters, and taking corrective action to prevent the database from failing. Database administrators are primarily interested in monitoring database trends; Chapter 10 discusses the use of STATSPACK for that purpose. Automatic Workload Repository (AWR) can also be used for monitoring database trends, but very few sites are licensed to use it.

Availability Management

Availability Management is *"the **Process** responsible for defining, analysing, **Planning**, measuring and improving all aspects of the **Availability** of **IT services**. Availability Management is responsible for ensuring that all **IT Infrastructure, Processes, Tools, Roles** etc are appropriate for the agreed **Service Level Targets** for **Availability**."*

Most of the database administrator's time can be taken up by tasks relating to availability management. Database tuning (Chapter 16), SQL tuning (Chapter 17), and hardware upgrades are required to keep performance at acceptable levels. Database backups (Chapter 12) are required as insurance against database failures, and recovery testing (Chapter 13) is required to validate the usability of backups and to measure recovery times. An unplanned outage is usually classified as a "Sev 1" issue, requiring the immediate attention of the database administrator.

Incident Management

Incident Management is *"the **Process** responsible for managing the **Lifecycle** of all **Incidents**. The primary **Objective** of Incident Management is to return the **IT Service** to **Customers** as quickly as possible."*

The Incident Management process is usually handled by the Service Desk. The Service Desk prioritizes each issue that comes to its attention and engages with the Operations team as necessary until the problem is resolved.

Problem Management

A Problem is *"the root cause of one or more incidents."* Problem Management is *"the **Process** responsible for managing the **Lifecycle** of all **Problems**. The primary objectives of Problem Management are to prevent **Incidents** from happening, and to minimise the **Impact** of **Incidents** that cannot be prevented. **Problem Management** includes **Problem Control**, **Error Control** and **Proactive Problem Management**."*

Incident Management is a reactive process, while Problem Management is a proactive process. An example of an incident is a database outage caused when the archived log area fills up. The incident may be resolved by removing the oldest archived logs, but the root cause of the incident must also be addressed. For example, disk space may be inadequate, and additional disk space may have to be procured. The Problem Management process ensures that chronic problems are identified and fixed.

Change Management

A Change is *"the addition, modification or removal of anything that could have an effect on **IT Services**. The **Scope** should include all **Configuration Items**, **Processes**, **Documentation** etc."* Change Management is *"the **Process** responsible for controlling the **Lifecycle** of all **Changes**. The primary objective of Change Management is to enable beneficial **Changes** to be made, with minimum disruption to **IT Services**."*

The Change Management process is tasked with ensuring that changes are appropriately authorized and tested before being applied to the infrastructure that supports the IT services required by the business. The Change Management process is also responsible for ensuring that the risks of the changes are understood and that conflicts are detected. For example, a change to the database may conflict with business tasks.

Configuration Management

A Configuration is *"a generic term, used to describe a group of **Configuration Items** that work together to deliver an **IT Service**, or a recognisable part of an IT Service. Configuration is also used to describe the parameter settings for one or more **CIs**."* Configuration Management is *"the **Process** responsible for maintaining information about **Configuration Items** required to deliver an **IT Service**, including their **Relationships**. This information is managed throughout the **Lifecycle** of the CI. The primary objective of Configuration Management is to underpin the delivery of **IT Services** by providing accurate data to all **IT Service Management Processes** when and where it is needed."*

In the terminology of Configuration Management, a database is a "configuration item." The configuration management process is responsible for creating a repository of information about each configuration item and recording changes made to each configuration item. Systematic Configuration Management improves the effectiveness of the other branches of IT Service Management. For example, ready access to configuration information can help in resolving incidents (Incident Management) and diagnosing chronic problems (Problem Management).

In Chapter 9, we saw how Remote Diagnostic Assistant (RDA) could be used to assemble information about a database into an HTML framework. In the terminology of Configuration Management, the information collected by RDA is called a "configuration record" and should be stored in a Configuration Management Database (CMDB). You can create a simple Configuration Management Database of sorts by linking your RDA collections into an Excel spreadsheet. RDA collections can be run at regular intervals and linked into the spreadsheet. This is an easy way to create and organize a historical record of changes to database configurations.

■Note An RDA collection is the simplest and quickest way of documenting a database environment.

Release Management

A Release is *"a collection of hardware, software, documentation, **Processes** or other **Components** required to implement one or more approved **Changes** to IT Services. The contents of each Release are managed, tested, and deployed as a single entity."* Release Management is *"the **Process** responsible for **Planning**, scheduling and controlling the movement of **Releases** to **Test** and **Live Environments**. The primary objective of Release Management is to ensure that the integrity of the **Live Environment** is protected and that the correct **Components** are* *released. **Release Management** works closely with **Configuration Management** and **Change Management**.*"

Release Management is concerned with major changes and additions to the IT infrastructure, such as installation of database software (Chapter 5) and database creation (Chapter 6). You should keep careful notes whenever you install database software and create a database so that the process can be standardized and repeated.

■**Note** Oracle provides the Service Level Management Pack for service level management, the Change Management Pack for change management, the Configuration Management Pack for configuration management, and the Provisioning Pack for release management, but few sites are licensed to use these tools because they are available only with Enterprise Edition and require extra license and support fees on top of those paid for Enterprise Edition.

Start with the End in Mind: The Ten Deliverables

In his best-selling book *The 7 Habits of Highly Effective People* (Free Press, 1989), Stephen Covey distills the secrets of effectiveness into 7 principles. In my opinion, the most important habit is *"Start with the End in Mind"*—how you want your work to be evaluated when you have completed it. When Big Bob turned responsibilities over to me, he had little more for me than the database passwords, a firm handshake, and good wishes— he left me very unhappy.

To be effective as database administrators, we must start with the end in mind—the moment when we hand over responsibilities to our successors. What will we give them other than the database passwords, a firm handshake, and good wishes?

Here are the ten deliverables of the database administration role—they map to the ten deliverables of the Operations team which are listed in the ITIL literature. In large organizations with many database administrators, these are shared deliverables.

1. *A database that meets the needs of the business*: This is the most important deliverable, if not the only one. The needs of the business include certain levels of *performance*, *security*, and *availability*. You must understand the needs of the business, you must have a way of evaluating how well the needs are met, and you must have a methodology for meeting those needs. Any chronic performance, security, and availability issues must be discussed with the incoming database administrator.

2. *A secure document library*: The absence of a document repository causes a lot of valuable information to be lost. Examples of documents that should be retained include service level agreements, network diagrams, architecture diagrams, licensing information, E-R diagrams, performance reports, audit reports, software manuals, installation notes, project notes, copies of important correspondence, and so on.

"Standard Operating Procedures" (SOPs) are another important class of documents; you will learn about them later in the chapter. Original software media and files should also be stored in the library for use if the database needs to be rebuilt or if additional databases need to be created. Note that the document library needs to be secure since it contains sensitive and confidential information.

3. *Work logs of service requests, alarms, and changes*: Work logs are important for many reasons. They bring transparency and visibility to the database administration function. From the Incident Management perspective, it is necessary to review the work logs and identify inefficiencies and root causes. From the Problem Management perspective, it is necessary to review the work logs and identify chronic problems. From the Availability Management perspective, it is necessary to review the work logs and identify availability issues. These are just some examples of how work logs help bring about improvements and efficiencies in your ability to provide good service to the business.

4. *Standard Operating Procedures*: Any database administration task that is done repeatedly should be codified into a Standard Operating Procedure (SOP). Using a written SOP helps efficiency and accuracy. We will return to this subject later in the chapter.

5. *Procedures and records for backup testing and failover testing*: It is absolutely essential that backup procedures and disaster recovery procedures be documented. The procedures should be periodically tested and records should be maintained.

6. *Maintenance and batch schedules, documentation, and records*: Chapter 14 discussed database maintenance. Database maintenance procedures should be documented and records should be maintained. If the maintenance procedures are automated, log records should also be automatically created. For example, an RMAN catalog can be used to store backup histories. Any repeating tasks or batch jobs that are the responsibility of the database administrator should also be adequately documented, and records should be maintained for them.

7. *Database administration tools*: Database administration tools include Oracle-supplied tools such as Database Control, Grid Control, and SQL Developer. The Management Packs, such as Diagnostics Pack, Tuning Pack, Change Management Pack, and Configuration Pack, are very valuable tools but most organizations don't purchase licenses to use them because of their high cost and because Enterprise Edition is a prerequisite. Other popular tools are Toad from Quest Software and DBArtisan from Embarcadero Technologies.

8. *Management reports*: Examples of database reports for management are reports on database growth, workload, and performance. STATSPACK and AWR histories should be retained for as long as practicable—the defaults (two weeks in the case of STATSPACK and eight days for AWR) are unsuitable. I suggest retaining data for

at least one year if you can afford the space. Baseline snapshots should be retained indefinitely. For example, you can designate the period between 9 a.m. and 10 a.m. every Monday morning as a baseline period so that the snapshots marking the beginning and end of the period are retained indefinitely.

9. *Exception reports*: This deliverable includes reports on SLA violations, security violations, backup failures, and the like. For example, a certain stored procedure or SQL statement may have been identified as critical to the business, and an exception report can be produced by mining STATSPACK data.

10. *Audit reports*: This deliverable typically refers to audit reports conducted by security auditors but can also refer to internal audits of compliance with organizational processes such as Change Management or database reviews by external consultants. The absence of audits indicates a lack of oversight of the database management function.

The Book You Really Need and the Art of the SOP

The book you really need will never be found in bookstores—it is the book containing all the procedures that you need to operate your databases. You're going to have to write that book yourself. Nobody can write the book for you, because you have a unique environment and nobody except you would write a book that caters to a unique environment.

Do you know how to start or stop a database? I thought I did—until I went to work in a large Network Operations Center. We had Solaris, AIX, HP/UX, Linux, and Windows. We had Oracle 8*i*, Oracle 9*i*, and Oracle 10*g*. We had VCS, HP Service Guard, Sun Clusters, Data Guard, and RAC. There were so many variations of the startup and shutdown procedures that I could not remember all of them.

A common task such as adding a data file to a database requires different methods depending on whether you are using cooked files, raw devices, or ASM. Additional complexities are introduced by RAC and Data Guard. Raw files in particular are notoriously difficult to manage—they make it easy to damage the database. And, in my experience, database administrators routinely forget the important step of backing up the data file immediately after it is created.

A TRUE STORY

A database administrator stopped a database using the `shutdown` command in preparation for moving some data files to a new location. Unknown to him, the database was managed by Veritas high availability software, which automatically restarted the database. The database was corrupted when the DBA moved the files.

It happened to me—it could happen to you.

Benefits of SOPs

Here are some of the advantages of SOPs:

- *They improve consistency.* A documented procedure is more likely to be executed consistently than one that is not documented.[4]

- *They improve quality.* It is easier to do a good job if you don't have to rely on memory or invent the procedure.

- *They facilitate continuous improvement.* It is easier to improve the quality of a procedure if it is documented than if it is not documented.

- *They promote transparency.* Would you hire anyone who insisted upon charging you a lot of money but refused to tell you what was involved?

- *They improve efficiency.* Things get done faster. They get done correctly the first time. Further, it is easier to improve the efficiency of a procedure if it is documented than if it is not documented.

- *They facilitate planning.* It is easy to quantify the labor involved in a written procedure than one which is undocumented. This facilitates planning and project management.

- *They can reduce cost.* SOPs established by senior personnel may be delegated to junior personnel who are paid less. Needless to say there is also a definite cost associated with making mistakes and inefficient execution.

---

4. I remember a case when a customer vociferously expressed dissatisfaction with the work performed by a certain individual, going so far as to suggest that he be dismissed from service. Management finally agreed that the real problem lay with the "process," not with the performer, and that written procedures would be a better solution than dismissing the performer. I believe that IT management in general is too eager to blame the performer rather than the process. Performers are evaluated every year, but organizational processes are rarely evaluated. I believe that improving organizational processes will inevitably lead to improvements in employee performance. The likelihood that "unwritten standards" will be violated is much greater than that written standards will be violated. Standards can be violated intentionally or unintentionally. An unintentional violation of unwritten standards usually results when a task is performed by a newcomer to the group or when a veteran performer forgets to use one of the elements of the standard. An unintentional violation of written standard usually results from inadequate training or from sloppy execution. Standards can also be intentionally violated. However, the violator has a convenient excuse if the standard is unwritten, and deliberate violations stem from the belief that the standard is imperfect. It is not difficult for experienced individuals to find something about a procedure that they might choose to do differently if left to their own devices, and therefore organizations that rely on "unwritten standards" are likely to experience steady erosion of standards.

- *They facilitate knowledge transfer.* "Tribal knowledge" is lost when the members of the tribe leave to join other tribes or is forgotten with the passage of time; written documentation is more permanent. "Tribal knowledge" is also subject to the "Telephone" game phenomenon.[5]

- *They reduce risk.* SOPs reduce the risk of things going wrong. These risks are exacerbated when the regular performers are unavailable because of vacations, illness, resignation, and so on. Mistakes made by IT departments in large organizations often make the front page of the newspaper.

- *They improve employee morale.* Employee morale is high if the organization works well. A dysfunctional organization has low employee morale.

- *They reduce blame games.* It's hard to blame a performer for following a well-established SOP. Responsibility for failure transfers from the performer to the SOP. Of course, the SOP needs to be improved for the next time around.

- *They improve customer satisfaction.* The previous advantages would satisfy almost anybody, but we cannot neglect to mention that SOPs must inevitably improve customer satisfaction. Which customer would not be satisfied with your attention to detail?

A common excuse for not writing SOPs is that most tasks are "simple enough." Consider the "simple task" of shutting down a database. Why does a custom SOP need to be written for this "simple task" or customized for each individual database? How customized, one might ask, can this "simple task" get? Well, the procedures for shutting down a database depend on the Oracle database version, the operating system, any high availability mechanisms such as VCS, HP Serviceguard, and Sun Cluster, and Oracle components such as RAC and ASM. And, here are some of the things a DBA might have to do *before* actually pressing the buttons that shut down the database:

- Confirm there are no conflicts with backup schedules.

- Confirm that there are no conflicts with batch schedules.

- Confirm that no incompatible activities have been scheduled at the same time.

- Confirm that there are no conflicts with the SLA for database availability.

- Obtain the permission of the business owners of all applications that are directly or indirectly impacted.

- Send advance notifications to the user community.

---

5. "Telephone" is a game in which each participant whispers a sentence to the next. Errors begin to accumulate and the last participant receives a highly garbled version of the original sentence.

- Determine the impact on replication mechanisms and take the appropriate steps to eliminate or mitigate the impact.

- Confirm the availability of other performers to bring down applications gracefully prior to shutting down the database.

- Confirm the access of all performers to databases, servers, and applications.

- Agree on communication mechanisms and performer handoffs.

- Establish escalation procedures for use if things go wrong.

- Establish procedures for use if users or jobs are still connected when the time comes to shut down the database.

- Blackout alarm mechanisms.

- Send broadcast messages to users just before the shutdown.

Another example of a "simple task" that can quickly become complicated is resetting a password. Metalink note 270516.1 explains the lengthy sequence of tasks that must be performed to change the SYSMAN password.

Structure of an SOP

In the following sections, I describe an SOP template that can be customized to each site's specific requirements and standards. Each SOP may be divided into the following sections.

Overview

The overview section is provided not so much for the benefit of those executing the SOP but for all those who are peripherally involved, such as customers who need the work done and managers or teams responsible for scheduling, approving, or supervising the work. A minimum of technical jargon should be used, and technical details should be suppressed if appropriate. The following points should be addressed:

- *Purpose*: This is the key section for nontechnical reviewers or managers.

- *Risks*: A clear description of risks helps in getting approvals to perform the task—it also helps educate the performer. There can even be risks if the task is *not* performed.

- *Labor and billing*: This section specifies the "standard fee schedule" which is the standard number of labor hours required to complete the work. In cases where a standard fee schedule cannot easily be constructed because of the variability of the work, guidelines are provided for estimating the work. In some cases, it is appropriate to specify billing details (for example, interdepartmental billing).

- *Scheduling*: This section specifies what advance notice is required, what information needs to be supplied by the requestor, what forms completed, and scheduling constraints if any.

- *Prerequisites*: Clearly documenting the prerequisites improves the chances that they will actually be met. You might want to include a "nice to have" section.

Testing

This section describes what testing should be completed in a laboratory setting before the "real work" can begin. Here are the reasons for testing:

- A standard operating procedure may not be perfect. Testing the procedure in a laboratory setting that duplicates the targeted production setting may uncover deficiencies in the procedure.

- Practice is good preparation. It may have been a long time since the performer last executed the procedure. Also, the Standard Operating Procedure may have omitted some of the details, and practice in a laboratory setting will allow a less experienced performer to supply them for herself or himself.

- Testing smoothens out the approval process. Note that in some cases, testing may not be considered necessary, because the work is truly routine; for example, adding a user. In other cases testing may not even be practical because of the huge effort required to duplicate the target environment in a laboratory setting. If testing is unnecessary or impractical, then the author of the SOP should indicate as much and explain why.

Approvals

This section describes whose approval is required and the protocols to be observed—for example, verbal approval, written approval, formal meetings, advance notice, and so on. I have observed that most IT organizations fall into one of two categories:

- Very little attention is paid to change management. The performers are given free rein to take suitable action. Performer morale is high but the situation is certainly not desirable from a management viewpoint.

- A huge amount of attention is paid to change management. Performers are not permitted to do the slightest work without the approval of "change czars." Performers chafe under the scrutiny and complain of delays and the effort expended in submitting paperwork before artificial deadlines, attending change management meetings, and answering questions from "change czars" who do not have expertise in the subject matter.

The approach I recommend is that the Standard Operating Procedure explicitly state whose approval is required. The following is a short list:

- The performers who will be actually performing the tasks.

- Managers of the performers required to perform the task or tasks.

- Representatives of users who will be affected by the task.

If all the necessary approvals have been obtained, the formal approval of the change czars becomes a mere formality.

Notification

This section describes who should be notified before the work begins and the mechanisms and procedures that should be used.

Backup

This section provides step-by-step instructions for creating backups in case the work needs to be undone.

Staging Activities

This section addresses all other preparation steps that are not covered by the approval, notification, and backup sections.

Execution

This section provides step-by-step instructions on how the work should be done.

Verification

This sections states what "successful" execution means. For example, it may require confirmation from a user that they are able to use the application.

Backout

This section provides step-by-step instructions on using the backups if it becomes necessary to reverse the change.

Signoff

This section describes who decides that the performer has executed the work correctly.

Record-Keeping

This section makes the record-keeping requirements explicit.

Quality Assurance

This section describes any quality assurance procedures that should be used to assess the quality and accuracy of the work.

KILL FIRST, ASK QUESTIONS LATER?

An article titled *A Day in the Life of an Enterprise DBA* was published in the March 1998 issue of *Oracle* magazine, published by Oracle. The protagonist used the Enterprise Manager tool to perform a variety of tasks. Here is how he diagnosed and fixed a slow system.

*"To find out who is hitting the system so hard, I start up TopSessions and look at the user-resource usage on the system. I sort based on redo activity to find the culprit. A developer is inserting data into the database and causing significant redo-log activity. A double-click on the user shows me the actual SQL that has been executed. Apparently, the developer is loading data onto the production system during production time. Should I call him before I kill his session? No—**kill first, call later**. He should know better. Soon after, the supervisors report that the system is running well again."*

This brings to mind the 2002 James Bond movie *Die Another Day,* starring Pierce Brosnan as James Bond and Rosamund Pike as the double agent Miranda Frost. In the movie, Frost describes Bond as follows:

*"He's a double O, and a wild one as I discovered today. He'll light the fuse on any explosive situation, and be a danger to himself and others. **Kill first, ask questions later**. I think he's a blunt instrument whose primary method is to provoke and confront ..."*

Your motto should not be "Kill first, ask questions later" but "Follow the SOP." That way, you won't light the fuse on explosive situations and be a danger to yourself and to others!

Suggested SOPs

Here is a list of common database tasks. As we have proved, even everyday tasks such as stopping and changing passwords can be nontrivial. If you don't have the time to write detailed SOPs, you should consider writing at least a few sentences on each topic.

1. *Connecting to a database*: This describes how the DBA connects to the database to perform database administration activities. This SOP is invaluable in an emergency when speed is critical or when the primary DBA is unavailable.

2. *Starting a database*: This describes how to start the database engine and associated components such as ASM, Data Guard, and database applications.

3. *Stopping a database*: This describes how to stop the database engine and associated components.

4. *Backups and recovery*: This describes how to perform an ad hoc backup and how to recover the database from backups.

5. *Removing archived redo logs*: This describes what to do when the archived log destination fills up.

6. *Standby database maintenance*: This describes how to fail over and fail back, as well as how to re-create the standby database if it gets damaged.

7. *Adding space*: This describes the process for adding data files or increasing the size of data files.

8. *Health checks*: This describes how to check the health of the database and of applications that use the database.

9. *Adding a user*: This describes special procedures and security rules to be followed when adding a user to a database; for example, specific privileges that might be needed by users of particular applications.

10. *Resetting a password*: This describes special procedures to be followed when performing password resets; for example, steps to prevent applications from malfunctioning.

11. *Clearing a lock*: This describes internal procedures to be followed when terminating a process that is blocking other users.

12. *Maintenance activities*: This describes daily maintenance activities, such as investigation of backup failures, review of the error log, and checking contents of trace files. It also covers weekly maintenance activities such as regeneration of statistics, monthly maintenance activities such as preparation for month-end batch processing, and quarterly maintenance activities such as preparation for quarter-end processing.

Summary

Here is a short summary of the concepts this chapter touched upon:

- IT services are managed using the principles of IT service management (ITSM). The Infrastructure Management team manages the hardware and software that power the services required by the business—it is divided into a Design and Planning (D&P) team, a Deployment team, and an Operations team. The Application Management team designs and develops the software applications underlying the services used by the business. The ITSM team is the interface between the business and the Infrastructure Management team. In particular, the Service Desk is the single point of contact for all users of the services.

- The database administrator is part of the Operations team. This is an intuitive classification, since the term "administration" suggests the day-to-day maintenance of an operational database. However, persons with that title can often be found in the Deployment team and the Applications Management team.

- Some of the processes of ITSM are strategic—Service Level Management, Financial Management, Capacity Management, Availability Management, and IT Continuity Management (a.k.a Disaster Recovery). Other branches are tactical—Incident Management, Problem Management, Configuration Management, Change Management, and Release Management.

- Oracle provides Management Packs for a number of ITSM processes, but most sites are not licensed to use them, because they are available only with Enterprise Edition and require extra license and support fees.

- Oracle makes it very easy to download, install, and activate software, but this causes organizations to be vulnerable to using unlicensed software. Particular care has to be taken in the case of the Management Packs, which few sites are licensed to use but which are automatically installed and activated during the installation process.

- Every database requires a disaster recovery plan. The three approaches that can be used are *hot standby*, *warm standby*, and *cold standby*. A cold standby is the cheapest option and is simply a plan for the procurement and provisioning of hardware at a previously identified location, complete reinstallation of software, and database recovery from backup tapes.

- STATSPACK reports can be used to monitor trends in workloads and performance. STATSPACK histories should be maintained for as long as practicable. Baselines should be retained indefinitely.

- Incident management is a reactive process—the goal being to restore service as soon as possible. Problem management is a proactive process—the goal being to identify and eliminate chronic problems.

- Configuration management is the linchpin of the other ITSM processes. Oracle provides the Configuration Management Pack but few sites are licensed to use it—RDA is a cheap and simple substitute.

- These are the ten deliverables of the database administration role: databases that meet the needs of the business; a secure document library; work logs of service requests, alarms, and changes; standard operating procedures (SOPs); backup testing and failover testing procedures and records; maintenance and batch schedules, documentation, and records; database administration tools; management reports; exception reports; and audit reports.

- Any database administration task that is done repeatedly should be codified into a Standard Operating Procedure (SOP). Using a written SOP has many benefits, including efficiency, quality, and consistency.

Exercises

- Download *Oracle 11g Licensing Information* from `http://tahiti.oracle.com`. Also download *Oracle Technology Global Price List* from `http://www.oracle.com/corporate/pricing`. Review the contents of the `DBA_FEATURES_USAGE_INFO` view in your database. Which extra-cost options and Management Packs have been automatically installed in the database? Which extra-cost options and Management Packs are already in use? For example, have AWR collections been automatically scheduled by the Oracle installer? Compute what the total licensing and annual support costs might be if your database was not solely for self-educational purposes.

- Download *ITIL V2 Glossary* from `http://www.best-management-practice.com`; the direct URL is `http://www.best-management-practice.com/gempdf/ITIL_Glossary_May_v2_2007.pdf`. Find the definitions of the boldfaced terms in the various ITIL definitions provided in this chapter.

- Write a Standard Operating Procedure to add a data file to your database. Include enough detail so that somebody who was unfamiliar with Oracle (for example, a Windows system administrator) would be able to perform this simple task. Remember to include the step of backing up the data file immediately after it was created.

Further Reading

Service Support. Office of Government Commerce, 2001. This book describes the tactical aspects of IT Service Management, specifically the Service Desk, Incident Management, Problem Management, Configuration Management, Change Management, and Release Management processes.

Service Delivery. Office of Government Commerce, 2000. This book describes the strategic aspects of IT Service Management, specifically the Service Level Management, Financial Management, Capacity Management, IT Continuity Management, and Release Management processes.

ICT Infrastructure Management. Office of Government Commerce, 2002. This book describes information and communications technology (ICT) management and its relationship to IT service management.

ITIL V2 Glossary v01. Office of Government Commerce, 2006. This is a glossary of terms, definitions, and acronyms used by ITIL Version 2. It can be downloaded from `http://www.best-management-practice.com`. The direct URL is `http://www.best-management-practice.com/gempdf/ITIL_Glossary_May_v2_2007.pdf`.

Jan Van Bon. *Foundations of IT Service Management: based on ITIL.* Van Haren Publishing, 2005. This book is much more affordable than the publications of the Office of Government Commerce and is suitable for beginners.

PART IV

■ ■ ■

Database Tuning

■ ■ ■

CHAPTER 16

Instance Tuning

Citius, Altius, Fortius—Swifter, Higher, Stronger

—Motto of the Olympic Games

Database tuning can be a complex exercise but it can be facilitated by a systematic approach. This chapter describes a systematic five-step approach to performance tuning. It also presents the most important tools provided by Oracle to help with performance tuning; Statspack is emphasized because newer tools such as AWR and ADDM require costly licenses and are not available at most sites.[1] In particular, you will learn a powerful method of mining the Statspack repository for data on performance trends. This data can be graphed by using tools such as Microsoft Excel.

I highly recommend that you download and review *Oracle Database 11g Performance Tuning Guide* from the Oracle web site after reading this chapter. I also recommend that you do the exercises listed at the end of the chapter—they will familiarize you with the most common tools for database tuning. The best way to learn is by doing.

Using a Systematic Five-Step Tuning Method

Once upon a time, a database tuning expert saw a drunken man on his hands and knees searching for something under a bright streetlight. "Have you lost something?" he asked the drunk.

"My keys," said the drunk.

The performance expert offered to help and he too got on his hands and knees to search for the lost keys. After concluding that no keys were to be found under the streetlight, he began questioning the drunk. "When was the last time you remember seeing your keys?" he asked.

"At the bar," said the drunk.

---

1. The president of a well-known consulting company reported that only 2 out of 70 clients had licenses for Diagnostics Pack. The list of clients included big companies such as AXA, Northrop Grumman, CVRD Inco, MDS, Fox Interactive, JDS Uniphase, Electronic Arts, Cinram, and Diageo.

"Then why are you searching here?"

"Because it is so much brighter here!"

The story is fictional, and the moral is that you must concentrate your efforts in the appropriate place. You shouldn't focus your effort wherever it is most convenient to do so—in fact, the problem might not even be in the Oracle database at all.

Here is an example of a case where poor performance was reported but the database was *not* the problem. The output shown in Listing 16-1 was produced by using the dbms_monitor.session_trace_enable procedure to trace a poorly performing batch process and then using the tkprof utility to summarize the trace data. The session was traced for about 40 minutes, and the data shows that the Oracle database spent only 140.08 seconds in executing SQL queries. The bulk of the time—2138.67 seconds—was spent waiting for further instructions from the program. This clearly showed that the database was *not* the problem.

Listing 16-1. *Sample Output of the tkprof Utility*

```
OVERALL TOTALS FOR ALL NON-RECURSIVE STATEMENTS
```

call	count	cpu	elapsed	disk	query	current	rows
Parse	14114	0.37	0.40	0	0	0	0
Execute	78466	107.84	109.89	195	1105246	26768	13139
Fetch	72200	19.88	29.78	2100	432976	0	84080
total	164780	128.09	**140.08**	2295	1538222	26768	97219

```
Misses in library cache during parse: 4
Misses in library cache during execute: 4

Elapsed times include waiting on following events:
```

Event waited on	Times Waited	Max. Wait	Total Waited
SQL*Net message to client	87649	0.00	0.09
SQL*Net message from client	**87649**	**0.57**	**2138.67**
db file sequential read	2295	0.26	10.80
SQL*Net break/reset to client	1084	0.00	0.07
log file sync	1813	0.15	18.02
latch: session allocation	8	0.29	2.14
latch: cache buffers chains	1	0.00	0.00
latch: library cache	3	0.00	0.01
log file switch completion	1	0.97	0.97
latch: redo writing	1	0.04	0.04

In his book, *The Art and Science of Oracle Performance Tuning*, Christopher Lawson outlines a systematic five-step method for solving any performance tuning problem:[2]

1. *Define* the problem. This requires patient listening, skillful questioning, and even careful observation. "The database is slow" is an example of a poorly defined problem. "The database is slow between 10 a.m. and 11 a.m. every day" is more precise. "This report now takes twice as long as it used to take only a week ago" is another example of a precisely defined problem. Ask the user for the history of the problem. Ask what previous efforts have been made to solve the problem. Ask what changed recently in the environment—for example, software or hardware upgrades. Ask whether all users are affected or only some. Ask whether the problem occurs at specific times of the day or week. Ask whether all parts of the application are equally affected or just parts.

2. *Investigate* the problem and collect as much pertinent evidence as possible. Examples include Statspack reports, graphs of database workload and *DB time*, and session traces. Study the environment and find out what may be affecting the database—for example, other databases and applications may be competing for resources with your database.

3. *Analyze* the data collected in the second step and isolate the cause of the performance problem. This is often the most challenging part of the performance tuning exercise. If the cause of the problem is not found, go back to step 1 or step 2.

4. *Solve* the problem by creating a solution that addresses the root cause. Solutions are not always obvious and, therefore, this step might require a great deal of ingenuity and creativity.

5. *Implement* the solution in a safe and controlled manner. An appropriate level of testing should be conducted. "Before" and "after" measurements should be obtained, if possible, in order to quantify the performance improvement. If the expected improvement is not obtained, go back to step 2.

Oracle Database versions may change, and software tools may change, but the five performance tuning steps never change. A problem may be simple and require only a few minutes of your time or it may be tremendously complex and require weeks of your time, but the five steps always remain the same. A simple example follows; you will be asked to duplicate it in the "Exercises" section at the end of the chapter:

---

2. This was presented in Chapter 11 as a general method of solving any performance problems; refer to the flow chart shown in Figure 11-2.

1. The users told the DBA that the problem was restricted to certain parts of the application only and that there had not been a problem the previous day. On questioning the application developers, the DBA learned that there had been an application upgrade the previous night.

2. The DBA used the `spreport.sql` script to generate Statspack reports for a 1-hour period for the previous day and the current day. The DBA also traced a number of database sessions by using the `DBMS_MONITOR.SET_SQL_TRACE` procedure.

3. Examination of the Statspack report for the current day showed large numbers of `enq: TM - contention` events; sessions were waiting, trying to lock an entire table. These events were not observed in the Statspack report for the previous day. The table in question was identified by searching through the trace files.

4. The `enq: TM - contention` event indicates an unindexed foreign key. If a foreign key is not indexed, Oracle must lock the entire child table when a record is deleted from the parent table in the foreign-key relationship. The DBA queried the `DBA_CONSTRAINTS`, `DBA_CONS_COLUMNS`, and `DBA_IND_COLUMNS` views to identify the missing index and brought this to the attention of the developers.

5. All that was left to do was to implement the solution in a safe and controlled manner. The developers followed the necessary change control procedures before creating the necessary index.

Tip A good question to ask during the investigation phase is, *"What changed?"* If you have installed RDA as suggested in Chapter 6, you can compare old and new RDA collections by using the `diff` option and determine whether the database environment has changed.

Analyzing DB Time

The best way to analyze database performance is to find out where the database is spending time. This is powerfully summarized by the Statspack and AWR reports. To demonstrate this, I used the Swingbench tool[3] to perform large numbers of transactions in my test database on my laptop. I then used the `spreport.sql` and `awrrpt.sql` scripts to generate the Statspack and AWR reports for a 1-hour period; the scripts can be found in `ORACLE_HOME\rdbms\admin`. Listing 16-2 shows the first page of the Statspack report; the AWR report contains similar information.

---

3. The Swingbench tool can be downloaded from `http://www.dominicgiles.com/swingbench.php`.

Listing 16-2. *First Page from a Sample Statspack Report*

```
STATSPACK report for


Database    DB Id    Instance     Inst Num  Startup Time    Release     RAC
~~~~~~~~  -----------  ------------  --------  ---------------  -----------  ---
          1202453053 orcl                  1 01-Jan-09 16:25 11.1.0.6.0  NO


Host Name               Platform                    CPUs Cores Sockets  Memory (G)
~~~~  ----------------  -----------------------  ----- ----- -------  ------------
      HP6910            Microsoft Windows IA (      2     0       0         2.0


Snapshot       Snap Id    Snap Time        Sessions Curs/Sess Comment
~~~~~~~~       ----------  -----------------  --------  ---------  -------------------
Begin Snap:        91 01-Jan-09 18:00:32        97       4.3
  End Snap:       101 01-Jan-09 19:01:05        99       4.4
  Elapsed:          60.55 (mins)
  DB time:       1,589.75 (mins)     DB CPU:        7.88 (mins)


Cache Sizes          Begin        End
~~~~~~~~~~~~~      ----------  ----------
   Buffer Cache:        12M              Std Block Size:        8K
   Shared Pool:        104M                 Log Buffer:    6,104K


Load Profile             Per Second     Per Transaction    Per Exec    Per Call
~~~~~~~~~~~~~~         -------------------  ------------------  -----------  -----------
       DB time(s):            26.3                1.1          0.24         0.17
        DB CPU(s):             0.1                0.0          0.00         0.00
        Redo size:        25,988.4            1,113.8
    Logical reads:           799.2               34.3
    Block changes:           183.7                7.9
    Physical reads:           63.4                2.7
   Physical writes:           34.9                1.5
        User calls:          152.1                6.5
           Parses:            84.0                3.6
      Hard parses:             1.8                0.1
 W/A MB processed:             0.1                0.0
           Logons:             0.0                0.0
         Executes:           107.6                4.6
        Rollbacks:             0.9                0.0
     Transactions:            23.3
```

Instance Efficiency Indicators
~~~~~~~~~~~~~~~~~~~~~~~~~~~~~~~~~~~~~

Buffer Nowait %:	99.90	Redo NoWait %:	99.59
Buffer Hit %:	92.07	Optimal W/A Exec %:	100.00
Library Hit %:	93.93	Soft Parse %:	97.82
Execute to Parse %:	21.95	Latch Hit %:	99.97
Parse CPU to Parse Elapsd %:	3.60	% Non-Parse CPU:	73.08

Shared Pool Statistics	Begin	End
	------	------
Memory Usage %:	88.91	88.54
% SQL with executions>1:	71.35	66.30
% Memory for SQL w/exec>1:	84.24	78.44

Top 5 Timed Events
~~~~~~~~~~~~~~~~~~~~~

			Avg wait	%Total Call
Event	Waits	Time (s)	(ms)	Time
db file sequential read	214,849	51,400	239	50.9
log file sync	91,814	39,109	426	38.7
log file parallel write	15,434	3,617	234	3.6
control file sequential read	5,507	1,498	272	1.5
db file parallel write	47,396	1,257	27	1.2

The most important section of the Statspack report is the "Top 5 Timed Events" section. It is preceded by details concerning the workload processed by the database. In Listing 16-2, you can see that the DB time was 1,589.75 minutes during an elapsed interval of 60.55 minutes. *DB time* is the sum of the response times of all database calls made by the connected sessions. The reason it is so much larger than the clock time is because many database sessions were simultaneously active. Note that actual CPU usage was only 7.88 minutes, less than one half of 1 percent of DB time. The rest of the time was spent waiting for overhead activities such as reading data from disk (db file sequential read operations) and writing redo information to the online redo logs (log file sync operations). Each db file sequential read operation retrieves one 8 KB block of data from disk. The average time for each operation was 239 milliseconds, which is totally unacceptable and indicates that the disks were the bottleneck; it should not take more than 5 milliseconds to retrieve a block of data. The average time for each log file sync operation was 426 milliseconds—more than four-tenths of a second—another indication that the disks are the bottleneck.

The best way to tune this database would be to get faster disks; another alternative would be to increase the size of the buffer cache so that less data has to be read from disk.

The ADDM report automatically analyzes the components of DB time and makes appropriate suggestions, some of which are shown in Listing 16-3.

Listing 16-3. *Recommendations from a Sample ADDM Report*

```
          Findings and Recommendations
          ----------------------------


Finding 1: I/O Throughput
Impact is 14.3 active sessions, 57.09% of total activity.
-----------------------------------------------------------
The throughput of the I/O subsystem was significantly lower than expected.

    Recommendation 1: Host Configuration
    Estimated benefit is 14.3 active sessions, 57.09% of total activity.
    ----------------------------------------------------------------------
    Action
       Consider increasing the throughput of the I/O subsystem. Oracle's
       recommended solution is to stripe all data file using the SAME
       methodology. You might also need to increase the number of disks for
       better performance. Alternatively, consider using Oracle's Automatic
       Storage Management solution.
    Rationale
       During the analysis period, the average data files' I/O throughput was
       498 K per second for reads and 276 K per second for writes. The average
       response time for single block reads was 235 milliseconds.


Finding 2: Undersized instance memory
Impact is 11.25 active sessions, 44.89% of total activity.
------------------------------------------------------------
The Oracle instance memory (SGA and PGA) was inadequately sized, causing
additional I/O and CPU usage.
The value of parameter "memory_target" was "252 M" during the analysis period.

    Recommendation 1: Database Configuration
    Estimated benefit is 11.24 active sessions, 44.87% of total activity.
    ----------------------------------------------------------------------
    Action
       Increase memory allocated to the instance by setting the parameter
       "memory_target" to 378 M.
```

Symptoms That Led to the Finding:

> Wait class "User I/O" was consuming significant database time.
> Impact is 13.83 active sessions, 55.22% of total activity.
> Hard parsing of SQL statements was consuming significant database time.
> Impact is 2.22 active sessions, 8.87% of total activity.

Finding 3: Commits and Rollbacks
Impact is 10.56 active sessions, 42.16% of total activity.

Waits on event "log file sync" while performing COMMIT and ROLLBACK operations were consuming significant database time.

Recommendation 1: Application Analysis
Estimated benefit is 10.56 active sessions, 42.16% of total activity.

Action
> Investigate application logic for possible reduction in the number of
> COMMIT operations by increasing the size of transactions.

Rationale
> The application was performing 1360 transactions per minute with an
> average redo size of 1125 bytes per transaction.

Recommendation 2: Host Configuration
Estimated benefit is 10.56 active sessions, 42.16% of total activity.

Action
> Investigate the possibility of improving the performance of I/O to the
> online redo log files.

Rationale
> The average size of writes to the online redo log files was 5 K and the
> average time per write was 232 milliseconds.

Symptoms That Led to the Finding:

> Wait class "Commit" was consuming significant database time.
> Impact is 10.56 active sessions, 42.16% of total activity.

Understanding the Oracle Wait Interface

Statspack gets its data from the Oracle *wait interface*—the collection of *dynamic perfor-mance views* that track all aspects of database activity. Performance monitoring tools can query these tables by using SQL. Some of the most important views in the wait interface are described in the following sections.

V$SYSSTAT and V$SESSTAT

V$SESSTAT and V$SYSSTAT contain almost 400 counters describing every aspect of the work-load handled by the database. V$SESSTAT contains session-level counters—almost 400 of them for each session—and V$SYSSTAT contains system-level counters, each one being the total of all the session-level counters of the same type. In other words, each row in V$SESSTAT gives us the value of a counter for one session, and each row in V$SYSSTAT gives us the total value for all sessions. Four of these counters (logons current, opened cursors current, session cursor cache current, and workarea memory allocated) represent current levels; the rest are cumulative counters that keep incrementing from the time the data-base was started.

Because the majority of these counters are cumulative, the way to monitor the rate of activity is to observe the values of these counters at fixed intervals and calculate the dif-ference; this is the approach used by the Statspack report. Some of the most important counters are described here:

- CPU used by this session is the amount of CPU used by one session in the case of V$SESSTAT. It is the amount of CPU used by all sessions put together in the case of V$SYSSTAT.

- consistent gets and db block gets are the number of blocks read in *consistent* and *current* mode respectively; current mode is used to find the most up-to-date ver-sion of a block, and consistent mode is used to find the state of a block at a prior point in time. The sum of consistent gets and db block gets is the number of *logi-cal reads* performed by the database.

- physical reads is the number of blocks that are not found in the memory cache and have to be physically retrieved from the disk.

- physical writes is the number of modified blocks that are written to disk.

- user commits and user rollbacks track transaction rates.

A complete list of the workload metrics tracked in the V$SYSSTAT and V$SESSTAT views is available in *Oracle Database 11g Reference*.

V$SESSION_EVENT and V$SYSTEM_EVENT

While V$SESSTAT and V$SYSSTAT track the workload handled by the database, V$SESSION_EVENT and V$SYSTEM_EVENT track the amount of time spent waiting in over 100 different categories—for example, waiting for I/O or waiting for a lock. All the counters are cumulative; V$SESSION_EVENT has session-level counters, and V$SYSTEM_EVENT has system-level counters. You saw some examples of these counters in the "Top 5 Timed Events" example earlier in this chapter; a complete list and explanations of each wait event is provided in *Oracle Database 11g Reference*. Here are some more examples:

- db file sequential read tracks the amount of time spent reading single blocks from tables.

- db file scattered read tracks the amount of time spent performing full table scans.

- enq: TX - contention is the amount of time waiting for row locks.

- enq: TM - contention is the amount of time waiting for table-level locks.

Mining the Statspack Repository

Statspack gets its data by performing *snapshots* of the dynamic performance tables such as V$SYSSTAT and V$SYSTEM_EVENT. This data is stored in tables that mimic the structure of the dynamic performance tables; for example, the STATS$SYSSTAT table corresponds to the V$SYSSTAT view, and the STATS$SYSTEM_EVENT table corresponds to the V$SYSTEM_EVENT view.

The Statspack repository can be mined for historical data that can be graphed by using tools such as Microsoft Excel. The graphs will show any historical trends and repeating patterns.

■**Tip** A stable database will exhibit distinct repeating patterns; for example, the workload may peak during the day and subside at night. These patterns are the signature of the database. Deviations from established patterns can be a sign that something is wrong with the database. The Statspack reports for the affected periods can be analyzed and compared with the reports for baseline periods.

In Chapter 10, you saw examples of SQL queries to mine the Statspack repository. Listing 10-8 showed an SQL query to track logical reads per second and physical reads per second over a period of time. That query is a good way to monitor trends and changes in the database workload; you can modify it to include other workload metrics. The corresponding graph is shown in Figure 10-2. Listing 10-9 showed an SQL query to extract performance information on specific SQL queries of your choice.

In Listing 16-4, you see another valuable SQL query; it provides the distribution of DB time for each available time period. It is a fairly long query, but you can download the text from the Source Code section of the Apress web site (http://www.apress.com). You have to specify a range of snapshots; the appropriate range can be obtained from the STATS$SNAPSHOT table. As I explained earlier in this chapter, the distribution of DB time is precisely the information you need to tune the database. CPU time is obtained from the STATS$SYSSTAT table, while the wait times for each type of event are obtained from the STATS$SYSTEM_EVENT table. The classifications in the V$EVENT_NAME view are used to group events into categories such as Application, Concurrency, Commit, User IO, and System IO. The PIVOT operator is used to convert rows into columns; this makes it easy to perform further analysis on the data. The LAG function is used to compute the amount of increase in each row of data. Finally, we divide CPU time and wait time by the length of the observed interval to compute *average active sessions* for each category of time.

Sample output of this query is shown in Figures 16-1 and 16-2; each graph shows data for the same database—one week at a time. Even if you knew very little about perfor-mance tuning, you could instinctively tell which week was a good week for the database and which week was a bad week. The graph in Figure 16-1 exhibits very regular patterns, indicating database stability. The graph in Figure 16-2 is for another week in the same database, but the regular patterns are missing. I hope these examples convince you of the importance of this query; it will show you the big picture and tell you where to focus your attention.

Listing 16-4. *SQL Query to Show Patterns and Trends in the Distribution of DB Time*

```
set linesize 132
set pagesize 10000
set tab off
set trimout on
set trimspool on
set sqlblanklines on

alter session set nls_date_format = 'yyyy/mm/dd hh24:mi';

column aas_cpu format 999.99
column aas_other format 999.99
column aas_application format 999.99
column aas_concurrency format 999.99
column aas_commit format 999.99
column aas_user_io format 999.99
column aas_system_io format 999.99
```

```
WITH

    timed_events AS

    -- Get wait time from the STATS$SYSTEM_EVENT table.
    -- Select snapshots between start_snap_id and end_snap_id.
    -- Convert wait microseconds into seconds.
    -- Merge some wait classes into the "Other" class (wait_class# = 0).
    -- Ignore the "Idle" class (wait_class = 6).
    -- Wait classifications are those found in the V$EVENT_NAME view.

    -- Get CPU usage from the STATS$SYSSTAT table.
    -- Select snapshots between start_snap_id and end_snap_id.
    -- Convert CPU centiseconds into seconds.

    (SELECT   snap_id,
              CASE
                    WHEN wait_class# IN (0, 2, 3, 7, 10, 11, 12)
                    THEN 0
                    ELSE wait_class#
              END AS wait_class#,
              time_waited_micro / 1000000 AS time_spent
       FROM   stats$system_event NATURAL JOIN v$event_name
      WHERE   snap_id between &&start_snap_id and &&end_snap_id
        AND   wait_class# != 6

              UNION ALL

     SELECT   snap_id,
              100 as wait_class#,
              VALUE / 100 as time_spent
       FROM   stats$sysstat
      WHERE   snap_id between &&start_snap_id and &&end_snap_id
        AND   name = 'CPU used by this session'),
```

```
    pivoted_data AS

    -- Create separate columns for each wait class and for CPU time.
```

```
(SELECT    *
    FROM    (SELECT * from timed_events)
            PIVOT (SUM(time_spent)
                FOR wait_class# IN ( 0 AS other,
                                     1 AS application,
                                     4 AS concurrency,
                                     5 AS commit,
                                     8 AS user_io,
                                     9 AS system_io,
                                   100 AS cpu))),
```

```
deltas AS

-- Use the LAG analytic function to determine the amount of increase.
-- Partition the rows by database startup time.
-- The STATS$SNAPSHOT view tells us when the database was started.

(SELECT    snap_id,

           snap_time,

           (snap_time - LAG(snap_time)
             OVER (PARTITION BY startup_time ORDER BY snap_id)) * 86400
             AS snap_time_d,

           cpu - LAG (cpu)
             OVER (PARTITION BY startup_time ORDER BY snap_id)
             AS cpu_d,

           other - LAG (other)
             OVER (PARTITION BY startup_time ORDER BY snap_id)
             AS other_d,

           application - LAG (application)
             OVER (PARTITION BY startup_time ORDER BY snap_id)
             AS application_d,

           concurrency - LAG (concurrency)
             OVER (PARTITION BY startup_time ORDER BY snap_id)
             AS concurrency_d,
```

```
            commit - LAG (commit)
              OVER (PARTITION BY startup_time ORDER BY snap_id)
              AS commit_d,

            user_io - LAG (user_io)
              OVER (PARTITION BY startup_time ORDER BY snap_id)
              AS user_io_d,

            system_io - LAG (system_io)
              OVER (PARTITION BY startup_time ORDER BY snap_id)
              AS system_io_d

    FROM    pivoted_data NATURAL JOIN stats$snapshot)
```

```
    -- Compute and print Average Active Sessions for each category of time.

    SELECT    snap_id,
              snap_time,
              cpu_d / snap_time_d AS aas_cpu,
              other_d / snap_time_d AS aas_other,
              application_d / snap_time_d AS aas_application,
              concurrency_d / snap_time_d AS aas_concurrency,
              commit_d / snap_time_d AS aas_commit,
              user_io_d / snap_time_d AS aas_user_io,
              system_io_d / snap_time_d AS aas_system_io

    FROM      deltas

    ORDER BY  snap_id;
```

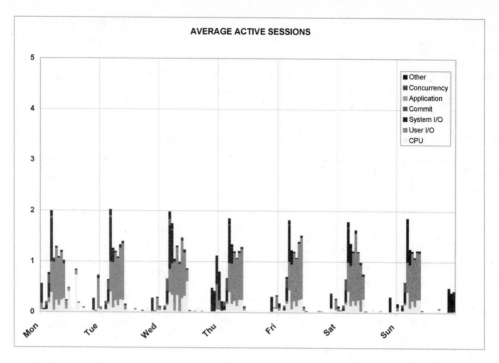

Figure 16-1. *A good week for the database*

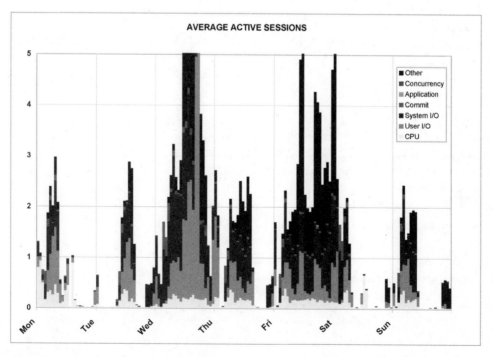

Figure 16-2. *A bad week for the database*

It is also useful to see at a glance the top five timed events for a range of time periods. The query shown in Listing 16-5 will let you do exactly that. The text of this query can also be downloaded from the Source Code section of the Apress web site (http://www.apress.com). Listing 16-6 shows some sample output; it is for the first six periods in the graph shown in Figure 16-1.

Listing 16-5. *SQL Query to Display the Top Five Timed Events for a Range of Time Periods*

```
set linesize 132
set pagesize 10000
set tab off
set trimout on
set trimspool on
set sqlblanklines on

alter session set nls_date_format = 'mm/dd hh24:mi';

column event format a30
column time_spent_d format 9,999,999.90
column aas format 9999.90
column percentage format 999.90


break on snap_id on snap_time skip 1

WITH

  timed_events AS

  -- Get wait time from the STATS$SYSTEM_EVENT table.
  -- Select snapshots between start_snap_id and end_snap_id.
  -- Convert wait microseconds into seconds.
  -- Ignore the "Idle" class (wait_class = 6).
  -- Wait classifications are those found in the V$EVENT_NAME view.

  -- Get CPU usage from the STATS$SYSSTAT table.
  -- Select snapshots between start_snap_id and end_snap_id.
  -- Convert CPU centiseconds into seconds.

  (SELECT   snap_id,
            event,
            time_waited_micro / 1000000 AS time_spent
```

```
   FROM    stats$system_event NATURAL JOIN v$event_name
  WHERE    snap_id between &&start_snap_id and &&end_snap_id
    AND    wait_class# != 6

           UNION ALL

 SELECT    snap_id,
           'CPU used by this session' AS event,
           VALUE / 100 as time_spent
   FROM    stats$sysstat
  WHERE    snap_id between &&start_snap_id and &&end_snap_id
    AND    name = 'CPU used by this session'),
```

```
deltas AS

-- Use the LAG analytic function to determine the amount of increase.
-- Partition the rows by database startup time.
-- The STATS$SNAPSHOT view tells us when the database was started.

(SELECT    snap_id,
           snap_time,
           event,
           (snap_time - LAG (snap_time)
             OVER (PARTITION BY startup_time, event ORDER BY snap_id)) * 86400
             AS snap_time_d,
           time_spent - LAG (time_spent)
             OVER (PARTITION BY startup_time, event ORDER BY snap_id)
             AS time_spent_d
   FROM    timed_events NATURAL JOIN stats$snapshot),
```

```
ranks AS

-- Use the RANK analytic function to rank the events.
-- Also compute the percentage contribution of each event.

(SELECT    snap_id,
           snap_time,
           event,
```

```
            snap_time_d,
            time_spent_d,
            RANK()
              OVER (PARTITION BY snap_id ORDER BY time_spent_d DESC)
              AS rank,
            decode(time_spent_d, 0, 0, time_spent_d / SUM(time_spent_d)
              OVER (PARTITION BY snap_id) * 100)
              AS percentage
      FROM  deltas
     WHERE  time_spent_d IS NOT NULL)


------------------------------------------------------------------------------


  -- Compute Average Active Sessions for each category of time.
  -- List the top 5 events.

   SELECT   snap_id,
            snap_time,
            rank,
            substr(event, 1, 30) as event,
            time_spent_d,
            time_spent_d / snap_time_d as aas,
            percentage
     FROM   ranks
    WHERE   rank <= 5
 ORDER BY   snap_id,
            rank;
```

Listing 16-6. *Sample Report Showing the Top Five Timed Events for a Range of Time Periods*

SNAP	SNAP_TIME	RANK	EVENT	TIME_SPENT_D	AAS	PERCENT
2201	01/07 01:00	1	CPU used by this session	127.05	.04	47.32
		2	RMAN backup & recovery I/O	74.75	.02	27.84
		3	control file parallel write	17.59	.00	6.55
		4	db file sequential read	16.89	.00	6.29
		5	control file sequential read	10.56	.00	3.93
2211	01/07 02:00	1	log file sync	269.49	.07	36.58
		2	log file parallel write	266.31	.07	36.15
		3	CPU used by this session	151.23	.04	20.53

4 db file sequential read	31.48	.01	4.27
5 control file parallel write	15.52	.00	2.11

2221 01/07 03:00

1 log file parallel write	867.97	.24	31.45
2 CPU used by this session	653.38	.18	23.67
3 log file sync	608.85	.17	22.06
4 db file scattered read	273.92	.08	9.93
5 log buffer space	121.16	.03	4.39

2231 01/07 04:00

1 log file parallel write	2,169.10	.60	30.36
2 CPU used by this session	1,362.13	.38	19.06
3 db file scattered read	1,308.39	.36	18.31
4 db file sequential read	871.71	.24	12.20
5 log file sequential read	606.94	.17	8.49

2241 01/07 05:00

1 db file scattered read	3,154.11	.88	82.63
2 db file sequential read	264.16	.07	6.92
3 CPU used by this session	102.78	.03	2.69
4 log file parallel write	101.61	.03	2.66
5 control file parallel write	84.06	.02	2.20

2251 01/07 06:00

1 db file scattered read	3,327.81	.92	71.27
2 CPU used by this session	827.02	.23	17.71
3 db file sequential read	261.75	.07	5.61
4 read by other session	122.51	.03	2.62
5 control file parallel write	58.31	.02	1.25

Using the Statspack Report

A Statspack report is generated from two *snapshots* of the database. These snapshots are a copy of the contents of the various dynamic performance tables that are continuously accumulating information about activity in the database. Automatic Workload Repository (AWR) and Automatic Database Diagnostic Monitor (ADDM) were offered as replacements for Statspack beginning with Oracle Database 10*g* and are no longer documented in the Oracle manuals. However, you can use AWR and ADDM only with Enterprise Edition and only if you have a license for Diagnostics Pack—an extra-cost option available only with Enterprise Edition. In my experiences, very few organizations have the requisite licenses. I therefore emphasize the use of Statspack and use it a lot in my own work. Note that Oracle did make several incremental enhancements to Statspack in Oracle Database 10*g* and 11*g*, thus further increasing its usefulness and relevance. However, you will have to refer to Chapter 21 of *Oracle Database 9i Performance Tuning Guide and Reference* for documentation on Statspack because it is not documented in the Oracle Database 10*g* and 11*g* manuals. A useful introduction to Statspack as well as installation instructions can be found in `spdoc.txt` in the `ORACLE_HOME\rdbms\admin` folder.

The Statspack report contains a wealth of other information that can help you diagnose and solve your performance problem. In Listing 16-2, you saw the first page of a sample Statspack report, of which the most interesting section was the "Top 5 Timed Events" section. Here is a list of other interesting sections of the Statspack report:

- "SQL Ordered by CPU" lists the SQL queries that consume the most CPU.

- "SQL Ordered by Elapsed Time" lists the SQL queries that take the longest time.

- "SQL Ordered by Gets" lists the SQL queries that perform the most logical reads.

- "SQL Ordered by Reads" lists the SQL queries that perform the most physical reads.

- "Instance Activity Stats" lists workload data from the `V$SYSSTAT` dynamic performance view.

- "File Read Histogram Stats" lists workload and performance metrics for each file in the database.

- "Segments by Logical Reads" and "Segments by Physical Reads" show which tables and indexes have the most logical reads and physical reads. They are available in only *level 7 snapshots*. Refer to Chapter 21 of *Oracle Database 9i Performance Tuning Guide and Reference* for information on the different snapshot levels and how to change them.

Summary

Here is a short summary of the concepts touched on in this chapter:

- When a performance problem is reported, the database might not be the cause. A systematic method should be used for identifying the root cause.

- The five steps for addressing any performance problem are define, investigate, analyze, solve, and implement.

- The best way to analyze database performance is to find out where the database is spending its time. This is summarized by the "Top 5 Timed Events" section of the Statspack report.

- Statspack gets its data from the Oracle *wait interface*—the collection of dynamic performance views that track all aspects of database activity. Important views include V$SYSSTAT, V$SESSTAT, V$SESSION_EVENT, and V$SYSTEM_EVENT.

- The Statspack repository can be mined for historical data that can be graphed by using tools such as Microsoft Excel. This is a good way to monitor trends and changes in the database workload and database performance. Performance of individual queries can also be tracked over time. It is also useful to see at a glance the top five timed events for a range of time periods.

- A stable database will exhibit distinct repeating patterns; for example, the workload may peak during the day and subside at night. These patterns are the signature of the database. Deviations from established patterns can be a sign that something is wrong with the database; the Statspack reports for the affected periods can be analyzed and compared with the reports for baseline periods.

- The Statspack report contains a wealth of information that can help you diagnose and solve a performance problem. Examples include "SQL Ordered by CPU," "SQL Ordered by Elapsed Time," "SQL Ordered by Gets," "SQL Ordered by Reads," "Instance Activity Stats," "File Read Histogram Stats," "Segments by Logical Reads," and "Segments by Physical Reads."

Exercises

In this set of exercises, you will duplicate the locking problem that was described in this chapter. You will need to use the HR sample schema as well as Statspack. If you did not install the sample schema when creating your database, you can use the hr_main.sql script in the ORACLE_HOME\demo\schema\human_resources folder. Instructions for running this script can be found in *Oracle Database 11g Sample Schemas*—you can download it from the Oracle web site. If you have not already installed Statspack in your test database, run the scripts spcreate.sql and spauto.sql in the ORACLE_HOME\rdbms\admin folder. The instructions are in spdoc.txt in the same folder.

Perform the following sequence of instructions once the HR sample schema and Statspack have been installed:

1. Query the DBA_CONSTRAINTS and DBA_CONS_COLUMNS views and confirm that the manager_id column of the employees table in the HR schema is a *foreign key* that links to the employee_id column of the same table. Use the following commands:

```
SELECT constraint_name
  FROM dba_constraints
 WHERE owner = 'HR'
   AND table_name = 'EMPLOYEES'
   AND constraint_type = 'P';
```

```
SELECT constraint_name,
       owner,
       table_name
  FROM dba_constraints
 WHERE constraint_type = 'R'
   AND r_owner = 'HR'
   AND r_constraint_name = 'EMP_EMP_ID_PK';

SELECT column_name,
       position
  FROM dba_cons_columns
 WHERE owner = 'HR'
   AND constraint_name = 'EMP_EMP_ID_PK';

SELECT column_name,
       position
  FROM dba_cons_columns
 WHERE owner = 'HR'
   AND constraint_name = 'EMP_MANAGER_FK';
```

2. Drop the emp_manager_ix index on the manager_id column of the employees table.
   Use the command drop index hr.emp_manager_ix.

3. Find the name of each employee's manager. Use the following command:

```
 SELECT e2.first_name AS manager_first_name,
        e2.last_name AS manager_last_name,
        e1.first_name AS employee_first_name,
        e1.last_name AS employee_last_name
   FROM hr.employees e1,
        hr.employees e2
  WHERE e2.employee_id = e1.manager_id
ORDER BY 1, 2, 3, 4;
```

4. Connect to the database as the HR user and update one of the records in the
   employees table; for example, issue the command update employees set
   phone_number=phone_number where first_name='Alexander' and last_name='Hunold'.
   Do not commit this transaction.

5. Connect to the database again and attempt to delete the manager of the employee
   whose record you just updated; for example, issue the command delete from
   employees where first_name='Lex' and last_name='De Haan'. This command will be
   blocked by Oracle.

6. Connect to the database as the `system` user. Query the `v$session_wait` table and find the session ID of the blocked session. Because you know that it is waiting for an `enq: TM - contention` event to complete, you can use the command `select sid as session_id, wait_time_micro from v$session_wait where event = 'enq: TM - contention'`.

7. Query the `V$SESSION` view and obtain the *serial number* of the blocked process. Use the command `select serial# as serial_num from v$session where sid=&session_id`.

8. Begin tracing the blocked session by using the `DBMS_MONITOR.SESSION_TRACE_ENABLE` session; issue the command `execute dbms_monitor.session_trace_enable(&session_id, &serial_num, TRUE)`. Refer to *Oracle Database 11g PL/SQL Packages and Types Reference* for a description of the `session_trace_enable` procedure.

9. Generate a Statspack snapshot by using the `statspack.snap` procedure. Using a special version of the procedure, capture performance information for the blocked session in addition to systemwide information; issue the command `execute statspack.snap(i_session_id => &session_id)`.

10. Now resume the first session and issue the `rollback` command. This will release the blocked session, and Oracle will display the error `ORA-02292: integrity constraint (HR.EMP_MANAGER_FK) violated - child record found`.

11. Identify the trace file for the second session by using the command `select tracefile from v$process where addr = (select paddr from v$session where sid = &session_id)`. Review the trace file and locate the lines similar to the following line:

    ```
    WAIT #4: nam='enq: TM - contention' ela= 855599225 name|mode=1414332421
    object #=71472 table/partition=0 obj#=-1 tim=198871373294
    ```

12. Confirm that the object number listed in the trace file corresponds to the `employees` table. Use the command `select owner, object_type, object_name from dba_objects where object_id=&object_id`.

13. Perform the experiment once more and confirm that additional wait messages appear in the trace file.

14. Navigate to the folder where the trace file is located and invoke the `tkprof` utility from the command line. You have to specify the name of the trace file and choose a name for the output file. Review the output file created by `tkprof`.

15. Generate another Statspack snapshot by using the `statspack.snap` procedure with the same parameter used in step 9. Use the command `execute statspack.snap (i_session_id => &session_id)`.

16. Connect to the database as the `system` or `perfstat` user and generate a Statspack report from the snapshots obtained in step 9 and step 15. Run the `spreport.sql` script by using the command `@?/rdbms/admin/spreport.sql`.

17. Review the Statspack report. In particular, review the "Top 5 Timed Events" section. Also pay attention to the sections of the report that provide information on the blocked session that you were tracking.

18. Finally, connect to the database as the HR user and re-create the index that you had dropped at the start at the exercise. Use the command `create index hr.emp_manager_ix on hr.employees (manager_id)`.

Further Reading

Oracle Corporation. *Oracle Database 11g Performance Tuning Guide.* Oracle Corporation, 2007. This is certainly the place to start if only because it is searchable and downloadable free of charge at `http://tahiti.oracle.com` or `http://www.oracle.com/technology/documentation/index.html`. It offers a detailed and comprehensive treatment of performance tuning methods, and the price is right. Printed copies can be purchased from Oracle's online store.

Oracle Corporation. *Oracle Database 9i Performance Tuning Guide and Reference.* Oracle Corporation, 2002. Searchable and downloadable free of charge at `http://tahiti.oracle.com` or `http://www.oracle.com/technology/documentation/index.html`. Chapter 21 of this reference guide explains how to install and use Statspack. Note that Statspack is not documented in the reference guides for Oracle Database 10*g* and 11*g* even though it is an essential tool for those who don't have a license for Diagnostics Pack.

Oracle Corporation. *Oracle Database 11g Reference.* Oracle Corporation, 2007. Searchable or downloadable free of charge at `http://tahiti.oracle.com` or `http://www.oracle.com/technology/documentation/index.html`. It contains detailed information on the dynamic performance views—for example, descriptions of the workload metrics visible in the `V$SYSSTAT` and `V$SESSTAT` views, and descriptions of the wait time metrics tracked in `V$SYSTEM_EVENT` and `V$SESSION_EVENT`. Printed copies can be purchased from Oracle's online store.

Shee, Richmond et al. *Oracle Wait Interface: A Practical Guide to Performance Diagnostics & Tuning.* McGraw-Hill Osborne Media, 2004. An excellent book on tuning by using the Oracle wait interface. Of great value are the explanations of how to handle the most common wait events.

Lawson, Christopher. *The Art and Science of Oracle Performance Tuning.* Apress, 2003. At the time of writing, this book has not yet been updated for Database 10*g* and 11*g*, but the systematic five-step method it teaches is as fresh and valid today as it was when the book was written. I highly recommend this book.

■■■

CHAPTER 17

SQL Tuning

Every limbo boy and girl
All around the limbo world
Gonna do the limbo rock
All around the limbo clock

—"Limbo Rock," recorded by Chubby Checker in 1962
(free.napster.com/search/results.html?query=chubby+checker&type=artist)

Perhaps the most complex problem in database administration is SQL tuning, and it may not be a coincidence that I left it for the very end. The paucity of books devoted to SQL tuning is perhaps further evidence of the difficulty of the topic.

The only way to interact with Oracle, to retrieve data, to change data, to administer the database, is SQL. Oracle itself uses SQL to perform all the work that it does behind the scenes. SQL performance is therefore the key to database performance; all database performance problems are really SQL performance problems even if they express themselves as contention for resources.

In this chapter, I will present some of the causes of inefficient SQL and some of the common techniques of making SQL more efficient, but we will spend most of our time working through a case study. I will present a fairly typical SQL statement and improve it in stages until it hits the theoretical maximum level of performance that is possible to achieve.

Defining Efficiency

The efficiency of an SQL statement is measured by the amount of computing resources such as CPU cycles used in producing the output. Reducing the consumption of resources is the goal of SQL tuning. Elapsed time is not a good measure of the efficiency of an SQL statement because it is not always proportional to the amount of resources consumed. For example, contention for CPU cycles and disk I/O causes execution delays. The number of logical read operations is a better way to measure the consumption of computing resources because it is directly proportional to the amount of resources consumed—the fewer the number of logical read operations, the less CPU consumption.

Identifying Inefficient SQL Statements

When an application is performing poorly or a batch job takes a long time, we have to identify SQL statements that are consuming a lot of resources and are candidates for tuning. The simplest way to do this is to watch the operation of the database by using a GUI tool such as Enterprise Manager or SQL Developer. In Figure 17-1, you can see a query being run by SYSTEM.

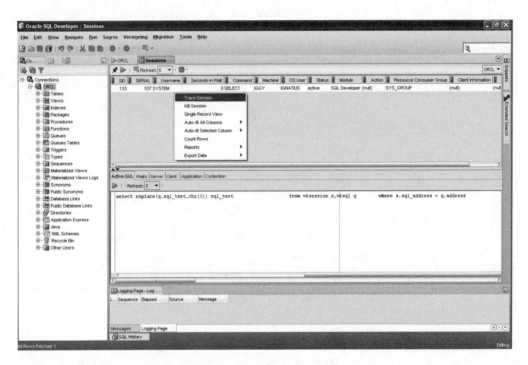

Figure 17-1. *Using SQL Developer to monitor sessions*

A systematic way of identifying tuning candidates in a batch job is to *trace* the job. If you ask Oracle to trace a job, it records SQL statements and execution details in a *trace file*. The simplest way to start tracing a session is to use Enterprise Manager or SQL Developer as in Figure 17-1. You can also use the SET_SQL_TRACE_IN_SESSION command as in the following example:

```
EXECUTE dbms_system.set_sql_trace_in_session(133, 537, true);
```

You can then use the tkprof tool to summarize the information in a more readable form, as in Listing 17-1. You can see that a particular statement was executed 163 times—execution statistics are also displayed. In this case, the number of logical reads—the number of buffers gotten for consistent read—is zero because the information is coming from dynamic performance tables, not from actual database tables.

Listing 17-1. *Using tkprof to Summarize a Trace File*

```
C:\app\IGNATIUS\diag\rdbms\orcl\orcl\trace>tkprof orcl_ora_6744.trc
output = orcl_ora_6744.tkprof

TKPROF: Release 11.1.0.6.0 - Production on Sun Sep 28 21:59:38 2008

Copyright (c) 1982, 2007, Oracle.  All rights reserved.

C:\app\IGNATIUS\diag\rdbms\orcl\orcl\trace>type orcl_ora_6744.tkprof

TKPROF: Release 11.1.0.6.0 - Production on Sun Sep 28 21:59:38 2008

Copyright (c) 1982, 2007, Oracle.  All rights reserved.

Trace file: orcl_ora_6744.trc
Sort options: default

********************************************************************************
count    = number of times OCI procedure was executed
cpu      = cpu time in seconds executing
elapsed  = elapsed time in seconds executing
disk     = number of physical reads of buffers from disk
query    = number of buffers gotten for consistent read
current  = number of buffers gotten in current mode (usually for update)
rows     = number of rows processed by the fetch or execute call
********************************************************************************

select replace(q.sql_text,chr(0)) sql_text
from v$session s,v$sql q
where s.sql_address = q.address
and s.sql_hash_value = q.hash_value
and s.sid = :SID

call     count      cpu    elapsed       disk      query    current       rows
-------  ------  -------- ---------- ---------- ---------- ---------- ----------
Parse       61     0.00       0.00          0          0          0          0
Execute     61     0.00       0.03          0          0          0          0
Fetch       61     0.00       0.02          0          0          0        305
-------  ------  -------- ---------- ---------- ---------- ---------- ----------
total      183     0.00       0.06          0          0          0        305
```

Misses in library cache during parse: 1
Misses in library cache during execute: 1
Optimizer mode: ALL_ROWS
Parsing user id: 5

```
Rows    Row Source Operation
-------  ----------------------------------------------------
     5  NESTED LOOPS  (cr=0 pr=0 pw=0 time=11 us cost=0 size=640 card=1)
     1   MERGE JOIN CARTESIAN (cr=0 pr=0 pw=0 time=0 us cost=0 size=108 card=1)
     1    NESTED LOOPS  (cr=0 pr=0 pw=0 time=0 us cost=0 size=39 card=1)
     1     FIXED TABLE FIXED INDEX X$KSLWT (ind:1) (cr=0 pr=0 pw=0 time=0 us cost=0
          size=26 card=1)
     1     FIXED TABLE FIXED INDEX X$KSLED (ind:2) (cr=0 pr=0 pw=0 time=0 us cost=0
          size=13 card=1)
     1    BUFFER SORT (cr=0 pr=0 pw=0 time=0 us cost=0 size=69 card=1)
     1     FIXED TABLE FIXED INDEX X$KSUSE (ind:1) (cr=0 pr=0 pw=0 time=0 us cost=0
          size=69 card=1)
     5   FIXED TABLE FIXED INDEX X$KGLCURSOR_CHILD (ind:1) (cr=0 pr=0 pw=0
          time=6 us cost=0 size=532 card=1)


*****************************************************************************
```

Another way to identify tuning candidates is to examine a STATSPACK report. STATSPACK reports were discussed in Chapter 16.

Understanding the Causes of Inefficient SQL

We may not even realize that we are dealing with inefficient SQL because powerful hardware can compensate for much inefficiency. In fact, one simple method of "improving" performance is simply to throw powerful hardware at the problem.[1] In other cases, a statement may take such little time to execute that we may not realize that it is inefficient. There are many different causes for poor performance of SQL statements, and there are many solutions; a short essay cannot do them justice.

We should also keep in mind that, given enough time, effort, and money, it is always possible to extract more performance out of an SQL statement. The example used in this chapter perfectly illustrates the point; we keep improving its performance until we hit the theoretical maximum level of performance. However, it is not usually possible to give so

---

1. In *Oracle on VMware*, Dr. Bert Scalzo makes a persuasive case for "solving" problems with hardware upgrades, saying that "*Person hours cost so much more now than computer hardware even with inexpensive offshore outsourcing. It is now considered a sound business decision these days to throw cheap hardware at problems.*"

much time and attention to individual statements. The amount of effort we are willing to expend is usually governed by business requirements and the return on our investment.

The most frequently cited cause of inefficient SQL is the failure of the query optimizer to generate an efficient query execution plan, but there are many others. Here are some examples:

- There are usually many ways to write the same query, and not all of them are equally efficient. In Chapter 2, you saw ten solutions to the problem of listing the status of all suppliers who supply hammers. Failure to use advanced features of the language is a common cause of inefficient SQL.

- Poor application development practices may increase the amount of inefficient SQL. For example, giving users the ability to generate new types of queries (a.k.a. *ad hoc queries*) is usually a perfect recipe for poor performance. Another example of poor application development practices is insufficient testing.

- Logical and physical database design can play a big role in SQL performance. Examples are inadequate indexing and partitioning of data, and insufficient attention to disk layouts.

- Inadequate database maintenance can cause SQL performance to degrade as time passes. A perfect example is the absence of an archiving strategy to keep the amount of data under control.

It bears repeating that hardware limitations—including CPU speed, memory size, and disk speed—play a big role in performance. If the system does not have enough memory, data may have to be frequently retrieved from disk. The workload handled by the database server also plays a major role in performance; your SQL statement will run slowly if it has to compete for resources with SQL statements submitted by other users. Often this is the result of poor coordination of workloads. For example, it is poor practice to perform batch processing during the day when most OLTP work is performed. Sometimes this is the result of poor capacity planning. For example, an online store may not have properly planned for the increase in transaction volumes during popular holidays.

Ways to Improve SQL

Given enough time, effort, and money, it is usually possible to extract more performance out of any SQL statement. However, it is not usually possible to give so much time and attention to individual statements. The amount of effort we are willing to expend is usually governed by business requirements and the return on our investment. The goal is usually to bring performance of poorly performing SQL statements to a level that is acceptable to the users of the database. The following sections describe some techniques that can be used to improve performance.

Indexes

A common reason for inefficient processing of SQL statements is the lack of appropriate indexes and other paths to reach the required data. Imagine how difficult it would be to find an item of information in a book if those items were not organized into appropriate chapters and there were no index of key words at the back of the book. We discussed indexes in Chapter 7.

Most tables have a primary key and therefore have at least one index—that is, the index on the items composing the primary key. This index is used to ensure that no two records contain the same values of these data items. The absence of such an index would make it harder to ensure this. Indexes should also be created for any *foreign keys* in a table, that is, data items that link the table to another table, unless the table in question is small enough that the lack of such indexes will not have an impact on performance. Indexes should also be created for data items that are restricted in SQL queries.

The dba_indexes and dba_ind_columns views show what indexes have been created, as in the following example from the tuning exercise in this chapter:

```
SQL> SELECT table_name,
  2           index_name
  3    FROM user_indexes
  4   WHERE table_name in ('MY_TABLES', 'MY_INDEXES');


TABLE_NAME           INDEX_NAME
-------------------- --------------------
MY_INDEXES           MY_INDEXES_FK1
MY_INDEXES           MY_INDEXES_I1
MY_INDEXES           MY_INDEXES_PK
MY_TABLES            MY_TABLES_PK


SQL> SELECT table_name,
  2           index_name,
  3           column_name,
  4           column_position
  5    FROM user_ind_columns
  6   WHERE table_name in ('MY_TABLES', 'MY_INDEXES');


TABLE_NAME           INDEX_NAME           COLUMN_NAME           COLUMN_POSITION
-------------------- -------------------- -------------------- ----------------
MY_INDEXES           MY_INDEXES_PK        OWNER                               1
MY_INDEXES           MY_INDEXES_PK        INDEX_NAME                          2
MY_INDEXES           MY_INDEXES_I1        INDEX_TYPE                          1
MY_INDEXES           MY_INDEXES_FK1       TABLE_OWNER                         1
MY_INDEXES           MY_INDEXES_FK1       TABLE_NAME                          2
```

| MY_TABLES | MY_TABLES_PK | OWNER | 1 |
| MY_TABLES | MY_TABLES_PK | TABLE_NAME | 2 |

Database designers have several kinds of indexes at their disposal; the most common are listed here:

- Most indexes are of the *b*tree* (balanced tree) type and are best suited for online transaction processing environments. Index entries are stored in a structure that has a root node, branches, and leaves, hence the name.

- *Reverse key indexes* are a specialized type of b*tree index in which the key values are reversed (for example, *IGGY* becomes *YGGI*) to prevent concentrations of similar entries in index blocks and consequent contention for blocks.

- *Function-based indexes* and indexes on *virtual columns* (columns defined in terms of other columns) are indexes not on the data values contained in columns—but on combinations of these values. For example, an index on UPPER(name) would be an example of a function-based index.

- *Bitmap indexes* are a specialized kind of index used in data warehouses for columns that contain only a few values—for example, model, year, and color. Each value is represented by a *bitmap* (an array of 0s and 1s), and each element of the bitmap represents one record in the table.

In addition to indexes, database designers have other data structures at their disposal. Examples include clusters, index-organized tables, and partitioned tables.

■Tip Oracle does not use an index unless the query optimizer perceives a benefit in doing so. You can verify that an index is being used by issuing the MONITORING USAGE clause of the ALTER INDEX command and reviewing the contents of the v$object_usage view after a suitable time has passed. If Oracle is not using an index, you can use the techniques in the following sections to increase the chances that it will do so. If an index is never used, you should consider whether it can be removed safely because indexes slow down insert, update, and delete operations and occupy valuable space within the database.

Hints

Hints for the optimizer can be embedded inside an SQL statement if the optimizer does not find an acceptable query plan for the statement. Each hint partially constrains the optimizer, and a full set of hints completely constrains the optimizer. In fact, a desirable query plan can be preserved by capturing the complete set of hints that describes it in a *stored outline*. For details, refer to *Oracle Database 11*g *Performance Tuning Guide*.

The most commonly used hints are in the following list; detailed information on these and other hints can be found in *Oracle Database 11g SQL Language Reference*:

- The LEADING hint instructs Oracle to process the specified tables first, in the order listed.

- The ORDERED hint instructs Oracle to process the tables in the order listed in the body of the SQL statement.

- The INDEX hint instructs Oracle to use the specified index when processing the specified table.

- The FULL hint instructs Oracle not to use indexes when processing the specified table.

- The NO_MERGE hint instructs Oracle to optimize and process an inline view separately from the rest of the query.

- The USE_NL, USE_HASH, and USE_MERGE hints are used in conjunction with the LEADING hint or the ORDERED hint to constrain the choice of Join method (nested loops, hash, or sort-merge) for the specified table.

Here is an example of an SQL query that incorporates hints to guide and constrain the optimizer. Oracle is instructed to visit the My_indexes table before the My_tables table. Oracle is also instructed to use an index on the index_type data item in My_indexes and an index on the owner and table_name data items in My_tables, if such indexes are available. Note that hints must come directly after the SELECT keyword and must be enclosed between special markers, for example, /*+ INDEX(MY_INDEXES (INDEX_TYPE)) */.

```
SELECT        /*+ INDEX(MY_INDEXES (INDEX_TYPE))
                  INDEX(MY_TABLES (OWNER TABLE_NAME))
                  LEADING(MY_INDEXES MY_TABLES)
                  USE_NL(MY_TABLES)
              */
    DISTINCT my_tables.owner,
             my_tables.table_name,
             my_tables.tablespace_name
       FROM my_tables, my_indexes
      WHERE my_tables.owner = my_indexes.table_owner
        AND my_tables.table_name = my_indexes.table_name
        AND my_indexes.index_type = :index_type;
```

Statistics

Statistical information on tables and indexes and the data they contain is what the query optimizer needs to do its job properly. The simplest way to collect statistics is to use the procedures in the DBMS_STATS package. For example, DBMS_STATS.GATHER_TABLE_STATS can be used to collect statistics for a single table, and DBMS_STATS.GATHER_SCHEMA_STATS can be used to collect statistics for all the tables in a schema. You will see some examples in the tuning exercise in this chapter.

However, the question of how and when to collect statistics does not have an easy answer—because changes in statistics can lead to changes in query execution plans that are *not* always for the better. A perfect example of how fresh statistics can degrade performance occurs when statistics are collected on a table that contains very volatile data. The statistics describe the data that existed when the statistics were collected, but the data could change soon thereafter; the table could be empty when the statistics were collected but could be filled with data soon thereafter.

Here is what various Oracle experts have said on the subject. The quote that ties all the other quotes together is the last; you have to *understand* your data in order to create a strategy that works best for your situation.

> *It astonishes me how many shops prohibit any unapproved production changes and yet reanalyze schema stats weekly. Evidently, they do not understand that the purpose of schema reanalysis is to change their production SQL execution plans, and they act surprised when performance changes!*[2]

> *I have advised many customers to stop analyzing, thereby creating a more stable environment overnight.*[3]

> *Oh, and by the way, could you please stop gathering statistics constantly? I don't know much about databases, but I do think I know the following: small tables tend to stay small, large tables tend to stay large, unique indexes have a tendency to stay unique, and nonunique indexes often stay nonunique.*[4]

> *Monitor the changes in execution plans and/or performance for the individual SQL statements...and perhaps as a consequence regather stats. That way, you'd leave stuff alone that works very well, thank you, and you'd put your efforts into exactly the things that have become worse.*[5]

---

2. Don Burleson in the web article "Optimizing Oracle Optimizer Statistics" at http://www.orafaq.com/node/9

3. Mogens Norgaard in the *Journal of the Northern California Oracle Users Group*

4. Dave Ensor as remembered by Mogens Norgaard and quoted in the *Journal of the Northern California Oracle Users Group*

5. Mogens Norgaard in the *Journal of the Northern California Oracle Users Group*

It is my firm belief that most scheduled statistics-gathering jobs do not cause much harm only because (most) changes in the statistics were insignificant as far as the optimizer is concerned—meaning that it was an exercise in futility.[6]

There are some statistics about your data that can be left unchanged for a long time, possibly forever; there are some statistics that need to be changed periodically; and there are some statistics that need to be changed constantly....The biggest problem is that you need to understand the data.[7]

Beginning with Oracle 10g, statistics are automatically collected by a job called GATHER_STATS_JOB that runs during a nightly maintenance window; this default strategy may work for many databases. The procedures in the DBMS_STATS package can be used to create a custom strategy. Complete details of the DBMS_STATS package can be found in *Oracle Database 11g PL/SQL Packages and Types Reference*, which can be freely searched and downloaded at http://tahiti.oracle.com. Here is a representative list of the available procedures:

- The ENABLE_JOB and DISABLE_JOB procedures can be used to enable and disable the GATHER_STATS_JOB job, respectively. The START_JOB procedure can be used to run the job immediately.

- The GATHER_*_STATS procedures can be used to manually gather statistics. For example, GATHER_TABLE_STATS can be used to gather statistics for a single table, and GATHER_SCHEMA_STATS can be used to gather statistics for all the indexes and tables in a schema.

- The DELETE_*_STATS procedures can be used to delete statistics.

- The EXPORT_*_STATS procedures can be used to copy the statistics to a special table. IMPORT_*_STATS can be used to import desired statistics. For example, statistics can be exported from a production database and imported into a development database; this ensures that both databases use the same query execution plans.

- The GATHER_STATS_JOB job retains previous statistics. The RESTORE_*_STATS procedures can be used to restore statistics from a previous point in time. The default retention period used by the GATHER_STATS_JOB is 31 days; this can be changed by using the ALTER_STATS_HISTORY_RETENTION procedure.

- The LOCK_*_STATS procedures can be used to lock statistics and prevent them from being overwritten. Oddly enough, locking statistics can be a useful practice not only when data is static, but also when it is volatile.

---

6.   Wolfgang Breitling in the *Journal of the Northern California Oracle Users Group*

7.   Jonathan Lewis in the *Journal of Northern California Oracle Users Group*

- Possibly the most important procedures are the SET_*_PREFS procedures. They can be used to customize how the GATHER_STATS_JOB collects statistics. The available options are similar to those of the GATHER_*_STATS procedures.

■**Caution** One class of statistics that is not collected automatically is the system statistics; an example is sreadtim, the time taken to read one random block from disk. System statistics must be collected manually by using the GATHER_SYSTEM_STATS procedure. For details, refer to *Oracle Database 11g PL/SQL Packages and Types Reference*.

Tuning by Example

Let's experience the process of tuning an SQL statement by creating two tables, My_tables and My_indexes, modeled after dba_tables and dba_indexes, two dictionary views. Every record in My_tables describes one table, and every record in My_indexes describes one index. The exercise is to print the details (owner, table_name, and tablespace_name) of tables that have at least one bitmap index.

Note that you will need the SELECT ANY DICTIONARY and ALTER SYSTEM privileges for this exercise. You may need the help of your database administrator or you may need to use your own Oracle database on your laptop or PC.

Creating and Populating the Tables

Create and populate the two tables as follows. When I performed the experiment, 1,574 rows of information were inserted into My_tables, and 1,924 rows of information were inserted into My_indexes.

```
SQL> /* Create the my_tables table */
SQL> CREATE TABLE my_tables AS
  2   SELECT dba_tables.*
  3     FROM dba_tables;

Table created.

SQL> /* Create the my_indexes table */
SQL> CREATE TABLE my_indexes AS
  2   SELECT dba_indexes.*
  3     FROM dba_tables, dba_indexes
  4    WHERE dba_tables.owner = dba_indexes.table_owner
  5      AND dba_tables.table_name = dba_indexes.table_name;
```

```
Table created.

SQL> /* Count the records in the my_tables table */
SQL> SELECT count(*)
  2    FROM my_tables;

  COUNT(*)
----------
      1574

SQL> /* Count the records in the my_indexes table */
SQL> SELECT count(*)
  2    FROM my_indexes;

  COUNT(*)
----------
      1924
```

Establishing a Baseline

Here is a simple SQL statement that prints the required information (owner, table_name, and tablespace_name) about tables that have an index of a specified type. We join My_tables and My_indexes, extract the required pieces of information from My_tables, and eliminate duplicates by using the DISTINCT operator:

```
SELECT DISTINCT my_tables.owner,
                my_tables.table_name,
                my_tables.tablespace_name
           FROM my_tables, my_indexes
          WHERE my_tables.owner = my_indexes.table_owner
            AND my_tables.table_name = my_indexes.table_name
            AND my_indexes.index_type = :index_type;
```

If you have some prior experience in SQL tuning, you will observe that we have not yet created appropriate indexes for My_tables and My_indexes, nor have we collected statistical information for use in constructing query execution plans. However, you will soon see that Oracle can execute queries and join tables even in the absence of indexes and can even generate statistical information dynamically by sampling the data.

Some preliminaries are required before we execute the query. We must activate the autotrace feature and must ensure that detailed timing information is captured during the course of the query (statistics_level=ALL). The autotrace feature is used to print the most important items of information relating to efficiency of SQL queries; more-detailed information is captured by Oracle if statistics_level is appropriately configured.

```
SQL> ALTER SESSION SET statistics_level=ALL;

Session altered.

SQL> SET AUTOTRACE on statistics
```

Here is the output of our first attempt:

```
SQL> /* First execution */
SQL> SELECT DISTINCT my_tables.owner,
  2                       my_tables.table_name,
  3                       my_tables.tablespace_name
  4              FROM my_tables, my_indexes
  5             WHERE my_tables.owner = my_indexes.table_owner
  6               AND my_tables.table_name = my_indexes.table_name
  7               AND my_indexes.index_type = :index_type;

OWNER                    TABLE_NAME               TABLESPACE_NAME
-------------------- -------------------- --------------------
SH                       FWEEK_PSCAT_SALES_MV EXAMPLE
SH                       PRODUCTS                 EXAMPLE
SH                       CUSTOMERS                EXAMPLE
SH                       SALES
SH                       COSTS


Statistics
----------------------------------------------------------
        114  recursive calls
          0  db block gets
        228  consistent gets
          0  physical reads
          0  redo size
        645  bytes sent via SQL*Net to client
        381  bytes received via SQL*Net from client
          2  SQL*Net roundtrips to/from client
          2  sorts (memory)
          0  sorts (disk)
          5  rows processed
```

Five rows of data are printed. The name of the tablespace is not printed in the case of two tables; the explanation is left as an exercise for you. But the more interesting information is that which relates the efficiency of the query; this has been printed because we activated the autotrace feature. Here is an explanation of the various items of information:

- *Recursive calls* result from all the work that is done behind the scenes by Oracle before it can begin executing your query. When a query is submitted for execution, Oracle first checks its syntax. It then checks the semantics—that is, it de-references synonyms and views and identifies the underlying tables. It then computes the *signature* (a.k.a. *hash value*) of the query and checks its cache of query execution plans for a reusable query plan that corresponds to that signature. If a query plan is not found, Oracle has to construct one; this results in *recursive calls*. The number of recursive calls required can be large if the information Oracle needs to construct the query plan is not available in the *dictionary cache* and has to be retrieved from the database or if there are no statistics about tables mentioned in the query and data blocks have to be sampled to generate statistics dynamically.

- *DB block gets* is the number of times Oracle needs the latest version of a data block. Oracle does not need the latest version of a data block when the data is simply being read by the user. Instead, Oracle needs the version of the data block that was current when the query started. The latest version of a data block is typically required when the intention is to modify the data.

- *Consistent gets*, a.k.a. *logical reads*, is the number of operations to retrieve a consistent version of a data block that were performed by Oracle while constructing query plans and while executing queries. Remember that all data blocks read during the execution of any query are the versions that were current when the query started; this is called *read consistency*. One of the principal objectives of query tuning is to reduce the number of consistent get operations that are required.

- *Physical reads* is the number of operations to read data blocks from the disks that were performed by Oracle because the blocks were not found in Oracle's cache when they were required. The limit on the number of physical reads is therefore the number of consistent gets.

- *Redo size* is the amount of information Oracle writes to the journals that track changes to the database. This metric applies only when the data is changed in some way.

- *Bytes sent via SQL*Net to client, bytes received via SQL*Net from client*, and *SQL*Net roundtrips to/from client* are fairly self-explanatory; they track the number and size of messages sent to and from Oracle and the user.

- *Sorts (memory)* and *sorts (disk)* track the number of sorting operations performed by Oracle during the course of our query. Sorting operations are performed in memory if possible; they spill onto the disks if the data does not fit into Oracle's memory buffers. It is desirable for sorting to be performed in memory because reading and writing data to and from the disks are expensive operations. The amount of memory available to database sessions for sorting operations is controlled by the value of PGA_AGGREGATE_TARGET.

- Finally, *rows processed* is the number of rows of information required by the user.

The preceding explanations should make it clear that a lot of overhead is involved in executing a query—for example, physical reads are required if data blocks are not found in Oracle's cache. There were no physical reads necessary when we executed our query the first time, indicating that all the required blocks were found in the cache. We can gauge the extent of overhead by flushing the *shared pool* (cache of query execution plans) and *buffer cache* (cache of data blocks) and executing the query again:

```
SQL> ALTER SYSTEM FLUSH SHARED_POOL;

System altered.

SQL> ALTER SYSTEM FLUSH BUFFER_CACHE;

System altered.
```

The numbers rise dramatically; 1,653 recursive calls and 498 consistent gets (including 136 physical reads) are required after the flush. The number of sort operations also jumps—from 0 to 37:

```
Statistics
----------------------------------------------------------
       1653  recursive calls
          0  db block gets
        498  consistent gets
        136  physical reads
          0  redo size
        645  bytes sent via SQL*Net to client
        381  bytes received via SQL*Net from client
          2  SQL*Net roundtrips to/from client
         37  sorts (memory)
          0  sorts (disk)
          5  rows processed
```

Let's now flush only the buffer cache and execute the query again to quantify the precise amount of overhead work involved in constructing a query execution plan. Recursive calls and sorts fall from 1,653 to 0, while consistent gets fall from 498 to 108. We realize that the amount of overhead work dwarfs the actual work done by the query. The number of consistent gets is 108; it will not go down if we repeat the query again. The baseline number that we will attempt to reduce in this tuning exercise is therefore 108. Notice that the number of physical reads is less than the number of consistent gets even though we flushed the buffer cache before executing the query. The reason is that the consistent gets metric counts a block as many times as it is accessed during the course of a query, whereas the physical reads metric counts a block only when it is brought into the buffer cache from the disks. A block might be accessed several times during the course of the query but might have to be brought into the buffer cache only once:

```
Statistics
----------------------------------------------------------------
          0  recursive calls
          0  db block gets
        108  consistent gets
        104  physical reads
          0  redo size
        645  bytes sent via SQL*Net to client
        381  bytes received via SQL*Net from client
          2  SQL*Net roundtrips to/from client
          0  sorts (memory)
          0  sorts (disk)
          5  rows processed
```

Executing the query yet one more time, we see that physical reads has fallen to zero because all data blocks are found in Oracle's cache:

```
Statistics
----------------------------------------------------------------
          0  recursive calls
          0  db block gets
        108  consistent gets
          0  physical reads
          0  redo size
        645  bytes sent via SQL*Net to client
        381  bytes received via SQL*Net from client
          2  SQL*Net roundtrips to/from client
          0  sorts (memory)
          0  sorts (disk)
          5  rows processed
```

Table 17-1 summarizes our findings. The first time we executed the query, Oracle had to construct a query execution plan but found most of the required data in its cache. The second time we executed the query, Oracle had to obtain all the data required to construct a query execution plan from the disks, and all the data blocks required during the actual execution of our query also had to be obtained from the disks. The third time we executed the query, Oracle did not have to construct an execution plan, but all the data bocks required during the execution of our query had to be obtained from the disks. The fourth time we executed the query, all the required data blocks were found in Oracle's cache.

Table 17-1. *Overhead Work Required to Construct a Query Execution Plan*

Metric	First Execution	Second Execution	Third Execution	Query Plan Overhead	Fourth Execution
Recursive calls	114	1653	0	1653	0
Consistent gets	228	498	108	390	108
Physical reads	0	136	104	32	0
Sorts	2	37	0	37	0

The number of consistent gets will not go down if we repeat the query a fifth time; 108 is therefore the baseline number that we will try to reduce in this tuning exercise.

Examining the Query Plan

It's now time to examine the query plan that Oracle has been using. A simple way to do so is to use the dbms_xplan.display_cursor procedure as follows:

```
SQL> SELECT *
  2    FROM TABLE (DBMS_XPLAN.display_cursor (NULL, NULL, 'TYPICAL IOSTATS LAST'));

PLAN_TABLE_OUTPUT
--------------------------------------------------------------------------------

SQL_ID  45b7a5rs8ynxa, child number 0
-------------------------------------
SELECT DISTINCT my_tables.owner,
                my_tables.table_name,
                my_tables.tablespace_name
           FROM my_tables,
                my_indexes
          WHERE my_tables.owner = my_indexes.table_owner
            AND my_tables.table_name = my_indexes.table_name
```

```
        AND my_indexes.index_type = :index_type
```

Plan hash value: 457052432

```
-----------------------------------------------------
| Id  | Operation              | Name         | Starts |
-----------------------------------------------------
|  1  | HASH UNIQUE            |              |    1 |
|* 2  |  HASH JOIN             |              |    1 |
|* 3  |   TABLE ACCESS FULL| MY_INDEXES  |    1 |
|  4  |   TABLE ACCESS FULL| MY_TABLES   |    1 |
-----------------------------------------------------
```

```
-------------------------------------------------------------------------------
| Id  | E-Rows |E-Bytes| Cost (%CPU)| E-Time    | A-Rows |   A-Time   | Buffers |
-------------------------------------------------------------------------------
|  1  |     8 |   800 |    30  (7)| 00:00:01 |      5 |00:00:00.04 |     108 |
|* 2  |     8 |   800 |    29  (4)| 00:00:01 |     15 |00:00:00.04 |     108 |
|* 3  |    15 |   735 |    15  (0)| 00:00:01 |     15 |00:00:00.01 |      58 |
|  4  |  1574 | 80274 |    13  (0)| 00:00:01 |   1574 |00:00:00.01 |      50 |
-------------------------------------------------------------------------------
```

Predicate Information (identified by operation id):

```
   2 - access("MY_TABLES"."OWNER"="MY_INDEXES"."TABLE_OWNER" AND
            "MY_TABLES"."TABLE_NAME"="MY_INDEXES"."TABLE_NAME")
   3 - filter("MY_INDEXES"."INDEX_TYPE"=:INDEX_TYPE)
```

Note

```
   - dynamic sampling used for this statement
```

The hash signature of the SQL statement is 45b7a5rs8ynxa and that of the query execution plan is 457052432. You may obtain different values when you try the exercise in your database. Oracle caches as many plans as possible for future reuse and knows how to translate a hash value into the precise place in memory where the SQL statement or plan is stored. Whenever an SQL statement is submitted for execution, Oracle computes its signature and searches for a statement with identical text and semantics in the cache. If a statement with identical text and semantics is found, its plan can be reused. If Oracle finds a statement with identical text but does not find one that also has identical semantics, it must create a new execution plan; this execution plan is called a *child cursor*. Multiple plans can exist for the same statement—this is indicated by the *child number*. For example, two users may each own a private copy of a table mentioned in an SQL statement, and therefore different query plans will be needed for each user.

The execution plan itself is shown in tabular format and is followed by the list of filters (a.k.a. *predicates*) that apply to the rows of the table. Each row in the table represents one step of the query execution plan. Here is the description of the columns:

- *Id* is simply the row number.

- *Operation* describes the step—for example, TABLE ACCESS FULL means that all rows in the table are retrieved.

- *Name* is an optional piece of information; it is the name of the object to which the step applies.

- *Starts* is the number of times the step is executed.

- *E-Rows* is the number of rows that Oracle *expected* to obtain in the step.

- *E-Bytes* is the total number of bytes that Oracle *expected* to obtain in the step.

- *Cost* is the *cumulative* cost that Oracle *expected* to incur at the end of the step. The unit is *block equivalents*—that is, the number of data blocks that could be retrieved in the same amount of time. The percentage of time for which Oracle expects to use the CPU is displayed along with the cost.

- *E-time* is an estimate of the *cumulative* amount of time to complete this step and all prior steps. Hours, minutes, and seconds are displayed.

- *A-Rows* is the number of rows that Oracle *actually* obtained in the step.

- *A-Bytes* is the total number of bytes that Oracle *actually* obtained in the step.

- *Buffers* is the cumulative number of consistent get operations that were *actually* performed in the step and all prior steps.

More than a little skill is needed to interpret the execution plan. Notice the indentation of the operations listed in the second column. The correct sequence of operations is obtained by applying the following rule: *Perform operations in the order in which they are listed except that if the operations listed after a certain operation are more deeply indented in the listing, then perform those operations first (in the order in which those operations are listed).* On applying this rule, we see that the operations are performed in the following order:

```
------------------------------------------
| Id | Operation          | Name         |
------------------------------------------
|*  3 |    TABLE ACCESS FULL| MY_INDEXES |
|   4 |    TABLE ACCESS FULL| MY_TABLES  |
|*  2 |  HASH JOIN          |            |
|   1 |  HASH UNIQUE        |            |
------------------------------------------
```

First, all the rows of data in the My_indexes table will be retrieved (TABLE ACCESS FULL), and a lookup table (a.k.a. *hash table*) is constructed from rows that satisfy the filter (a.k.a. *predicate*) my_indexes.index_type = :index_type. This means that a signature (a.k.a. *hash value*) is calculated for each row of data satisfying the predicate. This signature is then translated into a position in the hash table where the row will be stored. This makes it tremendously easy to locate the row when it is required later. Because My_indexes and My_tables are related by the values of owner and table_name, a hash signature will be constructed from these values.

Next, all the rows of data in the My_tables table will be retrieved (TABLE ACCESS FULL). After retrieving each row of data from the My_tables table, rows of data from the My_indexes table satisfying the join predicate my_tables.owner = my_indexes.owner AND my_tables. table_name = my_indexes.table_name will be retrieved from the lookup table constructed in the previous step (HASH JOIN) and, if any such rows are found, the required data items (owner, table_name, and tablespace_name) are included in the query results. Duplicates are avoided (HASH UNIQUE) by storing the resulting rows of data in another hash table; new rows are added to the hash table only if a matching row is not found.

Of particular interest are the columns in the execution plan labeled E-Rows, E-Bytes, Cost, and E-Time; these are estimates generated by Oracle. Time and cost are straightforward computations based on rows and bytes; but how does Oracle estimate rows and bytes in the first place? The answer is that Oracle uses a combination of rules of thumb and any available statistical information available in the data dictionary; this statistical information is automatically refreshed every night. In the absence of statistical information, Oracle samples a certain number of data blocks from the table and estimates the number of qualifying rows in each block of the table and the average length of these rows. This is indicated by the remark dynamic sampling used for this statement seen at the end of the preceding listing.

In our example, Oracle estimated that 15 qualifying rows would be found in the My_ indexes table and that 8 rows would remain after the qualifying rows were matched to the rows in the My_tables table. Oracle's estimate of the number of qualifying rows in My_indexes is surprisingly accurate, but its estimate of the number of rows that could be matched to rows in the My_tables table is less accurate. Every row in My_indexes corresponds to exactly one row in the My_tables table and, therefore, a better estimate would have been 15. The reason Oracle cannot estimate correctly in this case is that it is unaware of the relationship between the tables—we have not yet given Oracle the information it needs. Oracle therefore resorts to a rule of thumb; it estimates that each row in a table will match the same number of rows in the table to which it is joined—the number obtained by dividing the number of rows (or estimate thereof) in the table to which the row is being joined by the number of distinct values (or estimate thereof) in that table. (Another equally plausible estimate can be made by reversing the roles of the two tables involved in the computation, and Oracle chooses the lower of the two estimates.)

Indexes and Statistics

Let's create an appropriate set of indexes on our tables. First, we define primary key constraints on My_tables and My_indexes. Oracle automatically creates unique indexes because it needs an efficient method of enforcing the constraints. We also create a foreign key constraint linking the two tables and create an index on the foreign key. Finally, we create an index on the values of index_type because our query restricts the value of index_type. We then collect statistics on both tables as well as the newly created indexes as follows:

```
ALTER TABLE my_tables
ADD (CONSTRAINT my_tables_pk PRIMARY KEY (owner, table_name));

ALTER TABLE my_indexes
ADD (CONSTRAINT my_indexes_pk PRIMARY KEY (owner, index_name));

ALTER TABLE my_indexes
ADD (CONSTRAINT my_indexes_fk1 FOREIGN KEY (table_owner, table_name)
REFERENCES my_tables);

CREATE INDEX my_indexes_i1 ON my_indexes (index_type);

CREATE INDEX my_indexes_fk1 ON my_indexes (table_owner, table_name);

EXEC DBMS_STATS.gather_table_stats(ownname=>'IFERNANDEZ',tabname=>'MY_TABLES');
EXEC DBMS_STATS.gather_table_stats(ownname=>'IFERNANDEZ',tabname=>'MY_INDEXES');
EXEC DBMS_STATS.gather_index_stats(ownname=>'IFERNANDEZ',indname=>'MY_TABLES_PK');
EXEC DBMS_STATS.gather_index_stats(ownname=>'IFERNANDEZ',indname=>'MY_INDEXES_I1');
EXEC DBMS_STATS.gather_index_stats(ownname=>'IFERNANDEZ',indname=>'MY_INDEXES_FK1');
```

We find a substantial improvement both in the accuracy of the estimates and in the efficiency of the query plan after indexes are created and statistics are gathered. Oracle now correctly estimates that every qualifying row in the My_indexes table will match exactly one row in the My_tables table, and the remark dynamic sampling used for this statement is not printed. Oracle uses the index on the values of index_type to efficiently retrieve the 15 qualifying rows—this reduces the number of consistent gets from 108 to 55.

```
SQL> SELECT *
  2    FROM TABLE (DBMS_XPLAN.display_cursor (NULL, NULL, 'TYPICAL IOSTATS LAST'));
```

PLAN_TABLE_OUTPUT

SQL_ID 45b7a5rs8ynxa, child number 0

```
SELECT DISTINCT my_tables.owner,
                my_tables.table_name,
                my_tables.tablespace_name
          FROM my_tables,
                my_indexes
         WHERE my_tables.owner = my_indexes.table_owner
           AND my_tables.table_name = my_indexes.table_name
           AND my_indexes.index_type = :index_type
```

Plan hash value: 1434988034

| Id | Operation | Name | Starts |

1	HASH UNIQUE		1
* 2	HASH JOIN		1
3	TABLE ACCESS BY INDEX ROWID	MY_INDEXES	1
* 4	INDEX RANGE SCAN	MY_INDEXES_I1	1
5	TABLE ACCESS FULL	MY_TABLES	1

| Id | E-Rows |E-Bytes| Cost (%CPU)| E-Time | A-Rows | A-Time | Buffers |

1	15	945	17 (12)	00:00:01	5	00:00:00.02	55
* 2	15	945	16 (7)	00:00:01	15	00:00:00.02	55
3	15	465	2 (0)	00:00:01	15	00:00:00.01	5
* 4	15		1 (0)	00:00:01	15	00:00:00.01	2
5	1574	50368	13 (0)	00:00:01	1574	00:00:00.01	50

```

Predicate Information (identified by operation id):
---------------------------------------------------
```

```
     2 - access("MY_TABLES"."OWNER"="MY_INDEXES"."TABLE_OWNER" AND
            "MY_TABLES"."TABLE_NAME"="MY_INDEXES"."TABLE_NAME")
     4 - access("MY_INDEXES"."INDEX_TYPE"=:INDEX_TYPE)
```

Using SQL Access Advisor

If you are using Enterprise Edition and have a license for the Tuning Pack, you can use SQL Tuning Advisor to help you with SQL tuning. We've already created indexes and generated statistics; we now look to SQL Tuning Advisor for fresh ideas. The commands in the following example generate a recommendation report:

```
SQL> /* get recommendations from SQL Access Advisor */
SQL> VARIABLE tuning_task VARCHAR2(32);
SQL> EXEC :tuning_task := dbms_sqltune.create_tuning_task (sql_id => '&sqlID');
Enter value for sqlid: 45b7a5rs8ynxa

PL/SQL procedure successfully completed.

SQL>
SQL> EXEC dbms_sqltune.execute_tuning_task(task_name => :tuning_task);

PL/SQL procedure successfully completed.

SQL>
SQL> SET LONG 100000;
SQL> SET PAGESIZE 1000
SQL> SET LINESIZE 160
SQL> COLUMN recommendations FORMAT a160
SQL>
SQL> SELECT DBMS_SQLTUNE.report_tuning_task (:tuning_task) AS recommendations
  2     FROM DUAL;
```

The final SELECT in the preceding code retrieves the following report from SQL Tuning Advisor:

```
RECOMMENDATIONS
--------------------------------------------------------------------------------

GENERAL INFORMATION SECTION
-------------------------------------------------------------------------------
Tuning Task Name                     : TASK_21
Tuning Task Owner                    : IFERNANDEZ
Scope                                : COMPREHENSIVE
```

```
Time Limit(seconds)         : 1800
Completion Status           : COMPLETED
Started at                  : 09/30/2008 05:37:57
Completed at                : 09/30/2008 05:37:58
Number of Index Findings    : 1


---------------------------------------------------------------------

Schema Name: IFERNANDEZ
SQL ID      : 45b7a5rs8ynxa
SQL Text    : SELECT DISTINCT my_tables.owner,
                              my_tables.table_name,
                              my_tables.tablespace_name
                      FROM my_tables, my_indexes
                  WHERE my_tables.owner = my_indexes.table_owner
                    AND my_tables.table_name = my_indexes.table_name
                    AND my_indexes.index_type = :index_type


---------------------------------------------------------------------

FINDINGS SECTION (1 finding)
---------------------------------------------------------------------


1- Index Finding (see explain plans section below)
-------------------------------------------------

  The execution plan of this statement can be improved by creating one or more
  indices.

  Recommendation (estimated benefit: 100%)
  ----------------------------------------
  - Consider running the Access Advisor to improve the physical schema design
    or creating the recommended index.
    create index IFERNANDEZ.IDX$$_00150001 on
    IFERNANDEZ.MY_TABLES('OWNER','TABLE_NAME','TABLESPACE_NAME');

  Rationale
  ---------
    Creating the recommended indices significantly improves the execution plan
    of this statement. However, it might be preferable to run "Access Advisor"
    using a representative SQL workload as opposed to a single statement. This
    will allow you to get comprehensive index recommendations, which takes into
    account index maintenance overhead and additional space consumption.


---------------------------------------------------------------------
```

EXPLAIN PLANS SECTION

1- Original

Plan hash value: 1434988034

| Id |Operation |Name |Rows|Bytes|Cost (%CPU)|Time |

0	SELECT STATEMENT		15	945	17 (12)	00:00:01
1	HASH UNIQUE		15	945	17 (12)	00:00:01
* 2	HASH JOIN		15	945	16 (7)	00:00:01
3	TABLE ACCESS BY INDEX ROWID	MY_INDEXES	15	465	2 (0)	00:00:01
* 4	INDEX RANGE SCAN	MY_INDEXES_I1	15		1 (0)	00:00:01
5	TABLE ACCESS FULL	MY_TABLES	1574	50368	13 (0)	00:00:01

Predicate Information (identified by operation id):
----

   2 - access("MY_TABLES"."OWNER"="MY_INDEXES"."TABLE_OWNER" AND
           "MY_TABLES"."TABLE_NAME"="MY_INDEXES"."TABLE_NAME")
   4 - access("MY_INDEXES"."INDEX_TYPE"=:INDEX_TYPE)

2- Using New Indices

Plan hash value: 317787978

| Id |Operation |Name |Rows|Bytes|Cost (%CPU)|Time |

0	SELECT STATEMENT		15	945	8 (25)	00:00:01
1	HASH UNIQUE		15	945	8 (25)	00:00:01
* 2	HASH JOIN		15	945	7 (15)	00:00:01
3	TABLE ACCESS BY INDEX ROWID	MY_INDEXES	15	465	2 (0)	00:00:01
* 4	INDEX RANGE SCAN	MY_INDEXES_I1	15		1 (0)	00:00:01
5	INDEX FAST FULL SCAN	IDX$$_00150001	1574	50368	4 (0)	00:00:01

Predicate Information (identified by operation id):

```
   2 - access("MY_TABLES"."OWNER"="MY_INDEXES"."TABLE_OWNER" AND
             "MY_TABLES"."TABLE_NAME"="MY_INDEXES"."TABLE_NAME")
   4 - access("MY_INDEXES"."INDEX_TYPE"=:INDEX_TYPE)
---------------------------------------------------------------------------
```

SQL Tuning Advisor recommends that we create yet another index on the `My_tables` table. The new index would contain *all* the items of information required by our query and make it necessary to read the table itself. However, let's first make sure that Oracle is taking advantage of the indexes we have already created before creating yet another index.

Optimizer Hints

As I have pointed out before, hints for the optimizer can be embedded inside an SQL statement if the optimizer does not find an acceptable query plan for the statement. Each hint partially constrains the optimizer, and a full set of hints completely constrains the optimizer.[8] Let's instruct Oracle to use an index to efficiently associate qualifying records in the `My_indexes` table with matching records from the `My_tables` table:

```
SELECT          /*+ INDEX(MY_INDEXES (INDEX_TYPE))
                    INDEX(MY_TABLES (OWNER TABLE_NAME))
                    LEADING(MY_INDEXES MY_TABLES)
                    USE_NL(MY_TABLES)
                */
    DISTINCT my_tables.owner,
             my_tables.table_name,
             my_tables.tablespace_name
        FROM my_tables, my_indexes
       WHERE my_tables.owner = my_indexes.table_owner
         AND my_tables.table_name = my_indexes.table_name
         AND my_indexes.index_type = :index_type;
```

The `LEADING` hint specifies the order in which tables are processed, the `INDEX` hint specifies that an index be used, and the `USE_NL` hint specifies that tables be joined using the simple *nested loop* method (instead of the *hash* method used in previous executions). The use of the `my_indexes_pk` index reduces the number of consistent gets to 37.

---

8. The use of hints is a defense against *bind variable peeking*. To understand the problem, remember that a query execution plan is constructed once and used many times. If the values of the bind variables in the first invocation of the query are not particularly representative of the data, the query plan that is generated will not be a good candidate for reuse. *Stored outlines* are another defense against bind variable peeking. It is also possible to turn off bind variable peeking for your session or for the entire database; this forces Oracle to generate a query plan that is not tailored to one set of bind variables. However, note that bind variable peeking does work well when the data has a uniform distribution.

```
SQL> SELECT *
  2     FROM TABLE (DBMS_XPLAN.display_cursor (NULL, NULL, 'TYPICAL IOSTATS LAST'));

PLAN_TABLE_OUTPUT
--------------------------------------------------------------------------------

SQL_ID  dsh3tvd5p501p, child number 0
-------------------------------------
SELECT          /*+ INDEX(MY_INDEXES (INDEX_TYPE))
                    INDEX(MY_TABLES (OWNER TABLE_NAME))
                    LEADING(MY_INDEXES MY_TABLES)
                    USE_NL(MY_TABLES) */
      DISTINCT my_tables.owner,
               my_tables.table_name,
               my_tables.tablespace_name
          FROM my_tables,
               my_indexes
         WHERE my_tables.owner = my_indexes.table_owner
           AND my_tables.table_name = my_indexes.table_name
           AND my_indexes.index_type = :index_type

Plan hash value: 813127232
```

Id	Operation	Name	Starts
1	HASH UNIQUE		1
2	NESTED LOOPS		1
3	TABLE ACCESS BY INDEX ROWID	MY_INDEXES	1
* 4	INDEX RANGE SCAN	MY_INDEXES_I1	1
5	TABLE ACCESS BY INDEX ROWID	MY_TABLES	15
* 6	INDEX UNIQUE SCAN	MY_TABLES_PK	15

Id	E-Rows	E-Bytes	Cost (%CPU)	E-Time	A-Rows	A-Time	Buffers
1	15	945	18 (6)	00:00:01	5	00:00:00.01	37
2	15	945	17 (0)	00:00:01	15	00:00:00.01	37
3	15	465	2 (0)	00:00:01	15	00:00:00.01	5
* 4	15		1 (0)	00:00:01	15	00:00:00.01	2
5	1	32	1 (0)	00:00:01	15	00:00:00.01	32
* 6	1		0 (0)		15	00:00:00.01	17

```
Predicate Information (identified by operation id):
---------------------------------------------------

    4 - access("MY_INDEXES"."INDEX_TYPE"=:INDEX_TYPE)
    6 - access("MY_TABLES"."OWNER"="MY_INDEXES"."TABLE_OWNER" AND
              "MY_TABLES"."TABLE_NAME"="MY_INDEXES"."TABLE_NAME")
```

Extreme Tuning

It does not appear possible to reduce consistent get operations any further because we are already using indexes to maximum advantage. Here is a summary of the previous execution strategy:

- Using the my_indexes_i1 index, collect the addresses of rows of the My_indexes table that qualify for inclusion; this requires at least one consistent get operation.

- Using the addresses obtained in the previous step, retrieve the qualifying rows from the My_indexes table. There are 15 rows that qualify and, therefore, we may have to visit 15 different blocks and perform 15 consistent get operations; fewer operations may be required if multiple rows are found when a block is visited.

- For every qualifying row retrieved from the My_indexes table, use the my_tables_pk index and obtain the address of the matching row in the My_tables table; this requires another 15 consistent get operations.

- Using the addresses obtained in the previous step, retrieve the matching rows from the My_tables table; this requires another 15 consistent get operations.

- Finally, eliminate duplicates from the result. This does not require any consistent get operations.

If we add up the numbers in this analysis, we get 46. The actual number of consistent get operations may be slightly higher or slightly lower than 46 if multiple rows are found when a block is visited or multiple blocks have to be visited to retrieve a row of information from a table or from an index. It therefore appears that we have tuned the SQL statement as much as we can. After all, we need to use indexes to retrieve records quickly, and we cannot avoid visiting two tables.

However, there *is* a way to retrieve records quickly without the use of indexes, and there *is* a way to retrieve data from two tables without actually visiting two tables. *Hash clusters* allow data to be retrieved without the use of indexes; Oracle computes the hash signature of the record you need and translates the hash signature into the address of the record. Clustering effects can also significantly reduce the number of blocks that need to be visited to retrieve the required data. Further, *materialized views* combine the data from multiple tables and enable you to retrieve data from multiple tables *without* actually visiting the tables themselves. We can combine hash clusters and materialized views to achieve a dramatic reduction in the number of consistent get operations; in fact we will only need one consistent get operation.

First, we create a hash cluster and then we combine the data from My_tables and My_indexes into another table called My_tables_and_indexes. In the interests of brevity, we select only those items of information required by our query; items of information that would help other queries would normally have been considered for inclusion:

```
SQL> CREATE CLUSTER my_cluster (index_type VARCHAR2(27))
  2  SIZE 8192 HASHKEYS 5;

Cluster created.
```

Next, we create a materialized view of the data. We use *materialized view logs* to ensure that any future changes to the data in My_tables or My_indexes are immediately made to the copy of the data in the materialized view. We enable *query rewrite* to ensure that our query is automatically modified and that the required data is retrieved from the materialized view instead of from My_tables and My_indexes. Appropriate indexes that would improve the usability and maintainability of the materialized view should also be created; I leave this as an exercise for you.

```
SQL> CREATE MATERIALIZED VIEW LOG ON my_tables WITH ROWID;

Materialized view log created.

SQL> CREATE MATERIALIZED VIEW LOG ON my_indexes WITH ROWID;

Materialized view log created.

SQL> CREATE MATERIALIZED VIEW my_mv
  2  CLUSTER my_cluster (index_type)
  3  REFRESH FAST ON COMMIT
  4  ENABLE QUERY REWRITE
  5  AS
  6  SELECT t.ROWID AS table_rowid,
  7         t.owner AS table_owner,
  8         t.table_name,
  9         t.tablespace_name,
 10         i.ROWID AS index_rowid,
 11         i.index_type
 12    FROM my_tables t,
 13         my_indexes i
 14   WHERE t.owner = i.table_owner
 15     AND t.table_name = i.table_name;
```

Materialized view created.

```
SQL> EXEC DBMS_STATS.gather_table_stats(ownname=>'IFERNANDEZ',tabname=>'MY_MV');
```

PL/SQL procedure successfully completed.

It's now time to test our query again; we find that the number of consistent gets has been reduced to its theoretical limit of 1:

```
SQL> SELECT *
  2    FROM TABLE (DBMS_XPLAN.display_cursor (NULL, NULL, 'TYPICAL IOSTATS LAST'));


PLAN_TABLE_OUTPUT
--------------------------------------------------------------------------------


SQL_ID  45b7a5rs8ynxa, child number 0
-------------------------------------
SELECT DISTINCT my_tables.owner,
                my_tables.table_name,
                my_tables.tablespace_name
           FROM my_tables,
                my_indexes
          WHERE my_tables.owner = my_indexes.table_owner
            AND my_tables.table_name = my_indexes.table_name
            AND my_indexes.index_type = :index_type


Plan hash value: 1006555447
```

Id	Operation	Name	Starts
1	HASH UNIQUE		1
* 2	TABLE ACCESS HASH	MY_MV	1

Id	E-Rows	E-Bytes	Cost (%CPU)	E-Time	A-Rows	A-Time	Buffers
1	321	12198	1 (100)	00:00:01	5	00:00:00.01	1
* 2	321	12198			15	00:00:00.01	1

```
Predicate Information (identified by operation id):
---------------------------------------------------

   2 - access("MY_MV"."INDEX_TYPE"=:INDEX_TYPE)
```

But Wait, There's More!

Executing a query requires at least one consistent get operation. However, there is no need to execute the query if the query results have been previously cached and the data has not changed. Oracle 11g introduced the RESULT_CACHE hint to indicate that the data should be obtained from cache if possible. Note that this feature is available only with the Enterprise Edition. In the following example, you can see that the number of consistent gets has been reduced to zero!

```
SQL> SELECT          /*+ RESULT_CACHE */
  2        DISTINCT my_tables.owner,
  3                 my_tables.table_name,
  4                 my_tables.tablespace_name
  5           FROM my_tables, my_indexes
  6          WHERE my_tables.owner = my_indexes.table_owner
  7            AND my_tables.table_name = my_indexes.table_name
  8            AND my_indexes.index_type = :index_type;

OWNER                TABLE_NAME            TABLESPACE_NAME
-------------------- -------------------- --------------------
SH                   FWEEK_PSCAT_SALES_MV EXAMPLE
SH                   PRODUCTS             EXAMPLE
SH                   CUSTOMERS            EXAMPLE
SH                   SALES
SH                   COSTS

Statistics
----------------------------------------------------------
          0  recursive calls
          0  db block gets
          0  consistent gets
          0  physical reads
          0  redo size
        652  bytes sent via SQL*Net to client
        416  bytes received via SQL*Net from client
          2  SQL*Net roundtrips to/from client
```

```
        0   sorts (memory)
        0   sorts (disk)
        5   rows processed

SQL> SELECT *
  2     FROM TABLE (DBMS_XPLAN.display_cursor (NULL, NULL, 'TYPICAL IOSTATS LAST'));


PLAN_TABLE_OUTPUT
-----------------------------------------------------------------------------------


SQL_ID  cwht0anw8vv4s, child number 0
-------------------------------------
SELECT          /*+ RESULT_CACHE */
       DISTINCT my_tables.owner,
                my_tables.table_name,
                my_tables.tablespace_name
          FROM my_tables,
               my_indexes
         WHERE my_tables.owner = my_indexes.table_owner
           AND my_tables.table_name = my_indexes.table_name
           AND my_indexes.index_type = :index_type


Plan hash value: 1006555447
```

Id	Operation	Name	Starts
0	SELECT STATEMENT		1
1	**RESULT CACHE**	afscr8p240b168b5az0dkd4k65	1
2	HASH UNIQUE		0
* 3	TABLE ACCESS HASH	MY_MV	0

Id	E-Rows	E-Bytes	Cost (%CPU)	E-Time	A-Rows	A-Time
0			1 (100)		5	00:00:00.01
1					5	00:00:00.01
2	602	24682	1 (100)	00:00:01	0	00:00:00.01
* 3	602	24682			0	00:00:00.01

```
Predicate Information (identified by operation id):
----------------------------------------------------

   3 - access("MY_MV"."INDEX_TYPE"=:INDEX_TYPE)

Result Cache Information (identified by operation id):
------------------------------------------------------

   1 -
```

You saw four query plans in this exercise:

- The first query plan did not use any indexes because none had been created at the time.

- Qualifying records in My_indexes were efficiently identified by using the index on the values of index_type and were placed in a lookup table. All the records in My_tables were then retrieved and compared with the records in the lookup table.

- Qualifying records in My_indexes were efficiently identified using the index on the values of index_type. An index on the values of table_owner and table_name was then used to efficiently find the corresponding records in My_tables.

- A materialized view was used to combine the data from My_tables and My_indexes, and a *hash cluster* was used to create clusters of related records.

Summary

Here is a short summary of the concepts touched on in this chapter:

- The efficiency of an SQL statement is measured by the amount of computing resources used in producing the output. The number of logical read operations is a good way to measure the consumption of computing resources because it is directly proportional to the amount of resources consumed.

- Inefficient SQL can be identified by using tools such as Enterprise Manager and Toad, by tracing a batch job or user session, and by examining STATSPACK reports.

- Common causes for inefficient SQL are as follows: failure to use advanced features such as analytic functions, poor application development practices, poor logical and physical database design, and inadequate database maintenance.

- Hardware limitations and contention for limited resources play a major role in performance.

- The primary key of a table is always indexed. Indexes should be created on foreign keys unless the tables in question are small enough that the lack of an index will not have an impact on performance. Indexes should also be created on data items that are restricted in SQL queries. The `dba_indexes` and `dba_ind_columns` views show what indexes have been created. Most indexes are of the b*tree type. Other types of indexes are reverse key indexes, function-based indexes, and bitmap indexes. Clusters, index-organized tables, and table partitions are other options available to the database designer.

- Hints for the optimizer can be embedded inside an SQL statement. Each hint partially constrains the optimizer, and a full set of hints completely constrains the optimizer. A desirable query plan can be preserved by capturing the set of hints that describes it in a *stored outline*.

- Statistical information on tables and indexes and the data they contain is what the query optimizer needs to do its job properly. Table and index statistics are automatically collected by a job called `GATHER_STATS_JOB` that runs during a nightly maintenance window. The `DBMS_STATS` package contains a variety of procedures for customizing the statistics collection strategy. System statistics are not collected automatically; they should be manually collected by using the `GATHER_SYSTEM_STATS` procedure.

- One of the principal objectives of query tuning is to reduce the number of consistent get operations (logical reads) required. The theoretical lower bound on the number of consistent get operations is 1.

- The cost of creating a query plan can far exceed the cost of executing a query. Plan reuse is therefore critical for database performance. Dynamic sampling, necessitated by the absence of statistics, can dramatically increase the cost of creating a query plan.

- If you are using the Enterprise Edition and have a license for the Tuning Pack, you can use SQL Tuning Advisor to help you with SQL tuning.

Exercises

- Enable tracing of your SQL query by using the `dbms_monitor.session_trace_enable` and `dbms_monitor.session_trace_disable` procedures. Locate the trace file and review the recursive calls. Also review the `PARSE`, `EXECUTE`, and `FETCH` calls for your query.

- Re-create the `my_tables_and_indexes` materialized view with all the columns in `My_indexes` and `My_tables` instead of just those columns required in the exercise.

- Determine an appropriate set of tables and indexes for the materialized view created during the exercise.

- Insert new data into `My_tables` and `My_indexes` and verify that the data is automatically inserted into the materialized view.

Further Reading

Oracle Corporation. *Oracle Database 11g Data Warehousing Guide.* Oracle Corporation, 2007. This book pays much attention to SQL techniques that are particularly useful when working with large databases such as materialized views, pipelined data transformation, parallel operations, bitmap indexes, and star schemas. Searchable or downloadable free of charge at `http://tahiti.oracle.com`. Printed copies can be purchased from Oracle's online store.

Oracle Corporation. *Oracle Database 11g Performance Tuning Guide.* Oracle Corporation, 2007. This is certainly the place to start, if only because it is searchable or downloadable free of charge at `http://tahiti.oracle.com`. It covers all aspects of performance tuning, including SQL tuning. Printed copies can be purchased from Oracle's online store.

Antognini, Christian. *Troubleshooting Oracle Performance.* Apress, 2008. An excellent book on Oracle performance issues, covering database tuning as well as SQL tuning. The book is billed as "written for developers by an application developer who has learned by doing." If you had to buy just one book on performance tuning, this is the one that I would recommend.

Harrison, Guy. *Oracle SQL High-Performance Tuning (2nd Edition).* Prentice Hall, 2001. This book predates Oracle Database 9*i* and is fairly out-of-date but is one of only a very small handful of books devoted exclusively to the subject of tuning SQL for Oracle databases. Despite its lack of coverage of the latest techniques, it is an excellent work and recommended reading for serious students.

Lewis, Jonathan. *Cost-Based Oracle Fundamentals.* Apress, 2005. This book is a scholarly exposition on the inner workings of Oracle's query optimizer, suitable for the advanced student who wishes to gain some insight into how the optimizer makes its choices.

Tow, Dan. *SQL Tuning.* O'Reilly Media, 2003. No single query plan is optimal for all values of the bind variables when the data has a skewed distribution. In this book, Dan Tow develops the theory of the robust execution plan. Such plans have only moderate sensitivity to the values of the bind variables (which implies that they continue to perform well as your tables grow), and their cost is proportional to the number of rows retrieved. They may not be the most efficient plans in all cases but they are not very likely to be far off the mark. Such plans are conducive to stability and predictability and are obviously very desirable. Various techniques including hints can be used to guide the optimizer toward such plans.

Index

You Need the Companion eBook

Your purchase of this book entitles you to buy the companion PDF-version eBook for only $10. Take the weightless companion with you anywhere.

We believe this Apress title will prove so indispensable that you'll want to carry it with you everywhere, which is why we are offering the companion eBook (in PDF format) for $10 to customers who purchase this book now. Convenient and fully searchable, the PDF version of any content-rich, page-heavy Apress book makes a valuable addition to your programming library. You can easily find and copy code—or perform examples by quickly toggling between instructions and the application. Even simultaneously tackling a donut, diet soda, and complex code becomes simplified with hands-free eBooks!

Once you purchase your book, getting the $10 companion eBook is simple:

1 Visit **www.apress.com/promo/tendollars/**.

2 Complete a basic registration form to receive a randomly generated question about this title.

3 Answer the question correctly in 60 seconds, and you will receive a promotional code to redeem for the $10.00 eBook.